# Morality and the Human Future
## in the Thought
## of Teilhard de Chardin

# Morality
# and the
# Human Future
# in the Thought
# of Teilhard de Chardin

## A Critical Study

Joseph A. Grau

*Rutherford* ● *Madison* ● *Teaneck*
*Fairleigh Dickinson University Press*
*London: Associated University Presses*

© 1976 by Associated University Presses, Inc.

Associated University Presses, Inc.
Cranbury, New Jersey 08512

Associated University Presses
108 New Bond Street
London W1Y OQX, England

*170.924*

*977m*

*104082*

*March 1978*

**Library of Congress Cataloging in Publication Data**

Grau, Joseph A
  Morality and the human future in the thought of Teilhard de Chardin.

  Bibliography: p.
  Includes index.
  1. Teilhard de Chardin, Pierre—Ethics. 2. Human evolution. 3. Love. 4. Christianity—Philosophy.
  I. Title.
  B2430.T374G66      170'.92'4      74-4976
  ISBN 0-8386-1579-1

# Contents

# Foreword

BY CHRISTOPHER F. MOONEY, S.J.

In a remarkably revealing passage from a 1927 letter, Pierre Teilhard de Chardin said that what he desired to propagate was not a theory or system so much as a taste and perception of beauty. "I try to translate the species of calm intoxication produced in me by an awareness of the profound substance of things into theories (how I wish I could translate them into music!), but these theories really matter to me only by their vibrations in a province of the soul which is not that of intellectualism. Those who do not hear the fundamental harmony of the Universe which I try to transcribe. . .look in what I write for some kind of narrowly logical system and are confused or angry. . .Once again, it would be more to my purpose to be a shadow of Wagner than a shadow of Darwin."

Joseph A. Grau is well aware of this significance of theory for Teilhard, yet he does not for that reason underestimate either the value of the theory as theory or the value of that perception of beauty which is its source. In coming to terms with both, he has produced a careful, imaginative, and reflective work which is remarkable for both its scope and its control. The author's aim is to do what Teilhard did not do: present a comprehensive view of all aspects of his moral theory. Much of his success is due to his methodology. Teilhard him-

9

self used several different ways of approaching ethical issues, but Dr. Grau wisely chooses to center his reconstruction around Teilhard's analysis of love as a human phenomenon, and to underline its significance as the most unusual form of spiritualized human energy. This enables him more accurately to deal with those other forms of human energy seen by Teilhard as activations of the fundamental ethical drive of the species for "more-being." Such a morality of movement, or "moralization" as Teilhard calls it, easily encompasses such diverse phenomena as the aggressive impulse in war and scientific research, the political impulse in society, and the contemporary concern for education, eugenics, and technology.

This broad and generalized anthropology Grau allows to stand by itself in order to test its value under reasoned analysis. Inevitably certain parts of the system wobble or collapse under closer scrutiny, for, as Teilhard himself said, he was not aiming to construct a "narrowly logical system." Hence the author reminds the reader at each step of Teilhard's primary motivation, namely, to catch by his theories "vibrations in the province of the soul," "the fundamental harmony of the Universe." This is most effectively done in the lengthy ninth chapter, where each of the theories previously expounded is inserted into Teilhard's larger religious context and where these theories are shown to constitute in their entirety a theological anthropology, or, more accurately, a Christology. The mode of such insertion I find admirable, allowing as it does both for the clear limits and deficiencies of Teilhard's ethical theories as well as for their ultimate grounding in religious experience.

Dr. Grau does not pretend that, in pursuing his goal, he has been able to put together *the* Teilhardian ethic. He is well aware, as he says, that synthesizers inevitably color their tasks with their own peculiar concerns, which preclude any general agreement on method and emphasis. This is especially true of materials as fragmentary

and scattered as the writings of Teilhard on moral behavior. Grau's concern with the nature of freedom, for
example, gives him a prism by which he filters out what
he sees to be a profound ambiguity in Teilhard's morality of movement. Grau understands freedom to mean
autonomy, self-determination in some fundamental
sense, and therefore radical unpredictability. By trying
to insert such a phenomenon into an evolutionary
perspective derived from the subhuman biological world,
where everything develops in a determined and predictable way, Teilhard is forced to handle analogy badly. A
valid argument from analogy must be based on what is
continuous and similar in the two analogues. Yet what
Teilhard does is to proceed to a conclusion in a discontinuous area on the assumption that he is reasoning
from continuity. To locate at this point the root flaw of
Teilhard's phenomenological analysis is valid to the extent that one understands human evolution to be an
area discontinuous with what preceded it. Grau believes
this to be Teilhard's understanding and underlines the
subsequent inconsistency of his analysis. I for one am
not so sure Teilhard could feel comfortable with an idea
of human freedom which involved radical self-
determination as well as discontinuity with evolutionary
forces operating on the prehuman level. He would have
been far more aware of the various influences determining human behavior which have been recently described, for example, by B. F. Skinner. Unlike Skinner,
however, he would have insisted that humans exercise
their freedom precisely in and through their awareness
of these stimuli, their ability to choose some stimuli over
others, and their capacity freely to solve the problems of
life within such manipulative influences.

The point at issue, here, of course, is what Teilhard's
understanding of freedom was, since this will determine
whether or not he was inconsistent in his argument from
analogy. Dr. Grau makes a good case for inconsistency.
But then he makes a good case generally. The reader

will be challenged, as I have been, to come to terms with an interpretation that is rich, searching, and provocative. Teilhard's "theories" are recognized throughout for what they are: efforts to hold love of the world in one hand and love of God in the other, and by examining each closely to determine where and how synthesis was to be achieved. The author has the ability to be both stern and compassionate where he judges the synthesis to be weak or defective. But he never loses sight of the fact that what Teilhard wanted to make was not theories but music.

# Preface

What this study attempts to do is gather together and criticize pertinent materials from Teilhard's writings on morality, love, and the organization of human energy under the influence of personal love. The pattern for this critical synthesis will itself be derived from his thought, although some modifications will be introduced.[1] However, in order to view these materials in their proper perspective, it will be necessary first to recall certain essentials of his overarching world view and his generalized anthropology, which provide the base for his moral theory about human social growth.[2] For a sym-

1. See below, chap. 4, A for other details on the rationale behind the arrangement of the present study, which leans heavily on Teilhard's thought in his essay "Human Energy," 1937. Denis Mermod, on the other hand, has opted in favor of a structure derived from *PM*. See Mermod, *La morale chez Teilhard*, pp. 42-43.

2. For more complete treatment of Teilhard's overall vision, the following works are particularly important, even though some have a more or less specialized slant. Louis Barjon, *Le Combat de Pierre Teilhard de Chardin* (Laval, Québec: Les Presses de L'Université Laval, 1971) hereafter referred to as *Le Combat de Teilhard*; René d'Ouince, *un prophète en procès: Teilhard de Chardin et l'avenir de la pensée chretienne* (Paris: Aubier Montaigne, 1970), vol. 2, hereafter referred to as *Teilhard: la pensée chrétienne*; Robert L. Faricy, S.J., *Teilhard de Chardin's Theology of the Christian in the World* (New York: Sheed and Ward, 1967), hereafter referred to as *Teilhard: Theology*; Donald P. Gray, *The One and the Many: Teilhard de Chardin's Vision of Unity* (New York: Herder and Herder, 1969); Henri de Lubac, *The Religion of Teilhard de Chardin*, trans. René Hague, Image Books (Garden City, N.Y.: Doubleday and Co., Inc., 1968), hereafter referred to as *Religion of Teilhard*; and *Teilhard de Chardin: the Man and His Meaning*, trans. René Hague, Mentor-Omega Books (New York: New Ameri-

pathetic grasp of this basic anthropology, two other avenues of thought must also be examined. They are his
own motivation for exploring the meaning of life and
the method of his thought and expression.

Chapter 1 deals with Teilhard's motivation and a
background summary of his world view. Chapter 2 looks
to his ethical methodology, to how he derived and expressed his moral theory. The remaining chapters take
up the content of this theory, working out to particular
notions from general concepts.

The meaning of Teilhard's "Morality of Movement" is
explored in chapter 3. Love energy, as the highest form
of moral energy is examined in chapter 4. How love
energy would be organized and related to the other
types of human energy, "spiritualized" as well as "controlled" and "incorporated," occupies chapter 5 (the direction of aggression, by sublimation, to constructive research), chapter 6 (the politics of complementarity),
chapter 7 (education as transmissive and developmental
of spiritualized energy), and chapter 8 (technology as
controlled energy, eugenics as incorporated energy).

Chapter 9, finally, correlates the preceding with
Teilhard's understanding of the role of Christ and
Christian love in his morality of movement, both in its
general aspects, and in the particular facets as consi-

can Library, 1967), hereafter referred to as *Teilhard: Man and Meaning*; Chris-
topher F. Mooney, *Teilhard de Chardin and the Mystery of Christ*, Image Books
(Garden City, N.Y.: Doubleday and Co., Inc., 1968), hereafter referred to as
*Mystery of Christ*; Olivier Rabut, O.P., *Teilhard de Chardin: A Critical Study* (New
York: Sheed and Ward, 1961); Emile Rideau, *Teilhard de Chardin: A Guide to
His Thought*, trans. René Hague (London: Collins, 1967), hereafter referred to
as *Teilhard: Guide*; Piet Smulders, *The Design of Teilhard de Chardin*, trans. Arthur Gibson (Westminster Md.: The Newman Press, 1967) hereafter referred
to as *Design of Teilhard*; de Solages, *Teilhard: étude* and Norbert M. Wildiers, *An
Introduction to Teilhard de Chardin*, trans. Hubert Hoskins, preface by Christopher Mooney, S.J., Fontana Books (London: Collins, 1967). This last is
perhaps the best short introductory work available in English and its author is
the general editor of the official French text of the works of Teilhard. Christopher Mooney's preface has some excellent suggestions for a sequence of
readings from Teilhard's writings that would most easily lead into a grasp of
his thought. For a good selection of texts arranged according to Teilhard's
own short outline note, "Ma position intellectuelle" (1948), see Jean-Pierre
Demoulin, *Let Me Explain*, trans. René Hague *et al.* (London: Collins, 1970).

dered in chapters 4, 5, 6, 7, and 8. Chapter 10 stands by way of a brief summary of the main positive and negative elements in Teilhard's moral theory as they emerged in the course of the study.

# Acknowledgments

I would like to thank the following publishers for permission to quote copyrighted material: Ruth Nanda Anshen, for permission to quote from the *Perspectives in Humanism* series. These quotations are from the volume in *Perspectives in Humanism*, Planned and Edited by Ruth Nanda Anshen; *Letters to Two Friends, 1926-1952* by Pierre Teilhard de Chardin, New York, 1968.

Georges Borchardt, Inc., for permission to quote from *Letters to Léontine Zanta* (New York: Harper & Row; London: Collins), 1969. Reprinted by permission of George Borchardt, Inc., New York.

Collins, Publishers, for permission to quote from Pierre Teilhard de Chardin, *The Phenomenon of Man*, 1959, *The Future of Man*, 1964, *The Making of a Mind*, 1965, *Letters from a Traveller*, 1962, *The Divine Milieu*, 1960, *Writings in Time of War*, 1968, *Science and Christ*, 1969, *Human Energy*, 1969, *The Vision of the Past*, 1966, *The Apperance of Man*, 1965, *Man's Place in Nature*, 1966, *Letters to Léontine Zanta*, 1969, *Activation of Energy*, 1970, and *Let Me Explain*, arranged and selected by Jean-Pierre Demoulin, 1970. Reprinted by permission of Collins, Publishers, London.

Harcourt, Brace, Jovanovich, Inc., for permission to quote from Teilhard de Chardin, *Activation of Energy*,

17

1970, and *Human Energy*, 1969. Excerpts from *Human Energy* by Pierre Teilhard de Chardin are reprinted by permission of Harcourt Brace Jovanovich, Inc.; copyright © 1962 by Éditions du Seuil; copyright © 1969 by William Collins Sons & Co. Ltd.

The author thanks Harper & Row, Publishers, for permission to quote from Pierre Teilhard de Chardin, *The Phenomenon of Man*, 1959, *The Future of Man*, 1964, *The Making of a Mind*, 1965, *Letters from a Traveller*, 1962, *The Divine Milieu*, 1960, *Writings in Time of War*, 1968, *Science and Christ*, 1969, *The Vision of the Past*, 1966, *The Appearance of Man*, 1965, *Man's Place in Nature*, 1966, and *Let Me Explain*, arranged and selected by Jean-Pierre Demoulin, 1970. Reprinted by permission of Harper & Row, Publishers, New York.

Helicon Press, Inc., for permission to quote from *Teilhard de Chardin: A Biographical Study* by Claude Cuénot, translated by Vincent Colimore and edited by René Hague, Helicon Press, Baltimore, Md. © 1965 by Helicon Press, Inc.

Paulist Press, for permission to quote from Piet Smulders, *The Design of Teilhard*, translated by Arthur Gibson (Westminster, Md.: Newman Press, 1967). Copyright © 1967 by The Missionary Society of Saint Paul The Apostle, New York. Reprinted by permission of Paulist Press, New York.

I would also like to express my thanks for the encouragement and constructive criticism of the Rev. Charles E. Curran, Dr. Emily Binns, the Rev. Robert L. Faricy, S.J., and the Rev. Christopher Mooney, S.J. (for his Foreword to this book, and for his critical reading of the Christological summary in chapter 9). For special assistance in obtaining manuscript material of Teilhard's writings not otherwise available, I would like to thank the Rev. Robert L. Faricy, S.J., the late Minna Cassard, of the American Teilhard de Chardin Association, and the Rev. Emile Rideau, S.J.

# Morality and the Human Future
## in the Thought
## of Teilhard de Chardin

# Abbreviations

The following list of abbreviations is for major works of Teilhard or collections of his writings cited in the footnotes. Complete bibliographical information about these materials can be found in the Bibliography.

| | |
|---|---|
| *AE* | *The Activation of Energy* |
| *AM* | *The Appearance of Man* |
| *CB* | *Correspondence, Teilhard-Blondel* |
| *CE* | *Christianity and Evolution* |
| *DA* | *Les directions de l'avenir* |
| *DM* | *The Divine Milieu* |
| *EG* | *Écrits du temps de la guerre* |
| *FM* | *The Future of Man* |
| *HE* | *Human Energy* |
| *HU* | *Hymn of the Universe* |
| *I* | *Inédits* (unpublished French manuscripts) |
| *LF* | *Letters to Two Friends* |
| *LME* | *Let Me Explain* |
| *LT* | *Letters from a Traveller* |
| *LZ* | *Letters to Léontine Zanta* |
| *MM* | *The Making of a Mind* |
| *MPN* | *Man's Place in Nature* |
| *PM* | *The Phenomenon of Man* |
| *SB* | *Sur le Bonheur* |
| *SC* | *Science and Christ* |
| *VP* | *The Vision of the Past* |
| *WW* | *Writings in Time of War* |

# 1

# Introduction. The Problem of Compressive Socialization

## A. Morality in Teilhard's Evolutionary World

Teilhard saw the world as an evolutionary world become conscious of its responsibility to push the development of mankind forward and upward toward complete human fulfillment. But it was also a world in which social process had reached a critical phase. In his own terms, this is the phase of "compressive socialization." Moreover, the controlling energy that will determine success or failure in resolving the crisis, is, according to him, human moral energy. The reason seems to be clear enough, in that morality, regardless of the many theories about it, is fundamentally concerned with the orientation of responsible human choice, with the complex spectrum of human decisions bearing on how life should be lived in order to be lived well.

Although Teilhard's concern about morality and his evaluation of its importance is manifest in his earliest writings, he never did set himself the task of putting together a comprehensive synthesis of his ethical thought,

21

bringing together the different insights and conclusions he had reached about moral matters down through the years.[1] But it can be said, nevertheless, that his moral concern continued to deepen, and, particularly during the last two decades of his life, came to focus with particular emphasis on the critical problems of human unification on a global scale, which he saw generating so much turmoil and confusion about him.[2]

As he viewed the total situation, the proper understanding, development, and organization of love, which he considered the highest form of human energy, were the crucial factors affecting and effecting human growth. Moreover, central to grasping the meaning of love was an understanding of the meaning of human personality. Where all of this was coming to a head, he perceived, was in the arena of social process, development, and organization.

---

1. In the absence of a complete systematic presentation of Teilhard's moral thought, Mermod sees one possible explanation for the fact that he has not been attacked on these grounds, despite strong negative criticism in other areas. See Denis Mermod, *La Morale chez Teilhard* (Paris: Editions Universitaires, 1967), p. 142. The scattered character of Teilhard's ethical thought is also evidenced by the regrets and some misunderstandings expressed in the papers of several contributors to an International Symposium dealing with Teilhardian themes, as recently as the early seventies, about certain aspects of his thought. As will be seen from texts to be cited in the present study, while there are gaps enough, and bases for misunderstanding, not all of those lamented are as bad as might seem. The situation is rather one of certain significant materials tucked away in various essays and not readily accessible, even to serious readers. See *Teilhard de Chardin: In Quest of the Perfection of Man*, An International Symposium, ed. and comp. by Geraldine O. Browning, Joseph L. Alioto, and Seymour M. Farber, M.D. (Rutherford, N.J.: Fairleigh Dickinson University Press, 1973 hereafter referred to as *Teilhard: Symposim*). Particular papers indicative of this situation are those by Conor Cruise O'Brien, pp. 23-41, Ralph R. Greenson, M.D., pp. 180-94, Mark F. Ferber, pp. 195-209, and Pearce Young, pp. 210-25. To a greater or less extent, certain points raised in these penetrating, thought-provoking essays would have been illuminated by texts to be cited in the following chapters dealing with Teilhard's thought on aggression and matters political.

2. See Madeleine Barthélemy-Madaule, *La personne et le drame humain chez Teilhard de Chardin* (Paris: Éditions du Seuil, 1966), pp. 141, 144 (hereafter referred to as *La personne chez Teilhard*). See also Mgr. Bruno de Solages, *Teilhard de Chardin: témoignage et étude sur le développement de sa pensée* (N.p.: Edouard Privat, Éditeur, 1967) pp. 30-31 (hereafter referred to as *Teilhard: étude*).

## B. Teilhard's Faith Seeking Understanding

Long ago, Augustine, Bishop of Hippo, wrote, "To believe is nothing else than to think with assent. . . . If faith is not charged with thought, it is nothing."[3] Although Teilhard differed in many ways from Augustine, his work and intent, corroborated by the testimony of at least one who spent long hours discussing theological matters with him, reveal the same guiding spirit.[4] What stands in stark contrast to Augustine is, of course, the thought with which Teilhard's faith was charged, the thought of a twentieth-century scientist deeply concerned about the meaning of evolutionary theory for his faith.

From certain works of Teilhard, one can get the impression that his principal concern was to elaborate a new style of natural theology leading to religious belief, that he was working upward from generalized scientific reasoning to God and revelation. And it is true that his apologetic works, written with a scientific-humanist reader principally in mind, do come off this way.[5] Other texts convey the idea that he was indecisively and agonizingly in an insoluble dilemma, with an ardent love of the world and scientific research tugging his mind and heart in one direction and his love of Christ pulling him in another.[6] But the overall tenor of his life and thought

3. *De praedestinatione sanctorum* 5, (*PL* 44:963). Cited by Emile Mersch, S.J., *The Theology of the Mystical Body*, trans. Cyril Vollert, S.J. (St. Louis: B. Herder Book Co., 1951), p. 10.

4. See Gabriel M. Allegra, O.F.M., *My Conversations with Teilhard de Chardin on the Primacy of Christ: Peking, 1942-1945*, trans. by Bernardino M. Bonansea, O.F.M. (Chicago: Franciscan Herald Press, 1971), p. 27, for Teilhard's familiarity with St. Augustine, and p. 37 for Teilhard's apostolic intent. An excellent study of Teilhard's missionary orientation can be found in Henri de Lubac, "Teilhard de Chardin: Missionary and Disciple of St. Paul," in *Teilhard Explained*, trans. Anthony Buono, Deus Books (New York: Paulist Press, 1968), pp. 7-37.

5. Note the progression of his ideas, for example, as it can be seen in the plan for *PM* (1940), *MPN* (1949), and "The Singularity of the Human Species" (1954), *AM*, pp. 208-73. Also, "How I Believe" (1934), *CE*, pp. 96-132.

6. This reading of his psychological orientation can be derived, principally

leads to the first position, that his controlling commitment was religious. His overriding concern, then, was to interpret and enrich his and others' Christian beliefs through his experience of scientific-humanist culture. At the same time, he hoped to help those who did not share his beliefs to be disposed more favorably toward them.[7]

Examination of Teilhard's thought could, then, quite properly begin with his religious convictions and then go on to how they were affected by his experience of the world. However, the writings in which he presents the base of his moral theory start from his phenomenological thought and then go on to the relation of this thought to God. Principally because of this approach, this study follows a similar sequence.

While the weight of controlling priority was with Teilhard's religious faith, he really struggled with the difficult problem of how to explain the synthesis of his two faiths, which he was convinced did exist, but which he himself initially did not know how to formulate.[8] He did love the world and could write with sincere feeling

by over-weighting the manner in which he points up the problem of faith for modern man when he is leading into his discussion. See "Cosmic Life" (1916), WW, pp. 28-45, and "How I Believe" (1934), CE, 99-103.

7. For an early explicit expression of his apologetic, apostolic concern, see "Note pour servir à l'évangélisation des temps nouveaux" (1919), EC, pp. 367-81. His comment in "Creative Union" (1917), WW, p. 174, is also significant: ". . . the philosophy of creative union is simply the development-generalization, extension to the universe—of what the Church teaches us about the growth of Christ. *It is the philosophy of the universe expressed in terms of the notion of the mystical body.* It was primarily as such that I myself came to grasp it, and it is only so that it can be understood: by striving to love and hold Christ in all things" (emphasis Teilhard's). His best explanation of different levels of writing according to different objectives is found in "Outline of a Dialectic of Spirit" (1946), AE, pp. 143-51. Also see Barjon, *Le Combat de Teilhard,* on "Les raisons d'écrire," pp. 150-57, where he singles out for special comment in this regard a passage from "Forma Christi" (1918), WW, pp. 250-51. In this passage Teilhard expresses his regrets at the extrinsic and individualistic manner in which Christianity was being explained in his day.

8. In his autobiographical "Le coeur de la matiére" (1950), I, pp. 24-25, Teilhard relates how, when a young Jesuit in the Juniorate on the Island of Jersey, he was reassured by the Master of Novices that the God of the Cross looked to his natural development as well as his sanctification, but did not explain to him how or why.

about it.[9] Moreover, he believed intensely in the progress of the world through evolution, with special emphasis on man's creative research in recent centuries.
How to synthesize, integrate, and formulate in language
his convictions of this sort with his radical commitment
to Jesus and His Church as he understood it, was the
central synthesizing task of his inner life.[10]

The present study keeps this overall concern in view,
but its specialized focus is on how Teilhard resolved the
apparent dilemma in the context of what he called the
"compressive Socialization" stage in social process, and
how this resolution not only gave new clarity to his faith
in Christ, but also shed new light on his faith in the
world.


## C. Summary of Teilhard's Phenomenological Anthropology

"Compressive socialization" is an expression that
emerges in Teilhard's thought at a point well down the
line in his elaboration of his evolutionary world view. To
get at its meaning calls for a look at the fundamental
elements in this view that lead up to it.[11]

First are the key ideas in his particular type of

9. See, for example, "The Spiritual Power of Matter" (1919), *HU*, pp. 59-
71, especially the "Hymn to Matter" concluding it, pp. 68-71. On "passion"
and "passionate" in Teilhard, see Henri de Lubac's remarks in his *The Eternal
Feminine: A Study on the Poem by Teilhard de Chardin*, trans. René Hague (New
York: Harper & Row, 1970), hereafter referred to as *Eternal Feminine*, pp.
105-107. Roger Garaudy, the French Marxist, it might also be noted, has
found Teilhard's *joie de vivre* worthy of comment. See Claude Cuénot, *Science
and Faith in Teilhard de Chardin*, with a comment by Roger Garaudy, trans.
Noel Lindsay (London: Garnstone Press, 1967), p. 82, hereafter referred to as
*Science and Faith*.

10. See "Le coeur de la matière" (1950), *I*, pp. 24-25, where he describes
how he worked out his synthesis in theory and expressed it in the first chapter of *DM* (1927).

11. The principal sources for the outline presented here are *PM* (1940),
*MPN* (1949), "A Summary of my Phenomenological View of the World"
(1954), *LME*, pp. 71-74, and "The Singularities of the Human Species"
(1954), *AM*, pp. 208-73.

phenomenological perspective of the world. The next chapter will examine more in detail what he himself understood by the term *phenomenological*. Present concern is directed rather to the *content* of his vision, however it might be described, from a methodological angle. It will be helpful, and in a sense necessary, in order to grasp this content, to bear in mind what the main thrust of the term did and did not have for him. In using it he was consciously attempting to avoid what he understood to be technical philosophical, metaphysical thought. Rather, he had in mind to *describe* what *appeared* to his mind. Hence his choice of the word *phenomenon*. But, he did not want to limit his analysis and synthesis to merely the empirical data, the technically positive phenomena of the various empirical sciences. He proposed to start with this type of data, but he wanted to go beyond it into what he spoke of at one time as a "generalized biology." This would retain certain basic characteristics of the scientific method of hypothesis and test, yet transcend the limits of specialized scientific disciplines to the larger questions of human life and destiny—without getting into completely abstract philosophizing.[12]

What are the main lines of his vision of the world?

In the principal texts that present Teilhard's overall picture, preliminary material is consistently provided about the nature of the evolutionary process prior to the advent of life on earth. In his major work, *The Phenomenon of Man*, these considerations are lengthy.

The fundamental operative pattern, spoken of by Teilhard himself as the "starting point and key" for his whole system, is what he terms the *Law of Recurrence*, or *Complexity-Consciousness*.[13] Since it is so important, a close

12. For the expression *generalized biology*, see "Centrology" (1944), *AE*, p. 115 n. 8. This note is of special significance for helping to clarify, in Teilhard's own words, how he himself was reading "scientific" terms in his phenomenological writings. It also contains basic material for understanding how his thought proceeded analogically.

13. "A Summary of My Phenomenological View of the World" (1954), *LME*, p. 71.

examination of it is in order. There are two main questions to consider: 1) how does he derive the law? and 2) what does he mean by it?

The law emerges as the solution to a problem that he views as otherwise insoluble. At its root, the problem has to do with the relationship between matter and spirit. In its more developed form, it deals with the continuity of physics and biology. From a philosophical angle, it bears on the thorny question of finalism vs. determinism. He describes it as follows in *The Phenomenon of Man*:

> On the one hand, the materialists insist on talking about objects as though they only consisted of external actions in transient relationships. On the other hand the upholders of a spiritual interpretation are obstinately determined not to go outside a kind of solitary introspection in which things are only looked upon as being shut in upon themselves in their "immanent" workings. Both fight on different planes and do not meet; each only sees half the problem.[14]

What underlies Teilhard's concern here is, of course, his elemental intellectual passion for a unified vision of what seem to be antithetic components of the universe, a passion that runs through his writings with remarkable consistency from "Cosmic Life" down through the years.[15]

His solution to the problem is reached, in a sense, by undercutting it—treating a more basic question, answering that one, and then showing how the answer to this basic question provides an acceptable answer to the apparent dilemma he has described. The more basic question and the most general and fundamental of all can be put in broad scientific terms: how can one formulate a general descriptive law of evolutionary process?

In brief, he derives and formulates this law in the following steps:

First, a consideration of matter, minuscule, interre-

14. *PM* (1940), p. 53.
15. See, for example, the introductory pages to two essays at opposite ends of the time-spectrum of his writings; "Cosmic Life" (1916), *WW*, pp. 14-18, and "Le Christique" (1955), *I*, pp. 1-2.

lated, energized, and in movement. On analysis, matter yields to a breakdown into countless tiny particles. But these are not isolated from one another. In similarly countless ways there is a vast network of interconnection and dependence throughout the universe. Nor is this interconnection static. Material particles are energized, active, moving. What is the character of their dynamism? Some would incline to say, by virtue of the laws of Conservation and Dissipation of Energy, that they have a fundamental entropic drift, unifying, solely "downward" toward decomposition, leveling, and equilibrium. Teilhard admits the incontestability of the laws, but pleads that there is more to the story.[16]

Second, one cannot overlook, he insists, the phenomenon of "corpusculization." Material particles not only interact and break down, they also come together and combine. Furthermore, as one scrutinizes the range of material units, even below the level of life, one finds a considerable spectrum of *organized complexity*. True, there are certain groupings together that amount to the same type of combination one finds in a heap of sand. This is not what Teilhard has in mind. Rather, he would call attention to combinations with a certain recognizable center or core of energy binding the disparate elements into a new and, as such, observable unity.

In what can be distinguished as his third step, his thought leapfrogs ahead, so to speak, and then extrapolates in reverse. What has been seen up to this point had dealt with complexity—but nothing has been said about consciousness. To do so, he must go up the line in the universe to man and then come back. For in man and in man alone is consciousness aware of itself. Man alone "knows that he knows." Still, if one reflects, it is clear

16. For a clarification of contemporary scientific understanding of the meaning of entropy, quite different from the sense of the term as employed by Teilhard, see William C. Saslaw, "Entropy and the Universe," *The Teilhard Review* 3, no. 2 (Winter 1968-69): 76-79. Saslaw views Teilhard's conception of the term as no longer tenable, however current it may have been in Teilhard's formative years.

enough that a condition similar to consciousness is present in the "centering" of material bits, in bits even so humble as the simplest of atoms. There is even at this level a unifying bond of energy giving them each their peculiar identity, a real, however rudimentary, "self." Moreover, as one proceeds to examine more complex portions of matter, he perceives a more distinctive centering energy as he finds more and more complex bodies. There is a verifiable correlation between the complexity of organic structure and this peculiar "within" of things that gives each its special uniqueness. Plants clearly have more of an interior energy than nonliving things; animals, still more. In man, there is a special distinctive "within," which we know as "consciousness." At this stage—the human—it has a peculiar clarity, manifest in man's awareness of himself as a self, with a coordinated system of integral parts sustaining and developing that self. Below man there is no such patent awareness, but nonetheless there are undeniable counterparts.

What then, is the meaning of the Law? Bearing in mind the phenomena just observed and their special characteristics, one may formulate their dynamic pattern in a law, the Law of Complexity-Consciousness. In his "Postscript" to *The Phenomenon of Man*, where Teilhard sums up the essence of that study, he puts it in the following way:

> if the universe, regarded sidereally, is in the process of spatial expansion (from the infinitesimal to the immense), in the same way and still more clearly it presents itself to us, physico-chemically, as in process of organic *involution* upon itself (from the extremely simple to the extremely complex)—and, moreover, this particular involution "of complexity" is experimentally bound up with a correlative increase of interiorisation, that is to say, in the psyche or consciousness.[17]

Another version, from "A Summary of my

17. *PM* (1940), p. 301.

Phenomenological View of the World," puts it thus:

> Developing as a counter-current that cuts across Entropy, there is a cosmic drift of matter towards stages of arrangement of progressively greater complexity (this being towards—or within—a "third infinite," *the infinite of complexity*, which is just as real as the Infinitesimal or the Immense.) And consciousness presents itself to our experience as the effect or the specific property of this Complexity taken to extremely high values.[18]

As Teilhard saw it, the formulation of this general law of evolution helped him to meet satisfactorily the matter-spirit dilemma mentioned above. Through his conception of tangential energy, pertaining to the arrangement of particles and to radial energy, tied in with a thrust upward to higher consciousness, he was able to bring together in complementarity the Laws of Conservation and Dissipation of Energy and the Law of Complexity-Consciousness.[19]

As important as this Law is in Teilhard's thought for describing a fundamental mechanism of evolution, he associates it with yet another pattern: the ramification of living matter.[20] This latter is not technically a corollary of the first, for it is not deduced from it. Rather, it describes the curves of energy *branching* upward and forward in accord with the Law of Complexity-Consciousness. Much of his strictly scientific research and writing was devoted to analysis of this mechanism as

18. *LME*, p. 71. The significance of Teilhard's emphasis on the organized complexification of matter as a base for sympathetic dialogue with Marxist humanists can be seen in Roger Garaudy's remark that Engels himself had looked on the development of life from this perspective, and that Engels, had he been given the knowledge of human origins and development of Teilhard's generation, would probably have written something like *The Phenomenon of Man*—minus, of course, the theological implications Teilhard drew. See Claude Cuénot, *Science and Faith*, comment by Garaudy p. 79.

19. See *PM* (1940), pp. 62-66.

20. See particularly "The Singularities of the Human Species" (1954), *AM*, pp. 215-19, with regard to his use of the term *ramification*. The process is, however, clearly described in both *PM* and *MPN*.

it operated in the past. A great part of the first half of *The Phenomenon of Man* sums up this process on the pre-human level. Teilhard's central thesis here may be formulated as follows: the universe, that is to say, evolution, in its surge onward and upward toward higher forms of consciousness, branched out ceaselessly in variegated forms. In these, once the animal level was reached, the index of fuller consciousness became *cephalization*, a more intricate and highly developed nervous system. In this steady upward thrusting, the line of primates became axial, or radial, pointing toward the advent of man, whose role in the entire process would assume unique distinctiveness.[21]

With the appearance of man on earth, evolution, according to Teilhard, passed a critical threshold far more important than that passed by the first upsurges toward life—the threshold of reflection. The external biological arrangement of the aboriginal human group was achieved through a mutation, or series of mutations, quite similar to previous mutations along the various branches of living beings. But with this particular style of complexity in the nervous system, consciousness burst into the full daylight of awareness. With human awareness of awareness there likewise came a fuller spontaneity and a longer range of vision; inventiveness also—not merely the blind inventiveness of indefinitely groping chance, but calculating inventiveness, which meant creativity, foresight, and planning, and that unique variety of spontaneity too known as freedom, with its inescapable concomitants of responsibility, and the power to love or refuse love. Evolution itself was moving into the self-conscious stage; the all-important stage of the personal in life had risen upward and begun the development of a totally new type of "sphere" on the

21. See *PM* (1940), pp. 159, 163-80; *MPN* (1949), pp. 47-57; "The Singularities of the Human Species" (1954), *AM*, pp. 210-22.

planet: the sphere of thought—the *noosphere*.[22]
As with the rest of evolution, this last development was a long time aborning, with several miscarriages, or at least incomplete successes—the pre-hominids and neanderthaloids—prior to the arrival and spread of *homo sapiens*. But as mankind's proper and distant ancestors multiplied and fanned out across the globe, another special phenomenon came upon the scene, a phenomenon that in its advanced form provides the matter for central questions—that aspect or element in the hominization process known as *socialization*.[23]

22. The term first appears in Teilhard's essay, "Hominization" (1923), *VP*, p. 63. Perhaps his best extended treatment of this specific term occurs in the latter part of *MPN* (1949), chap. 4, "The Formation of the Noosphere," "I. The Socialisation of Expansion: Civilisation and Individuation," pp. 79-95, and chap. 5, "The Formation of the Noosphere," "II. The Socialisation of Compression: Totalisation and Personalisation: Future Tendencies," pp. 96-102. The most developed single essay is "The Formation of the Noosphere" (1947), *FM*, pp. 155-84. Moreover, despite the fact that he is not much preoccupied with the term itself in *PM* (1940), it would not be stretching a point to assert that "Book Three: Thought," pp. 163-234, and "Book Four: Survival," through the "Epilogue: The Christian Phenomenon," pp. 237-99, are concerned with noospheric origins and problems attendant upon its development, along with predictions about its future and conditions for success. Where his concern came to focus with regard to noospheric growth was especially in the area of socialization in what he described as its compressive phase—about which more shortly. For an excellent treatment of the principal ideas involved, see Faricy, *Teilhard: Theology*, chap. 2, "Evolution and its Direction," particularly pp. 51-72. Likewise de Solages, *Teilhard: étude*, chap. 6, "La Noosphere," pp. 137-66, chap. 6, "Le Point Omega," pp. 167-207, and chap. 7, "Une morale au service de la cosmogenese," pp. 208-34. Madeleine Barthélemy-Madaule, *Bergson et Teilhard de Chardin* (Paris: Éditions du Seuil, 1963), pp. 336-51, hereafter referred to as *Bergson-Teilhard*, has a special section on the noosphere, but the entire "Deuxième Partie: Le Personnel," embracing chap. 6, "La Personne Humain et la Phénomène Humain," pp. 303-62, chap. 7, "L'Univers Personnel," pp. 363-425, and chap. 8, "Le Divin," pp. 426-93, is concerned with important ideas pertinent to the growth and meaning of life in the noosphere. Her later book *La personne chez Teilhard* could, in effect, be taken as a work on the noosphere with emphasis on the personal perspective. Similarly, one could say that the present study can be looked at as a study of key elements in noospheric growth, with emphasis on ethical perspectives.
23. In addition to the texts of Teilhard cited above, p. 17, n25, regarding the noosphere, the bulk of the material found in the collections, *FM, HE*, and *AE* is relevant to Teilhard's thought about socialization. Commentators, depending on the particular angle from which they approach the question, draw up different lists of the essays or sections of books they judge most significant. To assemble a battery of such texts at this point in the present study seems unwarranted, in view of the fact that the texts the present writer has found most important have, regarding fundamental ideas, been mentioned already,

Teilhard correctly notes that certain forms of socialization—the organized clustering of individuals within a group, with differentiation of function for the corporate good—are observable in life other than human. One can also mark that this manner of coming together is, on a special plane, manifestation or corroboration of the Law of Complexity-Consciousness. However, on the subhuman level, socialization is always characterized by a certain mechanization, most aptly typified in the ant hill or the hive. It lacks the qualities attendant upon reflection: spontaneity, inventiveness, foresight, freedom, and love. It is *impersonal*.

Through socialization the noosphere is deployed and takes shape. Teilhard distinguishes two stages in this development. The first he describes as socialization of expansion; the second, that of compression.

First, the expansive phase. From the very beginning, as men multiplied, they lived in groups, with differentiation of function. In primitive nomadic hunting groups the organizational pattern was relatively simple, determined by the needs and functions of food gathering, protection from the elements and other forces, and the continuation of life in some sort of family unit. As men settled down, cultivated fixed plots of ground, and devised more sophisticated tools to meet their needs, more complex and highly organized styles of social living emerged. For century after century, as this process went on, men continued to spread out, and the human race expanded over the face of the earth.

In general, what characterize the compressive socialization stage and differentiate it from the expansive are three principal lines of development. First, the extraordinary escalation of population growth throughout the

and, with regard to specific aspects of the socialization process, will be cited in considerable detail in subsequent chapters. A quite comprehensive list can be found in Faricy, *Teilhard: Theology*, pp. 54-55 n36. See also, Barthélemy-Madaule, *La personne chez Teilhard*, p. 144, and Francois Russo, "La socialisation selon Teilhard de Chardin, *"Teilhard de Chardin et la pensée catholique: colloque de Venisse,* ed. Claude Cuénot (Paris: Éditions du Seuil, 1965), p. 171.

world, with its concomitant crowding of people into vastly larger and more densely populated urban centers and the progressive settlement of hitherto unsettled and open territory. Second, the rapid growth, in the last two centuries, of ever-more-sophisticated technology, as a consequence of scientific discoveries and their application through inventive engineering and the business of marketing. Particularly significant here have been the development of mass-production techniques, along with electronic means of communication in all forms, and the vastly improved methods of transportation, embracing the highly complex network of highways, railroads, and air traffic, together with the reduction of infant mortality and the prolongation of the human life span through use of the fruits of an expanding medical technology and more efficient methods of agriculture. Inextricably associated with these developments have been the more complicated and centralized styles of political organization and the bureaucratic structures inevitably found in their train. On the third level is what Teilhard speaks of as the gradual emergence of a kind of common consciousness, a shared awareness, which he attributes in a special way to the diffusion of scientific knowledge and its application in the development of the varied forms of technology.

These three stages or levels of human societal growth have, it is true, been present in some recognizable form from the beginning, centuries ago, of town and city life. But they are experienced now in much greater magnitude, and with increased intensity. The reason for this is that whereas at one time the phenomena were located in relatively scattered sites in various parts of the earth, from which people could always emigrate into new and undeveloped territory, men are now becoming aware, with concern bordering on panic for some, that the globe itself, not merely one part of it, is becoming crowded with people who are increasingly bound with ever-more-complex ties of economic and political dependence, made more intricate by almost instant communication and enormously accelerated and expanded methods of transportation.[24] What is less clear is the type and extent of world consciousness that is emerging. It is particularly at this level that the major ethical problem develops, the ramifications of which will occupy the bulk of this study.

The fundamental ethical question looks to the governing attitude, the orientational stance that mankind should take when faced with the brute facts of ever-increasing population, more complex styles of economic and political life binding people more and more into a global collective existence, and the universal diffusion of all types of knowledge. Teilhard was well aware of the impact of the developments described in this compressive process, and in his "Reflections on the Compression of Mankind," written only a few years before he died, he put down his impressions about the particulars in the following passage, under the ominous heading "The Agony of Our Age: A World that is Asphyxiating."

> unfortunately, the most directly perceptible result of this compression would appear to be, for our generation, a generally experienced agony—not to say a general worsening of our situation.
> For, in short, is it not under the influence—always the same influence—of an extreme demographic pressure that a linked series of disorders and evils is making itself felt, threatening gradually to make the world uninhabitable for us?
> This flood of sheer humanity which seeps up through every fissure, drowning all the best of us, and, in virtue of its very mass, one might say, escaping the governance of selection—
> This disappearance, so enervating both intellectually and physically, of solitude and of nature, in favour of the factory and the town—

24. One of Teilhard's best analytic descriptions of the network of ties binding human beings together in the modern world is found in his essay, "The Evolution of Responsibility in the World" (1950), *AE*, pp. 207-14. This essay will be examined closely below, chap. 3, in conjunction with Teilhard's moral theory.

This disagreeable closeness of intercourse, this continual friction between individuals who become more alien or even hostile to one another, the more numerous they are—
This mechanization of persons by enslavement to forms of work that are inevitably collectivized—
This complication, this burden, this increasing insecurity of daily life, which largely explains* the extreme nervous tension (or even the disturbing neuroses) of our time—
Not to mention the increasing danger of contagious influences and the exhaustion of resources in an overpopulated setting—
And all this because there are too many of us in too little room.

Faced with this type of global situation, what should mankind do? In an earlier essay, almost a decade and a half before, Teilhard isolated four main possible approaches, which in themselves are indicative of the difficulties found in the whole picture. In "The Grand Option" he outlined the character and implications of the inclination to 1) pessimistic withdrawal; then to 2) fundamentally optimistic but nevertheless retiring disengagement; 3) optimistic but divergent, dispersive individual fulfillment; and, finally, 4) positive commitment to convergent, yet differentiating personal communion.[26] In his own mind, Teilhard could see no successful issue for mankind in the nihilism of existential pessimism, nor in the premature disengagement from matter of Eastern mysticism, nor in a theory of evolutionary development that defied the convergent trend of complexity-consciousness and subordinated the development of human society to the *individual*, which he was careful to distinguish from the *person*. What this left him with, in the fourth option, is what the rest of this study is all about—the function of morality in the evolutionary process, and all that is involved in the derivation and

---

*The other (possibly the most important?) part of the explanation being the unvoiced anxiety experienced by a being momentarily lost in the immensity of a universe he no longer understands.[25]

25. *AE* (1953), pp. 341-42.
26. *FM*, 1939, pp. 37-60.

specification of what this means, both phenomenologically and theologically, whereby the person develops his
individual uniqueness to the full in the process of universal convergence.[27]

## D. Theology and Compressive Socialization

Up to this point human development has been viewed
with the focus on Teilhard's evolutionary phenomenology, and the problem of compressive socialization has
been described and located in that context. What happens when his theological preoccupations are brought
into play?

Put generally, the problem in its theological context is
the vexing one of the relationship between science and
religion. Teilhard saw it half a century ago in its particularly acute form in the confrontation between the concept of an evolutionary universe and a concept, whatever
metaphysic was bolstering it up, that could be described
as more or less "fixist" or static.[28]

Whatever may be the final judgment on the Galileo
case, it has stood for centuries as a symbol of religious
superstition and intransigence that resist the discoveries
of science. However simple and devout certain eminent
scientists may have been in their private lives, their scientific discoveries have, in fact, paved the way for considerable philosophic revolt against religion and especially against organized Christianity in the West.[29]

27. For an illuminating overview study of the connection between world
view and human society, framed in a Teilhardian context, see N. Max Wildiers, "World Picture and Culture," *Teilhard: Symposium*, pp. 64-87. The piece
is excellent for tracing the correspondence between a "cosmos" outlook with
rigid social structuring, and a "cosmogenetic" view of dynamic social process.
28. The opposition between "fixism," or "immobilism" and "progressivism,"
or "mobilism" is a constantly occurring polarity in Teilhard's writings. Where
it shows up with particular significance in connection with his moral theory is
in his description of the moral theory needed in an evolutionary world as being a "morality of movement," as opposed to a "morality of equilibrium," or
static morality. See below, chap. 3.
29. For an excellent study, written from a historian's perspective, with considerable material on this point, see Alan Richardson, *History: Sacred and Profane* (Philadelphia: The Westminster Press, 1964).

Yet Teilhard firmly believed that Christ, the God-man, came on earth to give eternal life to men of all times and that his Church was given the commission to continue his work. But Teilhard could not deny that there were many in high places in the Church and a vast number of faithful who judged that the modern scientific evolutionary world was, in practice if not always in theory, antithetic to their religious faith. For many, a pantheistic, immanent God of the world, if any God at all, was vying for men's allegiance and replacing the transcendent God of Judaism and Christianity.

Hence it was that the theological aspect of the problem of compressive socialization emerged, and with it the problem of synthesis for Teilhard. What place did Jesus of Nazareth, the Christ, with his Church and his Eucharist, have in this world created by him? This world he came to save was gradually assuming, under the impact of steadily mounting scientific evidence, a character very different from the world of the Scriptures and of centuries of fervent, thoughtful believers. Teilhard could not deny the evidence of science, nor could he deny his firm conviction that the world of science was authentically God's world. Moreover, he was convinced that mankind, struggling with the problems of compressive socialization, must have not merely a place grudgingly assigned to, but an essential need for, Christ.[30]

To bring together these two worlds—of his research and exploration in laboratory and of prayer and loyalty to his God—this was the root problem that Teilhard faced early in his career and to which he devoted countless hours of reflection, prayer, discussion, and writing. In his own mind, and in the judgment of many others,

---

30. The problem first appears in "Cosmic Life" (1916), *WW*, pp. 13-71, and is central throughout the World War I essays and correspondence. His most elaborate statement of a theoretical solution is *DM* (1927). Most of the writings in the collections *SC CE*, and *DA* relate to it in one way or another. Unfortunately, his spiritual autobiography, "Le coeur de la matière" (1950), and the important synthesis from his last year, "Le Christique" (1955), have not, at the time of this writing, appeared, even in the French edition.

he succeeded in resolving it, by elaborating and attempting to clarify over the years what can be described as a Christological anthropology of responsible social process, embodying a moral theory of growth and development, or movement.

To my mind, the last word is by no means yet in as to the success or failure of his efforts, nor as to what his real significance is, relevant to morality, for people of the world today. I am convinced that there is much of value regarding both ethical method and content in Teilhard's thought. I am also of the opinion that strong negative criticism is required in certain areas.

Because of the importance of method for understanding content, method will be treated first and at some length in the following chapter, after which the bulk of the study will focus on content.

## 2

# Ethical Methodology in Teilhard's
# Scientific Christian Humanism

## A. Background. Morality in Teilhard's Anthropology and His Own Moral Commitment

From the elements of Teilhard's world view already seen, it is clear that questions of morality and ethics, taken in the broad, fundamental sense, were important for him. Enough has also been seen for one to say that by and large what his writings present is a comprehensive anthropology that incorporates an ethical and moral stance as an integral and critical element. His writings, in their content and organization are not moral treatises, with their anthropological roots laid bare, but rather reflective pieces about the meaning of life that pursue this question into the area of moral decision.

It has been noted that the motivation for Teilhard's reflective writing stemmed from a firm moral commitment to a particular way of life. The character of this moral commitment should be kept in mind as inquiry into his ethical methodology is carried out, since there is a close connection between the two. In other words, how he validated the answers to fundamental questions of meaning for his own life is closely tied in with how he organized and presented the validation of his answers to questions of meaning and moral decision for human life in general.

Because of this connection, the line of inquiry to be followed in the present chapter will take off from the base of his own life orientation. What that orientation was has been sketched in the preceding chapter. In it analysis reveals three interconnected objectives: 1) to synthesize for his own conscience the apparently conflicting attractions of his faith in the world and his faith in God, 2) to share his own synthetic vision with his fellow believers, so that their anxieties about scientific discoveries might be quieted and the solution integrated into their own lives of faith, for both the peace of their own consciences and the development of a genuinely meaningful apostolate to the scientific humanist mind of the twentieth century, and 3) to present, precisely to this scientific humanist mind, a vision of human life wherein the essential aspirations of scientific humanism would be seen as not only compatible with, but disposed to acceptance of a Christianity that in itself had assimilated scientific-humanist insights. Teilhard's different writings reveal that in his reflective essays the second or third objectives are usually in the foreground, with at times one predominating without eclipsing the other. His own retreat notes and private journals are dominated, mostly, by the first.

## B. The Comprehensive Methodological Question and Its Answer

Against this background, there stands the comprehensive methodological question: How did he validate and formulate his answers about the fundamental meaning of human life, the major sectors of life calling for moral decision, and the conscience-decision process itself?[1]

Exact answers about how he reached his different conclusions in the realm of ethics are not easy to come by. The one piece overtly concerned with method, "Outline of a Dialectic of Spirit" (1946), is more directed to the successive stages of his apologetic than to how he derived the main lines of his thought.[2] It is helpful for understanding his method of presentation, but because of its particular intent it leaves much unsaid. An important work such as "How I Believe" (1934) can give the impression of tracing a chronological development in his thinking, but when examined closely and in comparison with the manifestly autobiographical "Le coeur de la

1. The alignment of elements in this comprehensive methodological question differs from the sequence of basic questions pertinent to ethics as put down by Henry David Aiken in an important essay two decades ago, and utilized by James Gustafson in his significant piece "Context Versus Principles: A Misplaced Debate in Christian Ethics," some dozen years later. Aiken indicated four levels of moral discourse, 1) the "expressive-evocative," unreflective, expressing negative or positive feeling, 2) the "moral," where men ask what ought to be done in a given situation, 3) the "ethical," in which justifying reasons are sought for a moral judgment, and 4) the "post-ethical," which asks about the grounds for being moral in the first place. In the sequence chosen in the present study, the "post-ethical" becomes, in effect, the "pre-ethical," with the grounds for moral decision presented first through consideration of Teilhard's basic anthropology, which flows out into indications of principal areas for moral decision. The third element, the conscience decision process, can be said to include both Aiken's second and third questions. Aiken's first is simply bypassed as not sufficiently relevant for present purposes. Gustafson's analysis of where the situation ethics debate has been located is incisive, as is his subsequent discussion of the four principal base points from which various writers have worked. Attention is called to his study here because it is presumed to be sufficiently well known, or at least available, and can provide a clarifying contrast as a backdrop for the framework of the present study. The reason for adopting a different framework here is principally derived from the manner in which Teilhard's thought unfolds, as indicated above. See Henry D. Aiken, "Levels of Moral Discourse," in *Reason and Conduct* (New York: Knopf, 1962), pp. 65-87, originally published in *Ethics* 62 (1952): 235-46, cited by James M. Gustafson, in "Context Versus Principles: A Misplaced Debate in Christian Ethics," *New Theology: No. 3*, ed. Martin E. Marty and Dean G. Peerman, Macmillan Paperback (New York: The Macmillan Co., 1965), pp. 71-72. (Gustafson's essay originally appeared in the *Harvard Theological Review*, April 1965.)

2. *AE*, pp. 143-51. For an excellent analysis and discussion of Teilhard's dialectic, see Barthélemy-Madaule, *La personne chez Teilhard*, pp. 13-48, "Introduction à la dialectique teilhardienne," where the genesis and implicit and explicit use of the process are examined in considerable detail.

matière" (1950), reveals a logical arrangement rather than an explanation of the steps in a time sequence by which he had reached the concepts and conclusions he presents. Moreover, "Le coeur de la matière" itself is more of a description of what happened to his conscious life, and when, than the methods by which his thought grew.[3] Consequently, in the absence of a complete exposition of his methods by Teilhard, the picture of his methodology will have to be pieced together from fragments found in various places in his writings, and, in some aspects, inferred from what is known about his manner of life and work. The same technique of looking for evidence from his life to fill in gaps in his expressed thought and to clarify or interpret ambiguities will also be used in regard to content.

This is not an altogether desirable heuristic or hermeneutic process because of the risk of putting things in his mind that may not have been there, or of twisting his statements in accord with the bias of the investigator. But it seems to be called for in the present circumstances in view of the occasional character of much of Teilhard's writing, as well as the highly personal character of his approach, with his own stress on coherence between thought and life. In attempting to understand Teilhard, the implications of Emerson's dictum about not touching a book but touching a man seem to have particular significance. With regard to certain questions, Teilhard's life is the main channel to his thought; with regard to others, it provides both clues to unraveling obscurities, and, unpleasant as they may be, pieces of evidence that serve even to heighten vexing ambiguities.

In what follows immediately, no sharp line will be drawn differentiating his method of thought as it pertains to the development of his total anthropological

3. These essays deal mainly with Teilhard's fundamental world view, it should be noted, and do not push very far into specific areas of moral concern, with the exception of the final section of "Le coeur de la matière," on "Le Feminin (ou L'Unitif)." See "How I Believe" (1934), *CE*, pp. 96-132, and "Le coeur de la matière" (1950), *I*, pp. 1-34.

synthesis from the methodology pertinent to his specifically ethical thinking. A major reason for this is that the
underlying methodology is the same, whether one looks
to his larger world view or to the avenues of moral
choice leading from it or the conscience-decision process
itself. To say this is not to deny that there will be a difference, ultimately, between anthropology, however
broad its scope, and an ethic, however deeply it pushes
into its human foundations. Consequently, after an
examination of the fundamental methodology of
Teilhard's thought, focus will be narrowed, to see more
precisely how this methodology does express itself in the
area of basic moral options and the conscience-decision
process.[4] Because of the close connection between the

---

4. The approach to Teilhard's methodology outlined here encompasses
and goes beyond the writing of commentators such as Bastide,
Barthélemy-Madaule, Blanchard, Danielou, de Solages, Grenet, and others,
where they are concerned mainly with the philosophical or nonphilosophical aspects of his thought. It likewise differs from Mermod, in that it goes beyond
Teilhard's natural ethic to the synthesized ethic of reason-informed faith. And
it explores areas not specifically treated by de Lubac, who has written extensively on Teilhard's spirituality, but not directed his inquiry into how this is
incorporated into what can be called his total ethical thought as such. Another
contrast would be with the thought of Crespy, who explores the relation between Teilhard's scientific style and theology, but does not pursue the ethical
implications. There are ethical implications of course, in the theological works
of d'Ouince, Mooney, and Smulders, but they are not drawn out, although
Mooney and d'Ouince have much pertaining to Teilhard's method of synthesis. The same can be said of Rideau's comprehensive study. The present
study is, in effect an extension and specification of Faricy's work, but Faricy
does not explore ethical methodology in detail. See Barthélemy-Madaule,
*Bergson-Teilhard*, esp. pp. 564-631, sec. X, "Peut-on parler de philosophie
teilhardienne?," *La personne chez Teilhard*, esp. pp. 13-48, "Introduction à la
dialectique teilhardienne," and, "Réflexions sur la méthode et la perspective
teilhardienne," *Les études philosophiques* 21 (1966): 510-32. The last piece is an
answer to the criticism of Teilhard's style of "reflexion" by Georges Bastide,
"Naturalisme et spiritualité: le statut de la réflextion dans la pensée de Teilhard
de Chardin," *Les études philosophiques* 20 (1965): 409-47. Bastide attempts to
put Teilhard outside the philosophical world and Barthélemy-Madaule gives
reasons for keeping him in it. Her "Introduction à la dialectique teilhardienne" is particularly valuable for her commentary on Teilhard's "Outline of a
Dialectic of Spirit," pp. 33-47. Abbé J. P. Blanchard, *Méthode et principes du
Père Teilhard de Chardin* (Paris: La Colombe, 1961), has the distinction of having written a book-length study on Teilhard's method, but he unfortunately
builds most of his case on one text he considers sufficiently typical, *La Groupe
Zoologique Humaine* (English trans., *MPN*). Jean Danielou, "Signification de
Teilhard de Chardin," *Études* 312 (Feb. 1962): 147-48, makes the point that
Teilhard, like the pre-Socratics, worked to a philosophy fresh from the sci-

second and third objectives in Teilhard's writing, there will be two main lines of consideration in what follows: 1) how he found meaning for himself, and 2) his manner of communicating what he discovered.

## C. Teilhard's Active-Contemplative Quest for Personal Meaning

Important for understanding Teilhard's personal search for meaning is the fact that from his earliest years as a Jesuit he was schooled in the spirituality of Ignatius of Loyola, which embodied a variety of techniques for developing an active-contemplative mentality within the Roman Catholic tradition. He went through the full thirty-day course of Spiritual Exercises as a Novice, and although he never completed Tertianship, he did make the thirty-day retreat once again prior to his induction into the army in World War I. As a mature priest, he made his yearly retreat of at least eight days, and he became habituated to daily reflective prayer on the purpose of his life in the context of what would be for the greater glory of God wherever he found himself and with whatever means were available or adaptable. The focal point of his prayer was the inspiration of Jesus of Nazareth, who toiled, suffered, died, rose again, and left behind, without really withdrawing from it, the mystery

ence of his time, with which point Norbert Wildiers concurs, in his "Foreword" to *HE*, pp. 13-15. De Solages, *Teilhard: étude*, focuses on Teilhard's method in his fourth chapter, "Point de vue. Plan intellectual. Méthode." pp. 60-78. The central preoccupation of Paul-Bernard Grenet, *Pierre Teilhard de Chardin ou le Philosophe malgré lui* (Paris: Beauchesne, 1961), is clear from the title of his work. Note esp. his concluding chapter on what he thought Teilhard ought to have done to maintain purity in his methodology and a correct liaison with philosophy, pp. 208-40. As for the remaining works cited, see Mermod, *La morale chez Teilhard*, esp. pp. 29-43, "Le fondement de la morale naturelle"; de Lubac, *Teilhard: Man and Meaning*, and *Religion of Teilhard*; Georges Crespy, *From Science to Theology: the Evolutionary design of Teilhard de Chardin*, trans. George H. Shriver (Nashville: Abingdon Press, 1968); d'Ouince, *Teilhard: la pensée chrétienne*; Mooney, *Mystery of Christ*; Smulders, *Design of Teilhard*; Rideau, *Teilhard: Guide*, esp. "The Operative Method," pp. 38-50; and Faricy, *Teilhard: Theology*.

of his Church. Teilhard saw Jesus living on in his Mystical Body and, in a special way, in the power of his Eucharist, radiating his life and energy to all men through the continuation of his Incarnation and, thereby, affecting the entire universe.[5]

It has always been essential to the Jesuit tradition that, wherever Jesuits found themselves, their efforts should be directed toward prayerful assimilation of the human culture and experience of their milieu, both for their own good and the good of those for and with whom they worked. In keeping with this tradition, Mateo Ricci became in effect a Chinese scholar in the seventeenth-century China he knew. Robert De Nobili and John De Britto entered into and absorbed the mores and customs of India, and in Europe, Latin America, and the United States as well, generations of Jesuit humanists and philosophers steeped themselves in the late- and post-Renaissance culture of their environment and strove to incarnate the life and love of Christ in it.

Teilhard was in full communion with this tradition. What was distinctive about him was the peculiar style

5. Literature on Ignatian spirituality is extensive and continues to grow. It has been enhanced particularly since the late 19th century by a wealth of documentation stemming from the initiation of the *Monumenta Historica Societatis Jesu* in the closing years of that period. Prior to that date, the original spirit of the Society was difficult to grasp, both because of the unfortunate hagiographic style used to present the life of Ignatius himself, and also from the well-intentioned, but nonetheless inaccurate emphases on the interpretation of the text of the *Exercises* by John Roothan, the first General of the restored Society, in the early 1800s. Teilhard went through his Jesuit formation too early to be affected by the impact of much important revisionary scholarship, but he seems to have escaped Roothan's rigidity in his approach to the *Exercises*. Because of its extremely cryptic and jejune, sixteenth-century, Basque-Latin style, the text of the *Exercises* itself is not the best source for an understanding of what entered so vitally into Teilhard's spiritual growth. For biographical material on Ignatius, the writings of James Broderick and Mary Purcell are excellent. For an understanding of the Jesuit apostolate and spirituality, the works of George Ganss, Joseph Conwell, Joseph de Guibert, and Ignacio Iparraguirre, particularly, could well be consulted. Perhaps the best, but not readily available, source for understanding contemporary Jesuit life in the context of North American culture would be the *Consensus Positions and Recommendations*, of the Jesuit Provincials, American Assistancy, issued at the Santa Clara Conference, Santa Clara, California, August 1967. This document manifests a sympathy with the modern world that Teilhard would have found quite congenial.

and breadth of human experience that penetrated his consciousness in his reflective, contemplative prayer, and that, in an all-important way, illumined his understanding of the redemptive, risen, Mystical, and Eucharistic Christ with its special practical implications for his own activity and life-style.

For Teilhard, the universe—from the core of the atom to the outer reaches of the stars, from the micro-elements of living tissue to the mind-body complex of the human person and the intricate network of technologized human society—this universe as he saw it, with its triple infinities of space, time, and complexity, was a vastly different one from that of Christians and other men in previous centuries. Moreover, he was aware of the mentality of many contemporaries and close associates, both scientific and religious, who could see no compatibility between the universe of scientific humanism and the God of Christianity. For many of his scientific friends, God himself had been transcended and become irrelevant. For a host of his co-religionists, the picture of the world drawn by scientific humanism was false in its major outlines because it contradicted their understanding of divine revelation. Moreover, they judged the stance of scientific humanists, sophisticated and nuanced as it might be, to amount to little less than an arrogant Promethean regression, doomed sooner or later to enslave mankind within the cold prison, however large, of its own ego.

In this setting, the root operative technique whereby he developed his synthesized vision of the meaning of life for himself and others was that of protracted prayerful reflection. Into it entered his grasp of what he judged the essential concepts of Roman Catholic Incarnational Christianity, the data of his scientific and philosophical contacts, and also the fruits of his poetic talents, along with the impact of what can perhaps best be described as certain significant life experiences.

To comprehend this better, several styles of know-

ledge and their experiential context are important. For
working purposes these elements can be grouped under
the following headings:

1. Understanding of revelation
2. Scientific and philosophical concepts
3. Poetic insights and artistic experience
4. The rather global category of "significant life experiences," which would include the complex of family
   and friend relationships, professional scientific teamwork, his years in the military during World War I,
   relations with ecclesiastical superiors on various levels
   and a rather remarkable mobility of habitat throughout a great part of his life. This last saw him alternat-
   ing between periods of residence in intellectual centers on several continents, with long sea voyages and
   exploratory treks into wilderness areas of China, India, Southeast Asia, and Africa, not to overlook some
   contact with the land masses of South America and
   Western United States.

In the above listing the first three deal specifically with
thought processes, with styles and modes of knowing,
whereas the last focuses on particular, significant areas
of life experience that would feed data, in one way or
another, into the three different styles of knowledge.

### 1. UNDERSTANDING OF REVELATION

How did the basic data of revelation work into
Teilhard's thought? In addition to his daily prayerful reflective meditation, which he integrated with the Mass
and his reading of the Breviary, he devoted considerable
intellectual energy to pondering certain areas of Scripture that he considered of critical importance and comparing their meaning—as he understood it in the light
of his own reflections and the thought of the Fathers of
the Church, especially the Greek—to the interpretation

and emphases in the scholastic theology of his time. He was particularly concerned with Pauline and Johannine texts pertaining to the centrality of Christ in the universe, and with patristic writings on the same theme. What disturbed him deeply about the speculative theology of his period was its juridical, essentialistic approach, its being wedded to a form of aristotelianism ill-suited to modern times.[6]

In the course of his theological studies at Hastings (1908-1912) he drew up for himself in his notebooks a small anthology of Pauline and Johannine texts that clustered around three leading ideas: 1) the rooting of all things in Christ, 2) the fullness of Christ extending to the limits of the universe, and 3) the ultimate unification of all things in Christ. His approach to interpreting these texts was not that of a trained exegete or Scripture specialist, nor that of a speculative theologian of his own era who would be working from a philosophical climate he could not accept.[7]

6. For a good sketch of the character of school theology in the twenties, basically the type of theology Teilhard had in mind throughout his critical writings against theologians, see d'Ouince, *Teilhard: la pensée chrétienne*, "L'homme dans L'univers selon la théologie Classique," pp. 31-49. Representative texts from Teilhard pertinent to a revamping of theology would be: "Note pour servir à l'évangélisation des temps nouveaux" (1919), *EG*, pp. 367-81, esp. 377-81; "Note on the Universal Christ" (1920), *SC*, pp. 18-19; "Christianity and Evolution: Suggestions for a New Theology" (1945), *CE*, pp. 173-86; "Action and Activation" (1945), *SC*, pp. 178-79; and his final synthesis, "Le Christique" (1955), *I*, pp. 1-13. For discussions of his style of theologizing, see: de Solages, *Teilhard: étude*, "Son attitude devant la théologie," pp. 342-54; Faricy, *Teilhard: Theology*, "Christian Faith and Theological Method," pp. 82-88; and d'Ouince, *Teilhard: la pensée chrétienne*, "De la doctrine scripturaire à la théologie classique," pp. 144-64. Teilhard's references to the Fathers are never lengthy, but they are a respectable staple in his argument. See, for example: "Cosmic Life" (1916), *WW*, p. 50; "Christology and Evolution" (1933), *CE*, p. 85; "Some Reflexions on the Conversion of the World" (1936), *SC*, p. 122; "Super-humanity, Super-Christ, Super Charity" (1943), *SC*, p. 165; "Catholicism and Science" (1946), *SC*, p. 189; "Reflections on Original Sin" (1947), *CE*, p. 191 n7. For his continuity with the Greek Fathers, see George A. Maloney, S.J., *The Cosmic Christ* (New York: Sheed and Ward, 1968), pp. 182-220.

7. For some extensive reflections on Teilhard's conformity with St. Paul, and also pertinent observations on his theological method, see Mooney, *Mystery of Christ*, pp. 66-111. Teilhard does not employ prolonged, detailed exegesis of scriptural texts, but his citation of Scripture is frequent throughout his Christological writings. Perhaps his capital texts could be designated

But Teilhard was no dilettante eclectic outside Catholic tradition, and he had little sympathy for Modernism. Evidence of this can be found in his acceptance of the infallible guidance of the Church and his concern with the Scriptures themselves—how they were understood by great thinkers in the early Church, and how one could get at and maintain essential Catholic dogma in modern times within the framework of what he accepted as legitimate Church authority.[8] In his judgment,

as: "In eo omnia constant" (Col. 1.17), "Ipse est qui replet omnia (Col. 2.10, cf. Eph. 4.9), and "Omnia in omnibus Christus" (Col. 3.11). He was accustomed to cite the Vulgate, but at times his memory was not quite accurate. D'Ouince, *Teilhard: la pensée chrétienne*, pp. 144-64, has an excellent analysis of his approach to Scripture, with considerable citation of pertinent scriptural texts. The most impressive battery of texts assembled in one place and credited to Teilhard as the compiler is found in "My Universe" (1924), *SC*, p. 54 n2. The problem with introducing this note as evidence of his range of citation is that both the French and English published editions of this essay assign the note to the editor. It is introduced, however, in view of the fact that there is likelihood of a publishing error, since de Solages, *Teilhard: étude*, p. 356 n50; Mooney, *Mystery of Christ*, p. 249 n45; and Faricy, *Teilhard: Theology*, pp. 96-97 n52, all assign the note to Teilhard, and were at the time of their writing presumably working from an unpublished copy of the text. Mooney, *Mystery of Christ*, p. 249 n46, provides a good rundown on Pauline texts most frequently cited by Teilhard. For a concise presentation of Pauline and Johannine sources, see de Solages, *Teilhard: étude*, "La sources de sa Christologie," pp. 355-56. Teilhard's basic agreement in his interpretation with such scholars as Lebreton and Prat is noted by d'Ouince, *Teilhard: la pensée chrétienne*, p. 149 n5.

8. For Teilhard's own judgment on Modernism, see his journal entry for June 9, 1919, where he speaks of the Modernists as "evaporating" Christ and disengaging him from the world, whereas he is trying to center the world in Christ (cited by de Solages, *Teilhard: étude*, p. 342.) Apart from this judgment, the content of Teilhard's Christology, with its insistence on the concrete historicity of Jesus for a base, would speak for itself. As for the infallibility of the Church, Teilhard did not write much about it. That he accepted it throughout his life is clear from his submission to Rome regarding censorship of his writings. A clear, if brief statement of his views on infallibility and his justification of them in line with his evolutionary ideas occurs in his "Introduction to the Christian Life" (1944), *CE*, p. 153, where he pursues the biological image of a phylum so far as to present the Councils as "the permanent organ of this phyletic infallibility," and goes on to speak of "an even more advanced concentration of Christian consciousness in the Pope (formulating and expressing not his own ideas but those of the Church)" as being "completely in line with the great law of 'cephalization' which governs all biological evolution." In one of his earliest writings he expresses an essential aspect of theologizing as thinking with the Church, when, in "The Soul of the World" (1918), *WW*, p. 189, he writes, "The work will have to be tested and pursued, as every advance in the Church must be, in a quest shared by all and maintained in prayer." See also "Christianity and Evolution: Suggestions for a New Theology" (1945), *CE*, pp. 173-74. Another significant expression of Teilhard's

the theologians of the schools and certain approaches manifest in Roman documents of later times incorrectly identified the thinking of a particular philosophical cast of mind with the religious truth itself. What Teilhard earnestly sought to do was to work out a valid and orthodox interpretation of central Catholic dogma through the use of his evolutionary phenomenology as he came to develop it.

This concern appears in a special way in his interest in the theory of the development of dogma. How much he was influenced by Newman is hard to say. In his later years he seems to have forgotten the enthusiasm he had had for him as a younger man, when he gave close study to the *Essay on the Development of Christian Doctrine*.[9] A short journal entry from 1921 is illuminating for the manner in which he sifts out different aspects of dogmatic texts with a view to getting at the central meaning, which would have to be maintained in true development.

> Every dogmatic text, whether of St. Paul or the Vatican, contains three elements:
> 1) a material "letter";
> 2) an intention, a spirit, and this *in two ways*:
> a) an *axial* view or intention (dogmatic core);
> b) a blend of this view with ephemeral temporal views (the range of past and future time—the historic origin of things—the mechanism of intellection—social order . . .)[10]

thought on this matter is contained in a remark he made to Bruno de Solages during a discussion they were having about some difficult dogmatic questions in 1935: "We are fortunate to have the authority of the Church! Left to ourselves alone, how far could we run the risk of going adrift?" (Cited by de Solages, *Teilhard: étude*, p. 341. Translation by the present writer.)

9. De Lubac in *CB*, pp. 120-21, provides thorough documentation concerning Teilhard's World War I reading of Newman, his sympathy with him, and his enthusiasm for his ideas on the development of dogma, as well as his lapse of memory, later on, about his earlier reflection. A representative expression of Teilhard's early appreciation of Newman can be found in his letter of July 22, 1916, to his cousin Marguerite, *MM*, p. 114, where he writes of Newman's thesis "that the intellectual function of the Church consists primarily in eliminating, in choosing, in selecting from within, the positive dogmatic development expressed primarily in the body of the faithful," as an idea that entered into his mind as something with which he was already quite familiar.

10. See de Solages, *Teilhard: étude*, p. 349 n34. (Translation by present writer.)

A journal entry from the previous year puts quite simply his estimate of where the main difficulty lay in dogmatic development—a rigid tenacity on the part of theologians in holding onto certain conceptions out of fear of losing the truth, without seeing that in their theses the truth must be distinguished from its expression.[11]

So it was that Teilhard went at the Scriptures, patristic writings, and the teachings of the Church as they came to him, seeking to find the central core of dogmatic faith and to give it an expression in keeping with evolutionary humanism. Despite the fact that he was not operating precisely as a professional theologian, the interpretative process he used was sound, and hardly an innovation. That his main Christological theses appealed to certain scriptural areas rather than others can be explained in the light of his basically missionary, apologetic orientation, seeking to interpret the traditional Christ for his own time.

Hence, while his theological method was not comprehensive in the sense of seeking how to feed all of revelation into his Christology, he was using a legitimate technique with the revelation data he judged necessary for his specific purposes. Certain critics are of the opinion that he failed seriously in important areas and radically distorted basic dogma, at least in his emphases. Others (and with these I agree) hold his fundamental interpretations to be sound and helpful, some of his ideas poorly formulated and confusing, and some questionable to the point of being untenable.[12]

11. *Ibid.*, p. 348 and 348 n28.
12. A representative summary of the principal objections offered by strongly negative critics of Teilhard's theological positions appears in *Osservatore Romano*, June 30-July 1, 1962, in an unsigned article commenting on the monitum of the Holy Office, dated June 30, 1962 (for which see *AAS* 54 (1962): 526). Here for example, Teilhard is attacked because of his theory on the gratuity of creation, lack of proper treatment of God's transcendence, his cosmic "third nature" of Christ, his synthetic approach to creation, Incarnation, and redemption, faulty explanation of spirit and matter, errors on original sin, and excessive worldliness in his ascetical theory. On a number of the points taken up, even Teilhard's sympathetic critics, such as de Solages, de Lubac, and Mooney, to mention only a few, also have serious reservations,

## 2. SCIENTIFIC AND PHILOSOPHICAL CONCEPTS

*The Problem of Identifying Teilhard's "Scientific" Approach*
  In developing his own understanding of the human, his work as a scientist in the fields of geology, paleontology, and paleoanthropology played an important part.[13] Work in these areas made him familiar with certain basic concepts and techniques for the discovery and verification of knowledge, which became almost second nature to him as he pursued his quest beyond the strict limits of the empirical disciplines themselves into the major questions about the meaning, value, and direction of human life. How he used these instruments and how he viewed what he was attempting to do, have not met with universal understanding, or approval, and have provoked considerable discussion. In *The Phenomenon of Man* and other pieces in the same vein, Teilhard described his approach as "scientific." His readers, however, have variously condemned or praised him in speaking of what he did as not really science, but poetry, philosophy, or mysticism.[14] Writings like those in the collection *Christianity*

which will be brought up where they are pertinent to the present study. Since there is no point in covering ground already thoroughly examined elsewhere, the reader is referred to authors of the sort mentioned, and others to be cited for detailed critique of Teilhard's theological theory. A French text of the monitum and the commentary on it can be found in Charles Journet, "Pierre Teilhard de Chardin, penseur religieux: de quelques jugements *récents" Nova et Vetera* 37 (Oct-Déc 1962): 289-95.

  13. Part of the phenomenon of Teilhard is that, along with other facets of his thought and life, his competence as a scientist has been questioned. On this matter, see the short note by Theodosius Dobzhansky, the distinguished geneticist, included in *LF*, pp. 219-27. Also Barjon, *Le combat de Teilhard*, chap. 5, "La carrière scientifique," pp. 71-107. For some of Dobzhansky's critical corrections of Teilhard's thought, in a work basically expressing sympathy with his insights, see, by the same author, *The Biology of Ultimate Concern*, Meridian Books (New York: The New American Library, 1967), chap. 6, "The Teilhardian Synthesis," pp. 108-37.

  14. Perhaps the most harsh reaction from a noted member of the scientific community was that of Sir Peter Medawar in his review, "Teilhard de Chardin in 'The Phenomenon of Man,'" *Mind* 277 (1961): 99-106, where he speaks of Teilhard's writing derogatorily as "natur-philosophie" and "typsy, euphoric prose-poetry." Sympathetic critics, such as Dobzhansky, have noted the poetic and mystical aspects. See Dobzhansky, *The Biology of Ultimate Concern*, pp. 114-15. For discussion of the philosophical character of his phenomenological thought, see above, n4. A good rundown of important criticism of Teilhard,

*and Evolution* are easier to put in a general category, such as speculative theology, whereby he attempted to reach a new interpretation of essential Christian thought through the application of insights derived from his phenomenological reflections on scientific data.[15] However, since his speculative theologizing is rooted, on the human experience side, in his scientific phenomenology, classifying his theological thinking in this way does not mean much unless one knows what he was doing with the phenomenology.

What, then, was he doing with his brand of phenomenological humanism? Two central points are clear from the general tenor of his writing: 1) he judged his mode of thought to be fundamentally scientific, in the sense of working with the scientific method of hypothesis and hypothesis verification through coherence and fecundity, and 2) the object of inquiry that he sought to investigate, using this technique, was not a part, or several parts of human existence, but human life as a *whole*, with all pertinent elements in their organic interconnection. This is what he meant by the human phenomenon.[16] Moreover, in this vein, he was con-

much of it bearing on the methodological question, can be found in Canon Raven's work on his thought of a decade ago. While dated at the moment, it is excellent, as far as it goes. His remarks about Medawar's approach are particularly illuminating. See Charles E. Raven, *Teilhard de Chardin: Scientist and Seer* (New York: Harper & Row Pub., 1962), pp. 197-214. Also see Robert Speaight, *The Life of Teilhard de Chardin* (New York: Harper & Row, Pub., 1967), pp. 273-75. Next to Cuénot's work, Speaight's biography is the most complete account available in English. For severe negative criticism of Teilhard's approach, from a scientist friend who knew him for many years, see George Gaylord Simpson, "The Divine Non Sequitur," *Teilhard: Symposium*, pp. 88-102. Simpson's frank comments are a good example of how a mind holding a strict understanding of "science" found Teilhard's use of the term unacceptable. A broader view of the scientific approach, more sympathetic to what Teilhard attempted, is expressed by physicist Robert A. Thornton, "Comments on Scientific Methodology," *ibid.*, pp. 177-79.

15. The same can be said for much contained in the collections *SC* and *DA,* and in the as yet unpublished paper "Le Christique" (1955).

16. Teilhard spends little time explaining the mechanics of the scientific method. In view of the audience he had in mind for most of his phenomenological writing, it was legitimate for him to assume that the basic concepts were understood by those who would read him. But it is difficult to deny that clarity would have been helped if he had structured his thought

cerned with how things happened, with the regular predictable sequence of events capable of formulation in a
law. But he insisted he was not looking to the *why* questions of deep, formal philosophical inquiry.[17] In doing
this, however, he admits that he was responding to his
own inner psychological drive to generalize, to draw on
common elements in different disciplines and, ultimately, to come up with conclusions and insights beyond the
scope of highly specialized scientific inquiry. His description of what he was attempting and urging others to try
was the development of a "hyperphysics" or "ultra-
physics" but not a "metaphysics."[18]

The crucial matter of what he meant by "the
phenomenon of man," or the total, as distinguished

more frequently within the framework, rather than writing for the most part
discursively in its atmosphere. In only two essays does he begin by point blank
laying down how he is going to operate within this framework, and then proceed to work ahead from there. See the introductory remarks to "Sketch of a
Personalistic Universe" (1936), *HE*, pp. 53-54, and his conclusion, pp. 89-90.
Also the opening remarks for "The Phenomenon of Spirituality" (1937), *HE*,
p. 94, and the conclusion, pp. 110-12. His concern to maintain the scientific
tenor of his thought is quite consistent, so as scarcely to need documentation.
See, for example, the Preface to *PM* (written in 1947, almost ten years after
he began the book), pp. 29-30, also the introductory note to *MPN* (1950), p.
13, and the Foreword, pp. 14-15. But there were moments when he was appreciative that others would not read him this way. In one of his earlier essays
with the title "The Phenomenon of Man" (1930), *VP*, pp. 161-62, he affirms
his scientific concentration, but admits, p. 167, that his interpretation "will
perhaps appear . . . more poetic than scientific." The same essay, in the introductory pages cited, also has a good sample of his concern about science viewing man as such, man in his entirety. The best sources for viewing extended
treatment of this concern are, as might be expected, *PM* and *MPN*.

17. His insistence that he is trying to avoid philosophy usually accompanies
his announced intent to remain scientific. One of the clearest formulations is
in the Preface to *PM*, mentioned above. The earliest precise statement, in a
work that was in a real sense a forerunner of *PM*, occurs in "Hominization"
(1923), *VP*, p. 51, the opening paragraph: "The following pages do not seek
to present any philosophy directly; they set out, on the contrary, to draw their
strength from the careful avoidance of all recourse to metaphysics. Their
purpose is to express as objective and simple a vision as possible of humanity
considered (as a whole and in its connections with the Universe) as a *phenomenon.*" The text is also quite clear documentation of the main point in n 16, above.

18. See *PM* (1940), p. 30, for the term *hyperphysics*. For *ultra-physics*, see
"Sketch of a Personalistic Universe" (1936), *HE*, p. 70. For all practical purposes, the terms are synonymous with Teilhard. The generalization referred
to here is, properly, but one aspect of what Teilhard describes as his "incoer-
cible need to universalize." See "Le coeur de la matière" (1950), *I*, p. 12. The
tendency, however, even had he not been reflexively aware of it and spoken
about it, is manifest from the writings themselves.

from the fragmented study of the human, can best be approached by looking to the central questions he asked when following out this line of inquiry. They present a simple series in themselves, but it is important to observe carefully what emerges when they are all put together and he applies his technique toward their answers. The questions can be formulated as follows: 1) how was human life prepared for in the history of the universe? 2) how did human life come into existence? 3) how, when human life appeared, did it differ from previous forms of life? 4) how, after its appearance, did individual and social human life develop? and 5) how, in view of the direction human life has been taking from its origins, should it be lived in order to reach its genuine fulfillment, and what, transcending the human, is required for that fulfillment to be reached?

In working with all these questions, Teilhard would insist that one remain within the *phenomenological* framework, in the sense of the experientially verifiable, the observable—that which could be formulated in a law of recurrence and tested by experience, the disciplined experience, to be sure, of an observer trained in the scientific method of hypothesis and testing, broadened to the scope of generalized inquiry demanded by the big human questions. He would be equally insistent that inquiry into the ultimate efficient causality of what was happening at any stage along the line would project one into the technically metaphysical and go beyond the limits of his ultra-physical inquiry.

How the "ultra" differs from the "meta" is precisely here. Both, admittedly, go beyond the "physical" sciences taken even in a broad way. The "ultra" goes beyond what have been the ordinary questions of physics, chemistry, biology, and empirical psychology, and would feed into the thinking process from any or all of these disciplines, depending on the level of questioning. For example, the first questions in the area about preparation for human life in the universe would begin with the history and development of inorganic matter insofar as chemistry and physics could probe backward into the depths of time, assisted by mathematics. With the appearance of life, biology would enter in, along with the other disciplines just mentioned. With man, psychology and the social sciences would be added. What would be "ultra" for the whole complex of disciplines would be the attempt to focus the resources of all of them *beyond* what would customarily be considered their specific, proper concentration, and to direct the knowledge derived from the entire complex to answering the larger basic questions about human origins, development, and future, in a generalized synthesis.

For Teilhard, the general line of ascent was from the extremely simple and multiple toward the extremely complex, ultimately unified in a special manner, in man, through consciousness—a consciousness that he, by extrapolation, would see reaching a higher unity in a higher form of human consciousness to become one with the requisite Omega Point, requisite because of the psychological necessity of such an ultimate personal Center to motivate and thus activate human love. All along this line, spirit is viewed as either the approach to consciousness or a state of higher consciousness than the preceding, while matter is viewed as the pre- or lower conscious stage of the developing observable phenomenon. In so speaking of matter and spirit, he was attempting to escape a metaphysical dualism of two really distinct types of being, juxtaposed, but radically discontinuous.

Here, again, he is clearly "ultra" and beyond the usual run of empirical scientific thinking. But there is a critical question that arises in examining his thought at this point. When he talks of consciousness, reflection, spirit, and, above all, the character of freedom and personal love in man, as he does, is he really staying in a generalized "scientific" thought terrain, however uncharted, or is he pushing on into the metaphysical and philosophical, using a method of thought derived from and analogous to, but ultimately different from, the scientific method? Is not the fifth question above, which for him was the all-important question, about human fulfillment and the need for transcendence, really a question that for centuries has been taken as a fundamental question of philosophical ethics?

A case can be made that he is doing precisely that, and as a consequence of his insistence that he is remaining in the realm of the phenomenological and the properly, although generalized scientific, he has unnecessarily drawn attack from both scientific and philosophical flanks.[19] It can be argued that if he had been aware and had avowed that he was developing a different style of philosophical thinking, with roots in the scientific method, but also with ties to certain lines of philosophical thought, especially those of Bergson on duration, time, and evolution, and those of Blondel and Le Roy on action—then much of the'controversy about how to label his thought could have been avoided and more attention directed to the validation of the thought itself.

That he was doing a kind of philosophical thinking, commentators have maintained, and it would further seem confirmed by the fact that a man skilled in scientific discipline, such as Julian Huxley, not unsympathetic to Teilhard's efforts, could follow him on human origins and the need for collaborative human effort to continue evolution, but could not go with him all the way to Omega Point.[20]

19. See above, n14.
20. Introduction to *PM* (1940), pp. 18-19. Even Huxley's explanation of where he does not agree with Teilhard about Omega fails to manifest an understanding of a characteristic of Omega that was important for Teilhard, namely, that Omega Point was, and is, a transcendent personal existing center, and hence much more than an ultimate "condition" of mankind. It is true that Teilhard's exposition of this matter, "The Attributes of Omega Point," *PM*, pp. 268-72, along with pp. 266-67 leading into it, could be more precise. It is also true that the sense in which Huxley took the term is one of the meanings he assigned to it. But that he apparently missed the other meaning altogether is in itself significant. Regarding four related senses of Omega, see Donald Gray, *The One and the Many*, pp. 96-102.

This fact has implications worth pondering. One of the constant characteristics of distinctively scientific thought is that its evidence and argument admit of general validation by those familiar with its techniques. To say this is not to ignore the disputes among scientists themselves about interpretation of the same data. On the other hand, the history of philosophy attests not only to variances among schools of philosophy, but within schools of the same general tradition. Empirical science, to the extent that it holds its questions and criteria on the empirical level, in the long run scores much higher on the scale of general agreement than philosophy. And, the closer it approaches a philosophical type of thought process, the more generalized its thinking becomes, the more scientists disagree.

It is true that this particular argument as to the nonscientific quality of Teilhard's thought is an extrinsic argument, and, because of disagreements among scientists in the same discipline, it is not conclusively probative. But it does have circumstantial evidence value, when taken in connection with the other considerations advanced, particularly those pertaining to the type of question Teilhard was putting, and above all to his self-confessed interest in Bergsonian and Blondelian thought.

*The Question of a Hidden "Metaphysic"*

Where Teilhard seems to be particularly open to the objection that he is arguing from a hidden metaphysical premise is in the line of thought he presents leading to the existence of Omega. The point will be taken up specifically below, but at the moment it can be noted that in working from the psychological exigency for adequate motivation to the existence of an all-attractive motivator of love, he seems to rest his case, ultimately, on a hidden premise on the nature of human desire, and not to be extrapolating scientifically on the basis of accumulated evidence of antecedent probability.

Nor is this the only point with regard to which the problem of hidden premises, postulates, or uncritically examined starting points occurs. He never reflexively examines, or clearly explains the foundations of his knowing theory.[21] He makes much of intuition, vision, seeing, feeling, of introspection directed to one's inner psychological states, as of special importance in grasping the points he wants to make.[22] But he does not seem to

21. See Henri de Lubac, *Religion of Teilhard*, pp. 187-88. De Lubac's regret that Teilhard did not provide a more fully worked out investigation of epistemological problems central to his approach is directed specifically to *PM*. But the absence of such investigation is felt with regard to other styles of thought as well. To Teilhard's credit, he is usually careful enough about telling the reader *what* he is doing, but he never seems to have felt a compelling need to explain *why* he was doing it that way, or to have sensed the difficulties that were going to arise in the minds of critical readers precisely because of that absence.

22. His own self-analysis about the bent of his mind is clear enough in a letter to his cousin Marguerite (June 29, 1919), *MM*, p. 106: "I believe that you're perfectly right in thinking that the sap of my thought and activity is sentient rather than intellectual. Even though the distinction between the two powers, the 'affective' and 'apprehensive' is much less sharp than at first appears, and that to feel intensely involves almost necessarily a very intimate vision of what is experienced (my poor friend Rousselot thought that all knowledge is 'sympathetic' and therefore reducible to love), there are temperaments in which intuition is born from an excess of tension or vital ardour much more than the methodical effort: and probably it's to this type that I incline. I am much more enthusiast than scholar (forgive that pompous word, too weighty for my qualifications)." For more on this quality of his approach as seen in his wartime correspondence, see (December 5, 1916) *MM*, p. 150, (on the intuitional root of his thought), (February 1, 1919) p. 281 (on his concern for the spirit, rather than the external presentation of his ideas), and (August 28, 1919) p. 302: "While reaching a more precise definition of my points of contact with my friends, I have also come to realize the turn of my mind that divides me from them. I'm less concerned than they are with the metaphysical side of things, with what might have been or might not have been, with the abstract conditions of existence: all that seems to me inevitably misleading or shaky. I realize that, to the very marrow of my bones, I'm sensitive to the real, to what is made of it. My concern is to discover the conditions for such progress as is open to us, and not, starting from first principles, some theoretical development of the universe. This bias means that I'll always be a philistine to the professional philosophers: but I feel that my strength lies in the fidelity with which I obey it. So I'll continue to advance along those lines."

For the manner in which he expressed this fidelity and "bias," from his wartime essays, down to the year of his death, see: "Cosmic Life" (1919), *WW*, pp. 14-28, 57; "The Mystical Milieu" (1917), *WW*, pp. 117-23; "Mon Uvivers" (1918), *EG*, p. 267; "Note on the Universal Element" (1918), *WW*, p. 272; "The Universal Element" (1919), *WW*, pp. 290-92; "The Modes of Divine Action in the Universe" (1920), *CE*, p. 30; "Hominization" (1923), *VP*, p. 51; "My Universe" (1924), *SC*, p. 37; *DM* (1927), pp. 43-44, 46-47, 131; *PM* (1940), pp. 31-35; "Trois choses que je vois (ou: Une Weltanschauung en trois

be concerned about the importance of the subjectivity problem unavoidable because of this stress, despite the fact that he was conscious of the impact of idealist philosophical thought on science, and held no illusions about the possibility of total objectivity in human thought processes.[23]

On another issue, the significance of analogy, despite his recognition that it was operative in his thought, he never seems to have followed its implications all the way with regard to his own use of the scientific method. He does have some passing remarks pointing in this direction, but he does not seem to have adverted to the extent to which he could have strengthened his position and forestalled opposition if he had devoted more thought and space to clarifying precisely how his scientific phenomenology shared certain definite characteristics with recognizably empirical scientific methodology,

points)" (1948), *DA*, pp. 162-63; "Comment je vois" (1948), *DA*, pp. 181-82; "Quelques remarques POUR Y VOIR CLAIR, sur l'Essence du sentiment mystique" (1951), *DA*, pp. 227-28; "The Energy of Evolution" (1953), *AE*, p. 364; "The Stuff of the Universe" (1953), *AE*, p. 376; and, "Le Christique" (1955), *I*, p. 1. While there is this consistency underlying his writings down through the years, there was also a progression from the more poetic symbolic, to a more rarefied scientific style. De Solages notes three main stages, that of poetic symbolism (from the time of his experience at the Front, to the completion of *DM*, 1927), of "impassioned dialectic" (down to his return from China after World War II), and of a certain scientific rigor (from that point to his death). See Bruno de Solages, *Teilhard: étude*, pp. 28-31.

23. See "Human Energy" (1937), *HE*, pp. 113-14: "Long ago Kant (and in fact the Scholastics before him) pointed to the connexions which make the perceiver and the perceived indissolubly one with the universe. But this fundamental condition of knowledge only perturbed the rare and somewhat unapproachable adepts of metaphysics. For investigators of nature, it seemed indisputably established that things are projected for us 'just as they are' on a screen where we can look at them without being mixed up in them. Scientists contemplated the cosmos without suspecting that they could be influencing it in any degree by the contact of their thought or their senses, without even being aware of belonging intrinsically to the system which they were analysing with such wonder. . . . It seems that, for decisive and interior reasons, we are today beginning to emerge from this naive extrinsicality. . . . When they reach a certain degree of breadth and subtlety, the theories of modern physics distinctly reveal the intellectual texture of the investigator's mind beneath the shifting pattern of his phenomena. . . . The old realism of the laboratories veers, therefore, by the very logic of its development, towards a scientific idealism: matter being malleable by the intelligence that informs it." A reflection of the same thought in somewhat more condensed form can be found in *PM* (1940), p. 32.

and precisely how and where it went beyond it, or precisely how and where his style of thinking resembled,
and differed from, the philosophical metaphysics he
strove to avoid.[24]

There is one capital instance of his rather fluid, im-
precise approach to philosophy and metaphysics. It is
particularly significant for the present study, not only
because the sense he attributes to "metaphysics" in this
text is one that can include his "ultraphysic," but because
in it he specifically discusses the connection between
metaphysic, as he takes it in this context, and morality.
Moreover, the hidden premise problem shows up again.

The text in point is the short note, "La morale peut-
elle se passer de soubassements métaphysiques avoués ou
inavoués?" (1945). What he has to say specifically about
the meaning of morality will be taken up in the next
chapter.[25] More directly pertinent here are the two other

24. The passages in which he speaks of the process of analogical thought
are clear and definite enough, but there is hardly a plethora of them, nor do
they really contain a probing, reflexive analysis of the process itself. See: "The
Mastery of the World and the Kingdom of God" (1916), *WW*, p. 83, text and
n1, (by the editors), esp. with the references to letters of April 29, 1934, and
Oct. 29, 1949; "Forma Christi" (1918), *WW*, p. 265, text and n13 (by
Teilhard); "Note on the Universal Christ" (1920), *SC*, pp. 18-19; "The Basis
and the Foundation of the Idea of Evolution" (1926), *VP*, p. 117; "The
Phenomenon of Man" (1928), *SC*, p. 91; *PM* (1938-40), p. 88; and "Centrology" (1944), *AE*, p. 115, n8, where, in talking about "generalized biology"
Teilhard is clearly speaking of the process, although the word "analogy" does
not occur. A good sympathetic analysis of his style of analogical thought is de
Lubac's chapter on "Dynamic Analogy," in *Eternal Feminine*, pp. 66-84. Blanchard's *Méthode et Principes* goes into the question of analogy in several places,
but does not bear down on Teilhardian texts with the same incisiveness as
does de Lubac's work. See pp. 85-94, 147-53, 172-78. Despite the limited textual analysis by Blanchard, it is to his credit that he saw the significance of
understanding analogy in interpreting Teilhard. For an admiring but nega-
tively critical examination of analogy in Teilhard, from a Thomist angle, see
Paul-Bernard Grenet, *Pierre Teilhard de Chardin: ou le philosophe malgré lui*
(Paris: Beauchesne, 1960), pp. 103-23.

The question merits a study in itself, not on the strength of what Teilhard
says about the process, but because of the way he used it against an evolutionary, developmental background, and the way it relates to important Teilhardian concepts such as coherence (distinguished from concordism), extrapolation, dialectic, parameter, creative transformation, sublimation, and differentiating union. What should be traced out is how, in all of these, aspects of
sameness and difference, continuity and discontinuity are operative.

25. See below, chap. 3.

principal matters treated, the meaning of metaphysic and the relation between morality and metaphysic. *Métaphysique* he describes as:

> every explanation or vision of the world (of life) "as a whole" (every Weltanschauung), whether this total explanation of the world imposes itself on the intelligence or whether one adheres to it categorically, as to an option or a postulate.

The relation between morality and metaphysic is one of "coherence":

> If in effect morality (in the strict sense) implies *coherence* of action (be it with a universal equilibrium—static moralities—or be it with a universal movement—dynamic moralities), it (morality) *presupposes* necessarily the categorical acceptance of a certain perspective of the world (in equilibrium or in evolution). If not, it rests "in the air," undetermined.[26]

For Teilhard, the relationship between the two is an essential pairing, arising out of structural necessity. "Egoist" moralities flow from philosophical emphasis on the individual. By the same token, philosophies where primacy is given to society, race, pleasure, knowledge, humanity, or agnosticism, have their counterpart moralities—social, "national-socialist," "hedonistic," research oriented, humanitarian, or a-moral. And in each case, obligation arises from the solidarity and dependence put by the philosophical system between the individual's liberty and the universe. To the extent the individual is aware of himself as an element, in the organic Teilhardian sense, of a universe wherein he finds fulfillment, the individual is conscious of an *inner* bond of duty, tying him to the laws of that universe. If the philosophy admits God as the transcendent personal

26. *DA*, pp. 143-44. (Translation by the present writer, here and in what follows.)

culmination of the universe, this inner bond of duty is reenforced by a *transcendent* obligation to love and obey God. If the objection be put that many people act morally out of instinct or temperament and have no such metaphysical roots for their choices, his answer is that fidelity in this area is incomprehensible apart from some implicit metaphysic of one sort or another.

What he says about the specific organic character of this relationship, however, is something that gives one pause:

> If in effect the choice of a morality flows logically from rational adherence to a metaphysic, a metaphysic in turn appears to us ultimately acceptable only in the measure that it brings desirable fullness to our action. . . . The test of a metaphysic is the morality that flows from it.[27]

Some observations are in order.

Metaphysic, as used in this text, has a meaning quite close to that assigned in other places to religion or mystique—that of an all-embracing world view. There is a differentiating connotation, however, namely, association with an atmosphere of inquiry, whereas religion carries with it a context of adoration, and mystique a kind of elevated experience of unifying vision. The qualifying remarks inject a methodological aspect when Teilhard speaks of whether this world view "imposes itself on the intelligence or whether one adheres to it categorically as to an option or a postulate." What he means by this is not immediately clear. He certainly seems to say that not all acceptance of a metaphysic comes from rational proof alone, although the possibility of one that could do so seems allowed. To talk about option, however, is to talk about choice, not mere cogency of evidence, and to speak of a postulate is, commonly, to speak of something accepted as indispensable for an in-

27. "La morale peut-elle se passer de soubassements métaphysiques avoués ou inavoués?" (1945), *DA*, p. 145.

tellectual process, but which in itself is more given than proved.

Later on a preference is indicated, but still so as to require clarification. Recall what is said on the choice of a morality and the way it flows from rational adherence to a metaphysic. What he adds in the same sentence is both illuminating and provocative, with regard to the validation of a metaphysic: a metaphysic, for acceptance, must in the last analysis attract choice, it must bring desired fullness to action. Then comes the curious statement: "The test of a metaphysic is the morality which flows from it."

The point seems to be that however cogent the rational evidence for a world view, men still have to see the picture satisfying some crucial need, desire, or goal for choice, or they will not embrace it. Reason can take one so far, but the last step is not understanding, but option, and option attracted by a moral system. Put in simple language, what he seems to mean 'is, "If a moral theory does not attract, people won't buy the metaphysic to which it is tied."[28]

At this stage, for a certain type of rigorous intellectualist, a chink in the Teilhardian armor is showing. If one supposedly has gone beyond the last rational step, by what norm does one know what is genuinely fulfilling action? Is it by a kind of instinct or intuition? Or by relying on a hidden philosophical premise? Teilhard himself, in a portion of the same note not mentioned thus far, speaks of "empirical" approaches to morality that rely on a notion of "success," as implicitly containing a metaphysic that gives content to this notion. Can one not apply his own reasoning here and ask whether he must

28. This concern of Teilhard about the attractiveness of a moral approach and its truth value derived from its attractiveness was not a late development in his thought. See "Note pour l'évangélisation des temps nouveaux" (1919), *EG*, p. 370, where he speaks sympathetically of difficulties people have with being interested in Christianity, precisely because it seems inferior to an expansive, active social humanism, and hence is lacking in appeal, since it seems to be less good and therefore less true.

not hold there to be an implicit technically metaphysical base for the notion of "desirability" that affects the choice in question? With due corrections for the necessary analogy, the situation seems to be one in which Teilhard is running the serious risk of being hoisted by his own philosophical petard.

What precise type of *coherent* relationship is present between morality and metaphysic brings up the same type of problem to be worked over in the next chapter, where the implications of his statements on morality as related to mystique and religion will be examined.[29] It is the same type of problem in that it involves the consistency, the internal coherence, of Teilhard's thought. It is not the same problem, in that subsequently the question will have to do with how morality flowers, issues, in some sense in a mystique, and how, on the other hand, morality needs religion for orientation. Here the question has to do with the manner of validation for acceptance of a metaphysic that is the ground for a morality as it is rooted in a particular metaphysic. The question is not simply the relation of one to the other, but the ground for accepting the two as related on the basis of the motivational attraction of the morality.

The core of the difficulty here is that what is surfacing in another form is the argument for the existence of an adequate motivator from the conscious awareness of the need for a special type of motivation. How does one answer the objection that Teilhard is either advocating blind faith in subjective intuition, or relying on a hidden philosophical premise (that an essential desire in man must have an adequate object)? If this disjunction holds, how is Teilhard's approach scientific as extrapolative? (The term *philosophical* here, it should be noted, is used not in Teilhard's global world view sense, but in the sense of the theoretical metaphysical.) Does Teilhard have an answer, consistent with his peculiar scientific

29. See below, chap. 3C(a).

phenomenology, that would substantiate his claim that he is utilizing serious extrapolation?[30]

It seems that one can be formulated along his lines, although he never put the steps together in the following fashion to meet this precise objection.[31] The stages in the argument would be:

1. The empirical evidence of millions of years of the evolutionary process points inescapably to the steady, gradual rise toward consciousness, in pre-life and

30. The word *extrapolation* itself does not occur too often, although he is definitely working with the technique, even when not talking about it, as in *PM* (1940), "Book Four: Survival," pp. 237-90. For significant texts where the term is used, see: "The Atomism of Spirit" (1941), *AE*, pp. 40-48; "Some Reflections on Progress" (1941), *FM*, pp. 70-71; *MPN* (1949), "The Formation of the Noosphere II," pp. 107-17; "The Singularities of the Human Species" (1954), *AM*, section 3, "The Terminal Singularity of the Human Species: An Upper Critical Point of Ultra-Reflexion?" pp. 244-70, and "A Defence of Orthogenesis" (1955), *VP*, pp. 272-74.

31. For a detailed analysis of Teilhard's "proofs" for the existence of God see Bruno de Solages, *Teilhard: étude*, pp. 240-54. De Solages isolates two along lines of finality, one, remarkable enough, based on efficient causality, and another, undeveloped but capable of elaboration, rooted in contingency. The argument in the present study would be associated with the first two, but attempts to avoid going into the metaphysics of finality. Also, see Henri de Lubac, *Religion of Teilhard*, pp. 202-14. Relevant expressions of Teilhard's thought in his published correspondence can be found in *MM*, p. 96, letter of March 27, 1916, *LF*, p. 57, letter of February 14, 1927, and *LT*, p. 176, letter of May 4, 1931. For pertinent material in his works, consult: "La Grande Monade" (1918), *EG*, p. 247; "Mon Univers" (1918), *EG*, pp. 270-71; "The Spirit of the Earth" (1931), *HE*, pp. 43-47; *PM* (1940), pp. 226-34, 257-71; "Super-Humanity, Super-Christ, Super Charity" (1943), *SC*, pp. 162-63; "Action and Activation" (1945), *SC*, pp. 174-86; "The Contingence of the Universe and Man's Zest for Survival" (1953), *CE*, pp. 221-38; "The God of Evolution" (1953), *CE*, p. 239; "The Death Barrier and Co-Reflection" (1955), *AE*, pp. 400-403; and, "Research, Work and Worship" (1955), *SC*, p. 216.

Although similarity can be noted in Blondel's and Teilhard's approach to the existence of God through their mutual concern for the significance of action, Teilhard's phenomenology sets his off as quite different. For an analysis of Blondel's thought in this area, see Henri Bouillard, *Blondel et le Christianisme* (Paris: Éditions du Seuil, 1961), pp. 172-77. It is unfortunate that no correspondence between the two thinkers is extant on this particular topic. The letters de Lubac has edited focus on Christology and asceticism. At the time of their writing, however, Teilhard had not yet elaborated his phenomenological path to Omega. Although Blondel was still alive when he had done so, there does not seem to be any record of his reaction to it. For another study on Blondel and Teilhard, see Christian d'Armagnac, S.J., "De Blondel à Teilhard, nature et intériorité," *Archives de philosophie* (avril-juin, 1958), pp. 298-312. Also, see Rideau, *Teilhard: Guide*, pp. 26, 294 n47, for Teilhard's appreciation of the significance of action in Blondel's thought.

lower life forms, and toward higher forms of consciousness in higher forms of life.

2. If the evolutionary process in the past has infallibly
and irreversibly supplied whatever forms of activating
energy were needed for the continuance of the process, it is reasonable to predict that on the basis of antecedent probability, somehow the universe contains,
and will continue to supply, the type of energy demanded for the process to go on toward ever higher
forms of consciousness in and through men.

3. If it can be shown, through introspection, other
forms of psychological analysis, and sufficient sharing
of common insights by a sufficient number of persons, that all people require, however obscurely perceived this may be in many minds, an all-attractive
personal Someone to activate adequately this
evolutionary process in its present and future stages,
then it is reasonable to extrapolate, on the ground
that evolution will continue to supply the energy
needed, that the love-energizing Omega does exist.

The central elements in this line of argumentation
that keep it on the phenomenological plane are the *empirical* validation of evolution's success so far, providing
the base for predicting it will continue, and the *experiential* psychological evidence of what is actually needed to
activate human love energy to continue human evolution. Where Teilhard's thinking is most vulnerable to objection on phenomenological grounds is with regard to
the second element, namely, the existence of a general
psychological human need for this type of motivation.
True, he was not unaware of this objection, and responded to it mainly by attesting to his own inner convictions about what he needed, to the testimony he had
received from others with whom he had discussed the
matter, and to the evidence he found that people who
denied this need were, without being aware of the fact,
acting on it anyway, and would, if they analyzed them-

selves more deeply, find that it was there.[32] In the last analysis, he admitted that he was not working with complete certitude here, but with a hypothesis that still demanded further research and testing for general verification.[33]

For this reason, as well as for the recognizable phenomenological character of the steps in the argument, it seems that the argument can be put in a manner that coheres with his own premises, and can be formulated so as to avoid blind subjectivism as well as a hidden metaphysical base. Building on antecedent probability enables one to escape subjectivism. Working from observable consistency of human desire, rather than from a metaphysical judgment about its intimate nature, avoids the hidden metaphysic. If one were to comment that what he was doing was providing the background or basis for strict metaphysical inquiry in this area, Teilhard would not object, but say that such inquiry was precisely in the area of the "meta," beyond his "ultra."

*Teilhard's "Philosophy" of Creative Union*

What he gets into when he does, in some instances, attempt to work consciously on a more metaphysical level, by going beyond his phenomenological ultraphysic into a philosophy of what he called "creative union," is another question. He first broached the matter in his World War I essay by that title and came back to it several times in his later writings. What he did has been described as a more generalized presentation of his phenomenological ideas, which he himself categorized as more of a synthesized empirical and pragmatic view of the universe than a precise metaphysical doctrine, a "point of view" that he hopes could be adopted and verified, once explained, but not demonstrably proved. He was self-critically not satisfied with his efforts in this direction and in his later

32. Note, for example, "Le Christique" (1955), *I*, pp. 1, 12-13.
33. See particularly "Degrees of Scientific Certainty in the Idea of Evolution" (1946), *SC*, pp. 192-96.

years did not pursue them to any great extent. They do raise some important questions, especially on the understanding of creation, but detailed inquiry into these is not pertinent here.[34]

### 3. POETIC INSIGHTS AND ARTISTIC EXPERIENCE

In Teilhard's broadly scientific phenomenological writings, he is prone to use a geometric imagery of vectors,

34. See the editorial comments introductory to "Creative Union" (1917), *WW*, pp. 151-52. His own objective in the essay is indicated in the opening paragraph, p. 153. The other main texts to be noted are: "My Universe" (1924), *SC*, pp. 39-53; "Comment je vois" (1948), *DA*, pp. 207-14, (in good part a mixture of his "philosophy" with speculative theology); and, "The Contingence of the Universe and Man's Zest for Survival: or How Can One Rethink the Christian Notion of Creation to Conform with the Laws of Energetics?" (1953), *CE*, pp. 221-28. In this last essay, the idea of creative union (a metaphysic of *Unire*, or *Uniri*) is worked in as more motivationally satisfying for the evolutionary mind than a metaphysics of *Esse*. In this sector he has been subjected to considerable critical commentary. See Mooney, *Mystery of Christ*, pp. 179-93; Rideau, *Teilhard: Guide*, pp. 153-60; Smulders, *Design of Teilhard*, pp. 77-85 (unfortunately limited principally to "Comment je vois" [1948]); de Solages, *Teilhard: étude*, pp. 313-23. Friendly critics, such as the above, make clear that Teilhard has no intent to deny the transcendent action of God in creation, but admit that his explanation does present difficulties in the realm of God's graciousness and efficiency. Donald Gray, in his *The One and The Many*, sees Teilhard's theory of creative union as central and controlling to understanding his thought and determinative of its development through his life. For Gray's explanation of the theory itself, see pp. 15-33. The remainder of his carefully worked out study is devoted to tracing the correlations and implications of creative union in the context of other leading Teilhardian concepts, especially in his earlier writings. That the implications are there, it is difficult to deny, if one insists on working on this particularly unclear, quasi-philosophical plane of Teilhard's thought. But the indications of Teilhard's concerns as found in the amount of material devoted to it seem to indicate that he himself was not particularly preoccupied with the theory and was, psychologically, more drawn to work on the level of his generalized scientific phenomenology, when thinking in a theoretical style. While granting, with appreciation, the insights into Teilhard's thought provided by Gray's correlations, I question the thesis that the creative union theory was actually as determinative, in point of fact, throughout Teilhard's development, as Gray would have it operating. The evidence of determinative concerns derived from what he wrote about would seem to point to a different level of conscious orientation, more pragmatically apologetic if you will, seeking to affect, in some way, unification of human minds, rather than to work out theoretical explanations of this unification. Apart from the quantitative argument that Teilhard simply did not write much about the matter, and that if he had thought it terribly important, he would have written much more, there is the evidence, difficult to avoid even if perhaps embarrassing, of his own witness to his concern more for spirit than for clear, systematic thought, for enthusiasm over scholarship. See on this point, above, n22.

cones, circles, spheres, and centers, which have a rarefied emotional atmosphere.[35] If one expands the notion of phenomenon, maintaining the core of observability, but extending it into the realm of descriptive imagery associated with his underlying total human concern, something closer to what is usually taken as poetic or artistic imagery is found. This shows up particularly throughout his correspondence, in certain of his World War I writings, such as "La Nostalgie du Front" and "La Grande Monade," but also much later in his reflections on the meaning of the Berkeley Cyclotron (1953).[36] In writings of this sort one finds a higher pitch of emotional intensity, proportioned to the vividness of the pictorial imagery, associated with broadly philosophic reflections, but not enclosed in the framework of hypothesis and test.

Passing on to certain of his religious writings, such as "Christ in the World of Matter" (1916), "The Spiritual Power of Matter" (1919), and "The Mass on the World" (1923), one finds the same type of emotionally charged imagery as in the pieces just mentioned, but here in the context of expressing and interpreting his central insights into religious faith.[37]

However, and this is a subtle point, even in his more geometric writing, there somehow comes through a sense of warmth and passion, which finds more open expression in his writing where his images are more concrete. Also, in these more imaginative pieces the effect is that of an intuitive vision grasped and communicated through the impact of the imagery and feeling it evokes, whereas in his more scientific phenomenological writing, the steps and structure of the scientific process are utilized to lead to his concluding insights. Finally, the

---

35. "Centrology" (1944), *AE*, pp. 99-127, is a good example of heavy concentration on this type of imagery. It is also considered by Barthélemy-Madaule to be of prime importance for an appreciation of Teilhard's peculiar dialectic. See: *La personne chez Teilhard*, p. 33.

36. "On Looking at a Cyclotron: Reflections on the Folding-Back upon Itself of Human Energy" (1953), *AE*, pp. 349-57.

37. *HU*, pp. 41-55, pp. 59-71, pp. 19-37.

cumulative impact, even of such a work as *The Phenome-non of Man*, with its *creative* formulation of ways to build a more human future, is, despite its heavily scientific flavor, that of a fundamentally "poetic" effort, when considered from this creative aspect.[38]

Moreover, despite the fact that there is little reference to art and its function in his evolutionary theory as he elaborated it, he was not unaware of the significance of artistic effort and in one place, at least, expressed some important insights about it. Talking to a group of artists in 1939, he made the following points, which are perti-nent for understanding the role of his own poetic style in his thinking and writing. Commenting on the often-formulated objection regarding art, about its apparent uselessness, Teilhard sketched his views as to its threefold and necessary function in the unfolding of the human spirit through the course of history. First, art gives a body to, and in some sense, materializes, those vi-tal impressions which would remain incomplete or be lost to others if they did not find expression in a ges-ture, a dance, a song, or a cry. Second, at the same time, and by the very fact of giving sensible form to a vital current of spirit, art idealizes it and partially intellec-tualizes it. This is not done by way of conveying a thesis or doctrine, for art is dominated by intuition, not reason. However, he adds:

> if the work truly springs from the depth of oneself, as rich music, we should not be afraid: in the minds of those touched by it, it refracts in a brilliant rainbow. More primi-tive than every idea, beauty persuasively reveals itself as the fore-runner and generatrix of ideas.

Finally, as the most important third function, he sees art as personalizing spiritual energy coming to life on earth. "The more the world becomes rationalized and mechanized, the more it stands in need of 'poets' as the

---

38. But *PM* (1940) has its passages, too, of what is usually considered sim-ple poetic imagery. See "Modern Disquiet," pp. 226-29.

saviors and ferment of its personality." For despite the originality of scientific and philosophical thought, it tends to be absorbed in the universality of the results it expresses.[39] What all this comes to, taken en bloc, is that to describe his thought processes accurately one must conclude that in his reflective writings what is manifest is not a man of different, compartmentalized thought styles, but a human person of genuine scientific bent and gifts who is likewise endowed with a sense of vivid imagery and creativity as well as a grasp of its significance and who at times responded with more emphasis to one inner current than the other, but who never lost the feeling for descriptive poetic imagery or the forward-looking vision of a "poetic" social designer, or the scientific cast of mind—no matter what type of thinking or writing he might be engaged in at a particular time. That his understanding of religious faith was always operative in one way or another in the background would be hard to deny. His fundamental motivational concerns, as have been seen, point to this, likewise, the manner in which, even in works for the most part focused phenomenologically, the God question tends to surface sooner or later, as well as, often enough, the relevance of Christianity to what he has been discussing.[40] In a real but at times not readily discernible manner, then, all the facets of his temperament

39. "Comment comprendre et utiliser l'art dans la ligne de l'énergie humaine," 1939 DA, pp. 95-97. (Translation by the present writer.) There is also a significant footnote to his observations on the forward development of the noosphere through research, in MPN (1949), p. 107. It bears quotation in full: "In this propulsive system, artistic research, we should note, even though the lines it follows (or a physiology of it) are still obscure and would call for a separate investigation, is not biologically separable from scientific research (which is the only form we are explicitly studying here) and constitutes an integral part of the same exuberant surge of human energy."
40. In PM (1940), the Epilogue on "The Christian Phenomenon," pp. 291-99, is a prime example of this. See also MPN (1949), p. 121; "The Singularities of the Human Species" (1954), AM, pp. 271-73; "The Spirit of the Earth" (1931), HE, pp. 43-47; "Sketch of a Personalistic Universe" (1936), HE, pp. 89-92; and "The Phenomenon of Spirituality" (1937), HE, pp. 108-12. The list could be extended considerably.

and concern can be sensed as operative throughout the stretch of his reflective works.

## 4. SIGNIFICANT LIFE EXPERIENCES

How the various "significant life experiences" fed into all the preceding varied from situation to situation in which he thought through one or another problem of human meaning. The setting of the Front in World War I bulks large in several of his pieces during that period. It is particularly important for contributing, by his own admission, to his first profound intuitions about the reality of human solidarity—the *experience* of this reality, that is, as expressed in "La Nostalgie du Front" and "La Grande Monade," later to be developed in his concepts about the noosphere.[41] So too is what he has to say about the experience of the aggressive drive and its value. When, toward the end of his life he wrote, in "Le coeur de la matiére," about the importance of "The Feminine," he did not go into details, but his wartime correspondence with his cousin reveals a warm and affectionate relationship that certainly must have influenced his insights, as well as his friendships with Léontine Zanta, Lucile Swan, and others.[42] When he discusses the future of general human collaboration in the conquest of the challenges of the earth, it is likewise clear that he is drawing on the, for him, primordial experience of collaboration with his scientific co-workers on several continents. And, in writings like *The Divine Milieu*, what he speaks of in regard to resistance to evil and true resigna-

---

41. The later formulation of his idea about the noosphere in phenomenological terms, after having first been intuited in a kind of poetic insight, should be noted as quite in line with Teilhard's remarks on the kind of "pre-vision" given the artist to a truth that is later given other expression. See above, n39. Teilhard's summation, not quoted in the text, is particularly pertinent: "To sum up, surrounding human energy in its growth, art represents the outermost zone of advance, that in which truths coming into being condense, preform, and take on life, before they have been definitively formulated and assimilated." *DA*, p. 96. (Translation by the present writer.)
42. See below, chap. 4, nn25 and 38.

tion could not have but been affected by his own attempts to follow the integrity of his conscience in his interior search for synthesis while ecclesiastical superiors held firm in their refusal to allow his thoughts a public hearing.[43] The other side of his religious experience is also important, namely, the sustaining fraternal charity of friends, deeply committed as he was, to the same religious goals.[44]

## 5. THE CHRIST DIMENSION

So would run an overview of the currents and cross-currents of consciousness that Teilhard mulled over in his prayerful meditation, occasionally quite protracted. What came out of this was a multi-colored outlook on the energies at work in global technological society, vitalized by the vision he had of the Cosmic Christ offering Himself so as to penetrate all, and thus giving light, warmth, and love to the totality of human effort and suffering. In his complete synthesis, the centrality of Christ cannot be overemphasized.[45] Even though in many of his writings Jesus may be hidden from direct view, what he does say when he speaks about Him makes the point clear enough. His earliest writings, "Christ in the World of Matter (1916), "The Priest" (1918) and "The Spiritual Power of Matter" (1919) are

43. Perhaps the best available account of his struggle in English, by one of Teilhard's close associates, is that of Henri de Lubac. See *LZ*, "The Trial of Faith," pp. 27-44 (de Lubac's introduction to the Zanta correspondence). René d'Ouince, for a time Teilhard's Superior at *Études* in Paris in the years following World War II, traces the whole story in considerable detail, from the early twenties down to his death. See *Un Prophète en procès: Teilhard de Chardin dans l'Église de son temps* (Paris: Aubier-Montaigne, 1970), pp. 100-187, (hereafter referred to as *Teilhard dans l'Église*). Also Louis Barjon, another *Études* associate, *Le combat de Teilhard*, pp. 274-283, and Bruno de Solages, a friend of many years standing, *Teilhard: étude*, pp. 41-49.
44. Particularly men like Auguste Valensin, Pierre Charles, Bruno de Solages, and Henri de Lubac.
45. Mooney's *Mystery of Christ* is the outstanding synthesis of Teilhard's Christology. See also Francisco Bravo, *Christ in the Thought of Teilhard de Chardin* (Notre Dame, Ind.: University of Notre Dame Press, 1967), and Faricy, *Teilhard: Theology*.

witness to this.[46] Add to these "The Mass on the World" (1923), *The Divine Milieu* (1926-27), "Christology and Evolution" (1933), "Christ the Evolver" (1942), and, in his old age, the powerful testimony of his "Prayer to Christ Ever-Greater," which concludes "Le coeur de la matière" (1950), and the full dynamic thrust of the last formulation of his total synthesis not long before his death, "Le Christique" (1955).[47]

In all this, it is important to emphasize, that not only does Christ give fullness of meaning to the breadth and depth of the human experience as Teilhard came to know and to live it, but the totality of his human experience in turn enlarged and gave fuller delineation to his understanding of Christ. As Teilhard put it, the sphere of the world he loved so passionately, sought and found Christ as its center of meaning; the Christ-Center of his loving faith, by fulfilling, "pleromizing," Eucharistic radiance, suffused the entire sphere of his universe.[48]

## 6. PERSONALISTIC ASPECTS

Whatever group he had in mind, secular humanists, or believers, one central, communicative, characteristic is present in his style, which can perhaps be described as *personalistic sharing*. Convinced as he was of the need for men to come to a unified vision of human existence acceptable to all, and preoccupied as he was with the totality of human unity, Teilhard was faithful, in his manner of presentation, to the logic of his own basic principle of differentiating union, applied to the psychological and

---

46. *HU*, pp. 41-55, *WW*, pp. 205-24, *HU*, pp. 59-71. These are by no means the only essays where his Christocentrism shows. It also surfaces, over and over again, in his wartime correspondence with his cousin Marguerite.

47. *HU*, pp. 19-37; *CE*, pp. 76-95; *CE*, pp. 138-50. The last two essays cited are unpublished. But this list, too, of later writings is only a representative sample. Works from *SC*, *CE*, *DA*, and the remaining unpublished group, could be chosen almost at random for documentation.

48. "Le Christique" (1955), *I*, p. 6. For an early approach to the concept, see "Mon Univers" (1918), *EG*, pp. 272-73. A variant, in which he speaks of the cosmic magnifying the Christic and the Christic amorizing the cosmic, can be found in "The God of Evolution" (1953), *CE*, p. 243.

ethical realms. What this meant in this instance was that the unique and individual capacity of each person for resolving his or her own problems of human meaning must be not only respected, but fostered. Hence, his approach was not the coercive push toward uniformity of a totalitarian brain-washer or an inquisitorial dogmatic imperialist.[49] Although at times his enthusiasm led him to question-begging adjectives in describing the position he favored, he was quite consistent in his stress that he did not want to *force* his ideas on anyone, but to present them, with all the impact he could muster, adapted as well as he could to the mentality of his audience, by way of a presentation of a *psychological experience to be shared*.

In effect, he asked his audience quite simply to enter his universe, breathe its atmosphere, look around searchingly, listen to its harmonies, test out its entire ecology, and then decide for themselves whether it was not *the* universe in which life made most sense. Often enough he was sketching probes into questions, or only tentative solutions, and was offering his ideas very much as a plea for help to work out together with him the problem or problems he saw.[50] He was operating in the spirit, almost second nature to him, of a dedicated research worker who looked upon himself and his audience as members of the same research team seeking the resolution of critical human problems.

The many and different approaches he took to what are often fundamentally the same themes can also be grasped by a striking observation he made once in his correspondence. He remarked to one of his friends in a 1927 letter from Peking, that he had recently clarified better just what he was trying to do:

49. How this was manifest, even in conversation, is attested to by Robert Garic, in *LZ*, p. 20 (his introduction to the letters). See also Lucile Swan, "Memories and Letters" in *Teilhard de Chardin: Pilgrim of the Future*, ed. Neville Braybrooke, Libra Books (London: Darton, Longman & Todd Ltd., 1965), pp. 40-49.

50. Note, for example, the introductions to "Cosmic Life" (1916), *WW*, pp. 14-18; "Creative Union" (1918), *WW*, p. 153; "My Universe" (1924), *SC*, pp. 37-39; "Comment je vois" (1948), *DA*, pp. 181-82; "Le Christique" (1955), *I*, p. 1.

It is that, fundamentally, what I desire so greatly to propagate is not exactly a theory, a system, a *Westanschauung*, but a certain taste, a certain perception of the beauty, the pathos, and the unity of *being*. This may even account for the incomprehension I encounter. I try to translate the species of calm intoxication produced in me by an awareness of the profound substance of things into theories (how I wish I could translate it into music!), but these theories really matter to me only by their vibrations in a province of the soul which is not that of intellectualism. Those who do not hear the fundamental harmony of the Universe which I try to transcribe (fortunately, many do) look in what I write for some kind of narrowly logical system, and are confused or angry. Fundamentally, it is not possible to transmit directly by words the perception of a quality, a taste. Once again, it would be more to my purpose to be a shadow of Wagner than a shadow of Darwin. Taking myself as I am, I see no better course than to strive by all means to reveal Humanity to Men.[51]

It is unfortunate that Teilhard never developed at length the point he was making in these remarks. Despite the poetic hyperbole, they do provide a key, not only to his general style of presentation, but also to his elaboration of variations on the same theme. Lest his negative remarks about intellectualism give pause here, it should be observed that obviously from the entire tenor of his life, he was not against working with ideas nor discounting their impact. He worked with them too hard and too much.[52] But he was against a dry, over-rationalized, unfeeling scientism, which was insensitive to the total human experience and ignored the heuristic value of human feeling in the interpretation of meaning in human life.

He was no mere emotional sentimentalist. What he was trying to do was integrate all the relevant contributory factors of human existence into a coherent picture, internally consistent among its elements and compatibile

51. *LF*, p. 59, letter of February 14, 1927.
52. In this context, de Solages's analysis of the stages in the development of his thought should be kept in mind. See above, n22.

with his religious faith. This was to be done with what he hoped would be contagious enthusiasm, which in itself would help toward sympathetic appreciation of his vision.

## D. The Movement from Basic Anthropology to Major Moral Options

What, finally, remains to be said about Teilhard's method of thought and formulation, when one moves on from the general questions of human meaning to more particular areas of moral choice, and to the application of understanding about these areas to day-to-day living in a running sequence of decisions of conscience?

When he is thinking on the phenomenological level, there are two fundamental intuitions that serve as ethical criteria. The first is his Law of Complexity-Consciousness, the formula he arrived at through a process of empirical observation and synthesis, which affirms that evolution proceeds by moving toward higher forms of complexity and consciousness. The second is that, with man, evolution has become conscious of itself and responsible for increasing complexity and consciousness at the highest evolutionary level—that of autonomous reflective, human love energy.

His ethical evaluation, then, on the phenomenological plane, of political, educational, economic, and other matters will be governed by these two basic parameters. He has left in writing the barest sketch of how this process operates, in the few pages to be examined shortly on his moral theory. But as one works through the different specific areas in the following chapters, it can be seen that the two are functioning, even though attention is not always drawn to them in a reflex, moralizing way. Underlying his expressions of ethical evaluation one will find, either expressed or implied, his radical concerns as to how what he is dealing with contributes to: 1) heightened complexity-consciousness in the human sphere, and 2) an augmentation of love energy, binding human persons together in their shared evolutionary task, in communion with Omega.

The manner in which he goes about this is not deductive, proceeding from principles to conclusions, but rather empirical in the sense of putting styles and modes of acting to the test of experience alongside his empirically derived parameters.

While Teilhard is thinking on the Christological level, his ethical process is more complex. His Christological parameters parallel the phenomenological. Here he is concerned 1) with whatever builds the Body of Christ, and 2) with achieving this through growth in charity (divinized, Christic, human love). His starting points are derived from revelation, but, as he proceeds into areas of specific human endeavor, the interpretation of these revealed norms is affected by his understanding of the two parallel phenomenological criteria. When he is thinking Christologically, his application of fundamental ideas to areas of action and thence to concrete actions would move according to the process of the discernment of spirits, into which would feed whatever elements from revelation or human experience would be judged appropriate.[53]

53. Mermod's work, *La morale chez Teilhard*, is devoted to constructing a phenomenological ethic on Teilhard's texts, in the sense that he gathers together the pertinent materials from various sources and presents them in a synthesis of his own construction, yet remains faithful to Teilhard's main thrust. Mermod intended this to be phase one of a two-phase study, the second part of which would explore Teilhard's theological ethic. See Mermod, pp. 7-10, p. 24 n9. For Claude Cuénot's recognition of two levels, dialectic, or cosmogenetic, and mystical, or Christian, in Teilhard's ethical thought, see his letter to Mermod of May 8, 1963, quoted by Mermod, *La morale chez Teilhard*, p. 8. Whatever may be the ultimate resolution of the debate about the existence of a distinctive Christian ethic as such discernibly different from a humanist ethic, the present study proceeds on the working premise that in Teilhard's writings, at least, there are two distinguishable aspects. For a discussion of this problem at its present stage, see Charles E. Curran, *Catholic Moral Theology in Dialogue* (Notre Dame, Ind.: Fides Publishers, 1972), pp. 1-23. The evidence of the present study, as it unfolds, could be used to substantiate up to a point the position taken by Curran as to the nonexistence of a distinctively Christian ethic, in the precise sense he uses the concept *ethical*,

How this phenomenological ethic would be conceived and be clarified will emerge in the following chapters, on the function of morality, love, education, aggression, research, political life, economics, technology, leisure, and eugenics. For a secular humanist, the thought processes corresponding to Teilhard's own Ignatian style of active-contemplative prayer would be a thoughtful reflectiveness implied by what Teilhard says about the meaning of research, carried on in a spirit of loving, daring hope, heading toward unification of humanity in love of Omega. What Teilhard would and did insist on as the starting point would be a sincere inward-looking inquiry into one's own self, and the meaning of one's life in the setting of an evolutionary, convergent, personalizing universe.[54] True, he himself did not develop his

namely, pertaining to ethical *conclusions, proximate* dispositions, goals and attitudes (p. 20). (Emphasis supplied.) In fact, Teilhard's purpose in developing his phenomenological approach could be said to be an attempt to elaborate a stance that humanists could hold *in common* with Christians, and vice versa. But the question remains as to whether, despite agreement in large areas, on conclusions, proximate dispositions, goals and attitudes, there would ultimately be universal agreement on all such matters, and hence whether, in the last analysis there would not be certain facets of a Christian's approach to ethics taken in Curran's precise sense, that would differ from those of a secular humanist. A case in point would be that of forgiveness of enemies, or, on a more explicit Teilhardian level, that of the style of gentleness, or kindness in disposition toward other human beings, be they adversaries, friends, or associates, or any other human being on the face of the earth, for that matter. The crucial point in resolving the difficulty would seem to be how one establishes a criterion of proximity. Taking a larger sense of ethics, which would include motivation, there would seem to be a strong case that could be made for saying that the remainder of Curran's book itself documents the position for the existence of a definite distinctiveness in a Christian ethical approach. It would be difficult to conceive a secular humanist ethicist discussing the problems taken up in the manner Curran uses, or, for that matter, being preoccupied much at all about dialogue with a theology of the Church (chap. 5). The efforts of such men as Roger Garaudy and Herbert Aptheker would not seem to be involved in such a dialogue, but rather with churchmen about a common humanistic core of ideas.

54. Writing to a friend from Tientsin, June 11, 1926, he advised, ". . . for you, as for everyone, there is only one road that can lead to God, and this is the fidelity to remain constantly true to yourself, to what you feel is highest in you. Do not worry about the rest. The road will open before you as you go." *LF*, p. 31. In a similar vein, to Léontine Zanta, October 3, 1923, "The truth is a question between you and God. No certitude, no human teaching, can go against the awareness you have of growing in light and strength in the direction you have chosen. You're perfectly right in thinking that the best criterion of truth is 'the power of making ourselves coherent, *when put to the test*.' There

methodological thought in any formal treatise on precisely these lines, but they seem to follow from what he did say. One could even put the case more strongly and say that what he was talking about in the materials to be examined in the following chapters, up to the chapter on his Christological ethic, was precisely that, but taken from the vantage point of his world view looking toward moral action, rather than starting with moral action and looking to its roots and processes in a supporting world view.

The relationship between his phenomenological ethic, in its details, and his Christological ethic will be explored at some length in chapter 9, below. There it will be seen that it is not enough to say simply that his own statement about revelation's *animating*, but not duplicating the work of scientific humanist inquiry and activity, takes care of all that emerges in the body of his thought as it pertains to ethical matters.[55] Moreover, what he held with regard to the process of dogmatic development should be kept in mind as one examines the material in the immediately following chapters, as well as in chapter 9.

is no trace of unsatisfactory pragmatism in this proposition, for we know that the truth when so recognized has a consistency and price outside our own success." *LZ*, p. 56. Despite the nuances of extreme subjectivism that could be read in that last quotation, it seems clear that Teilhard, from his constant insistence upon respect for phenomenological evidence outside oneself, was no blind subjective intuitionist. The best way to read his words would seem to be that they express in strong terms the fundamental reality that in the last analysis one has to judge on the basis of phenomena as one sees them, and that no one else can do that task for anyone. The same frank appeal for a person to be taken as he is shows forth, likewise, in his letter of October 12, 1951, to Fr. Janssens, the Jesuit General. See Pierre Leroy, S.J., "Teilhard de Chardin: The Man," printed at the beginning of *DM*, pp. 37-40, esp. p. 38. Among other texts, where the need for self-development is stressed as primary for personalization, see "Réflexions sur le bonheur," 1943, *DA*, pp. 121-39, esp. pp. 129-35, where he discusses the three steps or stages in personalization: centration, decentration, and supercentration. In speaking of the first, he concludes, p. 130, "To be, is, from the outset, to fashion oneself, to discover oneself." (Translation by the present writer.)

55. "The Death Barrier and Co-Reflection" (1955), *AE*, pp. 403-6, esp. p. 405 n6, "Appendix: Science and Revelation."

## E. The Conscience-Decision Process

When one moves, at last, from charting out the main lines of moral decision, or, in Teilhard's terms, from determining the general physiology and anatomy of the noosphere, on to the concrete decisions of daily life about the practical application of these ideas, one is faced with the same basic methodological processes, now focused sharply on action in the immediate present or the closely foreseeable future.

How Teilhard worked this out in the practice of his own theological ethic was in his daily meditative prayer, examinations of conscience, reflective reading of the Breviary, and in his offering of the Eucharist, whether he had to do the latter "vicariously" through his "Mass on the World," or could say Mass in the usual way. Moreover, the orientation of this prayerful reflection was renewed and set for him yearly in his annual retreat.[56]

What is particularly illuminating with regard to his style of Ignatian prayer is what shows up in the manner by which he adapted the Ignatian Exercises to his phenomenological insights. His retreat notes reveal important modifications of the literal structure, with serious concern to maintain the essential spirit. When the complete text of his journals and retreat notes becomes available, a thorough study should be made of this particular process, with all its implications, specifically pertinent to ethics.[57]

---

56. Cf., for example, the plans sketched at the end of his retreat notes for 1944 and 1945.

57. Relevant material can be found in de Lubac's *Teilhard: Man and Meaning*, particularly in chap. 10, "Spiritual Life," pp. 71-78; chap. 11, "Annual Retreats," pp. 79-88, and chap. 15, "The Ignatian Tradition," pp. 112-18. Also Rideau, *Teilhard: Guide*, "Teilhard's Spirituality and the Spiritual Exercises of St. Ignatius," pp. 211-20, along with "Critical Comments," pp. 221-30. Neither de Lubac or Rideau, however, correlates his material with current thinking about the integration of "spirituality" with the ethical process, taken in its fullest dimensions.

Some important points significant for the present line of inquiry would be the following, drawn from the text of Teilhard's available retreat notes, which are full of his phenomenological language in a Christological setting and of his concern for synthesis.[58] This shows up strikingly in his expression of concern about the need to grow in communion with God in his work, and particularly to be a living, kind, serene, transparent witness to his convictions about the union of God and the world.[59] But he also shows a clear awareness of his own weakness, fragility, and the obscurity, at times the uncertainty, in an evolutionary, changing world, about just what the correct moral choices should be.[60] Related to this would be more insistence on the radical problem of faith in God as the underlying foundation of the Exercises—a matter simply assumed in the Ignatian text itself.[61] Then, too, there are important transpositions of basic Ignatian formulas. The Ignatian "Tantum-Quantum," his parametric maxim about using creatures as they lead to God and staying away from them as they do not, becomes for Teilhard, "To draw from creatures their maximum of spiritual energy (power of union)."[62] And, the idea of furthering Christ's Kingdom is taken out of its cultural context of a Crusade to become the work of bringing Christ to completion in the universe, with the "Two Standards" of Ignatius interpreted as humanity divided into two camps of those who will work for Christic evolution and those who refuse to move and work. In this setting, for Teilhard, the "poor" man, dedicated to following Christ in poverty at all cost, becomes the "worker," dedicated to toil with Christ at all cost, in whatever work is needed and, needless to say, with

58. Retreat Notes: *I*, 1944, 2nd Day, 5th Day, 7th Day, 8th Day, Plan of Life; 1945, 2nd Day, 4th Day, 5th Day, 7th Day; 1952, June 28, June 29, June 30; 1953, 1st Day, 5th Day, 6th Day (also note of June 24).
59. Retreat Notes: *I*, 1944, 1st Day, 5th Day; 1945, 1st Day.
60. Retreat Notes: *I*, 1944, 3rd Day, 7th Day.
61. Retreat Notes: *I*, 1944, 1st Day; 1945, 1st Day.
62. Retreat Notes: *I*, 1944, 5th Day; 1952, June 23; 1953, special Note of Oct. 8; 1954, 1st Day.

whatever detachment from possessions—that is, with whatever poverty of spirit and actual poverty—such work would call for.[63]

How these filtered down into Teilhard's day-to-day living was, of course, through his daily reflective prayer, in which he was disciplined to place himself in the presence of God, to compare his life with his ideals, and to think them through to their immediate practical conclusions.[64] The logical counterpart of this, for a secular humanist, would be, rather simply, periodic protracted reflective thought, similar to a retreat, on the meaning of human life. This would be carried on in the light, Teilhard would hope, of the significance of Omega, or an equivalent. There would also be the follow-through of daily reflective meditation on how best to apply personalist human goals to continue the evolutionary process of convergence in human love carried to its fullest scope of awareness, utilizing the principles of Teilhard's morality of movement, as will be examined in the next chapter.

An important accompaniment of reflective prayer for Teilhard, as part of his living out his Jesuit spirituality, was continual consultation with competent advisers, who would not only help to avoid acting out of self-deception, but also assist in making a better decision. What is involved here is the use of Ignatian rules for the discernment of spirits in something of what could be called a team context. For the secular humanist, there would obviously be no discernment of spirits to determine the operations of grace, but the counterpart measures of consultation and advice are not difficult to fill in.

On the matter of Ignatian rules for the discernment of spirits, which should be taken in conjunction with correlative practices for making a sound "election," or

63. Retreat Notes: *I*, 1954, 5th Day, 6th Day.
64. The steps indicated in this sentence are, obviously, not original with Ignatius, nor peculiar to Jesuit life, but they are given special emphasis in that tradition.

life-orientation decision, it is regrettable that Teilhard never saw fit to follow out the implications of what he practiced for many years as an exact religious, and to write at some length about how these practices would have a bearing on the implementation of his moral theory. Had he done so, something similar to Karl Rahner's writing on the knowledge of the concrete singular might have emerged, and one could say that the basic elements of a Teilhardian theological ethic would have been presented, all the way down to the all-important decision process itself.[65] But he never did this, and this aspect of his ethical methodology has to be pieced together from what is known of his personal religious practice and from what is contained mostly in his journals, retreat notes, and occasional references in his correspondence.

---

65. See Karl Rahner's lengthy essay, "The Logic of Concrete Individual Knowledge in Ignatius Loyola," in *The Dynamic Element in the Church*, trans. W. J. O'Hara (New York: Herder and Herder, 1964), pp. 84-169. A valuable critical and interpretive study could be made, which would help immensely to pursue development of a Teilhardian ethic into the concrete decision-process realm, by a comparative analysis of what Teilhard wrote in his published works and especially in his currently unavailable journals and retreat notes, about the discernment of spirits, intuition, and vision, with the leading concepts developed by Rahner in this study. Such an inquiry would be particularly important with regard to what some might detect as an aspect of subjectivist situationalism in Teilhard's morality of movement.

3

# Moral Energy and Teilhard's Morality of Movement

## A.  Teilhard and Morality—an Overview

Beginning with his private journal of World War I, and going on through his essays and correspondence of that period and various subsequent notes, letters, and essays, Teilhard introduced, clarified, and enlarged his thinking about the function of morality in evolution and its proper character. Although as far back as the time of the first World War he was thinking about putting together a plan of moral studies, he actually wrote relatively little in what could be called the area of reflex, conscious, moral theory. The specific plan he envisaged never materialized under that heading, although "The Mastery of the World and the Kingdom of God," written during World War I, is considered to be what issued from his intent at that time.[1] His most significant clarifi-

1. Although an atmosphere of moral concern pervades most of his essays, and surfaces over and over again in his letters, the following texts would be the main sources of formal statement about morality. For significant quotes from his World War I unpublished journals, see de Solages, *Teilhard: étude*, pp. 208-14. World War I letters, contained in *MM*, are those of September 8, 1916, p. 126; January 1, 1917, p. 160; January 9, 1917, p. 166; January 13,

cations on morality as such date from the thirties, with the exception of his one short note on the relationship between morality and metaphysics in the forties. An important segment of his thought about morality is implied in what he says down through the years about human responsibility in the evolutionary process.[2] His specification of the organic, as distinguished from the juridical character of responsibility, emerges in the twenties and reaches final clarification in his study "The Evolution of Responsibility in the World," written in the early fifties, only a few years before his death. The implicit character of much of Teilhard's moral thought stands out strikingly in *The Phenomenon of Man*, considered to be his masterwork, where morality is scarcely mentioned, and yet the thrust of the latter part of the book, which he considered to be the most important part, is clearly toward heightening an awareness of the significance of human responsibility in the evolutionary task.[3]

1917, p. 168; January 29, 1917, p. 176; and February 5, 1917, pp. 181-82. For pertinent material from later correspondence, see *LZ*, pp. 49-50, letter of May 26, 1923, and *LF*, p. 125, letter of November 12, 1938. Texts from essays, throughout his life, are: "Cosmic Life" (1916), *WW*, pp. 36-38; "Mastery of the World and the Kingdom of God" (1916), *WW*, pp. 75-91; "Creative Union" (1917), *WW*, pp. 171-73; "Science and Christ" (1921), *SC*, p. 33; "My Universe" (1924), *SC*, pp. 48, 66-78; "The Basis and Foundations of the Idea of Evolution" (1926), *VP*, pp. 136-41; "Le sens humain," 1929, *DA*, pp. 21, 28-30; "The Spirit of the Earth" (1931), *HE*, p. 29; "Christology and Evolution" (1933), *CE*, pp. 91-93; "Christianity in the World" (1933), *SC*, pp. 99, 102-3; "Sketch of a Personalistic Universe" (1936), *HE*, pp. 71-72; "The Phenomenon of Spirituality" (1937), *HE*, pp. 105-10; "Human Energy" (1937), *HE*, pp. 125-26; "The Atomism of Spirit" (1941), *AE*, pp. 48-57; "La morale peut-elle se passer de soubassements métaphysiques avoués ou inavoués?" (1945), *DA*, pp. 143-46; "The Evolution of Responsibility in the World" (1951), *AE*, pp. 207-14.

2. See below, D.

3. In *PM* (1940), "ethics" is mentioned only twice, and then in passing, pp. 62, 164. The fact that Teilhard's explicit treatment of ethics is so sparse and scattered, coupled with the implicit treatment of it elsewhere, has led to varied treatment of the matter by commentators, some of whom, such as de Lubac, practically ignore it. De Lubac's statement, that for the most part his ideas on morality are approached as mystical and apologetical aspects of the problem of God and Christianity would seem to downplay them too much. See *LZ*, p. 107. De Solages, on the other hand, goes so far as to affirm, somewhat hesitantly it must be admitted, that the problem of moral attitude was, perhaps, Teilhard's dominant preoccupation, and he backs this position up with some strong statements from his early journals. See de Solages, *Teilhard: étude*, p.

Teilhard's central thesis about the function of morality is that the onward course of evolution is directly dependent upon man's awareness of his responsibility to further it and upon his acting in accord with this sense. In other words, if evolution is to be continued and the many problems facing the world at the compressive socialization stage are to be resolved, the pivotal role is going to be played by morality.

The gist of his clarifying reflections on the peculiar character of morality is that it is a direct extension of the biological and organic sphere, so direct that in considering the reality of energy in the universe, one should not speak of separate realms of physical and moral energy, but only of one: the physico-moral, which reaches its peak in human energy. If one takes the term *energetics* to mean the systematic organization of action, then morality becomes, in view of the central role of person and love in Teilhard's thought, the energetics of personaliza-

208. But the fact remains that despite this explicit concern manifest in his early notebooks, Teilhard never did bring much explicit moral writing to term and did approach ethical theory tangentially, or incorporate it in a larger picture. De Solages, pp. 208-34, provides a comprehensive sketch, taking up both phenomenological and Christological aspects. Mermod's book-length essay, *La morale chez Teilhard*, is, as noted above, chap. 2, n4, limited to the phenomenological. Barthélemy-Madaule has sections devoted to ethics in both of her book-length studies. See her *Bergson-Teilhard*, pp. 363-425, and *La personne chez Teilhard*, pp. 171-211. The pages cited in the latter work are those explicitly devoted to ethics and politics, but there is much more that is pertinent, particularly the material on freedom, love, and socialization. In fact, the whole book could be taken as implicitly a book on Teilhard's ethics, with explicit focus on the meaning of person in his thought. It should be noted, though, that in speaking of ethics as such, she stays within a sharply limited phenomenological area, separating it even from politics. Faricy incorporates his explicit treatment of the question in his chapter on "Christian Endeavor." See Faricy, *Teilhard: Theology*, pp. 175-81. Here again, the remainder of the chapter is pertinent, with its discussion of purity, love, charity, detachment, and holiness. Rideau tucks a short division on morality into his chapter on "Anthropology," but then takes up much that would be pertinent to Teilhard's theological ethic, as the present study is considering it, throughout his chapter "Spirituality." See his *Teilhard: Guide*, pp. 135-40 (morality), pp. 192-229 (spirituality). Smulders, on the other hand, does not take up ethics *ex professo* at all in *Design of Teilhard*, but does present considerable material relevant to theological ethics in his third section, "The New Spirituality—God in the Cosmos," pp. 199-256. What was just said about Smulders applies to much of de Lubac's writing also, where he treats of Teilhard's spirituality.

tion, the vital core of which is the development and organization of love-energy.[4]

## B. The Problem of Determinism and Freedom

What arises as a crucial problem for the very existence of a Teilhardian ethic, however, despite his strong emphasis on morality, responsibility, and above all, love, is the question of whether, in view of his insistence on the ultimate triumph of love in human unification, his thought does not contain in the last analysis a determinism that at its root annihilates human freedom, and thus destroys the possibility of any real ethic at all, leaving one with his central thesis about man's need to assume responsibility for continuing evolution stripped of meaning.

The problem is obviously of enormous import, and has to be met head on. Teilhard was well aware of the determinist aspect of his thought, which surfaced on other levels than that of love alone. He was charged with "determining" God, both in his explanation of the creative act or process as such, and of advocating, not only a human universe in which love must in some sense succeed, but, also a human universe in which moral evil, or sin, was in some sense a necessity.[5] The creation prob-

---

4. Of the texts noted above in n1, see especially "Creative Union" (1917), *WW*, p. 173; "Science and Christ" (1921), *SC*, p. 33; "The Spirit of the Earth" (1931), *HE*, p. 29; "Christianity in the World" (1933), *SC*, pp. 99, 102-3; "Sketch of a Personalistic Universe" (1936), *HE*, pp. 71-72; "The Phenomenon of Spirituality" (1937), *HE*, p. 105; and "Human Energy" (1937), *HE*, pp. 125-26.

5. Surprisingly enough, the article explaining the *monitum*, which appeared in *Osservatore Romano* June 30-July 1, 1962, takes Teilhard to task only with regard to his necessitating God in creation, and says nothing, not even in the section on sin, about the problem of human freedom. See Charles Journet, "Pierre Teilhard de Chardin, penseur religieux: de quelques jugements récents," *Nova et Vetera* 37 (Oct.-Dec. 1962): 289-95, esp. 290-91 (on creation), and pp. 293-94 (on sin). But critics such as des Lauriers and Tresmontant have focused on it with harsh censure. See Guérard de Lauriers, "La démarche de Teilhard de Chardin," *Divinitas* 3 (1959): 247, where he finds Teilhard stripping sin of culpability, and Claude Tresmontant, *Introduction a*

lem can be put aside, for the moment. But the matter of some human choices failing morally out of evolutionary necessity, and of the grand complex of human choices ultimately succeeding because of the same necessity, has to be faced.

On this point, there is a definite tension in Teilhard's thought. He insisted that man was free. He accepted human freedom as a given, a fact. And he expressed this acceptance of freedom in no uncertain terms.[6] He likewise was clear and forthright, in critically important texts, on the fact that the success of evolution was *conditioned* on man's responsible, free choice.[7] When he spoke of necessity, it was not in the context of an *individual* human person as having no freedom to either love or reject love, but in the context of what *large numbers* could be known to do, against the background of evolutionary movement. He spoke of a "statistical neces-

---

*la pensée de Teilhard de Chardin* (Paris: Éditions du Seuil, 1956), p. 118, where Tresmontant criticizes Teilhard for a mechanistic world view, with no attention to human interiority and freedom. Other commentators, such as Chauchard, de Lubac, de Solages, Mooney, and Smulders, write clearly and sometimes trenchantly, about the problem of human freedom in Teilhard's thought, but none of these accuse him of hidden premises or consequences negating its existence. See Paul Chauchard, *Man and Cosmos*, trans. George Courtright (New York: Herder and Herder, 1965), pp. 149-65; de Lubac, *Religion of Teilhard*, pp. 125-39; de Solages, *Teilhard: étude*, pp. 333-38 (here, among other matters, de Solages reports on his own discussions with Teilhard about God's being free in creation); Mooney, *The Mystery of Christ*, pp. 132-42; and Smulders, *Design of Teilhard*, pp. 131-33, 137-39, 140-62.

6. In addition to what would hold from the texts on morality, n1, as well as those on responsibility, below, D, the following texts contain either explicit, or clearly implicit acceptance of the reality of human freedom: "The Mystical Milieu" (1917), *WW*, p. 133; "Creative Union" (1917), *WW*, p. 172; Letter of August 14, 1918, *MM*, p. 226; "Forma Christi," *WW*, p. 257; "Operative Faith" (1918), *WW*, pp. 232, 234, 239; "Les noms de la matière" (1919) *EG*, pp. 424- 429; A Note on Progress" (1920), *FM*, p. 19; "Hominization" (1923), *VP*, pp. 72-75; "My Universe" (1924), *SC*, pp. 83-84; "The Planetization of Mankind" (1945), *FM*, p. 135; "Reflections on Original Sin" (1947), *CE*, p. 196; "Faith in Peace" (1947), *FM*, p. 152; "The Formation of the Noosphere" (1947), *FM*, pp. 166, 182; "Le néo-humanisme moderne" (1947), *I*, p 4; *PM* (1948 addition), pp. 307-8; *MPN* (1949), pp. 118-19; "Human Unanimisation" (1950), *FM*, p. 284; and "The Mechanism of Evolution" (1951), *AE*, p. 309.

7. Conditioned success is obviously implied in the acceptance of freedom, as indicated in the texts of n6 above. But for explicit confirmation in texts Teilhard considered refined expressions of his thought, see *PM* (1948 addition), pp. 307-8, and *MPN* (1949), pp. 118-19.

sity," not of a metaphysical, inner, causal determination.[8] That he should so speak was thoroughly consistent with his fundamental drive and concern to describe phenomenologically what has occurred and what could be predicted to occur in the future on the basis of past ascertainable data.

His position has a remarkable resemblance, although rooted in different grounds and ultimately with quite a different thrust, to the traditional Roman Catholic thesis that it is morally impossible for a human person to avoid serious sin, without any destruction of the integrity of human freedom, unless assisted by the grace of God.[9] The Catholic thesis is derived from scriptural sources attesting to human frailty and dependence on God. Teilhard's thesis, on the inevitability of some human failure in the area of freedom, is a particularization of his general evolutionary law that evolution proceeds forward through a series of indefinite strivings, or gropings, which entails some, in fact a large, number of failures. In predicting human sin, he simply applies this law to human groping in the area of moral energy.

It is important to recall, however, that Catholic theology's failure to explain *how* freedom operates in the situation of moral impossibility to avoid sin without grace does not imply that freedom is being denied. Similarly, one can affirm that Teilhard's prediction of what men will do, for good or evil, on the basis of what he reads as valid statistical evidence, in no way undermines his basic thesis that men are free and will continue to be so.

8. See "Cosmic Life" (1916), *WW*, pp. 26-27, 39; "Les noms de la matière" (1919), *EG*, p. 424; "Note on Some Possible Historical Representations of Original Sin" (1922), *CE*, p. 51; "Reflections on Original Sin" (1947), *CE*, p. 196; "Faith in Peace" (1947), *FM*, p. 152; "The Formation of the Noosphere" (1947), *FM*, pp. 182-84; "Le néo-humanisme modern" (1948), 1: 4; *PM*, (1948 addition), pp. 307-8; *MPN* (1949), p. 119.

9. The same point has been made by both Mooney and Smulders with regard to the inevitability, yet culpability of sin. See Mooney, *The Mystery of Christ*, p. 136, and Smulders, *Design of Teilhard*, p. 289 n42. For the Council of Trent's teaching on the matter, see *The Church Teaches: Documents of the Church in English Translation*, trans. and ed. John F. Clarkson, S.J., John H. Edwards, S.J., William J. Kelly, S.J., John J. Welch, S.J. (St. Louis: B. Herder Book Co., 1955), p. 230, §557.

Where he can be faulted is on the soundness of his statistical predictions. When Teilhard argues from the record of an increasing number of collaborators who have reached agreement, and concludes that there will be ultimate unanimity of love, many critics would begin by challenging the record. They would question the basic facts upon which he rests his case. They would do this, moreover, however much they might agree that on the accepted record of human sin in the past, one can predict, with high probability of moral certainty, that men will sin in the future. But there is a deeper argument against his extrapolation of future human unity in love. This criticism prescinds from whether one accepts his basic facts or not, and looks to the process of his reasoning.[10]

At this point, how one works with analogical reasoning becomes critically important, as well as one's understanding of the meaning of human freedom. Teilhard's basic argument for the convergence of human persons in love is rooted in the operation of the Law of Complexity-Consciousness. Since the universe did, according to his formulation and reading of the law, for millions of years gradually evolve, with decisive irreversibility, up to the critical complex-consciousness of the human person, it must be assumed that it will continue to evolve, in accord with whatever is demanded for higher complexity-consciousness in human existence. Since this demands convergence in love if it is to be realized, such convergence simply must come.

But there is serious weakness in this argument, and it stems precisely from a fact upon which Teilhard insists,

10. Smulders, *Design of Teilhard*, pp. 147-50, reaches much the same conclusion regarding Teilhard's faulty reasoning in this regard. See p. 150, "By placing conscious reflection and, in the last analysis, personal responsibility and freedom at the center of evolution, Teilhard is tracing a clear boundary line between the material phase and the human phase. Yet he proceeds to describe the freedom phase using material categories. This is a want of logic in the application of his own principles." The critique in the present study, formulated independently of Smulders, concurs with his, and attempts to pinpoint more precisely where the flaw in the logic lies.

the fact that in reaching the human stage, evolution passed a critical threshold, and that while there was definite
continuity in the development of man, a sharply distinctive discontinuity was introduced when man reflective
and *free* emerged on earth. If one accepts freedom to
mean autonomy, self-determination in some fundamental sense, one immediately introduces an element of radical *unpredictability*. Furthermore, if one conceives love to
involve, at its core, a free commitment, a free self-giving,
then one must admit an unpredictability, ultimately, as
to whether a human person will love or not. What
Teilhard does in his argument is to project into the discontinuous, unpredictable, and *undetermined* area of human choice a convergence of conscious human unity on
the basis of what has happened through millions of
years of continuous and *determined* subhuman development. A valid argument from analogy must be based on
what is continuous and similar in the two analogues.
Teilhard's argument, viewed as analogous here, proceeds to a conclusion in a discontinuous area on the assumption that he is reasoning from continuity. And the
main thrust of his argument would seem to rest precisely
on this assumption.

The character of the problem, as presented, was
never, to the knowledge of the present writer, recognized in this form by Teilhard, presumably because he
seems never to have been concerned to probe into the
implications of the precise meaning of the discontinuity
that emerged in evolution with human freedom. In explanation, if not ultimately in defense, one could argue
that to be consistent with a purely phenomenological
approach, one could incline toward avoiding probing
analysis of the inner meaning of the phenomenon of
freedom, and simply work with it. But then, the serious
objection can be raised, on the phenomenological level
itself, that the mere phenomenon itself contains the constitutive elements of autonomy, self-determination, and
unpredictability, and that to work with this phenomenon

must mean that one accepts these characteristics as part of the given, even though one does not plumb their metaphysical depths.

If the preceding analysis is accepted, Teilhard was in error for having built his firm predictions of future human unity in love on radically invalid grounds. A viable Teilhardian ethic, however, does not collapse, nor is it really undermined because of whatever judgment one might render on the accuracy of Teilhard's arguments predicting what free choices men would make in the future. The basis for his ethic stands firmly rooted in his insistence on accepting the reality of human freedom and on the success of evolution as being not determined, but conditioned by the use of that freedom and contingent upon it. A motivational aspect is weakened to the extent that hope for the future is based on the statistical necessity of human success. To the extent that Teilhard's ethic is influenced by this precise hope, it is flawed.[11] But one can argue that a conditioned hope, based on what human life can become *if* men freely love and not on an extrapolated vision that they will love, is also very much a part of Teilhard's picture. In more than one place he does stress the contingency of this hope, in that he speaks, almost agonizingly, of what would happen if men did not learn to live with zest and love.[12] Ultimately, it does not seem that the tension between these two strains of thought in Teilhard was satisfactorily resolved. Hence, one is faced here with regrettable, serious ambiguity.

As a consequence of the above considerations about the elements of discontinuity introduced into the stream of evolutionary energy by the appearance of human freedom, it seems clear that Teilhard's expressions about moral energy as a direct extension of the biological, with

11. For a critique of Teilhard's basis for a natural hope, see Smulders, *Design of Teilhard*, pp. 140-62.
12. Note, for example, "A Phenomenon of Counter-Evolution in Human Biology: or the existential fear" (1949), *AE*, pp. 183-95. Likewise the texts from *PM* and *MPN*, cited above, n7.

the unification of energy into one type, the physico-moral, must be taken analogically. If they are not, then monistic determinism is on the scene, full-blown. That Teilhard recognized the importance of analogy has already been noted in the preceding chapter.[13] However, that he did not always see the full implications of what analogy entailed in his thought would certainly follow from the immediately preceding discussion on the validity or invalidity of his extrapolations on human unity. Be that as it may, there seems to be good reason to allow him benefit of the doubt, and to give these terms an analogical interpretation, which would be consistent with his recognition of the dissimilarity and discontinuity introduced into the understanding of energy by the reality of freedom. How heavily one should weight the inconsistency appearing in his thought in this context is disputable. In judging his accuracy as a prophet, in the sense of one foreseeing the future, the weaknesses indicated would seem serious indeed. But it should be kept in mind that Teilhard does not hold the mere possibility of evil in human choice. His own speculations as to the character of original sin, for example, insist on a "statistical necessity" of human moral failure. Human sinfulness and the reality of moral evil were for him integral to the evolutionary process.[14]

To my mind there is, as it stands, unacceptable ambiguity in Teilhard's approach to ethical foundations, stemming on the one hand from the determinist atmosphere of his extrapolations that men will choose rightly, and on the other, an insistence, and fear, that if they do not so choose, evolution can fail. I believe that if Teilhard had ever clarified the formulation of his ethic, he would have been forced, out of simple logic, to tone down his assurance about the statistical necessity of ultimate human unification, and to emphasize more

13. See above, chap. 2 n24.
14. See below, chapter 9C (2).

strongly the precariousness and fragility of human freedom, as well as the risk of total disaster arising from human malice and weakness.

## C. Basic Moral Theory

The most concise formulation of what Teilhard means by morality is found in his short "Note" on the relation between morality and metaphysics, which has already been considered for its methodological import. Near the beginning of this piece he offers the following definition:

> In the widest sense of the word, we may give the name of morality to every coherent system of action that is accepted by necessity or convention (in this sense, one could speak of the "morality" of control ("d'une partie d'échec"). In the strict sense, it is a coherent system of action which must be *universal* (governing all human activity) and *categorical* (involving some form of obligation).[15]

What the main characteristics of such a system would be in his convergent world is best explained in the third and concluding part of his essay, "The Phenomenon of Spirituality," where he treats of "Moralization." It is the lengthiest, most detailed, and, in fact, the only exposition of moral theory as such in the corpus of his writings.[16]

In this section, having affirmed his fundamental thesis about the importance of morality in constructing the world and organizing personal human energies as the higher development of mechanics and biology, he ex-

---

15. "La morale peut-elle se passer de soubassements métaphysiques avoués ou inavoués?" (1945), *DA*, p. 143. (The translation used here is that found in *LME*, p. 111, with the exception of the first parenthetical clause, omitted from the text of the collection.)

16. *HE* (1937), pp. 105-10. Although this is the only text of its kind, careful examination of the battery of texts listed above in n1, the main morality texts, will reveal consistency and coherence with the development of thought in the present text.

plains what this morality would be like. That it would be something new and different, in his judgment, is clear from the introductory material on the origins of morality, in which he contrasts a morality of movement with the older morality of equilibrium.[17] (That this is an oversimplified and to an extent inaccurate contrast will be argued later in this chapter.)

Teilhard sees the roots of morality to be what was centuries ago experienced as an empirical need for intelligent beings to guard against mutual encroachment. It was, thus, defensive in origin and became set against change.

> Morality has till now been principally understood as a fixed system of rights and duties intended to establish a static equilibrium between individuals, and at pains to maintain it by a *limitation* of energies, that is to say, of force.[18]

In this type of morality, the basis was a concept of the individual as a sort of absolute to be protected from external encroachment. But with man's development of an awareness of his own destiny to complete the growth of consciousness and personality in the universe, morality loses its protective emphasis and is conceived as guiding him onward toward this progressive enlargement of personality.

> The moralist was up to now a jurist, or a tight-rope walker. He becomes the technician and engineer of the spiritual energies of the world. (p. 106)

A statement of three, for him axiomatic, normative principles initiates his exposition of the main lines of a morality of movement. They are: 1) in the last analysis, what is *ultimately* good is what contributes to the growth of spirit; 2) *whatever* contributes to this growth is in some way good; and 3) the *best* is what most tends to develop

---

17. Valuable background along this line, to an extent corroborative of Teilhard's fundamental position, is contained in N. Max Wildiers, "World Picture and Culture," *Teilhard: Symposium*, pp. 64-87.
18. *HE*, p. 106.

spirit (pp. 106-7). With regard to these, it can be noted in passing, that they are not three really distinct principles, but three variants of the same underlying theme, the goodness of increasing spirit, which for Teilhard means consciousness in the form of personal, thought-informed love.

How these modify or complete the idea of goodness is then enlarged upon.

In conjunction with the first rule, certain things that were allowed by a morality of equilibrium turn out to be forbidden by a morality of movement. In general, previously, if a man did not encroach on his neighbor's wife or property, he could do pretty much as he pleased, using what he wanted or letting things lie fallow. But now, "No promise or custom is lawful if it does not tend to *the service* of the power within it" (p. 107). Examples from three areas serve to clarify his thought. For the morality of money, the governing rule was once that of exchange or fairness, but now the use of money is good only to the extent it works for the benefit of spirit. In love morality, the family-founding, procreative aspect was given primacy, with love itself allotted a secondary rank. But now love's fundamental object must be taken as developing spiritual power between husband and wife. Finally, the individual, once restrained from doing harm, must in the future recognize that neutrality and "inoffensiveness" are not enough; he must "free his autonomy and personality to the uttermost" (p. 107).

The implications of the second rule are an expansion on the last point made with regard to the first. Much, wrong according to equilibrium norms, is now permitted or obligatory. Previously much energy was wasted because the thrust of concern was merely to keep things running smoothly. There was no exploration. The unrocked boat was a kind of ideal. But now, whatever enlarges consciousness is judged fundamentally good: "All that has to be done is to isolate that goodness by analysis and to disengage it by sublimation" (p. 108).

Consequently, a new idea of *moralization* emerges as

one reflects on the implications of the third rule. It becomes "the indefinitely continuous discovery and conquest of the animate powers of the earth." For the "closed morality" of a morality of equilibrium, the moral world was boxed in, confined. However, the "open morality" of movement sees this world as rich in unknown powers to be explored and developed, whence the most important and basic moral law: "to try everything and force everything in the direction of the greatest consciousness." On the negative side, then, sin, or moral evil, consists in the limitation of force, or strength, unless the limitation itself is subordinated to the expansion of strength (p. 108).

The precise meaning here of the French word *force*, with its somewhat Nietzschean overtones, does provoke a question. That the editor of the French text felt uncomfortable about it is clear from the note appended, pointing out that in the larger context of Teilhard's thought it should be taken as referring to love (p. 108 n2). This is acceptable enough, and the need for clarification would be attributable to the imprecision of a "working paper," such as this essay was.[19] It does serve to highlight, however, the problem of determining just what Teilhard means by love and what connotation emerges from the various contexts in which he uses the word.

That the ideas just advanced seem absurd outside evolutionary perspectives, Teilhard avers; within them, he sees an irresistible appeal. But for them to succeed, to be reduced to practice, "a palpable center of attraction" is demanded, all of which leads him to the place of God in the morality scene (p. 108).

How he situates God in the two moralities could come as a surprise to some. Viewing the morality of equilibrium as preoccupied in good part with the balanced operation of a closed system, he sees such a morality as logically capable of ignoring God and being agnostic. It can

---

19. *Ibid.*, p. 13, "Foreword," by N. M. Wildiers.

close in on the mechanism and ignore all else (pp. 108-9). In effect, although he did not put his thought in this language, it can develop into a pharasaic legalism of the worst sort, in which preoccupation with the operation of the system becomes the real psychological ultimate, blocking out both some sort of law-giving God who might be given lip-service but not real personal love, and the needs of persons whom presumably law was meant to serve. What would be present in this instance would be the practical, if not theoretical, agnosticism of Ignace Lepp's "unbelieving believers," who despite pious profession and practices, live more for ritualistic mechanism than for loving concern of persons with whom God had identified himself.[20] On the other hand, the connection can also be drawn, although it was one he did not make in this particular context, between this type of legalism and the impersonalized bureaucratic ant-hill or beehive society he strongly decried as possibly developing evolutionary regression, away from spirit and increased personalization.[21]

A morality of movement, on the contrary, personalized as it must be, has to be going toward Someone, or it can have no drive. What this implies gives rise to two essential conditions regarding the type of God required for such a morality. He must, first of all, be "a God of cosmic synthesis in whom we can be conscious of advancing and joining together by spiritual transformation of all the power of matter," and, also, he must be personal, "a first nucleus of independent consciousness," whom we love.[22] The origin of the present moral crisis in the world is, moreover, attributed by Teilhard to the absence of precisely this type of God in men's minds and hearts.

20. Ignace Lepp, *Atheism in Our Time*, trans. Bernard Murchland, C.S.C., Macmillan Paperbacks (New York: The Macmillan Co., 1964), pp. 156-60.
21. See *PM* (1940), p. 257. "So we get the crystal instead of the cell; the ant-hill instead of brotherhood. Instead of the upsurge of consciousness which we expected, it is mechanisation that seems to emerge inevitably from totalisation."
22. *HE*, p. 109.

## 1. THE IMPORT OF PERSONALIZATION

Teilhard's phenomenological approach to the existence of God has already been seen, and needs no further examination here, from the angle of viewing it as a proof.[23] But it will not hurt to recall it for its value in clarifying the role and importance of the notion of person in his thought, particularly as it pertains to moral theory. The connection between Omega, person, and morality is quite plain, for example, in the sequential development followed by Teilhard in *The Phenomenon of Man*, where the convergence of the person and Omega are discussed under the headings "The Personal Universe" and "The Personalising Universe," after which, immediately he makes the transitional point: "Which brings us to the problem of love." The next topic developed is the key topic in his moral theory, "Love as Energy."[24]

What, then, does "personalization" mean to Teilhard, and what clarifications regarding his moral theory stem from it, in the context of a personal Omega?

At its root, he separates personalization from the notion of an absolutistic individuation and he places genuine human fulfillment in his understanding of the social or universal personal. Man advances to fuller being, not by going off in isolation by himself, but by sharing freely and fully in common human concerns.[25] Collaboration in scientitic and artistic research toward the mastery of needed material and spiritual resources, development of a higher quality of human life through better education and improved techniques of social and political organization—these are just such, but the *techniques* alone of collective research and development are not enough. An atmosphere of sympathy, of *conspira-*

23. See above, chap. 2C (2).
24. *PM* (1940), pp. 257-68.
25. See, "Sketch of a Personalistic Universe" (1936), *HE*, pp. 64-65; *PM* (1940), pp. 258-59, 261, 263; "Centrology" (1944), *AE*, p. 117; *MPN* (1949), p. 117.

*tion*, of genuine human love and free, willing collaboration on all organizational levels is also essential.[26] Moreover, it will be recalled, Omega is precisely the Personal Center ultimately required for activating the love-energy capable of bringing about the collaborative atmosphere needed for full personal development, or *Omegalization*.

To grasp the meaning of this term, certain aspects of personalization must be pursued further. Basically, Teilhard takes a person to be a conscious center, capable of free, reflective, inventive thought. As such, it is a peculiar type of centered reality: it finds completion, paradoxically, in the mysterious "excentration" of love, responding to the attraction and needs of other persons, striving dynamically toward fuller union with them and with the supreme Personal Center, Omega.[27] In this creative response, ranging through all the manifold possibilities of love between men and women, members of the human race in society, and human persons with a cosmos personalized through Omega, transcendent, yet immanent everywhere—there is the psychological possibility of a rich interior act: on the one hand, an awareness of cooperating in a great universal work, and, on the other, a *cooperation* meaning *incorporation* in a living reality whereby positive action signifies communion. *Omegalization* is precisely this unification of all human effort in a grand, total, and "totalizing" action.[28]

26. The term *conspiration* in this special sense is taken by Teilhard from Edouard LeRoy. See "Hominization" (1923), *VP*, pp. 60, 73; "The Moment of Choice" (1939), *AE*, p. 17; "The Compression of Mankind" (1953), *AE*, p. 345. Also see below, chap. 4, regarding general aspects of love.
27. Representative texts would be: *PM* (1940), p. 261; "The Atomism of Spirit" (1941), *AE*, pp. 45-46; "Centrology" (1944), *AE*, pp. 118-22; *MPN* (1949), pp. 116, 121.
28. In this context note especially, "The Atomism of Spirit" (1941), *AE*, pp. 54-57. For a lengthy treatment of "totalization," see "Human Energy" (1937), *HE*, pp. 146-54, and, below, chap. 4D (3), for commentary. What Teilhard is doing here in his phenomenological vocabulary is formulating a phenomenological description of what would be, in a Christological background, the abiding awareness of finding God in all things characteristic of the "contemplative in action." The question can well be raised as to whether he is actually describing a phenomenological mystical experience, or

Moreover, because this is an organic union, controlled by the love dynamics of creative union, the personal centers do not become merged in one homogeneous mass, robbing them of their uniqueness. Rather, since "union differentiates," they become their own proper, fulfilled, selves the more they unite organically in this love with each other and Omega.[29]

What this means for the problem of compressive socialization is of enormous significance. For it does sketch the essential elements required for resolving the problem: the possibility of adequate directional motivation that reconciles, controls, and integrates the human drives otherwise in danger of disruptive, dispersive individualism, or of mechanical, impersonal, ant-hill type of collectivism.

## 2. MORALITY AND RELIGION

With these concepts as background, the question of the relationship between morality and religion, the ques-

merely, without realizing it, transposing into his generalized scientific language, his own Christological experience, such as is found in "The Mass on the World" (1923), *HU*, pp. 19-37, or *DM* (1927), to mention only two examples. I prefer the latter explanation, in view of what is known about Teilhard's bent of mind, and, to my knowledge, the scarcity of testimony from what could be described as "pure Omega mystics," if, indeed, such could be said to exist in the light of Roman Catholic teaching on God's will to save all mankind and the universal, if hidden, operation of divine grace involved in it.

29. In his unpublished retreat notes for June 25, 1952, Teilhard put down "*Union differentiates* (personalizes) (Peking 37)," as the second of the five major insights he had experienced in his life. (The first, the Divine Milieu (1927), the third, complexity "generating" consciousness (1942), the fourth, the growth of reflection, and the fifth, the convergence of evolution.) However, as has been indicated in the works of de Solages, Gray, Mermod, and Mooney, he actually was working with the concept well before that date. Gray has an excellent inventory of early materials incorporating the journal entries to be found in Gray, *The One and the Many*, p. 178 nn20, 21. Also, de Solages, *Teilhard: étude*, pp. 197 n103; 191 n88; 268 n1; 271 n16. For Mermod's materials, see *La morale chez Teilhard*, p. 55 n1 and for Mooney's, *Mystery of Christ*, pp. 239-40 n22, 278 n81. Gray dates the first explicit use of the formula to "How I Believe" (1934), *CE*, p. 117 n5, but earlier passages as far back as World War I come so close as to make the point almost a semantic quibble. Perhaps Teilhard's best explanations of what he means are to be found in "The Phenomenon of Spirituality" (1937), *HE* pp. 103-4, "Human Energy" (1937), *HE*, pp. 144-45, and above all, "Centrology" (1944), *AE*, pp.

tion that instigated the narrowing of focus on Omega and person, can now be considered more at length. What will be seen here will help to emphasize and clarify the intimate connection Teilhard sees between the two. It will also serve to complement the consideration of the preceding chapter, where his ideas on the relationship between morality and metaphysics were taken up in a methodological context.[30] Both texts to be examined reflect the basic Teilhardian thesis seen earlier about the connection between a total, all-encompassing vision of life and the moral choices that enter into day-to-day living. In considering them, one should keep in mind that Teilhard, as also has been noted, was not primarily writing as a moral theoretician, seeking a base for moral theory, but more as a generalizing anthropologist, taking his anthropology all the way to the full sweep of human destiny, and noting the moral steps to be taken on the journey. Taken in the context of what is known about Teilhard's manner of thought, the passages can be utilized for their clarification value, without receiving the possible over-emphasis of two isolated expressions of his thought viewed by themselves.

In his essay "Christianity in the World" (1933), speaking of religion in general terms, he advances the same basic thesis seen above as put forward in "The Phenomenon of Spirituality," but in somewhat different language. He sees its function as:

> precisely . . . to provide a foundation for morality, by introducing a dominating principle of order, and an axis of movement, into the restless and undisciplined multitude of reflective atoms: something of supreme value, to create, to hold in awe, or to love.[31]

---

116-17. Gray's preference for translating "l'union differencie" as "Union personalizes," (*The One and the Many*, p. 121) is disputable, on the grounds that it is precisely the manner in which Teilhard explains differentiation that clarifies what he means by personalization.
30. See above, chap. 2C (2).
31. *SC*, p. 99.

On the other hand, in "The Atomism of Spirit" (1941), he speaks as follows:

> No moral system can hold together without religion. Or, to put it more precisely, no moral system can live without developing a nimbus of worship. The measure of an ethics is its ability to flower in mysticism.[32]

What he says about mysticism and its relation to morality does, at first glance, look like an inversion of the relationship noted in "Christianity in the World." The relative interchangeableness of "mysticism" and "religion" in this instance is clear enough from the second text cited, granted their difference in connotation. But a problem does arise about the relationship of the common core of these two terms with morality.

In one piece, he seems to be saying that ultimate meaning determines, governs, *causes morality*. In the other, that morality generates, brings about, *causes* an *idea of ultimate meaning*. Is there confusion, change of mind, or what?

One should remember, first of all, Teilhard's basically descriptive outlook, attending to observable phenomena with consistent, predictable patterns, and not to the metaphysical causal nexus among these phenomena. In both texts, the existence of a close mutual interaction of morality and mysticism-religion is affirmed. By insertion of a few qualifications, the two texts can be read as describing the same phenomenon from two different stances. Read, "Mysticism-religion directs morality" as "Mysticism-religion is always *present as necessary guiding motivation* for morality." Then read, "Morality always issues in mysticism-religion" as "Morality can never function *unless it has a mysticism-religion to guide it*." Both texts, then, can be read as describing the consistently observed association of a moral pattern with a motivating ultimate. (Note that they both, also, do not deal with the question

32. *AE*, pp. 53-54.

of whether that ultimate, through revelation, may have provided, in addition to motivation, specification for moral choice, i.e., a revealed moral law or set of directives.) The "Christianity" text looks at the association from an angle that first sees the ultimate and then its role, orientational, for the moral pattern. The "Atomism" text looks at the association from an angle that first views the moral pattern and then its orientation to an ultimate. If one can so read the two texts as limited to thus describing the same association from two different directions, the apparent contradiction disappears.

Another analysis that could be advanced, if one were to attempt second-guessing Teilhard on a philosophical level, would be to see the "Christianity" text speaking in terms of final causality, with the "Atomism" text looking to the element of efficient causality. Again there is one and the same reality, the total moral process, but considered in the light of two integrally complementary causal factors. But it does not seem likely that Teilhard, with his phenomenological bent of mind, was consciously thinking that way. What some might see, though, is "the philosopher in spite of himself" appearing once again.

The fact, highlighted by the preceding discussion, that morality as conceived by Teilhard is intimately bound up with motivation toward a goal in some sense "religious," points to a fundamental aspect of his morality of movement. It is a kind of *teleological* morality, but with a peculiar teleology of *process*, not a teleology looking to a static term, sharply defined. What the ultimate resolution of evolution would be at its climax is a question not probed thus far, except indirectly in speaking of the communion of all men in and with Omega.[33] That there must be *some* terminal situation incorporating these elements—of this Teilhard was sure. But he did not ex-

33. The question of the ultimate term for evolution will be taken up more in detail in chap. 9, in the context of Teilhard's Christology of the Second Coming.

trapolate what the concrete details of this would be. In fact, it is most important to note that his type of teleology does not call for a clear delineation of its term. (Even his religious faith in Christ's Second Coming does not do this, although it does clarify it more.)

What should be grasped here is that the type of goal-motivation of which he speaks is a realizable goal of creative communion, attainable and discernible in the continuing process. This is a goal that can be worked toward as reachable in some way *now*, short of the ultimate climax, regardless of the need to recognize the existence of some such ultimate as necessary, and despite the demands of his theology for the divinizing action of grace and the insufficiency of human effort alone to bring full completion. Moreover, since the ultimate "Omegalized universe" will be established by free creative acts of men in union with Omega, Teilhard cannot extrapolate *what* they will be like, but only *that* they will probably occur. Hence, the goal is not a blueprint to be concretized in the long run, but the very process of creatively drawing up the design, modifying it, and then working toward its actualization.

## D. Responsibility

Reference was made, in the opening paragraph of this chapter, to the notion of responsibility in Teilhard's thought, and some indication was given as to how it developed. The obvious importance of the concept for moral theory warrants closer examination.

In his earliest writings, without clarifying precisely what he means by the term through a descriptive formula or definition, he is nevertheless concerned with how it operates and from what foundations. The bases of which he speaks are two, which run subsequently through the entire course of his thinking, namely, man's role as the key element in the contemporary and future evolutionary process, and the role of the Christian to cooperate with God in creation and to carry out his mandate to develop the earth.[34]

Subsequently Teilhard enlarges on his exhortations to the Christian to put forth ever more generous effort in developing the human in the world and the world for the human.[35] His most complete statement of this side of his thought can be found in *The Divine Milieu*, of the late twenties. Here human responsibility is approached from the angle of its divinization, its incorporation of action and effort in a faith, as well as of acceptance and resignation when one's efforts have been exhausted.

For more precise specification of the character of just what is to be divinized, one must turn to his reflections on the role of man in the evolutionary process itself. In a 1920 essay he speaks forcefully about what the impact is on mankind of its increased knowledge of the world.

When Plato acted it was probably in the belief that his freedom to act could only affect a small fragment of the world, narrowly circumscribed in space and time; but the man of today acts in the knowledge that the choice he makes will have its repercussions through countless centuries and upon countless human beings. He feels in himself the responsibilities and the power of an entire Universe.[36]

But it was six years later, when writing on the moral consequences of transformism in an essay on the founda-

34. See "Cosmic Life" (1916), *WW*, pp. 62-65; "Mastery of the World and the Kingdom of God" (1919), *WW*, pp. 87-89; "Note pour l'évangélisation des temps nouveaux" (1919), *EG*, pp. 378-79; "A Note on Progress" (1920), *FM*, pp. 18-19; "Science and Christ" (1921), *SC*, p. 32; "Hominization" (1923), *VP*, pp. 75-77.

35. See "My Universe" (1924), *SC*, pp. 66-78; "Christianity in the World" (1933), *SC*, pp. 106-12; "Christology and Evolution" (1933), *CE*, pp. 91-93; "Some Reflections on the Conversion of the World" (1936), *SC*, pp. 122-24; "Super-Humanity, Super-Christ, Super-Charity" (1943), *SC*, pp. 167-71; "Introduction to the Christian Life" (1944), *CE*, pp. 168-70; "Christianity and Evolution: Suggestions for a New Theology" (1945), *CE*, pp. 183-86; "The Religious Value of Research" (1947), *SC*, 199-205; "Le Christique" (1955), *I*, pp. 10-11; "Research, Work, and Worship" (1955), *SC*, pp. 214-20.

36. "A Note on Progress" (1920), *FM*, p. 18.

tions of the idea of evolution that he explicitly introduced the distinction between the organic concept of responsibility, as he conceived it in an evolutionary world, and the juridical concept of responsibility in a static universe.[37] What is particularly significant about the way in which he looked at responsibility in this setting is how he saw it linked to the brotherhood of men, the all-important idea of universal human solidarity. He saw an evolutionism of convergence as alone capable of developing a "sense of universal responsibility and love." Evolutionists who talked of men's common origin, but then spun out the future as divergent in shape, were doomed to failure in this regard.

> They may make all men and everything else in the world into brothers as firmly united in the womb of Demeter as in that of any Eve. But brothers can be enemies; and if they are not, it is for reasons other than their common origin. Birth, after all, is only a memory. The existence of love depends on a common growth in the womb of a single future.[38]

Although only five years after writing this he pushed his analysis more deeply into the origin of duty, finding it ultimately in "the fact of being born and developing *as a function of a cosmic stream*," and, despite his continuing concern in his writing about the fact and implications of responsibility, it was not until a few years before he died that, in "The Evolution of Responsibility in the World" (1950), he put together his most penetrating analysis of the concept.[39] The essay reaffirms certain themes from earlier years, and then looks more deeply into what these mean. Because it is his major expression of thought on this topic, and the only essay devoted explicitly and entirely to it, the work calls for a close look. Not only does it supply a more detailed background for his gen-

37. "The Basis and Foundations of the Idea of Evolution" (1926), *VP*, pp. 136-41.
38. *VP*, pp. 138-39 n2.
39. "The Spirit of the Earth" (1931), *HE*, p. 29; *AE*, pp. 207-14.

eral theory about morality of movement, but, in capsule form, it presents his world view in an atmosphere of the heightened urgency for moral decision to build a better earth. In this piece, he first takes up a common notion of responsibility and then indicates how he will work with it. As frequently held, he sees it to be:

a moral compulsion that makes it impossible for the being to develop without having to some extent to make allowance for the development of the other beings around him.[40]

Since this is a *moral* compulsion, or subjugation, one is therefore faced with the much-discussed philosophical problem of the objective foundation of *obligation*. However, speaking as a biologist, not a philosopher, he declares his objective to be an explanation of how the sense of responsibility in man is the manifestation, on the reflective level, of a primary, necessary property of "the universal Given."[41] The rest of the essay is concerned with detailing the characteristics of this "Given" and its consequences. In the end he has a much stronger concept than the first he presents.

Under the heading "The Convergence of the Universe and the Rise of Cosmic Solidarity," he discerns three zones of cohesive arrangement (or levels of consciousness) and derangement. Derangement and arrangement alike assume different forms, depending on the stage of progress toward higher spiritualization, or, viewed from the other angle, on the level of materialization present. On the level of the inorganic material, derangement takes the form of desegregation, or disintegration and decomposition. Among living beings, there is the disorder of suffering. With men, fault occurs, which amounts to free irresponsibility (or, in effect, sin). Corresponding-

40. *Ibid.*, p. 207.
41. *AE*, p. 207. (My translation here and in the subsequent texts from this essay. Pagination conforms to the English text.)

ly, arrangement, or solidarity, on the inorganic level is evidenced by physicochemical interdependence among bodies, by symbiotic relations on the level of life, and by reflective, responsive interaction among free human beings.[42] Consideration of these relationships leads him to say:

> The altruism of the moralists is nothing other than the form taken, in hominization, by the basic interconnection of bodies composing, at every level, the stuff of the world, which, in the course of time not only condenses, but centers on itself. Which means that, taken in its roots, responsibility reveals itself as co-original and co-extensive in its genesis with the totality of time and space.

This means that:

> the evolution of responsibility is nothing other than a particular face of cosmogenesis.

Or, more precisely:

> It is cosmogenesis itself, observed and measured not as commonly, by the degree of organic complexity or psychic tension, but by the degree of inter-influence continually mounting at the heart of a multitude progressively gathering itself together in a convergent milieu.[43]

Proceeding to "Planetary Compression and the Rise of Human Responsibility," he notes that the spread of man over the planet brings not only mounting compression (the compressive socialization seen in chapter 1), but also variation in the range of individual action. In modern times, man finds not only differentiation and expansion, but concentration and totalization brought to new fullness. Developments in transportation and communication have brought greater *extension*; various scientific advances have enabled psychological penetration of greater

42. *Ibid.*, pp. 207-9.
43. *AE*, p. 209. (These three quotations are in direct sequence on the same page.)

*depth*; technological developments, ranging from the size of ships and aircraft to the atomic bomb, have enlarged the scope of one man's influence in *volume*.[44]

Concomitant with this progress are many problems that in turn give evidence of increasing human responsibility:

> For not only consciousness and evil, but also *solidarity*—we would say, are the three great realities subject to simultaneous growth (in intensity, if not—in the case of evil—in quantity) along with the arrangement, more particular as well as global, of a convergent system.

Which provokes the question:

> Is this sole fact not sufficient to found a new ethic of the Earth?

And the reason, summarizing:

> At no moment in history has man been found, as he is today, so bound, actively and passively, in the depth of his being, to the value and perfection of everyone around him.[45]

In his conclusion he contrasts the biological, *organic* type of responsibility he has been describing with what he calls a "juridical" type, derived from an Aristotelian or Platonic, static, nonevolutionary concept of nature, where matter and spirit, body and soul, are put in two different worlds. He sees a radical transformation in process, not only objective, but subjective, pertaining to the consciousness of human responsibilities. It is not just a matter of a surprising expansion of the range of human influence on other human beings; the evolutive value assumed by the social arrangement of mankind on itself brings with it an impressive solidity (*consistance*). What this ultimately means is:

44. *Ibid.*, pp. 210-11.
45. *AE*, p. 212. (The quotations are in direct sequence.)

As long as we thought we had before us only more or less arbitrary precepts of man relating to other men, we could think of possible evasions or infractions. But the moment we perceive, with shock, that socialization entwines us in a network, not of inventions, but of organic ties—then we begin to realize in our spirit the grandeur and the true seriousness of the human condition.

For the juridical always enabled one to come to some sort of compromise. But the organic, violated, grants no pardon.[46]

These concluding remarks are strong meat indeed, and if taken literally would ultimately make unintelligible the loving forgiveness of a merciful God, a religious truth that Teilhard accepted. If they are to be interpreted in line with his Creed, they must be taken as hyperbole and understood with some qualification. For they would also seem to imply that relations between men, once ruptured, could not be repaired, that divisive misunderstandings, or even hatred, could not be transformed into mutual acceptance and love. That they do highlight the inevitable, far-reaching consequences of wrong choices, and the extreme difficulty, because of the complexity at times of communication methods, of reestablishing relationships that have deteriorated, could well be argued. A governmental decision, for example, to terminate financial support of a certain program involving the economic well-being of thousands of workers and their families, could strongly alienate those affected from the decision-makers, in a fashion far more difficult to smooth over than would be possible in a less complicated, less highly organized, less technological society. But even in this instance, apologies, if they are necessary, can be made, and mistakes *can* be rectified, despite the fact that damage, quickly done, may well take a great deal of time and enormous effort to correct and heal.

Thus interpreted and qualified, the remarks can be saved, and their valid stress acknowledged. But as they

46. *AE*, p. 214.

stand, it must be admitted that they indicate a blind spot in Teilhard's thinking regarding the redemptive love of Christ, and failure to think through the implications, in this context, of his own theories and practice of personal love, of the gentleness noteworthy in his own character, and of the creative, consciousness-expanding force of forgiveness and reconciliation in human relations.[47]

## E. Teilhard's Critique of Moral Theory

Ethical historians can justifiably blanch at Teilhard sweeping generalizations concerning what morality was like in earlier times. On the other hand, many contemporary moralists would applaud his indictment of a certain type of moral thinking that he describes in his sketch of a morality of "equilibrium."

It would be difficult to deny that there was a type of humanist and Christian moral approach that involved an individualistic, defensive, protective legalism, elevated to a kind of systemic absolute. Nor can one say that it has as yet disappeared. Witness the moral theology of the "manualists," of Teilhard's era and even later. Political moralists who seem to be preoccupied mainly with the protective, regulatory functions of the state, give evidence of over-concern for individual autonomy and harmonious balance in social affairs at the expense of positive social growth and development. People are not wanting who look to "happiness" and the security of an ordered system, rather than the risks of creative free-

47. See below, chap. 4E (2). More on this point will be taken up in chapter 9, when looking into Teilhard's Christology of redemption. In general, it can be said for the present that the problem centers around how the notion of expiation has any meaning in Teilhard's emphasis on the constructive value of the Cross. The concept of expiation can only mean that someone has injured, or disobeyed, someone else, and that restoration of relationships will entail acknowledgment of fault and offer of compensation on the one hand, along with a willingness to forgive on the part of the offended. These particular factors are, to all intents and purposes, ignored in Teilhard's treatment of redemption, despite the fact that he insists he is not excluding, but merely emphasizing less, the expiatory element.

dom, as portrayed in Dostoevsky's parable of the Grand Inquisitor.[48] Nor is it impossible to find those "unbelieving believers" of Ignace Lepp, mentioned above.[49]

But to maintain that these thought styles sum up the history of ethical thought and practice prior to the advent of a morality of movement as described by Teilhard, simply does not square with the facts. Wherever the Gospel was accepted and thought through, there emerged a practical ethic in Christian life that was not cribbed, cabined, or confined to keeping people in somewhat isolated boxlike lives. Chaucer's Ploughman would be a good type of this, the true and good worker, who for Christ's sake would dig ditches without pay. Moreover, where the sacramentality of marriage was not lost to view, husbands and wives were concerned with profound personalizing enrichment, not merely with reproduction, as they prayerfully tried to live out St. Paul's urging to be as Christ to each other. Nor, for those who took Aquinas seriously on the communal nature, ultimately, of the goods of the earth, was there narrow individualism about property, which Teilhard deplored. More evidence could be assembled, but to do so would go beyond the limits of the present study. At any rate, what has been seen will, it is hoped, justify the need for modifying Teilhard's over-monolithic description of past moral approaches.[50]

## F. "Movement"

When one reflects on the concept of *movement* in Teilhard's theory, what is there distinctively characteristic about its dynamism? On the strength of evidence

---

48. Fyodor Dostoevsky, *The Brothers Karamazov*, trans. Constance Garnett, Signet Books, (New York: The New American Library, 1957), pp. 227-44.
49. See above, n28.
50. The variety of approaches in Christian ethical systems alone can be documented by consulting a work such as Edward LeRoy Long, Jr., *A Survey of Christian Ethics* (New York: Oxford, 1967).

seen, it obviously does not involve mere change for the sake of novelty. Nor does it entail a moving away from God to Promethean autonomy. Basically, it is movement in the sense of *constructive conquest* of the earth and growth upward and forward to more heightened consciousness, through personalizing, differentiating union in a shared evolutionary striving—a striving shared not only with human persons, but with Omega-God. If one were to bring in H. Richard Niebuhr's approach for comparison, one could surmise that, whereas Niebuhr focused on and wrote about *The Responsible Self* as he looked at the world and asked, "What is God *doing* and how should man respond?", Teilhard could well have written a book on *The Constructive Self* as he looked at the world and asked, "What is God *building*, and how can man share, responsibly, in this constructive effort?"[51]

Moreover, the thoughts seen above on Teilhard's approach to organic responsibility have their own nuances to add to an understanding of this sense of dynamism. They bring in a concretization of both the vast scope of interdependent ties existing among men and the expanded range of power now possessed by men to act in accord with phenomenologically verifiable patterns and laws of social process. People can not only see more clearly now than ever before how they progress or stagnate or fall back, together, but they also have an immensely increased store of resources and instruments with which to respond to the needs that they can discern. The *urgency* to act is proportionately intensified with the increase of knowledge and power, for now men

51. See H. Richard Niebuhr, "The Meaning of Responsibility," *The Responsible Self* (New York: Harper & Row Pub., 1963), pp. 47-68, esp. pp. 60, 67. Faricy describes Teilhard's ethic as an "ethic of conquest," and even provides the French equivalent, *morale de conquête*. I have searched in vain for this precise expression in the French text. *Religion de conquète* does occur, however, in the French "Le Christianisme dans le Monde," Oeuvres 9, p. 136. (English, "religion of conquest," "Christianity in the World," SC, p. 103). With Faricy's interpretation I would heartily concur, but judge that the expression should be kept in that realm, which may well have been Faricy's intent. How his passage is to be taken is not perfectly clear. See Faricy, *Teilhard: Theology*, p. 176.

can see more clearly what the consequences of acting or not acting would be, and they know, with the controls of immense energy currents in their hands, that they cannot blame God, or chance, or fate, if those currents are not channeled for human growth. Hence, along with this urgency comes, at least in certain areas, a clearer sense of *direction*, a more well-defined orientation for moral choice. All the questions now being asked about air and water pollution and their control, would be, for example, of the sort that would have import in this context.

## G. Meliorism

Another aspect of Teilhard's thought that calls for some comment here is his tendency to be concerned with striving not merely for what is acceptable, or passable in human effort, but for what is *more* constructive, what will bring *greater* expansion of consciousness. It is true that no place in his analysis of the human good does he condemn as specifically evil those acts which are not better or best. He does not, in fact, raise this specific question. But over and over again he is urging people to try, and to try harder. His exhortations are perfectionist, in the best sense of the term. And while he does show a certain contempt for unwillingness to try, it would be unfair to accuse him of pharisaic judgmentalism.[52] His respect for the individual conscience, struggling in whatever way to find the light, precludes that.

If one were to attempt an explanation of the background for Teilhard's hortatory meliorism, it would not be far-fetched to find a strong influential factor in

52. See, for example, *DM* (1927), pp. 51-52, "There is no need for us to consider the wayward or the lazy who cannot be bothered to acquire an understanding of their world, or seek with care to advance their fellows' welfare—from which they will benefit a hundredfold after their last breath—and only contribute to the human task 'with the tips of their fingers.'"

his Ignatian spiritual training. A Jesuit was and is schooled, from his earliest days of training, to think in terms of "the greater glory of God," not to settle for a minimal good, but, out of love for Christ, to strive incessantly toward discernment and enactment of the better, to give with limitless generosity, and not to count the cost.[53] Now, while moral analysts have long distinguished between necessities for salvation and acts of perfection, and while Teilhard himself was no formal advocate of breaking down the barriers between ascetical and moral theology, it seems that what he declares as the basic moral principle of striving constantly to increase consciousness through discerning love, does come to a transposition into his own terms of the Ignatian appeal for the greater, so as to transmute practically what many still consider to be an ascetical, perfective norm, into a universal moral norm.[54] If he did just that, and it seems he did—unconsciously enough—then he is open to the criticism, not of *imposing* the more difficult, theoretically, but of *expecting*, too much from a great many people. Such expectations, it could be added, would be quite in keeping with his optimistic predictions about ultimate

53. Cf. one form of what is spoken of as St. Ignatius's prayer for generosity: "Lord, teach me to be generous, to serve you as you deserve, to give and not to count the cost, to fight and not to heed the wounds, to toil and not to seek for rest, to labor, and to ask for no reward, save that I know I am doing Your will." That Teilhard would have read this as avoiding a morality of mere intention, is clear. See *DM* (1927), pp. 53-56. But there is little doubt as to his whole-hearted acceptance of the spirit of struggle and conquest for Christ, provided that the struggle and conquest were understood as directed toward developing, and building a more human personalized earth divinized in union with Christ.

54. To bring together into one comprehensive synthetic ethic, the different branches Teilhard had known as moral, ascetical, and mystical (or spiritual) theology, would have been in keeping, it would seem, with his inclination to unify and synthesize. But he left nothing in writing about interdisciplinary synthesis as such in this area, although much evidence is available that he brought them all together in his own "totalizing" vision and activity, as well as in much of his writing, without being aware of what he was doing, other than that he knew he was striving to elaborate a unified vision. For Mermod's view on what he describes as Teilhard's "maximalism," see *La morale chez Teilhard*, pp. 134-38.

human unity in love, which, as has been seen, are based on faulty logic.[55]

While Teilhard's tendency to urge people to work toward the better envelops his teaching with an atmosphere of strictness, and even a certain rigidity of discipline, the very fact that his morality of movement does involve abandonment of previously held positions and acceptance of new ones, gives rise, paradoxically, to an appearance of relativism. In this context it must be noted that while he does have the changes in man's moral options depend on the growth in human knowledge, and hence, in that sense, relative to it, this sort of dependence does not entail a purely subjective relativity of whim or flux of circumstances.[56] What he says about changes in moral choice resting on solid, rational know-

55. See above, B. A serious difficulty arises in view of Teilhard's emphasis on the better—or the greatest. The problem is whether he has actually *synthesized* the older divisions of moral and ascetical theory, or, quite simply, *replaced* moral by ascetical, at least with regard to what he is urging people to do. The practicability of his ethic would, in the minds of a good number of people, be diminished by what they would judge to be the impact of human sinfulness on many human lives, which limits their love-capacity to the minimum needed for survival and in some—God knows how many—imperils even that. It seems clear that Teilhard would object to such reading of the factual situation, but it seems equally clear that there are those who for good theological as well as experiential reasons would read Teilhard's stand here as indicating a lack on his part of appreciation of the concrete impact of sinfulness on the limitations of human existence. On this matter of the importance of taking human sinfulness into account, see Curran, *Catholic Moral Theology in Dialogue*, pp. 122-23, where he speaks of the problem of John XXIII's excessive "optimisim" in Pacem in Terris, and p. 225, where he introduces Paul Ramsey's difficulty of the same order. (Granted the drift of the first four parts of the Encyclical, it is somewhat surprising that Curran does not even allude to Pope John's description, in the fifth part, of the immensity of the task of implementing pastorally what he has written about earlier—an "immensity" that, in the context, would seem to have to take sinfulness into account.) Moreover, it is not easy to establish, in the long run, whether an ethic that asks too little is not as unrealistic as one that asks too much. There are those who would argue, in Teilhard's favor, that psychological evidence can be found that would point to the unexpected energies, moral as well as physical, that can be released when persons are presented, encouragingly, with a challenge they might think beyond their reach.

56. To explore the similarities and dissimilarities of Teilhard's moral theory with natural law theories would go beyond the scope of the present study, but it would be a valuable piece of correlative research. For significant Teilhard texts on the impact of increased knowledge on morality, see "A Note on Progress," 1920, *FM*, pp. 17-19, and "The Grand Option," 1939, *FM*, pp. 59-60.

ledge of organic ties of functional interdependence, injects a strong, stabilizing note of calm reflective rationality into the entire process. Obscurity and difficulty, often failure, in discovering and acting upon the implications of increased "Omegalization"—these he would admit. But in his scheme of things, acceptance of Omega as a loving Personal Center was an *absolute* necessity if human personalization were ultimately to succeed, and the need for man to seek Him was equally unconditioned.

## H.   Sublimation—a Clarification

Finally, the term *sublimation*, as seen above, has a dynamic, changing meaning that calls for some examination.[57] Teilhard does not expand on it in the text where it occurs, but it is an important concept, as will be clear from the following chapters, with regard to his thinking about the evolution of sexual love and chastity (chapter 4), and aggression (chapter 5).[58] Some guidelines for handling it are therefore in order. What he means by it, basically, in the various places where he uses it, is the direction of an energy from a form of conscious experience to which it is immediately drawn to a higher form of conscious experience—higher because more unitive with love of Omega, and all that that implies. The unitive affective drive of sexual love, then, would be directed upward beyond sexual intercourse, or mere emotional absorption of two people in each other, toward a more spiritual thought-union looking to intensifying warmth and affection in the larger human society and with Omega. The competitive, aggressive drive would, in turn, be directed beyond attacking other persons and toward the challenges of research and world develop-

57. See above, C.
58. A good explanation by Teilhard of what he means by sublimation can be found in "Introduction to the Christian Life" (1944), *CE*, pp. 169-70.

ment. What provides the sense of direction, of course, is the analysis, the discernment process preceding the sublimative choice, by which all the implications of organic responsibility are painstakingly examined and creatively tested, in accord with the overall picture of his world view.

# 4

# Love, the Highest Form of Spiritualized Human Energy

## A. The Place of Love in Teilhard's Scheme of Human Energetics

In *The Phenomenon of Man*, Teilhard speaks of energy's standing with plurality and unity as one of the "three faces of matter."[1]

> Under this name, which conveys the experience of effort with which we are familiar in ourselves, physics has introduced the precise formulation of a capacity for action or, more exactly, for interaction. Energy is the measure of that which passes from one atom to another in the course of their transformations. A unifying power, then, but also, because the atom appears to become enriched or exhausted in the course of the exchange, the expression of structure.[2]

While such a formulation might have been adequate enough when dealing with the phenomenon of pre-life, he found it incomplete in his attempt to explain the total range of interacting realities from pre-living up through

1. *PM*, p. 40.
2. *Ibid.*, p. 42.

the plant and animal realms to the human, in accord with his Law of Complexity-Consciousness. He could not deny the laws of thermodynamics, as he understood them nor, what was equally clear to him, the steady rise in the history of the cosmos, of entities more and more characterized by the qualities of spirit and consciousness. The upshot of his reflections on the need to provide a unified, albeit analogous, not univocal, concept of energy to deal with the complete energy spectrum in a genuine synthesis, was his affirmation of the essentially psychic, and hence, in some sense, spiritual, nature of all energy, with two distinct component facets, *tangential* and *radial*.

By means of the tangential aspect of this fundamentally psychic power, he was able to account for the interplay of energy forces described by the scientific thermodynamic Laws of the Conservation of Energy and Entropy. The drive of the radial component forward toward increased complexity and centricity enabled him to explain the ascent from pre-life to the highest forms of conscious existence. It is this radial energy component that develops ever greater clarity of interiority and higher forms of psychic spirituality as one goes up the scale of beings, which in the last analysis is the predominant component of the two, despite the fact that in the lower forms of existence its presence is almost totally obscured by the tangential. When one reaches the level of human existence, radial energy becomes manifest especially in the affective, volitional, and intellective activities of human consciousness, with all the impact of their controlling dynamic, yet with no denial, all the while, of the tangential component, which, through the forces of light, air, food, and the like, sustains the powers of thought and love, even as it is guided by them.[3]

3. The terms *radial* and *tangential* are introduced in *PM* (1940), and are important to the exposition of Teilhard's thought there. See *PM*, pp. 53-66, chap. 3, "The Within of Things," esp. pp. 63-66, "Spiritual Energy"; also, pp. 168-69. For further *PM* texts see the Index, p. 316, "Energy." Somewhat surprisingly, despite his constant concern for the "within" of things and con-

Human energy, then, for Teilhard, is both tangential and radial, with the primary evolutionary thrust coming from the radial, from the forces of the human spirit supported by the tangential. The moral energy, which in the last chapter was seen to be described as a unified physico-moral energy can be interpreted in the present context, by pairing "tangential" with "physico-" and "radial" with "moral." In so doing, though, one must bear in mind that this pairing of "tangential" with "physico-" in compound with "moral" maintains the connotation stress of "spiritualized" and is not to be taken in the gross "material" sense. It should be recalled that, for Teilhard, both tangential and radial energy are "psychic" and that while tangential energy looks more to the "without" of things, it is not cut off from the "within"—the preeminently psychic.

In his lengthy essay on "Human Energy," written not long before he developed the tangential-radial concepts in *The Phenomenon of Man*, his approach to the meaning of human energy is presented differently. In it he distinguishes three types or forms: incorporated, controlled, and spiritualized. Incorporated pertains to the energy of that "natural machine," the human body; controlled looks to the energy around man that he succeeds in mastering with power from his own body by means of "artificial machines"—all the energies of scientific technology as extensions of man, so to speak; spiritualized energy he speaks of as "localized in the immanent zones of our free activity, which forms the stuff of our intellectual processes, affections, and voli-

sciousness, the concepts do not even appear in *MPN* (1949), and occur only twice, briefly, in "The Singularities of the Human Species" (1954), *AM*, pp. 241, Fig. 20, 265 n1. In "The Activation of Human Energy," *AE*, p. 393, *axial* is used for *radial* in conjunction with *tangential*. Moreover, a consistency problem with regard to the unity of energy arises from his thought as it is formulated in this later essay, where he speaks definitely of two different energies, rather than two components of a single fundamental energy. However, in view of the fact that in this context he insists that he is dealing with duality, not dualism, it would seem that the substance of his thought has not really altered.

tions." However, working from a premise derived from Bergson, that the distinction between the natural and the artificial is conventional, he notes the difficulty in the last analysis of drawing hard-and-fast lines between the three types or levels. Taking a broad biological view, he asks whether ultimately there is a difference between the wing of a bird and that of an airplane. Furthermore, despite the fact that spiritualized energy goes beyond the physico-chemical in its strict sense, it does derive power from it, and, in a measure, contains it. Aware of the difficulty, he proceeds, nonetheless, to elaborate his thoughts on the organization of human energy within the framework of the three levels.[4]

He never correlated his thinking about incorporated, controlled, and spiritualized energy with what he later formulated in terms of the tangential and radial. It would seem clear enough that what he says about radial energy embraces the same realities as those contained in his description of spiritualized energy, and that one can find a tie between the levels of incorporated and controlled energy and tangential energy in the human sphere, with a certain edge of clarity to the earlier conceptualization, particularly from the angle of providing a working base for constructing a synthesis of his ethical thought. It was, in fact, this particular aspect of this approach in "Human Energy" that led me to take the working framework of the next chapters, with certain modifications and additions, from "Human Energy" rather than from *The Phenomenon of Man*.

4. "Human Energy" (1937), *HE*, pp. 115-16. This essay is a lengthy piece, running to almost fifty pages in the English text. In it he expands, pp. 125-37, on the organization of human energy in accord with the levels or divisions here indicated. While accepting these levels as working concepts, the present study employs a different sequence in its development of the subsequent chapters in order to achieve a smoother flow of continuity from the consideration of love energy into the other types of energy forms and their specifications expressive of love. The essay is Teilhard's most important piece for demonstrating how on a fairly large scale he conceived of morality in terms of human energetics. For Barthélemy-Madaule's comparison of his treatment of love in this essay with his approach in "Sketch of a Personalistic Universe," see her *Bergson-Teilhard*, pp. 387-89.

Love involving both affective and volitional components, as well as important ties with the intellective, obviously comes up for discussion as a form of spiritualized energy. An item of special concern, at this phase of the study, is the relationship of love to incorporated and controlled energy. That relationship has two facets, one of dependence and one of domination. Human conscious life in all its aspects is quite dependent on the operations, both of the human body as its immediate locus of function, and on the use of a steadily mounting system of tools to supply food, clothing, shelter, transport, and communication. But this conscious life (and here, in it, the directive, orientational activity of reflective love is most important) likewise has a certain measure, continually increasing, of control over both the manifold functions of the human body and the structures and functions of the instruments it has devised to support and extend its vital activity.[5]

Because of the preeminence assigned by Teilhard to love as the highest form of human energy and also because, with its volitional component, it is so closely allied to the realities of moral choice, I decided to take up the examination of love as the highest form of spiritualized energy first, and then, in subsequent chapters, examine other affective and intellective activities, along with those elements and facets of human individual and societal life associated with them in an ethical context.[6] The progres-

5. In other words, one is dealing here with both the psychosomatic and somatopsychic of contemporary psychology.
6. Consideration of the place and meaning of love in Teilhard's thought varies with the stance and controlling purpose of different commentators, analysts, and critics. Denis Mermod, in the only *ex professo* study of his ethics available at the present time, takes up the subject when he considers interior moral forces, and his limited examination is incorporated in a series of reflections on zest (*goût*). See Mermod, *La morale chez Teilhard*, pp. 95-102. For some excellent probing criticism of Teilhard's thought on love in the context of "The Redemption and the Mystery of Evil" and "The Church and the Parousia," see Mooney, *Mystery of Christ*, pp. 131-55, 161-77. Gray, in his *The One and the Many*, pp. 75-95, devotes a good part of a chapter to "Love: The Energy of Unification," but also touches on it in his next chapter, "Christ: Omega," pp. 95-112, especially in his analysis of Teilhard's thought on "The Cosmic Function of the Church," pp. 109-111. (For an essay by the same au-

sions, then, is from the zones of spiritualized energy and their organization and transmission, outward to controlled energy and the spiritualized activities involved in its development and mastery, with consideration of incorporated energy coming at the end.

In the course of this inquiry, the relationship of love to other forms of spiritualized energy will become clearer, but the main ties can be sketched at the outset. The relationship with intellective energy is one of mutual interdependence: the searching mind reveals what is lovable, while the loving mind is drawn on to search more and more. The principal affective energies with which Teilhard was concerned were fear, the aggressive drive, and hope. Teilhardian love, with its constructive movement toward union, will emerge as a peculiar synthesis with hope. This hopeful love, through its dynamic, will moderate and control fear, eliminate, ultimately, the negative, killing aspects of the aggressive

thor, "Teilhard's Vision of Love," see n10 below.) De Lubac's major efforts in this sector appear in his book-length study, *Eternal Feminine*. (See below, n35.) Barthélemy-Madaule, in her *Bergson-Teilhard*, incorporates her specific remarks on love, pp. 387-99, in the chapter on "L'univers personnel," as a portion of a rather lengthy consideration of Teilhard's ethical thought, pp. 363-426, with some relevant material in the earlier pages under the discussion of "Humanité," pp. 379-85. In her later work, *La personne chez Teilhard*, the principal treatment occurs in Part I. "Le personnel," chap. 3, "La personne et L'amour," pp. 110-35, but certain important concepts appear in other sections. See chap. 1, "Une expérience authentique de la personne," "La rencontre de l'autre...," pp. 51-58, and section 3, "Tous ensemble et le prochain," pp. 65-74. Also Part II, "L'universal," chap. 6, "Le drame humain," section 2, "Le drame de l'humanité," pp. 229-51. Faricy has a significant section on the development of Teilhard's thought on love in *Teilhard: Theology*, pp. 185-95, in his chapter on "Christian Endeavor," pp. 173-208. (See n9 below.) Particularly valuable for citation of material from Teilhard's unpublished journals is the short section pertinent to love in the chapter devoted to "Perspective morales," by de Solages, *Teilhard: étude*, pp. 219-26; but relevant material is also found in his first chapter where he writes about Teilhard's twofold love (the World and Christ), pp. 3-7, and toward the end of his study in his reflections on Teilhard's spirituality, pp. 260-62 and 363-73. Pierre-Louis Mathieu, *La pensée politique et économique de Teilhard de Chardin* (Paris: Editions du Seuil, 1969), in the chapter treating of "Un neo-Christianisme de l'action," pp. 162-82, has a section, "Un monde construit par amour," pp. 179-82, with some significant correlations between Teilhard's thought and that of the Sillonist, Marc Sangier, and also that of the sixteenth-century Dominican, respected in certain Marxist circles, Giovani Domenico Campanella. (Hereafter, this work will be referred to as *La pensée politique de Teilhard*.)

drive, and find support in the sublimated positive thrust to sustain evolutionary effort and overcome whatever obstacles present themselves.

In all the relationships indicated above (those between love, incorporated and controlled energy), concern in the present study arises from the questioning point of view as to how love can and *should* operate *responsibly*. Hence, with regard to the bipolarities and mutual interdependencies noted, emphasis is placed more on love's controlling and directing activity, rather than on its receiving sustenance from another energy source. If this is kept in mind, the particular relationship between cosmic love and incorporated and controlled energy will stand out with greater clarity. It will be found to involve, certainly, a response of loving wonder and gratitude to Omega's goodness manifest in the energies of the human body as well as in the devices created by human ingenuity to complement the body. But Teilhard's concern goes beyond that to love's constructive response seeking to master the forces of incorporated and controlled energy in the Omegalization process of striving to develop the world further.

## B.  Development in Teilhard's Thought on Love

The connection alluded to in the preceding paragraph becomes clear at the outset, when one follows Teilhard's thinking down through the years, from his World War I correspondence to his last essays.

In his wartime correspondence and essays, the question of the meaning of love is almost always approached from the angle of an attempt to penetrate or clarify the meaning of Christian charity. There is very little in these writings of what could be called a pure phenomenology of love.[7] Moreover, even in later years, when he would

7. Ideas pertinent to the meaning and practice of charity surface from

broach an analysis in a phenomenological context alone, it is not uncommon to find a correlation of the two strains of thought before the essay is finished.[8] His approach to the study of love is yet another concretization of how, throughout his thinking, one finds faith seeking understanding to be the controlling influence.

Again, while it is true, as Faricy pointed out, that the elaboration of his phenomenology of love took place in the thirties, with his thought on charity finding clarification in the forties and a final synthesis with human love in the fifties, still, what development took place with regard to central issues was more by way of clarification, expansion, and emphasis than through radically new discovery.[9] The roots of key concepts, such as the convergence of masculine-feminine love in God, a unifying bond tying all mankind together in the evolutionary

time to time in the World War I letters, especially from August 1915 to July 1917. See *MM*, pp. 63, 81, 85, 105, 107, 117, 132, 146, 163, 164, 180, 181, 192, 197. During roughly the same period, what could be taken as phenomenological observations are less frequent. See *MM*, pp. 55, 121. In the wartime essays, the following can be cited as the main phenomenological passages having a bearing on the meaning of love: "The Struggle Against the Multitude" (1917), *WW*, pp. 97-102; "Creative Union" (1917), *WW*, pp. 170-71; "La Grande Monade" (1918), *EG*, p. 243; "The Eternal Feminine" (1918), *WW*, pp. 192-96; "The Promised Land" (1919), *WW*, pp. 278-85; "The Spiritual Power of Matter" (1919), *HU*, p. 62. By contrast, the following give indication of his proportionate concern about charity, the love of God, and solidarity in Christ: "Cosmic Life" (1916), *WW*, pp. 48, 52, 65, 69; "The Mastery of the World and the Kingdom of God" (1916), *WW*, pp. 83, 88-89; "Christ in Matter" (1916), *HU*, pp. 52, 54; "The Struggle Against the Multitude" (1917), *WW*, pp. 94 (the scriptural citations from St. John are significant here), 102-3, 107-12; "The Mystical Milieu" (1917), *WW*, pp. 120, 125-27, 128-36, 143-46; "Creative Union" (1917), *WW*, pp. 172-74; "The Soul of the World" (1918), *WW*, pp. 187-89; "The Eternal Feminine" (1918), *WW*, pp. 197-202; "The Priest" (1918), *WW*, pp. 208, 215, 218, 222; "Operative Faith" (1918), *WW*, p. 246 (much of what he says here about faith is implicitly about love); "Forma Christi" (1918), *WW*, pp. 254, 257, 259, 266; "Note pour L'évangélisation des temps nouveaux" (1919), *EG*, p. 378; "The Promised Land" (1919), *WW*, p. 286; "The Universal Element" (1919), *WW*, pp. 296-97; "The Spiritual Power of Matter" (1919), *HU*, pp. 59-71 (the whole essay is really about the love of God coming through matter).

8. For example, "The Spirit of the Earth" (1931), *HE*, pp. 43-47, "Sketch of a Personalistic Universe" (1936), *HE*, pp. 89-92, "The Phenomenon of Spirit" (1937), *HE*, pp. 108-12, "Human Energy" (1937), *HE*, pp. 155-60.

9. Faricy, *Teilhard: Theology*, pp. 185-96. I would agree with Faricy's main stages, but, for reasons indicated below, prefer to make clearer the existence of the main seminal ideas in the earlier writings.

task, the dynamism as opposed to the static quality of Christian charity—all of these can be found in discernible form in the wartime writings.[10] Nor is there evidence of fundamental alteration or change in the direction of

10. The idea of masculine-feminine love converging on God can be noted as early as a letter to his cousin of December 2, 1915, MM, p. 81. It occurs again, June 19, 1916, MM, p. 101, in "Creative Union" (1917), WW, pp. 170-71, and especially in the second section of "The Eternal Feminine" (1918), WW, pp. 197-202. Since the appearance of this central concept in his thinking on sexuality antedates his "L'évolution de la chasteté" (1934) by a good decade and a half, Sullivan would seem to be placing too much emphasis on his age as a factor controlling his thinking, with his comments about Teilhard's being in his mid-fifties when he came to grips with the problem. See Dan Sullivan, "Psychosexuality: the Teilhard Lacunae [sic]," Continuum 2 (1967): 254-78.

The question of general human solidarity and a universal human love can be seen surfacing in "Cosmic Life" (1916), WW, pp. 36-37 (basic phenomenological concepts) and pp. 49-52 (Christological organic solidarity); "The Mystical Milieu" (1917), MM, p. 202; "Creative Union" (1917), WW, pp. 172-73; "La Grande Monade" (1918), EG, especially p. 243, although the entire essay is about Teilhard's rising consciousness of human unity; "The Priest" (1918), WW, p. 222; "The Promised Land" (1919), WW, pp. 282-83; and "The Universal Element" (1919), WW, p. 296.

His thinking on the dynamic quality of charity presents something of a problem. In a letter of August 4, 1916, MM, p. 117, he admits to a baffling mystery about charity, and the difficulty at that date of synthesizing in his thought what he understands charity to mean with what seems to be the need to give a preeminence to "the force that organizes, disciplines, selects." Also, in a letter of February 5, 1919, MM, p. 181, he speaks of charity as static, and furthermore, in his "Note pour l'évangélisation des temps nouveau" (1919), EG, p. 378, he complains about the gap in the theology of his time as to relating human and divine love. (Cf. Faricy's inferences from these texts, Teilhard: Theology, p. 185.) However, the evidence is present in his wartime writings that the main direction of his solution for the problem is already surfacing. In "Cosmic Life" (1916), WW, p. 52, the Body of Jesus is spoken of as "the bond that holds together all fruitful effort," and later in the same essay, p. 65, he asks why concern for progress and the cult of the earth could not be transformed into "a great virtue, as yet un-named, which would be the widest form of the love of God, found and served in creation?" Moreover, in "The Struggle Against the Multitude" (1917), WW, p. 109, he specifically writes, "Christian brotherly love seeks to do much more than to make good the harm done by selfishness, and ease the injuries inflicted by human malice. It is much more than a soothing lotion poured by the Good Samaritan into the wounds of society. There is an organic and 'cosmic' opus operatum of charity. By bringing souls together in love, charity gives them the fertility that enables a higher nature to form from their union." And in the next paragraph, by way of ex professo denying the static character of charity, he adds, "In real fact, no terrestrial effort is more constructive, more progressive than Christ's. It is not arrogant strength, but the holiness of the gospels, that maintains and continues the authentic effort of evolution." True, the synthesis of effort and charity was not yet precisely formulated, but the drift of his thought is clear enough. Moreover, not many years later, in the early twenties, he did give poetic synthesis to the two in "The Mass on the World" (1923), HU, p. 36, when he prayed that true charity be recognized as a "vigorous determination that all of us together shall break open the doors of life."

his thinking, even though at one period of his life he might be more concerned with certain aspects of the problem of love than with others. The shift of emphasis or focus is best explained by the particular concerns he found significant for himself in his thought environment at the time.

## C. The Meaning of Love

### 1. GENERAL ASPECTS

For Teilhard, the roots of love are to be found in the same way one traces the roots of responsibility and consciousness. Love, in its origins and history, can be identified with cosmogenesis itself. Its distant roots are found in the primeval affinities and attractions of cosmic particles seeking union, prior to the advent of life. Closer analogues can be found in all the affinities and attractions ranging through the levels of life as consciousness sharpened with complexity. It finally emerged in human form with the advent of human reflection as something critically distinct from its predecessors.[11]

There are four fundamental general aspects of love which appear when Teilhard speaks about it. These are attraction, affinity, sympathy, and synthesizing energy.[12]

11. Poetic expression of this is found in "The Eternal Feminine" (1918), WW, pp. 192-96. For a definite discursive statement, see "The Spirit of the Earth" (1931), HE, pp. 33-34.

12. See "The Spirit of the Earth" (1931), HE, p. 33; "Human Energy" (1937), HE, p. 145; PM (1940), pp. 264-68; "The Rise of the Other" (1942), AE, p. 70; "Life and the Planets" (1945), FM, p. 119; "The Planetisation of Mankind" (1945), FM, p. 135; "The Spiritual Repercussions of the Atom Bomb" (1945), FM, p. 147; "The Formation of the Noosphere" (1947), FM, p. 177; "The Directions and Conditions of the Future" (1948), FM, p. 235; "Comment je vois" (1948), DA, pp. 201-2; and "Human Unanimisation" (1950), FM, pp. 284-88. Gray inclines to consider the model of magnetism as a central image in understanding Teilhard's ideas on love, although he admits he finds the image applied to Omega only once in a 1939 essay, "The Salvation of Mankind," SC, pp. 145-46. However, to put so much emphasis on a physical model, demanding constant analogical correction for ethical viability, seems a questionable enterprise. Even if it could be granted that magnetism is

They occur consistently in his observations about the meaning and function of love with different nuances in different contexts. Central to understanding them will be attention in what follows to how he operates analogically in this area. A more complete grasp of their meaning calls for a close look at the main varieties of love, but a preliminary analysis of these generic elements will provide helpful background, as well as recapitulation of points already sketched.

Teilhard himself did not analyze these four concepts in a single context whereby they are taken in the progression listed above. They are arranged as they are here because, looking at them in sequence, a certain narrowing of focus and specification can be discerned. The concept of *attraction* provides a sense of direction, to which Teilhard usually gave a dual aspect, that of being drawn toward the Center of the universe, while also drawing the elements of the world together among themselves, center to center. When he speaks of *affinity*, he highlights an analogously higher level of attraction among human beings, which he stresses is internal, not superficially tangential. The weight of emphasis here is on the center-to-center character of being drawn together. A more specific picture of this mutual internal centrality emerges in the concept of *sympathy*. Here again the duality noted above is manifest. For example, in "The Planetisation of Mankind," although the Center of the Universe is referred to vaguely, he remarks:

> What we . . . see is a flood of *sympathetic* forces spreading from the heart of the system . . . sympathy in the first place

a prime concrete image to clarify one aspect of love (the element of attraction) still, since Teilhard's ethic, as has been seen, and his theory of love embodied in it, depend so much on man's autonomous, free determination, the stress on magnetism runs the risk of overplaying the role of the nonfree element in love, and of underplaying the distinctively human, the conscious, free, self-determined, and controlled response called for in a human person. See Donald P. Gray, "Teilhard's Vision of Love," in *Dimensions of the Future*, ed. Marvin Kessler, S.J. and Bernard Brown S.J. (Washington: Corpus Books, 1968), pp. 91-96, and pp. 196-97 nn43, 46, 48, 49.

(an act of quasi-adoration) on the part of all the elements gathered together for the general impulse that carries them along; and also sympathy (this time fraternal) of each separate element for all that is most unique and incommunicable in each of the co-elements with which it converges in the unity, not only of a single act of vision but of a single living subject.[13]

Moreover, he affirms that the role of sympathy in bringing love into being involves the shared experience of being "ardently intent upon a common object."[14] The ardor of intent about which he speaks is of special import, because it highlights the distinction he makes between passive sympathy, which can exist merely on the level of shared ideas, and active sympathy, which builds on a commonality of consciousness through an infusion of affective energy toward center-to-center, personalizing union.[15]

Love as the *synthetic energy* of personalizing union presents a further determination in this sequence of basic aspects, and it is an aspect that Teilhard did enlarge on at some length, working from the term *totalization*. When he speaks of love as the "totalizing principle of human energy," he is concerned with bringing together into a conscious "wholeness" or "totality" both the activities of the individual person within himself and the activities of many individual persons in society. What he is describing is a process that others might well prefer to put in terms of integration, unification, or the orientation, the organization of consciousness by a single life motive. Moreover, when this process is considered in the light of his basic thought on creative union (to create is to unite), it can be seen to be a fundamentally creative synthesis about which he speaks. Consequently, love emerges as a radically developmental energy, bringing into being,

---

13. *FM* (1945), p. 135.
14. "The Spiritual Repercussions of the Atom Bomb" (1946), *FM*, p. 147.
15. "The Formation of the Noosphere" (1947), *FM*, p. 177.

through its energy of creative synthesis, new forms of individual-personal, and societal-personal, conscious life. It is, therefore, truly an evolutionary power.

Certain aspects of societal, creative synthesis have already been seen in the sketch of Omegalization given earlier, and more will be seen shortly in the consideration of the human sense or societal love. Prerequisite for this larger, noospheric synthesis, is the inner synthesis of the individual's personal conscious life, which Teilhard describes in terms of two intimately connected processes, the totalization by love of individual actions and the totalization of the individual "on himself" by love, with the unifying principle consisting in the love of the supreme personal Center, Omega.[16] In developing his thought here, what Teilhard is doing is probing more deeply into the meaning of one facet of the duality of centering, noted above, in what he has to say about attraction, affinity, and sympathy—the facet or aspect of complete human love, which looks to center-to-center communion with a universal, common, personal Center of the universe.

These two intrapersonal totalizations are not easy to distinguish from each other in Teilhard's description of them. If one has the first, it is difficult to see how the second is not present. They call for some analysis.

He explains what he means by totalization of individual actions by citing the psychological fragmentation of pluralist man, a man whose life finds no focal point of love energy for his activities in Omega. (What he says here should be noted for its similarity to his thought, in another context, about purity.)[17] Such a person's actions,

---

16. The place where he specifically develops his thought on this point, using this phenomenological "totalization" vocabulary, is in "Human Energy" (1937), *HE*, pp. 146-54. But quite similar thought content, in Christological language, can be found elsewhere. See "The Mystical Milieu" (1917), *WW* "The Circle of Person" pp. 144-47, and "Super Humanity, Super-Christ, Super-Charity" (1943), *SC*, pp. 169-71, where he describes the manner in which charity is synthesized.

17. See, for example, "The Struggle Against the Multitude" (1917), *WW*, pp. 107-8; *DM* (1927), pp. 132-34.

whether they are of his feelings, his limbs, or his thoughts, are compartmentalized, or dissipated. They have no central core, no heart to unify them. They are actions of a human being, but not of a whole man. Even a life of intense scientific thought can end up dry and disillusioned, if the mind only, and not the personality, has been at work. On the contrary, when all one's activities are organized under the impulse of responding to the love of Omega, the least action has meaning in view of this wholly motivating love. In even the most insignificant acts, contact can be made with the universe, in and through Omega, and with the totality of oneself, consciously acting with this orientation.

What, then, is involved in the totalization of the individual "on himself"? Teilhard talks of man's various activities becoming totalized, merging in a single act, because they have become individually totalized, in the sense seen immediately above. That this happens under the truly synthetic impact of love, uniting and differentiating, is his thesis. Precisely *how* vision, thought, understanding, love, giving, receiving, growing, shrinking—even living and dying—retain their uniqueness while combining into a common whole or sum, is not explained with illuminating clarity. What happens in loving Omega is similar to, but far transcends, what happens by way of unifying wholeness when a person acts in response to a noble, elevating love of woman. But his comparison of two analogous complex experiences does not really tell one any more about either of them in detail.

An explanation that seems to make sense, but that Teilhard himself does not elaborate, is that if one makes a serious conscious effort over a period of time to organize his various activities in accord with his awareness of what response is required for Omegalization, sooner or later, either in a flash of insight, or by a slow, hidden growth of a state of mind, a person sees how all his varied activities fit into one complex, yet organically unified stream of love-imbued thought. In seeing how all the parts, so to speak, fit together in an organic whole, one sees their uniqueness, and also sees them combined into a "common sum." In the totalization of individual actions, *each act* is seen related to Omega and united to the source of the whole. In the totalization of the individual on himself, *all one's acts* are seen in their organic *interconnection* among themselves as coming from oneself, responding to the love of Omega. When this overall view has been seen, and is retained in the form of an abiding awareness, the totality of the individual's life has a new "wholeness," consciously possessed. In accord with this explanation, the distinction, then, between the two totalizations would be the distinction between two phases of development in a psychological growth process. The description of the process would seem, furthermore, to be a description in phenomenological terms of much the same reality as is described, in some literature, as mystical union, contemplation in. action, or, in another Teilhardian vocabulary, growth in awareness of the Divine Milieu.

## 2. CRITIQUE: DETERMINISTIC ATTRACTION, RECIPROCITY, RESPONSIBILITY, LOVE, AND REFLECTION

A serious problem presents itself because of the manner in which Teilhard approaches his theorizing about love, with considerable stress on the notions of attraction and affinity. The precise character of the problem arises from the emphasis on the aspect of the affective, automatic response of love, with consequent obscuring of, or disproportionate lack of emphasis on, the all-important free, volitional, self-giving element in truly human love. If one were to read only those texts in which Teilhard speaks of the mounting attraction of personal centers for Omega and for each other, one could easily lay at his feet the ancient charge of equating knowledge and virtue, or the more recently developed mechanism of psychological determinism.

Again, there is the problem of serious and regrettable

ambiguity. What would have been necessary to acquit him of the charges of both determinism and ambiguity would have been a more decisive emphasis on the *active* element in sympathy, with all its implications of self-directed effort, as well as clarifications of the sort indicated above in chapter 2, about his thought on freedom and responsibility, and the analogical transformation of concepts applied to the human after having first been used in pre-human deterministic contexts.[18]

When all his related statements are taken into account, one cannot accurately say that his theory of love negates or denies free self-donation or responsible commitment. But because of the misleading emphases, derived in good part from his own failure to make qualifications, he remains open to criticism that the uniquely human element in human love, the free, volitional, is underdeveloped in his theoretical exposition. The elements are there, implied, especially in what he says about the need for responsible effort to transcent narrow egoism, but explicit attention to this as integral to the radical freedom of human love is wanting. Even his lengthy explanation about the totalizing, synthetic energy of love is not helpful, because what he is describing in these passages is the effects of love, but not the inner workings. Further complications, moreover, arise when the implications of his love theory are viewed in the context of divine agapeic love.[19]

As for reciprocity, in the considerations on the varieties of love to be taken up shortly three different but analogous types of reciprocal need emerge.

On the level of sexual love Teilhard bypasses completely anything like a detailed consideration of the meaning of physical sexual love and focuses his attention

18. See above, chap. 3B (regarding freedom) and D (regarding responsibility).

19. Complete consideration of Teilhard's thought on love calls for analysis of how his treatment of Christian charity fits with the notion of agape. The agape question, because of its importance in understanding his Christological thought, will be taken up specifically in chapter 9 below.

mainly on the mutual enrichment, the reciprocal spiritual energizing that arises from mutual affective attraction, with the constant insistence that this mutuality must not develop into an "egoism of two," but lead to a higher mutual sharing of dedication to a higher object of love, hopefully the supreme Personal Center, Omega, and not merely an impersonal cause or ideal. What should be noted is that at this level there is a real I-Thou permeation of sympathy, or empathy, a center-to-center sharing of thoughts, feelings, ideals, along with the higher sharing of love of the supreme Personal Center.

On the level of societal, or generalized human love, such intimate intercentricity on the horizontal personal level does not exist. There is a mutual reciprocal attraction and sympathy, but it arises not from an intimate sharing of one's interior life, but rather from the awareness of a shared common challenge and task converging on and motivated by a love of Omega. It is not so much the sharing of individual personal centers with each other—although a great deal of this is possible in genuine friendship—but of individual centers sharing the awareness that they share a common Omega Center to complete fulfillment, a sharing not passively accepted, but actively to be achieved.

Cosmic love contains all the preceding and adds the further dimension of including in the sense of shared convergence the entire spectrum of cosmic elements beyond the human as they participate in the movement of the universe, through man, to Omega. The universe needs Omega as a unifying ultimate Center of attraction, and, mysteriously, the transcendent and supreme Omega, ultimately self-sufficient, still needs cosmogenesis, and cosmogenesis through human love, once it is understood that he has initiated an evolutionary universe. Moreover, with this Omega, transcendent yet also immanent, there is possible a center-to-center intimacy of mutual permeation between an indefinite number of human personal centers and Omega himself, far surpassing the most intimate intrahuman I-Thou relationship.

What also is important is that reciprocity in the sense described here is not a *quid pro quo* type of love based on a kind of mutual exchange-of-payment basis, but rather a back-and-forth sharing rooted in the experience of sharing a complementarity needed for mutual fulfillment. In personal terms, it would come to this: "I do not love you on the condition that you love me, or in payment for your love of me, but simply because I recognize that I need you and that you need me—either sexually, or in a larger societal sense, or cosmically."

Further clarification of the fundamental meaning of Teilhardian love can be had by noting more precisely the relationship between love and responsibility, alluded to above.[20] Teilhard does not spell out the correlation between the two, but what he says reveals that the four basic elements of love are very much a part of the same picture he described in speaking of a sense of responsibility. Allowing for analogical adjustments below the human level, one can affirm the same cosmic roots for both love and responsibility. They are found in the intimate organic connections of every particle of the cosmos with every other particle, which connections assume a special definition in the human person. To speak, for example, of active personal sympathy is to speak of a sense of oneness with another person, leading each out to the other for mutually cooperative effort. The sense of responsibility is, in effect, a reflex awareness of what this sympathy presents to the person in the context of a free decision that must be made if the capacity for active sympathy is to be realized, as it should be, in conformity with particular, known, organic relationships of attraction and affinity. Love, therefore, as responsible, rests on knowledge of the organic ties one has with other persons and of the need to act freely in accord with these ties.

20. See Chap. 3D above (regarding responsibility).

To say this is to bring to the surface another elemental characteristic of love, its reflective aspect, by pointing to its close connection with the intellective spiritualized energy of "research." Human awareness of the gamut of organic ties just mentioned does not come about by accident, but is derived through conscious inquiry. This is emphasized by Teilhard's second rule for moral goodness, wherein he speaks clearly of the need to isolate goodness by analysis.[21] The authentic affinity attracting persons to each other (despite what can be at times valid spontaneous initial impulses) and the goals drawing them together for hopeful effort—all require reflection for full validation. If the loving act is not preceded by this careful analysis, nor subjected to reflective criticism in the course of a series of loving acts, the dynamic energy of love can be squandered. More accurately, what seems to be love can turn out to be pseudo-love and hence not love at all.

## D.  The Varieties of Love

At various places in his early writings Teilhard does have things to say about the attraction of men and women to each other, about a sense of solidarity with other human beings (or the difficulty of achieving it), as well as the attraction of the beauty of the universe exercising its impact on him.[22] And, of course, he wrote about the love of God and Christ. But it was not until the thirties that he brought these concepts together and expanded on them in one setting. Nor did he, later in life, update a systematic synthesis of his thinking on love along the same lines. Particular aspects he would probe more deeply, in a number of different ways, but no lengthy study appeared gathering his thoughts together in the same framework. The extended reflections of the thir-

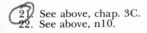

21. See above, chap. 3C.
22. See above, n10.

ties are mainly on the phenomenological level. Because of this fact, and also because they do present his principal expanded analyses on the subject, their tripartite framework will be used as the base for what follows, on sexual, societal, and cosmic love.[23]

## 1. SEXUAL LOVE

### a. Meaning and Significance

The significance of woman, profound as it was for Teilhard, dawned on him, by his own admission, relatively late, in his thirtieth year. Prior to that time, concern with the impersonal and general had absorbed him almost to the point of his ignoring sexuality.[24] He was, however, obviously attached to his mother, his sisters, and, in a special way, his cousin Marguerite, as is evident enough from the tone and atmosphere of his many letters to her. Presumably it was this last who provoked his particular reflections, initially, and in a remarkably profound way, about the significance of woman for man. His understanding was deepened over the years by several other close and warm friendships with women, as well as his opportunity to observe and reflect on family life in his relatives and friends, and to express these reflections in several talks given at marriage ceremonies, in addition to incorporating them in his essays.[25]

23. The core text with the tripartite division is "Sketch of a Personalistic Universe" (1936), Section V, "The Energy of Personalization," *HE*, pp. 71-84. In "The Spirit of the Earth" (1931), Section IV, "The Sense of the Earth," *HE*, pp. 31-38, he has divisions that treat of love and humanity, but nothing directly on cosmic love. Material pertinent to this concept does occur, however, in Section V, "The Future of Spirit," pp. 38-43, and Section VI, "The Arising of God," pp. 43-47. The three-level consideration is not peculiar to this essay. Years later, in "From Cosmos to Cosmogenesis" (1951), *AE*, p. 266, it occurs, without development, when he is discussing, in Section III, "A New Form of Human Energy: Love of Evolution," pp. 264-67. Reference can also be found in "Le coeur de la matière" (1950), *I*, p. 33, at the opening of his Clausule on "Le feminin, ou l'unitif." The elements, moreover, can be discerned in *PM* (1940), in the material on love as energy, pp. 264-68.

24. "Le coeur de la matière" (1950), *I*, p. 33.

25. The principal texts containing his thought on sexuality are: "The Eternal Feminine" (1918), *WW*, pp. 192-202, and "L'évolution de la chasteté" (1934), *DA*, pp. 67-94, along with portions of "The Spirit of the Earth" (1931),

What his reflections led him to over the years, as he integrated them with his insights into the meaning of matter and spirit in a convergent personalistic universe, are some rather striking observations that were, no doubt, quite disturbing to many of his religious confreres, on the one hand, and paradoxically, to his scientific humanist friends as well, although for different reasons.

When he asks about the essence and direction of passionate love in a personalistic universe, he notes that in its early stages sexuality was inevitably preoccupied with propagation. With the advent of personality in man, however, a more essential role could be discerned as emerging, namely, the necessary synthesis of two principles, male and female, in building human personality. (Prior to a certain maturation of human life on earth, this mutual-development role of sexuality was admitted but considered of secondary importance. The relationship between man and woman was considered to be primarily for the benefit of the child. But now, particularly with the threat of overpopulation and all the problems of compressive socialization, there is increasing need to reverse emphases.) For evolution to continue forward, spiritual energy must be expanded, amplified to its fullest capacity. In Teilhard's thinking, woman is precisely the isolation-breaking, energy-activating complement man needs for this energy expansion.[26] To this

*HE*, pp. 32-34, "Sketch of a Personalistic Universe" (1936), *HE*, pp. 72-77, and the final section or Clausule, of "Le coeur de la matière" (1950), "Le feminin ou l'unitif," *I*, pp. 33-34. Three of his marriage sermons (1928, 1935, 1948) are also significant and available in *SB*, pp. 65-91.

For understanding his relationship with women, valuable material is found in his published letters to his cousin Marguerite, *MM*, and *LT*, although not all of the latter collection consists of letters to her. Also, *LZ*. The identity of the two friends in *LF* remains officially anonymous, but they are known to have been women. For some valuable clarifying remarks about his purpose in writing "L'évolution de la chasteté," see *LŻ*, p. 111. On the question of his personal life and his women friends, see Claude Cuénot, "Teilhard de Chardin: Sketch for a Portrait," *The Teilhard Review* 6, no. 1, (Summer 1971): 7-9. The article is a short but excellent sketch of Teilhard as a person.

26. See "The Spirit of the Earth" (1931), *HE*, pp. 33-34, and "L'évolution de la chasteté" (1934), *DA*, pp. 76-78.

impact he gave frank testimony, in his later years, when he wrote in his spiritual autobiography that, from the time he passed the critical threshold of maturation and self-realization, "... nothing developed in me except under the gaze and influence of Woman." As he saw it, for full humanity, a further step beyond intellectual reflection is needed, the step of amorization through feminine attraction. As a consequence, the basic human unit is not the thinking monad, but the complete human molecule, man and woman together, the affective dyad.[27]

### b. Moral Implications

What moral implications follow for channeling this type of love energy? First, since, as always, true union differentiates, there should be no absorption, no fusion merging two lovers so as to negate personal identity. Rather, there should develop a genuine spiritual differentiation bringing out the unique best in each person. The opposite risk is that of plurality, which would mean no union at all, but egoistic use of each other through preoccupation with the joys of mere physical possession. Evil, misuse, and offense here do not therefore entail any defilement with something unclean, but rather a squandering of energy or confining it to the narrow limits of an "egoism of two," which can become a "universe of two." The second important rule has to do precisely with the opposite of the last-mentioned offense. Lovers constituting the human molecule as the affective dyad must look beyond themselves in two directions: toward social groupings in the larger human world, and to God, the ultimate center of convergence.[28]

How these rules differ from earlier rules shows up in a special way when one sees their implications for the

---

27. "Le coeur de la matière," *I*, pp. 33-34.
28. "Sketch of a Personalistic Universe" (1936), *HE*, pp. 74-76. Also, marriage sermons, Bacot-Teilhard (1928), *SB*, pp. 74-75, Goublaye (1935), *SB*, pp. 85-86, Dresch-Haardt (1948), *SB*, pp. 89-91.

meaning of purity. According to earlier norms, purity in the sense of virginal chastity called for the separation of the sexes. In its highest form, man and women entered into a direct alliance with God, eschewing any mutual relationship that would divide the heart. But now, purity does not mean absence of a mutual love relationship, however much Teilhard ultimately opts for virginity as more spiritual than marriage. The celibately pure can be genuinely in love, without physical sex relations, because of their mutual adherence, center to center, to the Supreme Center above them, where they join in the love of Someone greater than themselves. Hence, some of Teilhard's favorite descriptive terms in this context: not suppression of the spiritualized energies of matter but sublimation, conservation, and transformation. The more pure lovers of this sort love each other, the more they love God; and the more they love God, the more they love each other. Teilhard's strong language about the need and value of heterosexual affection, even for the dedicated celibate, is obviously what would upset many of his religious brethren. But equally upsetting to the scientific humanist mentality of many of his friends would be his difficult-to-avoid implication that the more and higher marriage evolved as a relationship, the more it would tend to sublimate physical sex in order to reach a highly spiritualized, celibate form of marriage, granted that the basic needs of sustaining the species be met.[29]

It is to the credit of his insight and intellectual consistency that he does, in accord with his premises about the spiritual energies of matter, see that there is at least an argument for spiritualized sex relations divorced from reproduction.[30] However, since the main thrust of his thought in pondering the question is in the direction of validating celibacy, he does not draw out the corollary

29. "Sketch of a Personalistic Universe" (1936), *HE*, pp. 76-77, "L'évolution de la chasteté" (1934), *DA*, pp. 87-92. Teilhard is much more explicit on the point of gradual diminution of physical sex relations in a letter to August Valensin, November 11, 1934, quoted by de Lubac, *Eternal Feminine*, p. 56.
30. "L'évolution de la chasteté" (1934), *DA*, pp. 85-92.

that would seem legitimate enough. In addition to marriage that would involve reproduction to meet the needs of the species and then become celibate, there would seem to be a place for marriage, reproductive as needed, but with continued physical relations, nonreproductive yet spiritually energizing. Teilhard's point that the act of physical sex somehow consumes part of one's "absolute" in the experience is crucial to his argument for a natural base for celibacy, and is, clearly enough, advanced as a "possibility," not definitive proof. There is a real difficulty and a serious one here in that the same argument could be extended to scientific, poetic, or musical experience of discovery as well, to the extent that they contain a "flash of ecstasy." Obviously, to apply it thus would be to negate his whole thrust toward research, with all that it implies. Furthermore, to argue as Teilhard does here seems inconsistent with his entire basic argument about the spiritual power of matter. Above all, it seems to imply that something very important in the sacrament of marriage is, in itself, somehow incapable of full sacramentalization. Moreover, on the empirical side, evidence from sexual psychology could also be advanced to dispute the totality of absorption he attributes to sexual intercourse, which is the empirical base of his argument.

The debate about a natural basis for celibacy will probably continue, apart from whether it is strictly accurate to speak of it as a superior state in an organically complementary social universe, where various roles have their own specific functional value and are, as a consequence, difficult to rank hierarchically. (This is not to deny that a strong case has been made for centuries on the grounds of closer imitation of Christ.) A strong natural argument, however, although not a new one, that Teilhard might have used in consistency with his general line of thought, would be the need, in a highly complex noospheric organism, for certain persons to be freed from the organic ties of family responsibilities so as to be more mobile and flexible in meeting the demands of certain necessary types of work, with their own peculiar absorbing bonds. However, the line of argument Teilhard pursues, unfortunately lends itself to the charge that it ends up as a highly qualified, tentative, sophisticated, yet subtle denigration of physical sex, with, ultimately, unavoidable Manichean implications.[31]

## c. Critique

Conjugal Love. It has been charged that there are not only lacunae in Teilhard's thought about sexuality, but errors as well. His treatment of conjugal love is admittedly skimpy, and it would be folly to claim that he had touched on more than certain basic themes in treating the vastly complex question of familial love. The meaning and value of physical sex relations for spiritualization, while implicit in his theory of matter moving toward spirit, is not developed. He attempts no in-depth analysis of the distinction, yet interconnection between exclusive affective attraction and the free—in a sense beyond emotion—intellectual and volitional commitment of the marriage bond. While he does speak of sharing the intimacies of feeling, thought, and ideals, he does not speak of this sharing and commonality under the form of that peculiar type of friendship love acknowledged to be important for marriage.[32] What is rather

31. Critics like Sullivan (see above, n10) whose bias is clearly on the other side, have not failed to point this out. Moreover, O'Day's critique of Sullivan's article, claiming breakthrough rather than lacuna in Teilhard's thought on sexuality, leans heavily on his attempt to find a natural base for celibacy as the main breakthrough factor. But O'Day merely accepts Teilhard's "possibility" and does not discuss the critical difficulties indicated above. See Michael O'Day, "Lacuna or Breakthrough: Review Article," *The Teilhard Review* 4, no. 2 (Winter 1969/70): 93-97.

32. The only text where he explicitly speaks about the matter of sharing thoughts, feelings, etc., by husband and wife is in the marriage sermon of 1928, referred to above, n28. To speak of the love involved in this type of intimacy as "sexual" simply because it is between members of the opposite sex seems questionable, although this has been done by C. W. Freible, S.J., in "Teilhard, Sexual Love, and Celibacy," *Review for Religious* 26 (1967): 288. Semantic dispute about the various meanings of *sexual* can be endless and unfortunately often fruitless, but here it would seem that clarity would better be served to refer to the material as describing the friendship element of a con-

surprising is that in his marriage discourses, while he does stress the union of marriage partners in love of God, he neglects specific and explicit discussion of an aspect that one would have thought would surface readily in his mind: that of the sacramentality of Christ's love and its significance in this context. Nor does he explore the enormously important areas of parent-child relationships in the family setting. The educative impact on children of parents looking to their social and cosmic responsibilities beyond the family circle is certainly a matter he would have affirmed, and could, if one takes what he says in the context of his thought on education, in a sense be said to have implied.[33] But explicit statement on this is missing.

By way of explanation concerning these lacunae, it can be advanced that his life situation was simply not the sort that brought him into direct confrontation with the need for making explicit the import of his basic theory in the context of family life. Moreover, it is plausible to claim that here, as in the area of practical politics, his concern was for the underlying drift, the direction of the current, rather than the guidance of the ship itself.[34] So far as this concern goes, one could justifiably claim that the central emphases he did make, pertinent to the quality of marital union, mutual respect of marriage partners for each other's uniqueness, and the need for husband and wife to strive for the betterment of society in union with God—these emphases would stand out as of undeniable importance for the solution of a host of problems in family life, and as definitely significant fundamental guidelines.

*Celibacy and Sexuality.* If Teilhard's life situation was not such as to impel him to explore family morality in

jugal relationship rather than something distinctly sexual. The reason for so urging would be that the intimacy of thought and feeling exchange has long been considered characteristic of the friendship relation, apart from the sex of the parties involved.

33. See below, chap. 7, on education.
34. See below, chap. 6A.

depth, it was, on the other hand, one to encourage him to a much more probing analysis of the character of sexuality in celibate life. Evidence of this concern can be found throughout his wartime correspondence with his cousin, and in several essays dating from that period on.[35] To many schooled in the traditional asceticism of celibate life, his apparent advocacy of heterosexual emotional involvement, or at least his frank admission of its positive value, would seem erroneous on the grounds of too ready an assumption of the possibility or probable practicality of the requisite sublimation—to put the objection in minimal terms.

The problem is admittedly delicate and difficult. To the extent that he hardly ever wrote without having some intention of influencing ecclesial life, the charge of advocacy has some strength. But that is obviously not the central issue. Moreover, much of his thought on this problem was by way of tentative, exploratory analysis of his own experience and an attempt to reach a solution to what must have been a concrete personal problem, a solution that would be coherent and in accord with both his inner psychological life and a viable Christian understanding of celibate purity.

That there is definite psychological evidence to corroborate his principal observations about the value of affective feminine influence on personality development is

35. See above, n10, for examples from his correspondence with his cousin. An extensive study of "The Eternal Feminine" (1918), *WW*, 192-202, has been done by de Lubac, *Eternal Feminine*, referred to above in n6. It is undoubtedly the best work available as a base for a complete study of the text, although more as a background, explanatory, source study than as a critical analysis. Significant aspects explored are the genesis of the essay as seen in Teilhard's notes and letters, the liaison between his ideas on love and Platonic love theory, and the meaning of analogy and symbol in his thought. "L'évolution de la chasteté" (1934), *DA*, pp. 67-92, focuses specifically on the meaning and rationale of chastity, particularly in the sense of religious celibacy, in an evolutionary world. In view of Teilhard's emphasis here, and of the concern he manifests about the value of celibacy in his other writings, Rideau's concern seems excessive with regard to his thought being too heavily biased toward marriage rather than sufficiently appreciative of celibacy. See Emile Rideau, S.J., "La sexualité selon le Père Teilhard de Chardin," *Nouvelle revue théologique* 90 (1968): 173-90, esp. p. 187.

difficult to challenge.[36] Further, there seems to be evidence enough also that where the two parties are sufficiently mature and deeply committed to virginal life, with a firmly rooted career interest and profound love of God, affective ties can sublimate, and have been and are being sublimated much as Teilhard has described the process. However, on the other side of the ledger, there is evidence that this sublimation is, as a matter of fact, too difficult in practice for a great many people, despite a deep love of God, and that the maintenance of strong affective ties outside marriage has a deleterious rather than wholesome ultimate impact on personality growth within religious dedication.

What the evidence points to is that Teilhard was probably correct in his analysis of his own experience and in his belief that what worked for him would work for others in rather closely comparable situations. He was also correct to the extent that he presented his opinions on an enormously important problem tentatively, for analysis and evaluation, without zealously pleading for their uncritical universal acceptance. If, and to the extent that, he held them presently applicable on a large scale, he was probably wrong. Where he seems to have been most probably in error with regard to his understanding of the ultimate development of rather wide-

36. See above, n32, C. W. Freible, "Teilhard, Sexual Love, and Celibacy." Rideau, "La sexualité selon Père Teilhard de Chardin." p. 188, disagrees with Teilhard's position on the extent of the need for feminine influence for personality development. For a cautious, carefully worded, but forthright statement on the matter of male religious and relationships with women, see *Consensus Positions and Recommendations* by the Jesuit Provincials of the American Assistancy, from "The Santa Clara Conference," Santa Clara, California, August 1967, chap. 7, "Psychological Development," pp. 35-37. The American Provincials would seem to side more with Teilhard than Rideau, although they are careful not to affirm a categorically universal need in all circumstances. "In order for a man to love God, he must have that capacity to love which is developed by the experience of human love, and this experience is not always exhausted by one man's love for another. A man's love for a woman and her response can add dimensions in sensitivity that might not otherwise be attained" (p. 36). The cautionary remarks against excessive emotional absorption and for a truly prayerful union in God are likewise similar to Teilhard's ideas.

spread sublimation of sexual affectivity to the extent of by-passing physical sex, was in his projection of such sublimation into the married state—even in the distant future. Such a projection not only seems to run counter to the experience of conjugal intimacy, but also to be inconsistent with his own thinking on the spiritual power of matter, his own enthusiasm about being a priest ordained for war, and with the implications of the Christian tradition about the sacramentality of sex in marriage.[37]

*The Equality of Women.* To accuse Teilhard of blatant male chauvinism is as unfair as to call him a racist, or, for that matter, a fascist. On the strength of his basic premises on complementarity in human life, it can be asserted that he would, in the last analysis, have held a radical equality of personal worth, along with complementarity and hence nonidentity of functional roles. He says little about the question explicitly, but his encouragement of people concerned with the problem, such as his cousin, and especially Léontine Zanta, is well known.[38] On the basis of what he did say, however, he would be faulted by a good many with regard to his judgment about precisely what is the complementary role of woman. His analysis of mutual sexual influence is one-sided, understandably enough, simply because his immediate experience is masculine. He writes of the im-

---

37. See above, n30. For a view of Teilhard's thought on sexuality, corroborative of the position taken in the present study, see Robert T. Francoeur, "Conflict, Cooperation, and the Collectivization of Man," *Teilhard: Symposium*, pp. 226-44, esp. pp. 232-36, "Critique of Teilhard's Virginal Universe."

38. His comment in "The Mastery of the World and the Kingdom of God" (1916), *WW*, p. 77, about giving woman her generous place in the sun may seem condescending and perhaps, unconsciously, it was. But the fact remains that in his spiritual direction there is ample evidence of his respect for the priority and integrity of the person, regardless of sex. See Cuénot's sketch, cited above, n25, for comments of friends on this characteristic of Teilhard as a director. Also, his letters to his cousin, *MM*, pp. 38, 66-68, 69, 127, 128, 129, 137, 148, 256, and to Léontine Zanta, *LZ*, pp. 53 (his comments on feminism and the status of Chinese women he has observed), and 56, 60, 62-63 (on the need for women to organize and act in assertion of their rights).

pact of woman on man, but practically nothing of the impact of man on woman. Moreover, in what he does write, he conveys the definite impression that woman's proper role is that of catalyst, of indirect activator, but not really that of a principal direct agent in the work of the world. Ambiguity arises from what he says about this indirectness and the positive encouragement he gave to women who were active in more than an indirect way.[39]

To assign women that many would consider an inadequate complementary role as person in the active world, still recognizes essential feminine personhood. But the manner in which Teilhard speaks of woman as symbol raises the more serious objection that in so doing he has in effect negated women's personality.[40] There can be no question here about the fact of his symbolic language, in both his essays and personal retreat notes. Woman is spoken of as symbol of the world; the Virgin Mary is assigned a special symbolic role; the Church and his own religious order are viewed under feminine sym-

39. The text that can most easily be used against Teilhard is found in his World War I correspondence with his cousin, and is a clear statement of sympathy for a catalytic view of woman's role. See *MM*, p. 121. But it would seem unfair to lean too heavily on this single statement written in a letter from the Front in 1916, particularly in view of the views expressed and implied in his later correspondence with Léontine Zanta and his ever-mounting insistence on the significance of the person. See above, n38, especially the letter of January 25, 1924, *LZ*, pp. 62-63, on the need for women to organize. Implicit in these other materials is the right of women to be active participants, not merely "idealizing" catalysts. There is tension, obviously, between these two positions, which Teilhard seems to have been resolving, unconsciously, in favor of active participation. What enters in here also is how one interprets his use of woman as symbol. See below, n42. André Devaux, in his sympathetic essay, *Teilhard and Womanhood*, trans. Paul Joseph Oligny, O.F.M., and Michael D. Meilach, O.F.M., Deus Books (New York: Paulist Press, 1968), supports the catalytic interpretation of feminine complementarity with considerable enthusiasm. See esp. chap. 4, "Woman has a Special Mission," pp. 31-38, and chap. 5, "An Anthropology of Woman," pp. 41-50. Unfortunately, he does not even raise the question of the ambiguity referred to above. The essay is a good overall presentation of the position that can be formulated by stressing certain Teilhardian texts and ignoring what would seem to follow from such things such as the aforementioned encouragement he gave to people like Léontine Zanta.

40. Such is Dan Sullivan's contention in the *Continuum* article cited in n10 above, p. 256.

bolic aspects.[41] But, does depersonalization necessarily follow from this?

It can be granted that symbolization does generalize, abstract, and thus depersonalize by focusing attention on certain aspects or qualities rather than on personal uniqueness. This is true regardless of who is being considered as symbol, someone masculine or feminine. (Does it, however, follow that from transformation of a woman or "womankind" into a symbol, existing women are depersonalized in one's understanding of them and in one's relation with them? )

Whether this happens or not depends on how symbolic thought functions in individual consciousness. If one takes symbol to be in practice the same as stereotype, and if one's interpersonal relationships are based on stereotyped thinking rather than on the existing reality of the person one meets, then, obviously, symbol depersonalizes. But, if a symbol is a means of conveying the possibility of a profound general truth being concretized in a unique manner in this or that existing person, symbolization can be a guide, alerting one to a special facet of personality in others, and not depersonalize at all. It can help sensitize one to a quality or set of qualities realized in a particular person in his or her own incommunicable way. If symbol functions this way, then the value of symbolization as such is not in question, but the accuracy of the symbol must be closely scrutinized.

With regard to Teilhard and woman as symbol, two questions arise. When he speaks of woman in this way, is the content correct? In the concrete, does he think and

41. For women as symbol of the world, see, "The Spirit of the Earth" (1931), *HE*, p. 33. On the Virgin Mary, "The Eternal Feminine" (1918), *WW*, pp. 200-201. De Lubac's comments on this in his *Eternal Feminine*, pp. 118-19, are significant in that he reads the universal feminine as symbolic of Mary, rather than the other way around. See also, Retreat of 1944, *I*, 6th Day, where Teilhard speaks of the Church and the Society of Jesus as "Mother," and of "Mary—face and feminine influence of Christic evolution."

speak and deal with depersonalized feminine stereotypes? The evidence of his spiritual direction and the testimony of women who knew him would hardly validate the charge that he stereotyped them. One of his characteristic traits was, as has been seen, to accept people for who and what they were in themselves, and to encourage them to develop their unique selves. His writings bear out the same point. The content he gave to the meaning of woman as symbol, however, is seriously questioned, as mentioned above, on grounds of the dubiousness of assigning a merely catalytic role to women in the effort of cosmogenesis.[42]

## 2. SOCIETAL LOVE

*a. Meaning and Significance. The Motivational Problem.*

Concern about human solidarity in general was a lifelong preoccupation with Teilhard, to the extent that it could, in one way, be considered his overriding, controlling preoccupation as he pondered the future of mankind on earth. In other words, his concern about the nature and resolution of the problem of compressive socialization was precisely the same concern—viewed from another angle—as that of the process of human unification considered concretely in its present critical stage. The expression "societal love" does not itself appear in his reflections on the matter, but it is clear that when he speaks of "the human sense" he is thinking of a

42. Sullivan's claim that *The Mass on the World* is in fact a Black Mass ("Psycho Sexuality: The Teilhard Lacunae," *Continuum* 2 (1967): 256, 274-75), seems to rest on a confused inversion of the meaning of woman as symbol of the world with Teilhard's extension of the Eucharist to cosmic dimensions. What Sullivan almost seems to be saying is that the world is a symbol of woman, which is the exact opposite of Teilhard's thought. The Cosmic Christ never was for Teilhard the Cosmic Woman, however much this may lower him in the esteem of those who are concerned about the masculine bias in Christianity and Teilhard's apparent failure to correct it. Teilhard's sensitivity to this masculine bias, was, as a matter of fact, manifest in his fostering of the importance of Mary precisely as a corrective, and in his approaching God as a great maternal force. On this, see de Lubac, *Eternal Feminine*, pp. 125-26.

genuine love-bond knitting men together on a global human scale.[43]

As early as his World War I essays, he has expressed the fundamental idea which he will develop from different points of view in later writings. It is that human beings somehow have to discover the reality and implications of their *common* responsibility to transcend individual, family, national, and other group ties and *collaborate* in a common *human effort* to advance mankind.[44]

What he uses as the phenomenological base for what men *should*, ethically, strive for, is what he observes has been developing as a matter of *fact* through the emergence, from scientific research and reflection, of a

43. See, for example: "Cosmic Life" (1916), *WW*, pp. 41-42; "The Basis and Foundations of the Idea of Evolution" (1926), *VP*, pp. 137-41; "The Spirit of the Earth" (1931), *HE*, p. 36; "The Planetisation of Mankind" (1945), *FM*, pp. 135, 138; "Faith in Man" (1947), *FM*, pp. 191-92; and "Human Unanimisation" (1950), *FM*, pp. 282-88. Note particularly, "Sketch of a Personalistic Universe" (1936), *HE*, p. 72, "The physical structure of the universe is love. . . . It seems to me to reveal itself to our consciousness in three successive stages: in woman (for man), in society, in the All—by the sense of sex, of humanity and of the cosmos." Here Teilhard, granting a certain primacy of origin to the feminine, still seems clearly not to confuse sexual love with universal human love or the love of God. To say that a basic sensitivity to and for love is stimulated by feminine influence is one thing. To affirm that universal human love and love of God are sublimations or transformations of sexual feminine love is quite another. If one means that as there is process from one love to another the type of loving is transformed to another type of love, similar to the preceding but different from it, then the successive stages could be considered as sublimations and/or transformations. The problem in the terms seems to be that sublimation, at least, would seem to convey the perduring of the feminine on all levels, rather than the emergence of a uniquely different type of love, with resemblance to the feminine and sexual. On this, see de Lubac, *Eternal Feminine*, chap. 5, "The Transformations of the Feminine," pp. 85-108. De Lubac would seem to interpret Teilhard as holding to a pervasive continuation of a spiritualized feminine on the other levels. Precisely what this would be is not clear, particularly in view of the fact that many of those to whom universal human love is extended are simply not feminine, but very masculine indeed, and however Fatherly or "Motherly" one might conceive God to be, God is, in the last analysis, personal beyond sexuality. To simply invoke dynamic analogy here would not solve the problem, but it would help to clarify it, by enabling one to focus on the question of what precisely continues as fundamentally the same through the different types of love, and where discontinuity enters in to bring about the dissimilarity among the types. The common element seems to be personal communion; what differs on the levels is the particular character of what is attractive and what is shared.

44. See n10 above for World War I period seminal texts.

sense of time (duration, progress, evolution, development), and with it the awareness of the unity of mankind over the entire planet and the organic ties binding
men together in the task of furthering evolution. In an
essay written in the late twenties, he traces the development of this "human sense" at some length, with considerable stress on the obligation to recognize that has happened and is happening among serious thinkers, to embrace their insights, and to further them. What seems to
be the main problem standing in the way of developing
this needed universal human love is not that men refuse
to love each other as brothers, but that so many of them
simply do not see *that* or *how* they are linked together in
genuine, universal brotherhood. The resistance of official Catholicism to evolutionary theory he judges to be a
serious fault, which will take considerable effort to correct.[45]

He is quite convinced that if one is exposed properly
to the evidence, the understanding about the fact of a
common human bond will come. But how to interpret
this in terms of a genuine brotherly love, he admits, is
not easy. The problem he is grappling with, the age-old
problem of how to really love all of one's neighbors, first
seems to have surfaced for him in the form of the problem of universal charity he knew he should practice as a
Christian, and it shows up early in his World War I correspondence.[46] The human base for resolving the problem to his own satisfaction was to be clarified in his
phenomenological writings, mostly in the thirties and
forties.[47]

45. See "Le sens humain" (1929), *DA*, pp. 21-32, for the development of
this sense and one meaning Teilhard assigns to it; pp. 32-44, contain his reflections on its implications for Christianity.

46. See above, n10, texts on charity, latter part of the note.

47. Probably his most popularly known statement on human solidarity in
the task of constructing the world is found in "The Spirit of the Earth"
(1931), *HE*, p. 37. Curiously enough it occurs in the section on scientific research, rather than in the section on human unity immediately preceding, pp.
34-36. "*The age of nations has passed. Now, unless we wish to perish we must shake
off our old prejudices and build the earth.*" (The emphasis is Teilhard's.) More will
be seen on the constructive aspect of research in the following chapter. The

Perhaps his most analytic description of the root of the problem from the psychological point of view occurs in an essay from the late thirties.[48] He accepts as a fact that in general people tend to view "the other," at first contact, as a rival and an obstacle. Between human beings as human beings, there is simply no strong, initial attraction such as is experienced by two people who fall in love. The reason he assigns for the difference in the two situations is that awareness of human solidarity does not directly touch the persons involved, but something surrounding them, and that the impression of dislike for the other arises from the fact that this something is not perceived, or associated with the other person to make him appear attractive. In effect, this something surrounding all human beings is their organic tie to each other in the common evolutionary task. But to speak as he does about this tie as extrinsic to the person, immediately provokes the critical question, "How can one genuinely love another person for himself because of something which is not intrinsic to him and therefore not himself?"

It is true that this is the only essay in which he speaks so clearly in terms conveying such extrinsicism. Because of his emphasis on love generally as involving a "center-to-center" relationship, one could question how literally

other principal works from the thirties important here are: "Sketch of a Personalistic Universe" (1936), *HE*, section on "The Sense of Humanity," pp. 78-81; "The Phenomenon of Spirituality" (1937), *HE*, the division on "Personalization," pp. 100-104; "Human Energy" (1937), *HE*, the materials on "Organization of Total Human Energy: the Common Human Soul," pp. 131-37, and on "Totalization by Love of Individuals in Humanity," pp. 150-54; finally, the whole thrust of "Book Four: Survival," in *PM* (1940), pp. 237-90.

As de Solages has noted in his *Teilhard: étude*, pp. 30-31, the genesis of the noosphere and its destiny become a central theme for Teilhard in the forties and early fifties. Texts bearing on this point, as well as some already cited, and others relevant to the growth of human solidarity, will come up for discussion as the focus of the present study narrows to more specific factors contributing to human solidarity in the socialization process. See also, Barthélemy-Madaule, *La personne chez Teilhard*, "Le phénomene de socialisation," p. 144.

48. "Sketch of a Personalistic Universe" (1936), *HE*, p. 78.

his words should be taken when he speaks of something surrounding and not really *in* the person.[49]

But the problem is compounded as he continues his explanation of love beyond sexual love by gathering, and to some extent analyzing, the existing evidence for saying that there is such a thing as another, more general type of interhuman cohesion.

First he speaks of friendship, arising from a certain amount of individual attraction, but most of all from the awareness of a common interest. The background of his own World War I experience and his years in the Jesuit Order, as well as years of collaboration in scientific research, show here when he speaks of such a common interest deriving from the pursuit of an ideal, the defense of a cause, and the ups and downs of research. As friendship develops, he does not detect much permeation of one by the other but a sense of joint forward movement and progress in building a new world—the "something surrounding" mentioned above. Moreover, relationships of this sort are open to many people at once, not restricted by the limitations or exclusiveness of sexual love.

Unfortunately, the specter of extrinsicism rises again in his remarks on friendship, and in so doing flies in the teeth of much that has been written about the nature of the relationship over the centuries. This happens to be the only place where he says much about friendship as such, and if he is to be taken literally, he is denying what the experience of countless friendships in the history of the human race have affirmed: that two friends, regardless of sex and apart from any kind of affective exclusivity do in a sense permeate each other when a close and

49. The texts cited above about love as sympathy (n13; nn14, 15) certainly indicate a type of core-to-core permeation. See also "The Atomism of Spirit" (1941), *AE*, p. 47; "The Rise of the Other" (1942), *AE*, pp. 71-72; "Centrology" (1944), *AE*, pp. 118-20; and "The Compression of Mankind" (1953), *AE*, p. 345.

profound friendship develops.[50] Casual, occupational associations, which do not allow for sufficient exchange of
thoughts and feelings or sharing of experience to bring
about an I-Thou relationship do fit the description a-
bout which he writes. They can be warm, cordial, and
find their principal bond in a "something other" not
much more than a shared goal or common interest. But
his analysis would have been more satisfying if he had
distinguished these two levels. As it is, the only in-depth
interpersonal relationship he describes is the heterosexual, with its peculiar affectivity and closeness, its interchange of thoughts, feelings, hopes, and prayers.[51]

Two other aspects he ascribes to friendship, its openness to many and its base in a common interest, are generally admitted. But there is another, which he does not
bring up and is important. Since the attraction element
of friendship is usually at its outset based on the intellectual awareness of a common interest more than on spontaneous emotional attraction, the friendship bond is initiated, sustained, and developed more in a relatively
quiet, free, thought-through commitment and acceptance than is the sexual relationship. Certainly conjugal
love, to be truly human, needs this intellectual element,
but it also contains a note of emotional exclusivity peculiar to sexual attraction, whereas the emotional attraction
in friendship is of a different, more universalized type.

The core ideas of *common interest*, capable of being

50. What he says here runs contrary also to the tone of friendship that
emerges from even a cursory reading of his correspondence with his cousin
and Léontine Zanta, and from the testimony of other friends. See Cuénot's
remarks, above, n25. Particularly significant would seem to be the same author's comments about Teilhard's kindness and compassion in his *Teilhard-
Biography*, p. 384. Likewise note the impression conveyed by Lucile Swan,
"Memories and Letters," pp. 40-49, and George B. Barbour, *In the Field with
Teilhard de Chardin* (New York: Herder and Herder, 1965), p. 21, where he
makes particular reference to Teilhard's "immense gift for friendship." Not
all of these relationships, obviously, were on the same level, but there is no
hint in any of the accounts of merely cold, hard, impersonal functional ties.
This would not deny that Teilhard, like most human beings, had his reserved
and withdrawn moments.

51. See above, n32.

shared and developed *by many*, run through the remainder of his development about societal bonds in this essay.[52] Some human groups are rather loosely articulated, arising from artificial or forced links, and do not have much of a common soul. Others can stem from deep common reactions and lead to considerable intimacy. Thus, in one way or another, Teilhard sees a variety of large collective aggregates active or emerging on the contemporary scene: political movements, such as Communism, Fascism, Nazism; social groups of one sort or another; sporting and educational organizations, to mention some. None of these would he call primitive gregarious regressions. All are considered modern noospheric developments embodying a special homogeneity of consciousness tied with rapid intercommunication. In these he sees the possibility attendant upon compressive socialization, of reflective masses, as contrasted with the dispersive, migratory waves of groups like the Huns or Mongols; and in them also, evidence of the rise of attraction, rather than repulsion, within and among the elements of the noosphere.

To the objection that the movements he describes are, with all their ramifications of urban, industrial, and economic organization, mechanizing rather than personalizing, he answers on two levels. On the predictive descriptive level, he expresses renewed confidence in the consistency of the evolutionary process and avers that since evolution has not failed up to this point to personalize as it intensifies complexity, there is no reason to doubt that collectivization will ultimately "super-animate" and that machinelike rematerialization will not triumph, despite indications of its appearance. On the ethical, responsible level, he urges that one should accept the trend to more highly organized life, accepting in the

52. "Sketch of a Personalistic Universe" (1936), *HE*, pp. 79-80. See also, above, n43. The themes are present in these texts, even though in different language.

process whatever brings greater individual or collective personalization. Ultimately, what his ethical exhortation comes to is that people must learn to love each other to escape the ant hill.[53]

In his thought at this juncture, once again, the predictive descriptive, the argumentative, and the hortatory are mingled. For society to be personalized, he affirms, it must lead to Someone, or mechanization is inevitable. Societal love, the "sense of humanity," must be *love*, and love cannot exist on the scale required unless there is this personal Center of universal consciousness at the end and apex of evolutionary process. On the one hand he argues for the necessary existence of a supreme Personal Center, from what he accepts as the descriptive psychological base of the needs for the motivation of human choice. On the other, he urges the responsible, free, loving acceptance of this Center as the only way toward activating a truly personalized collectivity.

The problem of extrinsicism in universal human love arises again in the context of a union of many by common focus of love on a common Center. How does one really love another human being for himself by sharing with him a love of Someone else? Paradoxically enough, it is precisely in his language about an ultimate union with Omega that he does speak in terms that convey a real breaking down of barriers between persons and allow them to mingle by an interpersonal center-to-center relationship among themselves. It is curious that when speaking about the fulfillment of personality, earlier in the same essay in which he speaks so clearly of the extrinsic "something other," he does use language that in-

53. "Sketch of a Personalistic Universe" (1936), *HE*, pp. 80-81. See also, "Cosmic Life" (1916), *WW*, pp. 39-40; *PM* (1940), pp. 256-57; "The Grand Option" (1939), *FM*, pp. 52-57; "The Rise of the Other" (1942), *AE*, pp. 64-75. One could likewise consult the observations of Francois Russo, S.J., "La Socialisation selon Teilhard de Chardin," in *Teilhard de Chardin et la pensée catholique: Colloque de Venisse*, pp. 178-81, and Mathieu, *La pensée politique de Teilhard*, pp. 44-45, 181-82. Barthélemy-Madaule's *La personne chez Teilhard* could be viewed from one angle as a book-length study of this problem.

dicates real permeation and intimacy.[54] It is the universal, omnipresent immanence of the common Center, distinct from, yet closely bound to the human center, which gives some plausibility, on the theoretical level, to his argument. If Omega is *in* everyone, then everyone can be loved because of Omega in him, in somewhat the same way, no doubt, that speaking as a Christian he would refer to love of other human beings because of Christ "in" them. But whether one speaks phenomenologically or Christologically, the immanence of Omega or Christ in no way eliminates distinction or transcendence. In this fashion, the central issue is merely relocated, not resolved. What accentuates the difficulty is that on more than one occasion, as seen above, he conveys the impression, even apart from speaking of convergence on Omega,

54. "Sketch of a Personalistic Universe" (1936), *HE*, pp. 68-69. The paradox, however, becomes painfully clear within a space of a few lines, even in this passage. At one point Teilhard writes of "perfect mutual transparency," and shortly after speaks enigmatically of persons being "interior to one another in the interiority of the supreme center that envelops them. . . ." Robert O. Johann, *Building the Human* (New York: Herder and Herder, 1968), writing on "Teilhard's Personalized Universe," pp. 105-7, speaks of Teilhard's thought here as a central insight into the problem of how to conceive of a universal human love. He has some excellent clarifying remarks, but still fails to explain precisely wherein resides the *unique* lovableness of human persons because of their sharing in the love of God. To say "I cannot truly love God without extending my love to all those to whom He stands in the same mutual relation as He does to myself," seems, by speaking of the *same* mutual relation to be destructive of that very uniqueness essential to personality. However, there does seem to be a solution, derived from Teilhard's own concept of the organic ties and interrelationships existing among persons in his evolutionary universe, although, to my knowledge, he never spelled it out in precise terms. If, instead of speaking as a person merely as a center, one explicitly adds the note that a person is a *responsive* center, responsive to all others, including God-Omega, in a uniquely different yet complementary way, and goes on to stress that this particular characteristic of responsiveness to the host of other persons is a constituent element of a person as a center, then, since the network of interrelationships involving response for each person is obviously different for each, the uniqueness of *this* person, whoever he may be, is safeguarded, and when grasped, effects a complex of lovable traits shared by no other. In the sense that God loves all other persons, there is a sameness, truly enough, but the love is different also, because each person has uniquely different characteristics, particularly by virtue of a different relation-complex, rooted in varying talents, capacities, qualities, and powers. What is loved in another human person, and is capable of stimulating love, is not, then, simply that he or she shares the love of God, but that this love is shared in a peculiarly unique and incommunicable way.

that universal human love is somehow center to center.[55]
To so speak does not cohere with talk about love shown
to a person because of an aura or atmosphere around
him.

One possible explanation of how he could speak in
such incompatible terms is that when thinking from his
*generalized* phenomenological perspectives, he could see
that love had to be "center to center" in some way, on
any level, in order to be personal love. But when he actually set out to describe the *concrete* psychological
phenomena of certain relations and associations, the picture he saw was one that emerged couched in paracen-
tric rather than intercentric language. It, nevertheless,
remains surprising that one so insistent on coherence
did not spot the discrepancy. If he had, in speaking of
the concrete phenomena, taken the stand that he was
describing what *appeared* to be "something other" than
the person, and from there had gone on to assert, as
well as he might have done, that the core of personality
really includes certain organic ties to others, then the
difficulty of extrinsicism would not so readily have ari-
sen. But it could arise, of course, relocated, this time in
more subtle fashion, if one were to press the question as
to how such ties could enter into the constitutive character of personality itself.[56]

The approach taken in the analysis of Teilhard's
theory of societal or general universal human love has,
up to this point, attempted to work from his own basic
thinking, which has strong emphasis on interpersonal attraction and center-to-center attraction with a type of
core-to-core permeation. It has been followed because of
the emphasis appearing in the considerable body of texts
in which he addresses himself to the problem. In his
own thinking, it seems, he was aware of the elements of
continuity and discontinuity as he went from one type of

55. See above, nn18 and 49.
56. See above, n54.

love, the masculine-feminine affective dyadic, to another, that of the broader human, which for him included friendship. The source of the difficulties examined in the immediately preceding paragraphs would seem to be his tendency to overstress the continuities, with a certain blindness to important discontinuities as one proceeded into the operational consciousness of the other ways of human binding together.

If he had sharply and insistently called attention to the precise manner in which his dynamic analogical thought was progressing in this context, much of the perplexity noted above could have been forestalled. What this would have amounted to would have been a frank admission that, as soon as one goes beyond the limits of close "I-Thou" ties, be they sexual or friendly, there must, by sheer psychological necessity, be an attenuation of the core-to-core permeation of personal communion. This does not mean that there is no sense of sharing or communion, but that the root cause of this sense has shifted from intimate, person-to-person attraction and mutual self-revelation to the awareness of sharing in the omnipresent, immanent love of Omega, and with it the awareness of sharing in the challenging, inspiring, cosmic task of Omegalization, building the earth, striving to bring the conscious life of the noosphere to ever-fuller maturation.

If this would have to be called "extrinsicism," then one would simply have to be content with making the most of it, out of the psychological impossibility for secondary interpersonal relationships, at their outset at least, to bear the same *kind* of closeness as primary relationships. In certain contexts, conceivably, what would begin as mere consciousness of sharing a global human task, could develop, with sufficient contact and mutual interchange of ideas and feelings, into a high and close level of friendship. On this level, the working toward this type of close communion would proceed from Omega consciousness to interpersonal human consciousness. On the other hand, the path from heterosexual intimacy has been seen, in order to escape the confines of an "egoism of two," or a "Universe of two," as a path outward toward Omega and Omegalization for full personalization.[57] The upshot would be a legitimate analogical connection between the types of loving, because of the sufficient similarity of sharing an elemental reality of communion, genuinely binding people together in conscious unity. But the initiating and continuing impulse on a universal level would be different, as well as the pitch of intensity in the experience of oneness.

### b. The Problem of Societal Love and Friendship

Where Teilhard's analysis is most vulnerable is in his failure to set friendship love and generalized human love in different categories. It is possible to get involved in semantic quibbles here, but on the basis of general experience of human relationships it would seem preferable to see the love of friendship, on grounds of warmth and intimacy, situated more closely to sexual love, yet as a type of loving distinct from it. Friendship then would, in a sense, be a type of loving intermediate between sexual love and generalized human, societal love. Because of the intimacy factor, it would be associated with the sexual. Because of its openness to many, it would look to the societal. Friendship would differ from societal love in that it is psychologically impossible to achieve, apart from some frequency of contact, the closeness of friendship, despite the possibility, on the basis of simple awareness of common human sharing, of being kind, considerate, and well-disposed to all. Sexual love and friendship love would share a common "I-Thou" aspect. Societal love, then, would rank similarly as a type of love, but with an "I-You" aspect, characterized by personal well-wishing, which would differentiate it from the impersonal "I-It."

57. See above, D (1).

### 3. cosmic love

*a. Fundamental Characteristics*

Working from the nuclear ideas of affinity and attraction, Teilhard finds yet one more variety of love drawing the human person out of himself into communion. He calls it "the cosmic sense," and describes it, initially, as "the more or less confused affinity that binds us psychologically to the All [au Tout] which envelops us." Evidence of its existence he traces back to the feelings experienced by primordial man when first he stood contemplative before the impressive vastness of forest, sea, and stars. How to place this experience psychologically, though, is not a simple task. For some, it is hardly recognized, or taken as an aberrant, perhaps embryonic form of spiritual energy. Others recognize it but see little value in it, relegating it to the level of some residual animal feeling. Still others are frightened by it, since it seems to overwhelm by its call to dissolve oneself in the infinite depths of the cosmic ocean. However, for Teilhard it falls quite easily into place in a personalistic universe:

> it represents the more or less obscure consciousness in each one of us of the reflective unity in which he is added to all the rest.[58]

What he seems to be saying here is that this "reflective unity" is a special kind of "something other" associated with the human person. But it is not perceived here as uniting one merely with other human beings. Rather, union is achieved in this context with the manifold and variegated spectrum of realities in the entire universe. Hence it embraces, in some way, all previously considered love-ties, and adds a multifaceted set of cosmic dimensions.

How can this meaning be further refined? As a

58. "Sketch of a Personalistic Universe" (1936), *HE*, p. 82.

physico-moral magnitude (because it is conscious,
person-based) it is capable of growth and development.
Again one confronts an aspect coherent with a converging universe but difficult to explain in one that is dis-
persing and disintegrating. As consciousness of a universal Center intensifies, this sense becomes more and more
a fundamental element in human psychology. The infinite range of appealing elements in the cosmos is increasingly seen as radiating a common if variously
analogized energy from a common source and converging on this common center. As awareness of this sort
grows, centration takes place. The element centers itself,
in harmony with all other centers, on the ultimate
Center of the supreme personality. What this last sentence seems to mean, when translated from its centric
terminology, is that the conscious person, in harmony
with other conscious persons, becomes aware of his own
internal identity and unity as a self by recognizing and
activating his capacity for responding in love to these
other conscious persons on a human level, but on a
transformed human level, lifted to a higher plane by
awareness that all share the common love of Omega and
can and should respond to Him, as all together strive to
develop the universe further.[59]

Unification of human love in Omega love has already
been introduced on the levels of sexual and societal love.
What happens here, with the addition of the cosmic context, is that the cosmic sense as described by Teilhard,
which in its initial manifestations could seem to be a
vague if profound and deeply stirring impersonal emotion, is found as it assumes greater clarity in human consciousness to emerge as an eminently personal love. The
constant, immanent presence of Omega, attracting, on a
variety of complex and inter-connecting levels, all elements to Himself, is known to be conscious, loving, u-
nique, complementary to the realities of the elements, and

59. "Sketch of a Personalistic Universe" (1936), *HE*, pp. 82-83.

personal. For Teilhard, because of the intimate connection of all below-personal elements and all personal elements with the Supreme Personal Center, it is therefore possible to *love the universe* in a personal way. The basic structural law of cosmogenesis, the law of differentiating union, maintains the integrity and distinction of those united in love. In this way, the best of man's pantheist tendencies and intuitions are satisfied at the same time he is provided with the fundamental law of moral perfection, the law of a truly universal love, now expanded to the depth and breadth of the cosmos itself.[60]

*b. Critique. The Problem of a Personal Love for the Cosmos*

What Teilhard is describing here seems to be a phenomenological version of his oft-repeated Christological theme about loving Jesus as a World, with all its implications regarding Pauline pleroma texts and their subsequent Patristic interpretation—and later neglect in ecclesial thought. However he manages to phrase it, there will always be, in many minds, extreme difficulty in grasping how one can love stars, water, rocks, trees, even the friendliest of animals with a genuinely personal love. To appreciate their beauty, to stand in awe before the vastness of the skies, to feel a genuine warmth toward a pet animal of any sort—the authenticity of these experiences is not in question. Nor is it difficult for many to see these elements of the universe as gifts of God, reflecting his goodness, power, and beauty, and in many ways expressive of his person and personal love. To take Teilhard literally in his statements about loving the cosmos personally, or loving evolution in the same manner, would seem to run counter to his basic understanding of personal love.[61] It would also go against other important

60. "Sketch of a Personalistic Universe" (1936), *HE*, pp. 83-84.
61. Clearly the underlying problem emerging from this text, which is only one sample of many by Teilhard on the same basic idea, is the problem he endeavored to resolve, from World War I on, with his own clarifications of the meaning of pantheism. The following are some significant representative texts about the pantheist problem in his writings: "Cosmic Life" (1916), *WW*, pp.

statements that make it quite clear that the main thrust of his love goes beyond the attractiveness of things to God creatively immanent in them.[62] The critical problem, ultimately, would not seem to be maintenance of a personal love of God and the avoidance of pantheism, but rather what kind of love is extended to the creature and for what specific motive. So far as the infrahuman cosmos is concerned, the problem is not a serious one, theoretically. Clearly the nonpersonal elements of the universe, whatever their shape or form, are not capable of giving or responding to personal love. A personal love of the cosmos in its infrahuman elements must, therefore, be analogous to, and hence not on the same level as, personal love. To the extent that it is personal, it is directed to God immanent in the cosmos, yet transcendent. When the notion of cosmic love is taken to include other human persons, either in sexual love or in general human love, it would be said to include all that has been seen with regard to these analogous levels of love, but add the multidimensional breadth and depth arising from considering them in the context of their extraordinarily rich and manfold organic bonds to the entirety of the Omegalizing cosmos. Men and women, all human persons, would be seen as related not only to each other and Omega, but to everything else that ever was or would be, from the smallest, submicroscopic particle to the farthest, yet-unknown galaxies, with their own stars and planets.

28-32; "Christ in Matter" (1916), *HU*, p. 53; "Pantheism and Christianity" (1923), *CE*, pp. 56-75; "My Universe" (1924), *SC*, p. 59; *DM* (1927), p. 116; "Le coeur de la matière" (1950), *I*, pp. 7-8. For comments on the problem and other texts, see Mooney, *Mystery of Christ*, pp. 191-92, 277-78; Rideau, *Teilhard: Guide*, pp. 149-50, 499-501; de Solages, *Teilhard: étude*, pp. 291-95; Claude Cuénot, *Nouveau lexique Teilhard de Chardin* (Paris: Éditions du Seuil, 1968), pp. 145-55 (a valuable section differentiating the various types of pantheism about which Teilhard wrote). The treatment by d'Ouince, *Teilhard: la pensée chrétienne*, pp. 138-43, is particularly significant for the present context in that he examines the matter in the setting of his chapter on "Sens cosmique et sens Christique."

62. See "My Universe" (1924), *SC*, pp. 73-78, where he is talking about the mystical milieu and communion. "Preadhesion" to God in love of everything else is central to his thought here. Also, *DM* (1927), pp. 72-73.

## E. Obstacles to Love

### 1. TEILHARD'S APPROACH

The ethical implications of all that has been seen thus far about the nature and varieties of love are not too difficult to draw out in general, provided that one accepts the theory Teilhard presents. The fundamental implication is that one must do all one can to grow in authentic love in accord with the uniqueness of one's temperament and life-situation, and to foster this growth in love among those with whom one lives.

Teilhard was well aware that this development and growth in love was no simple matter. If it is accurate to say of Teilhardian love that in the last analysis it consists in the personal completion through interpersonal communion of human persons with each other through convergence in a common love of Omega as the supreme immanent yet transcendent Person, then the radical blockage to love is going to be found in whatever tends to isolate one person from another. But in view of the fundamentally dynamic character of Teilhardian love, it must be kept in mind that this communion is never the communion of more or less static embrace, or its equivalent in an enduring state of harmonious interpersonal equilibrium. At root it is the communion of persons striving and struggling together in love to build. Consequently, at whatever level one looks at love, be it sexual, universal-human, or cosmic, there are two possible underlying inhibiting forces—not only those which lock the person in on himself, but also those which take away his zest for constructive effort. Ultimately what inhibits love for Teilhard is not merely what isolates, but what isolates and simultaneously deactivates.

Although the basic concepts can be found in his earliest writing, perhaps the clearest formulation of his thought on the fundamentals of the problem is contained in an essay from the late forties where he is concerned with what he describes as counter-evolution.[63] Despite the fact that the term *love* appears very little in this piece, it is quite clear that concern about it pervades the whole. What he focuses on explicitly is the notion of fear, fear in confrontation with the immensity of the material universe, its imprisoning power, despite its size, and its hostility. He writes also of fear of the immensity, the opacity, and the impersonality of the human world. Before these threats, there is, he feels, the genuine risk of the human person's turning inward on himself in panic and losing heart, both as to looking outward to others and toward their common task.

In an earlier essay, from the thirties, Teilhard writes more in detail from the angle of the difficulties, or "pains" of personalization.[64] Above all, what must be fought is the everpresent drag toward fragmentation, toward plurality. In this context he enumerates a list of obstacles to love that would apply alike to heterosexual

63. For an early indication of isolation and deactivation inhibiting human development, see "Cosmic Life" (1916), *WW*, pp. 29-31. Here he is writing about "The Temptation of Matter," and the drift toward self-centered, sluggish passivity that he has observed takes place by absorption of the wrong sort in the material universe, an absorption that leads to a more or less static self-complacency, stultifying the desire for personal growth. Also see letter of January 1, 1917, *MM*, p. 163, where he describes the "pain of isolation" with its numbing immobilization, and "The Struggle Against the Multitude" (1917), *WW*, pp. 98-102, where he discusses "The Evil of the Multitude," and in so doing, this fragmenting, pluralizing, isolating pain. What he says about sin here, pp. 102-3, will be taken up below shortly. On counter-evolution, see "A Phenomenon of Counter-Evolution in Human Biology: or the Existential Fear" (1949), *AE*, pp. 183-95. A brief statement of the same basic themes can be found in *PM* (1940), pp. 226-29, where he discusses "Modern Disquiet" under the heading "The Problem of Action." What should be noted here is that when Teilhard speaks of fear, and also of boredom, the psychological situation he is describing has important resemblances to both *anomie* and *alienation*, as well as to *angst*, all of which can and do have a crushing, immobilizing, self-limiting impact on human growth. Obviously, Teilhard was approaching the problem from a different over-arching world view from that of other authors, but this fact should not obscure a basic underlying similarity. If this had been grasped, a critic like Ferkiss would hardly have been so severely negative in his judgment about Teilhard's opinion that boredom is the real "public enemy number one." See Victor C. Ferkiss, *Technological Man*, Mentor Books (New York: New American Library, 1969), pp. 88-89.

64. "Sketch of a Personalistic Universe" (1936), *HE*, pp. 84-88. See also "Spirit of the Earth" (1931), *HE*, p. 35, and *DM* (1927), p. 145.

and friendly love. He speaks of the chances of compatible persons simply never meeting at all, of the difficulty of maintaining contacts even if they do meet, of the mazes in which people hear but cannot find each other, of the inevitable barrier even in a close union to completeness this side of final consummation, and of the many inevitable misunderstandings and estrangements that take place.

In overcoming obstacles of the sort he has just described there is the added difficulty of summoning up the will to struggle, to face the blunt fact of the need for effort to achieve union, to accept the pain of change, renunciation, and self-giving.

When he probes from another angle, he finds the age-old problem of concupiscence of the flesh and its associate, concupiscence of the mind, robbing men of interior unity, and hence true self-love, along with the capacity for loving others.[65] This last can ultimately lead to several manifestations of barriers to love. Even though not panicking and running in fear, men can become so self-centered that they retreat to themselves and the fruit of their own conquests in complacent arrogance. Or their arrogance can express itself in dominance, with contempt for one's associates. Another attraction to isolation is found in a kind of mystique of separation, of simple withdrawal, which even though not characterized by any sense of Promethean superiority, would nonetheless effectively cut a person off from fellow human beings.[66]

That unchecked human aggression in its most brutal form, war, was one of the major roadblocks to the unification of the earth through a universal human love, was clear to Teilhard and he was concerned about the problem. What he had to say about aggression and its subli-

65. "Struggle against the Multitude" (1917), *WW*, pp. 102-3. See above, n63.
66. See "The Grand Option" (1934), *FM*, pp. 45-49.

mation is more than can be sketched here and will occupy a good part of the next chapter.

Associated with war as an obstacle to love would also be the use of coercive force to effect unity in society. Teilhard was definite in holding that love could develop only where men were free, as much as possible, from coercion, although, as will be seen, he did hold it to be necessary at times and hence not essentially incompatible with love.[67]

## 2. CRITIQUE: MISSING ELEMENTS

In all of what has just been examined or indicated, it can be noted that while the theological language of sin has been absent for the most part, the realities of human sinful existence, weakness, and finitude are very much present. Texts that provide the basis for the preceding synthesis would, one hopes, at least serve to mitigate, if they could not put to rest, charges about Teilhard's "naive optimism" concerning evil in human life.

However, despite the fact that it can hardly be said that Teilhard was ignorant of the problem of evil, his analysis of obstacles to love lacks, among other things, specific considerations of the all-important notion of refusal to forgive. To phrase that concept positively, one could say that the creative thrust of *merciful* love toward the building of society has been left out. While, in a sense, the notion of repentance is included in the concept of resistance to evil in oneself, as he speaks of it in *The Divine Milieu*, still, forgiveness could be said to come

67. See *MM*, pp. 108-9, letter of July 10, 1916, and pp. 128-29, letter of September 18, 1916. In the first letter Teilhard acknowledges, surprisingly enough, the practical need of even such things as the Roman Index. See also, "The Directions and Conditions of the Future" (1948), *FM*, p. 235, and "The Essence of the Democratic Idea" (1949), *FM*, pp. 240-43. In this last essay he speaks of the need for "a judicious mixture of *laissez-faire* and firmness," in discussing the problem of freedom in society. (This point will be taken up again, specifically in chaps. 6 and 7 in the context of Teilhard's political and educational thought.)

into his thinking only to the extent that it would be implicit in both what he has to say about the value and need of gentleness, and in the manner in which in his own life he proved himself to be both gentle and forgiving.[68]

The lack is a serious one, and does give strength to the criticism that despite Teilhard's awareness of the reality of evil, his analysis is missing in desired depth, particularly in this sector, with all of its important implications for his theological thought regarding redemption.

When one considers the manifold tensions in society throughout history, the need for a spirit of willingness not only to admit one's own weakness and selfishness, but to accept these same qualities in others and to extend genuine forgiveness in a desire for conciliation and reconciliation stands out as of prime importance. It is doubtful that Teilhard, if faced bluntly with this ques-

---

68. See *DM*, 1926-27, "Our Struggle with God against Evil," pp. 83-84, and especially, "True Resignation," pp. 90-93. One of the few texts where Teilhard specifically refers to repentance as such is found p. 92, n5. Implicitly, the concept is present in the numerous texts where he talks of the need to exert effort to change in order to love actively. See above, n63, and also early texts in *DM*, pp. 70-72, where he talks of detachment in action. Although he does not say so in so many words, the texts clearly imply that one recognize false values that may be held, reject them effectively, and turn to personal, active love of Christ—which is what repentance and metanoia are all about. Teilhard's personal kindness, gentleness, and compassion have been clearly established. See Cuénot, *Teilhard-Biography*, pp. 384-85. Also, by the same author, "Teilhard de Chardin: Sketch for a Portrait," *The Teilhard Review* 6, no. 1 (Summer 1971): 4, 7. Teilhard does not have much to say about gentleness, but note, for one example, his letter of May 28, 1915, *MM*, p. 55. Why he never expanded on the topic, in view of the importance he obviously gave to it in his own life, is something of a mystery. One could argue that his insistent plea for sympathy, understanding, and love among men amounts to a strong implicit plea for gentleness—and forgiveness—which would be true. But explicit development of the subject could have forestalled bothersome objections about his insensitivity and ignorance of the significance of an essential redemptive element. Against the backdrop of the preceding, it would seem that one should not take literally, or should interpret accordingly, his remarks in "Christology and Evolution" (1933), *CE*, p. 91, " 'There has been too much talk of lambs. Give the lions a chance.' Too much gentleness and not enough force. Those symbols are a fair summary of my feelings and my theme, as I turn to the question of readjusting the gospel teaching to the modern world." "Gentleness" here is best read as "passivity" and "force" as "energetic drive to action." To give the terms a Nietzschean interpretation would run counter to both Teilhard's other thinking in this area as well as the interpretation of his thought to be derived from his life.

tion, would have denied its significance. But the fact is that he never did come openly to grips with it. Despite his meditations on the positive value of suffering, he did not write anything comparable about the positive value of forgiveness, and the enormous creativity, warmth, and intensity of mutual love-energy generated by forgiving love among human beings, both by the act of forgiving and by its acceptance.

What helps to explain his neglect of forgiveness would seem to be his aloofness from depth-probing into the mystery of evil as an important human phenomenon worthy of close analysis. Evil as inertia, fear, loneliness, isolation, separateness—these types of human evil, clearly enough, Teilhard did examine. But human evil as hatred, enmity, lying, and mendacity—all the forms of human evil as *malevolence* toward others—these types get no more than passing explicit mention, or, at the most, indirect, and even then not lengthy, consideration, as in his thought on the need to sublimate aggression.[69] Teilhard was so concerned with certain types of interior psychological and moral inhibitors of constructive action, that he seems to have been blinded to the destructive force of what human will can do when, through weakness or deliberate malice, it definitely turns against other human persons—and God. Because of this major lacuna in his treatment of human evil, or sinfulness, I would claim that his ethical thought has serious limitations, as it

69. The next chapter will go into Teilhard's thought on aggressivity. To my knowledge, hatred as an obstacle to human unification is mentioned explicitly only twice in his essays, and one of these times the passing reference is relegated to a footnote. See "The Struggle against the Multitude" (1917), *WW*, p. 105, and "The Human Rebound of Evolution" (1947), *FM*, p. 203, n1. He does speak of hatred in "Life and the Planets" (1946), *FM*, p. 119, but only to dismiss it as yielding to love. The same footnote indicated above, *FM*, p. 203, n1, contains his sole observation on the lie as an obstacle to noospheric union, although he does, in his correspondence, condemn Soviet deceitfulness. See letter of May 29, 1952, *LT*, p. 328. His lack of emphasis on mendacity as an obstacle to human unity is an obviously serious gap, and comes more sharply into focus when one contrasts his failure to emphasize it with the outspoken condemnation by the late Jewish theologian, Abraham Joshua Heschel. Cf. the television interview of Heschel by Carl Stern, NBC network, February 25, 1973.

stands in writing, for a large bloc of humanity. True, he seems to have been writing most of the time for there whom he judged to be men of good will, for whom the limitations would not be so great.[70] But the problem remains, even for these, since men of good will must always deal with the reality of living among men of bad will, and must take serious heed of how to cope with them, if they are to develop a comprehensive ethical stance.

Further, in a critical direction, one may ask if and to what extent the immediacy of contact about which Teilhard speaks in relation to love is all that necessary, or, in the context in which it has been seen, whether absence of contact is that much of an obstacle.

The answer depends both on what kind of love one is talking about and on what kind of contact. The experience of many cannot be denied, that a certain type of affective love, sexual or friendly, attenuates with physical absence. But there are also situations—and Teilhard in writing to his cousin speaks of one such—in which correspondence can maintain and increase such a bond.[71] Along with the divisive force of excessive self-concern, or sinfulness, the major obstacle to universal human love, and, on the theological plane, to universal charity, seems to lie more in the lack of a solid, firmly grasped

70. For what is perhaps the clearest statement of the type of reader Teilhard had in mind, and his own explanation of why he does not stress sinfulness, see *DM* (1927), p. 44. While one could say that, *DM* was a particular work clearly written for dedicated people of good will, searching for meaning in their lives, this text can be taken as typical of Teilhard's approach throughout. The human milieu with which he found himself most constantly involved, whether scientific or religious, seems to have been of this cast of mind. Teilhard was concerned with what he thought were their most immediate problems of interior motivation. But this concern still would not, as I see it, excuse him from ignoring the malevolence factor.

71. Teilhard saw advantages, at times, to correspondence over conversation. See letter of April 14, 1919, *MM*, p. 290, ". . . it's good for friends to be separated sometimes; it makes them collect and clarify what they have to say to one another, and forces them to put it into words. I told you that, with you away, Paris rather gives me the impression of being empty. What makes up for this, I think, is that affection then becomes more concentrated and spiritualized. That's why letters have something that conversation can't be a substitute for."

conviction about the dignity of every human person as a
fellow-worker in building either the earth or the Body of
Christ, than in the lack of close association.

There seems to be adequate enough empirical evidence that, once a solid grasp of shared task and ideals
is developed that would involve a kind of a priori acceptance of *whoever* is, so to speak, on the same team, it is
possible for a real respect and genuine feeling of solidarity to be at work effectively. This can be found in the
type of esprit de corps in certain organizations, particularly groups with an intensive formation in a common
spirit, and, quite patently, in good humanists and Christians alike, the world over, who have profoundly medi-
tated upon and assimilated the tenets pertinent to human union on rational or intuitive grounds alone, or on
grounds that add the dimension of faith in Christ to
fundamental human insights. When people of such mentality meet *anyone*, a sense of respect, caring, and warmth
can be experienced, even if they have never met before,
or may, for that matter, never meet again, or only casu-
ally. While not on so high a level of intensity as close
friendships, such a relationship could be described as a
type of genuine center-to-center encounter and acceptance, based on conviction of real personal worth.[72]

The prime obstacle to cosmic love would again seem
to be located in the area of conviction, insight, and understanding, which could be hampered for want of a
certain type of contact. Here the problem has in part to
do with affective response to natural beauty and power,
which can be a serious problem for thoroughly ur-
banized human beings, who are cut off in many instances from vital contact with those elements of

72. For an excellent treatment of this basic problem, which has a number
of striking resonances with Teilhard's thought, as well as several valuable
clarifications, see Mary Perkins Ryan and John Julian Ryan, *Love and Sexuality:
A Christian Approach*, Image Books (Garden City, N.Y.: Doubleday and Co.,
Inc., 1969) pp. 108-121, chap. 6, "Loving One Another in Truth." In the
same work, p. 185, for a Marxist view, see the quotation from Roger Garaudy,
*From Anathema to Dialogue* (New York: Herder and Herder, 1966), pp. 123-24.

stimulus to affectivity about the universe which are central to the experience Teilhard describes. This is one of the problems of technologized living that Teilhard ignored, probably because, in his own experience, travel, work, and vacation periods did not deprive him of this type of closeness to nature. Even with it, though, the other serious problem of the apparent impersonality, or nonpersonality, of the universe remains. As was seen above, there is a difficulty, not with regard to the existence of a personal God immanent in the universe, although that is obviously a block for many, but with regard to identifying love of God present in all things with love of the things themselves.

A further obstacle to cosmic love directed to a personal Omega-God would be the counterpart, in this relationship, of hatred and enmity on the human personal level. The existence of this is recognized in what Teilhard has to say about the Faustian and Promethean spirit, as well as acceptance of the reality of hell. But no analysis in depth ever appears in his writings.[73] Moreover, his neglect to explore this aspect of human sinfulness, both in human and divine interpersonal relations, helps to explain why next to nothing appears in his writings on the subject of repentance and forgiveness. Failure to attend closely to the intimate nature and implications of human malice would, understandably enough, lead to neglect of what is required to counteract and heal the wounds it causes.

## F. Love and Justice

Teilhard's repugnance to an over-juridical approach to morality may well be the best explanation why the vo-

73. Regarding the Promethean and Faustian spirit, see "Faith in Man" (1947), FM, pp. 188-89. On hell, see "Cosmic Life" (1916), WW, pp. 68-69; DM (1927), pp. 146-49; "Introduction to the Christian Life" (1944), CE, pp. 164-65. In none of these passages does Teilhard explicitly consider the factor of personal hatred.

cabulary of justice receives so little attention in his writings.[74] In only one essay does he go into the problem of the rights of man as such. Discussion among ethical theorists about the relation between love and justice has been spirited, complicated, and with precious little satisfactory resolution.[75] Limitations of the present study preclude any lengthy correlation of Teilhard's thought with this debate, but some observations are in order.

Teilhard does not write about justice as such. He does not raise the question as to whether the whole of ethical reality should be taken under the umbrella of love, or whether one should devote special concern to justice apart from love. Since he does not go into this particular problem, one is faced again with a gap in his ethical thought, and is forced to attempt a correlation of what he did say with an issue he never faced directly.

Since, of the two concepts, the only one he does write about is love, and since he writes extensively about it, the temptation is real to put him in the category of "love monist."[76] If categorization is dependent upon such criteria, he could be put there, but as a love monist with some important qualifying characteristics. Teilhard is far too insistent about the need for careful analysis and research in working out the expression and organization of love to warrant condemnation on the grounds of gross affective oversimplification. He can be criticized, it is true, for not having more clearly brought out the connection between his thinking on love and research in this particular ethical context. But the fact of the con-

74. See above, chap. 3C and E regarding Teilhard's thought on juridicalism in morality.
75. A good short study of the complexity of the problem relating the two can be found in Robert Johann, S.J. "Love and Justice," in *Ethics and Society*, ed. Richard T. De George, Anchor Books (Garden City, N.Y.: Doubleday and Co., Inc., 1966), pp. 25-47. Johann's approach, through an analysis of the implication of creative responsibility, manifests a definite similarity with Teilhard's thought.
76. See James M. Gustafson, "Love Monism: How does Love Reign?" in *Storm Over Ethics* (Philadelphia: United Church Press, 1967), pp. 26-37, and Joseph Fletcher's response in "Situation Ethics Under Fire" (same vol.) pp. 157-60.

nection can be established, not only from his inclusion of analysis in the working of his moral principles, but also from the implications of his thinking on responsibility and responsible love, on the very foundations of moral obligation and duty. Love is to be exercised in accord with the framework of discernible, organic ties binding men together in the evolutionary task. It is these organic ties, established by research, that would supply the objective context called for by the theoreticians of justice.[77] In writing about these ties, he would seem, if one is to judge him in all fairness and accuracy, to be writing about what men *owe* to each other, about what is *due*, in the light of objective relations in the vast and complex network of noospheric functions and structures.

Consequently, to ask the question whether there is any place for justice in Teilhard's system, or whether justice is really reduced to love, can be answered differently, depending on what principles of reduction one is invoking. If one insists on using the more strictly verbal criteria, and looks mainly to the fact that Teilhard writes much about love, and incorporates his thinking on duty, obligation, and human rights in a context of love, with no mention of justice or the problem of the relation of love to justice, then one would have to say that by inclusion, although not by critical exclusion, Teilhard does "reduce" justice to an expression of love. On the other hand, if one bears in mind that Teilhard does devote attention to the foundations of justice—the organic ties binding persons to each other as the basis for what is due them by right—then one could say that he speaks of the matter of justice as something distinguishable from love, although he never puts down the clarifications about the problem that many ethicists would like to see.

77. See, for example, Thomas E. Davitt, *Ethics in the Situation* (New York: Appleton-Century-Crofts, 1970), pp. 89-90. For Teilhard's thought on human rights, see his "Some Reflections on the Rights of Man" (1947), *FM*, pp. 193-95. For his thinking on the organic character of human responsibility, see especially "The Evolution of Responsibility in the World" (1950), *AE*, pp. 207-14, also the treatment of the question in the preceding chapter above.

5

# The Organization
# of Spiritualized Energy:
# (a) Beyond Aggressive War
# to Conquest by Research

## A. Aggression in Teilhard's Thinking
on Spiritualized Energy

Teilhard's moral stance, with its emphasis on putting out sustained effort to overcome obstacles in the way of mankind's development toward higher forms of personalization, has a definite element of aggression contained in it. What to do about the relationship between love and aggression has been a perennial problem for ethicists and has surfaced with considerable impact in the psychological realm also, as the well-known split between Freud and Adler will attest.

If one takes aggression in the broad fundamental sense of an affective drive against what is considered to be an obstacle in the path of desired movement, analysis reveals three basic types of obstacles, with correspondingly different implications for the ethics of aggression in an evolutionary universe.

181

First, one can view the material world, with its opaqueness to human understanding and its resistance to human control, as presenting a challenge to human inquiry and creative, mastering manipulation. Included here would be the automatic processes of the human psyche, below the conscious level of responsible control, as well as all that would go into the realms of biological process (Teilhard's sphere of incorporated human energy) and whatever would be involved in scientific, technological mastery of the physical, chemical, and organic world necessary for human development (Teilhard's sphere of controlled energy). As will be seen shortly, much of what Teilhard has to say about research pertains to this sector.

With regard to this type of obstacle to human progress, the ethical implications of Teilhard's thinking on *dynamic* charity and the component of hope locked into his theorizing on love are important. What is at the core of Teilhard's notion of dynamic love is a concept of love-motivated *struggle* and effort to develop the material and human potential of the universe through ceaseless courageous striving against all obstacles in one's path.[1] But involved in this concept is his understanding of the awareness of sharing in this struggle as itself the important foundation for a universal human love.

Where hope enters into this picture is precisely by way of providing strong and solid motivation that the effort needed in the struggle can succeed. Problems attendant

---

1. See texts cited above, chap. 4, n10, for the roots in his earliest writings of this dynamic quality of charity. Relevant material from later essays can be found in "My Universe" (1924), *SC*, p. 68; *DM* (1927), pp. 142-46; "Le sens humain" (1929), *DA*, p. 39; "Christology and Evolution" (1933), *CE*, p. 92; "Human Energy" (1937), *HE*, pp. 145-56 (this is the section on love as a higher form of energy); *PM* (1940), pp. 264-67; "The Atomism of Spirit" (1941), *AE*, pp. 52, 53; "The New Spirit" (1942), *FM*, pp. 93-96; "Super-Humanity, Super-Christ, Super-Charity" (1943), *SC*, p. 169; "Introduction to the Christian Life" (1944), *CE*, pp. 152-156; "Christianity and Evolution" (1945), *CE*, pp. 184-85 (*dynamized* charity), "Comment je vois" (1948), *DA*, pp. 218-19; and "Le Christique" (1955), *I*, pp. 7, 12. In the last essays, after 1945, he uses a more generalized vocabulary than in those of the preceding decade, but the direction of thought is unchanged.

upon the phenomenological basis for this hope have already been examined in chapter 3 and call for no further examination here.[2] How it can be firmed up from a solid Christological base will be taken up in chapter 9.[3] What is important at the moment is the fact that the ethical imperative to struggle for progress ultimately has to rest on some acceptable base for hope. In my judgment, that base does exist in Teilhardian thought, with certain qualifications concerning its phenomenological component (as noted in chapter 3), and in a quite acceptable sense for believers in his Christological approach to the meaning of the resurrection of Christ.

The same bases for hope in the struggle have import for the second and third types of obstacles, with their peculiar facets of aggression. These obstacles exist in the ultimately more difficult sphere of human interpersonal relations and consist in what arises when men take aggressive action against each other, rather than against impersonal forces. The second type consists of persons or a person who gets in the way of what another person or group wants to do, and who are attacked for what could be described as motives of selfish, arrogant dominance. The third type, which can be classified as the unjust aggressor, is the sort against whom one can speak of action taken in justifiable self-defense. What one is confronted with here, under a single heading, is the problem of the war phenomenon.

Pierre-Louis Mathieu has noted, in his important study of Teilhard's political and economic thought, that Teilhard did not approach this phenomenon as a moralist.[4] The observation needs qualification. The point is well taken, to the extent that it calls attention to an aspect of Teilhard's thought, noted earlier in this study,

---

2. See above, chap. 3B.
3. See below, chap. 9F.
4. Mathieu, *La pensée politique de Teilhard*, pp. 257-58. Mathieu's analysis of Teilhard's thought on war and peace runs from pp. 255-62. My conclusions, derived independently of Mathieu's work, concur with his, for the most part, but extend into certain questions Mathieu does not explore.

that pertains to much of what he has to say about matters of moral concern in general. Significant concepts about what he thinks men should do are incorporated as elements of his larger vision of the world and are not treated from the stance of an *ex professo* moral theorist. This would be true of a good part of what has just been considered, in the previous chapter on love. It is also true about what will be seen, subsequently, on education. And it is particularly true with regard to war and all that this involves about human aggressivity. Nevertheless, the present study will argue that a moral attitude toward war as aggressive coercive force is contained in Teilhard's thought, and that it has important links with his thought on love and research.

In the light of what has just been said, and also by way of setting the stage for the inquiry to follow immediately, the concrete linkage between love, aggression, and research, in the realm of spiritualized energy, can be sketched briefly.

Spiritualized energy embraces those zones of human energy covered by the terms affective, intellective, and volitional. Love (both volitional and affective), for Teilhard, is the highest form of this energy, but it is a complex form. Where aggression relates to it most closely is in Teilhard's foundation for societal love, the sense of *comradeship in attack* against the material obstacles to human personalization and also against the psychological and moral obstacles assembled under the general heading of "obstacles to love," which would include unjust aggressors, and unjust repressors. For Teilhard, the spiritual energy of aggression is a necessary thrust in cosmogenesis—and also in his understanding of pleromatic Christogenesis. It relates to love in two ways: love must guide it, but love, when it would falter, must also take sustenance from it. Research, the zone of spiritualized energy most characterized as intellective, has a similar relation of dependence and sustenance. Research must rely on the motivation of dynamic love to pursue inquiry toward fuller personalization, and yet understanding of growth in personalization is in turn dependent on research.

## B. Warfare

### 1. BASIC CONCEPTS

The leading ideas in Teilhard's understanding of the meaning of war in human existence took shape during his service as a stretcher bearer in the trenches of World War I. Later these were clarified and amplified, particularly as World War II approached and ran its course, with its implications for the future of mankind, especially in the light of developments in control of atomic energy through production of the A-bomb. First, then, an outline of his approach to the meaning of war, and after this, an examination of certain questions arising from aspects of his approach as they were clarified in his correspondence and essays.

Although Teilhard, if one reads him carefully, was no apologist for the glory of war—he bears ample testimony to its grimness and horror—he was affected by the grandeur of a cataclysmic struggle. Nor did he look on warfare as always in itself an unmitigated evil. He judged World War I as justified defense, by the Allies, of human dignity, culture, and freedom. Moreover, he could not avoid the testimony of his inner experience about the impact of World War I on himself, nor what his observation confirmed about its impact on others. It unified his people, brought them out of themselves. At the Front he found an experience of penetrating the unknown, of freedom and profound interior peace, which he had not met elsewhere.[5]

5. Teilhard's reflections on World War I as contained in his correspondence with his cousin Marguerite present a wide range of reactions and insights, summarized, in part, in her introduction to *MM*, pp. 25-29. Some of

World War II presented certain ambiguities to him, but they did not affect his fundamental stance that warfare could be morally good when engaged in to defend what was noblest in the human spirit—especially when this was under attack by brute or "immobilist" ideologies.[6]

Nevertheless, he held that mankind must go beyond the brutal competition of the jungle. What was perfectly clear to him as a biologist, about what had held sway in the evolution of life up to man, was equally clear to him as not to be judged normal for advancing human growth. The experience of attack and teamwork in combat must be directed, as mankind progresses, to researching the energies of the universe and to unifying

the points in these letters he developed more at length in certain wartime essays. In the following inventory of correspondence texts from *MM*, they have been grouped according to four main categories: 1) the character of the war; 2) its impact on society and the individual; 3) the meaning of war experience; and 4) how the war relates to Christ. All references are to *MM*, and the dates range from 1915 to early 1919, shortly after the war's end. For the sake of brevity, only page numbers will be cited. Regarding the *character* of the war: its grimness, p. 151; Teilhard's distrust of "worship of war," p. 201; his view of it as a clash of impersonal forces, p. 218; as a clash of two moralities, p. 170; of two civilizations struggling, p. 56; the war as a form of evolutionary struggle, pp. 71, 110. War *impact* on society and the individual: development of comradeship, p. 218, and faith, p. 245; moral formative influence, as a melting pot for civilization, pp. 66, 125; leading the individual to renounce self, p. 101, yet with depersonalizing effect, p. 153; projecting one into a dream world, p. 153. The *meaning of war experience*: war as another world, p. 71, generating a certain nostalgia for the Front, as a critical moving boundary of human experience, pp. 201, 203, 205 (more on this shortly, in connection with Teilhard's essay on the topic); sense of his country driving him ahead, p. 211; peculiar happiness of solitude in the midst of war, pp. 273, 283; the meaning of friendship with war comrades, p. 283. The *relation of the war to Christ*: as expression of pain, of struggle, shaping the future, p. 119; bringing spiritual maturation, p. 135; enabling Teilhard as priest to bear the burden of life in all forms, p. 183.

6. See, for example, his letter of October 6, 1939, *LF*, p. 135, where he expresses how he found it difficult to understand and feel what was going on in Europe, along with his impression at the time that there was a certain *abortive* character about the struggle. Also, his "obscure feeling" that the Allies were fighting more for defense of stability, or immobility, than for progress, construction, and movement (letter of December 13, 1949, *LF*, p. 138). Teilhard's thought on the legitimacy of using force against refractory elements, inhibiting human personalization from developing on the required global scale, can be found, put in trenchant fashion, in his letter to Léontine Zanta, January 26, 1936, *LZ*, pp. 115-17. Further development of the idea is contained in "The Salvation of Mankind" (1936), *SC*, p. 144.

the peoples of the earth in friendly rivalry, not in brutal competition that kills off one's adversaries.[7]

It is true, more than once he conceded that mankind in its present immaturity needed warfare to concretize the experience of attack and victory.[8] But he looked on this as a developmental phase in the human psyche that he was confident would be outgrown. For him, wars were crises of growth, not destruction.[9] When the atomic bomb was discovered, he concluded, paradoxically enough, that a significant step forward had been made. For he judged that its excessive destructive power put war in the category of the unthinkable, whereas the unlimited challenge of exploration and conquest thereby opened up provided mankind with a more fitting object for its aggressive instincts. These instincts, once absorbed in war, could now be directed to constructive research.[10]

As a consequence of all this, his view of peace, for which he earnestly pleaded, was that it should not be considered a fixed established order or equilibrium, but rather an organized sublimation of aggressive drives toward intensified research and development of a unified mankind bound together in a team spirit engendered by the highest possible common goal.[11] In view of the fact

7. Teilhard's basic thesis on the sublimation of aggression from attack on persons to attack against impersonal forces and energies in the way of developing higher consciousness, is indicated as early as his World War I writings, particularly in "The Promised Land" (1919), WW, pp. 284-85, where he writes of the challenge for construction presented by peace. See also, "My Universe" (1924), SC, p. 82; "Human Energy" (1937), HE, pp. 135-36; "The Natural Units of Humanity" (1939), VP, pp. 212-13; "The Spiritual Repercussions of the Atom Bomb" (1946), FM, p. 147; and "The Phyletic Structure of the Human Group" (1951), AM, p. 162.

8. See "My Universe" (1924), SC, p. 82; "Human Energy" (1937), HE, p. 135.

9. The idea is implicit in his basic understanding of conflict preceding synthesis in evolution. Adumbration of it can be found in his World War I correspondence texts cited above, (n5). See also, PM (1940), p. 210, for a general formulation. For specific statements, see: "The Salvation of Mankind" (1936), SC, pp. 141-42; "The Moment of Choice" (1939), AE, pp. 14-17; "The Rise of the Other" (1942), AE, pp. 61-62; and "Faith in Man" (1947), FM, p. 187.

10. "The Spiritual Repercussions of the Atom Bomb" (1946), FM, p. 147.

11. The idea is clearly implicit in what has been seen so far. For Teilhard's

that this thesis can be seen as a statement in different language of his central thesis about mankind's corporate responsibility to continue evolution, one can affirm that despite the scarce material from his pen about peace as such, his entire ethic is, at its roots, a peace ethic, conceived in dynamic, developmental terms, which accepts the reality of conflict in human history and seeks to supersede it by the societal, universal human love examined earlier. One could further affirm, in view of his notion that this struggle is pointed toward freeing human consciousness for ever-higher reaches of knowledge and love, that his ethic is, with equal radicality, an ethic of liberation, with, as will be seen, important implications in the political realm, at a time when the terms *development* and *liberation* have become a center of controversy.

## 2. QUESTIONS AND CLARIFICATIONS

If one accepts what has been said above as his main concepts on war and its significance, what questions do they provoke, and what clarifications or further questions do his texts provide?

### a. *The Justice of Warfare*

First, how does he come at the question of the moral goodness or evil, the justice or injustice of warfare? Certainly, not in direct fashion. At no place in his writings does he work with the body of teaching that has grown up through the centuries on the theory of a just war. That is to say, at no time does he put down the classical canons and apply them to the situations of armed strife

definite statement on the point, see "Faith in Peace" (1947), *FM*, p. 153. For a good short treatment of Teilhard's thought on war and peace, see Jerome Perlinski, "Teilhard's Vision of Peace and War," *The Teilhard Review* 3, no. 2 (Winter 1968-69): 52-59. Perlinski's treatment of the peace question in Teilhard can be looked on as confirmation of my stand that Teilhard's ethic can be considered a peace ethic, particularly in view of his stress on effort to construct a human world unified in love.

that concern him. Nor does he make more than passing reference to the problem over which many sincere, intelligent persons have agonized, the problem of whether any human being, even in defense, ever has the right to take another human life.

When he writes about war, it is for the most part about a concrete situation of strife, or danger of strife, against the background of his broad evolutionary perspectives. With regard to World War I, especially in "La Nostalgie du Front," and "The Promised Land," it is the experience of this particular war in which he was or had been immersed, that he is trying to interpret.[12] As tensions developed in the years following, the same overall view is found in "The Salvation of Mankind" (1936) and in "The Moment of Choice," written after the outbreak of hostilities in 1939.[13] The same holds for other papers in which he tries to analyze human strife during the years of World War II: "The Natural Units of Humanity" (1939), "Some Reflections on Progress" (1941), "The Rise of the Other" (1942), and "Universalization and Union" (1942).[14] After World War II, his attention focuses more directly on elements, factors, and influences to be worked with in the concrete task of constructing a peaceful world, regardless of the evidence of tensions. Particularly important here are his reflections on "The Spiritual Repercussions of the Atomic Bomb" (1946), "Faith in Peace" (1947), "Faith in Man" (1947), "Reflections on the Rights of Man" (1947), "The Essence of the Democratic Idea" (1949), and "The Phyletic Structure of the Human Group" (1951).[15]

In all of the above writings, when he is wrestling with the problems of strife and harmony specifically, he situates them in his larger picture, and when he makes

12. See *EG*, pp. 199-214; *WW*, pp. 277-88.
13. *SC*, pp. 128-50; *AE*, pp. 11-20.
14. *VP*, pp. 192-215; *FM*, pp. 61-81; *AE*, pp. 59-75; *AE*, pp. 79-95.
15. All essays but the last are contained in *FM*, pp. 140-48; 149-54; 185-92; 193-95; 238-43. For the last essay see *AM*, pp. 132-71.

pertinent remarks almost in passing, they are set in the same large context. Throughout, he simply assumes that the use of armed force has been necessary and good for human progress—at least up to 1946. Without consciously adverting to what he is doing, he seems to be working with certain basics of the just war theory: that the cause can be determined to be just, that excessive force not be used, that there be no personal hatred for the opponent, and that there be reasonable hope for more good than evil emerging from the conflict. But again, note, he never states the criteria in so many words. As he read the facts of the historical situation in World War I, and, later, in World War II, a brutal way of life had to be resisted by armed force if evolution was not to regress. His judgment after the discovery of the atomic bomb that war was indefensible can be seen to rest, in part, on the norm pertaining to excessive force.[16]

### b. The Meaning of War Experience

But there is another factor that complicates his approach here, namely, the impact on him of the experience of war, and his reflections on the meaning of that experience. Despite his revulsion from the suffering brought on by war, he could not avoid pointing to what might be described as enormously important by-products of engaging in warfare. In "La nostalgie du Front," he

16. *FM*, p. 147. From all that can be discovered in his writings about the meaning of total war, one is led to the conclusion that Teilhard, despite his recognition of its brutality, still looked on it as having the possibility of legitimacy. See, for example, his analysis in "Universalization and Union" (1942), *AE*, pp. 82-86. There is no evidence of the agonizing soul-searching such as appeared in the *Christian Century*, or the reflections of Reihold Niebuhr and John Bennett during the same period in *Christianity and Crisis*. Teilhard never seems to have pushed his own thinking into the horrible implications of the progression from strategic to obliteration bombing. Perhaps he never got news of Hamburg and what its destruction meant, cut off as he was on the other side of the world. For an excellent study of the ethical dilemmas being faced at the time, see Roland H. Bainton, *Christian Attitudes Towards War and Peace* (New York: Abingdon Press, 1960), pp. 211-29. A statement of the *Christian Century* position, as well as some pertinent observations of Niebuhr and Bennett, can be found on pp. 222-23. Apparently the Atom Bomb was required, with its terrifying destructive force, for Teilhard ultimately to speak of war in modern times as unthinkable.

writes of the exhilaration of being on the crest of the unknown, of the immense freedom, the deep interior peace, and the unification of men drawn out of their petty selves that he felt in the trenches.[17] In "The Promised Land," he speaks of the boredom of "peace," of the need not to lose the zest for life and also of the need for a noble cause, such as he had seen take hold of so many around him in the preceding years.[18] Later he would write of the "need" for ever-greater weapons, so that men would know the concrete experience of attack and victory, while at the same time he would claim that these instruments had to be and would be outgrown, when the sense of teamwork in combat could be directed not against other human beings, but against nonhuman forces in the way of human progress toward unity in love.[19]

What comes out of his ideas here is that while he would never urge battle for the sake of the experience, he would still affirm the positive value, even the need, of the experience of a just battle, if mankind at its present state of evolution were to summon up the energy demanded by progress and to achieve the level of understanding about human unification derived from the

17. *EG* (1917), pp. 206-12. (Why this essay has not been included in the English edition of the wartime writings, along with "La Grande Monade" (1918), remains something of a mystery in the selection process of scholarly editing.) Henri de Lubac insists that when Teilhard writes of nostalgia for the Front, it is not a nostalgia for war. "In this piece, which is all symbol, even though the war was its occasion—an occasion forced on the writer—and the place it occupies for a time, . . . The source of the symbolism is the front, the front line." See de Lubac, *Eternal Feminine*, pp. 113-16. While the distinction might seem over-subtle, it seems legitimate to the same extent that the present study points to the experience Teilhard eulogizes as a positive by-product of what in itself was a horrible reality. However, despite the fact that he deplored the brutality of war, it is clear that, as has been seen, he held, at least until the time of the atom bomb, an evolutionary need for it to stimulate the sense of attack. On this point also, see de Lubac, *Eternal Feminine*, pp. 81-82, where he presents his synthesis of Teilhard's thinking on war and peace. For Barthelémy-Madaule on these matters, see her *La personne chez Teilhard*, pp. 206-11.

18. *WW* (1919), pp. 278-88.

19. "Human Energy" (1937), *HE*, p. 135. This text was cited earlier, n8. Teilhard's thought is more strongly worded here than in the "My Universe" text of 1924.

welding together of large numbers of people in an urgent common task.

Whether mankind actually did pass an important psychological threshold with the discovery of the atomic bomb, so that now it can and will devote its spirit of conquest to the energy forces before it in the universe, rather than other human persons, is, of course, a moot point. Guerrilla warfare has not declined in the past quarter century, nor has there been any abandonment of massive destructive force with the use of more sophisticated conventional airborne explosives, as in Southeast Asia. What Teilhard well might have appealed to for an output of common, global energy, had he lived long enough for the issue to achieve the urgency appearing today, would be the need for planetary cooperation to prevent reckless technological exploitation of the earth from smothering human life in a series of steadily worsening ecological disasters.[20]

His evaluation of the morality of warfare, implicit as it was, can perhaps best be summarized by setting it in the framework of his basic premise of a morality of movement: that whatever would bring an enlargement of personal consciousness in love would be good. Defense of higher values against brute force would therefore be good. The experience of attack, victory, and teamwork in combat found in this defense, would also be good—if viewed as an experience to be drawn on to derive energy for conquering matter, not men, and consequently bringing men to a common conquest in which all would share in mutual love.

*c. Critical Observations*
*The Experience of Attack and Disapproval of Coercion.*
Teilhard's understanding of the positive by-product in

20. Teilhard was aware of the seriousness of planetary overcrowding, with its implications regarding food supply and energy reserves. See his review of the French edition of Fairfield Osborn's *Our Plundered Planet* (Boston: Little, Brown, 1948) in *Études* 262 (Dec. 1949): 402-3. He was also familiar with the works of J. de Castro and Ch. Galton-Darwin. On this point, see Mathieu, *La pensée politique de Teilhard*, pp. 212-16.

battle experience is quite consistent with his views on wars being crises of growth. In addition to providing the positive element noted, conflicts, even mortal, would, in the last analysis fall in the category of one of the types of evil inevitable in the long, upward struggle of life to higher consciousness. War, despite its horror, would fit into the overall picture wherein conflict precedes harmony in evolutionary development.[21]

It must be admitted that his views on the necessity of war to provide evolving man with a sense of attack and victory are not easy to fit in with his at times unqualified insistence that in human life mortal competition has no place and that coercion brings about only a pseudo-unity among people. What adds further complication is his assertion in "The Essence of the Democratic Idea" that, while maximum freedom should be allowed human personality to develop, still a mixture of laissez-faire and firmness is required.[22] To speak of firmness here as he does seems to imply that coercion at times is not ruled out. And, if one gives some weight to his remarks in his 1936 letter to Léontine Zanta about the reasonableness of constructive warfare or of mankind to control its onward development by using force on less progressive or recalcitrant segments of the race, the paradox, if not the dilemma sharpens.[23] He never seems to have juxtaposed all these elements so as to be aware of the problems they assemble.

Once again the question arises whether on his own premises the apparent oppositions can be resolved or whether he was caught in inconsistency but failed to catch sight of it. A solution seems possible here by introducing certain qualifications in keeping with his overall world view.

The ideal toward which mankind is gradually evolving is that of cooperation, collaboration in universal sympathy, in daring love, by which men strive incessantly

21. *PM* (1940), p. 210.
22. *FM* (1949), pp. 242-43.
23. *LZ*, pp. 116-17.

toward fuller consciousness and more harmonious social union. But mankind has not yet reached this advanced stage of development, and hence as it works upward through the process of growth it will still carry with it certain facets of the process that characterized prehuman evolution—namely, certain drives and tendencies toward brutal elimination of an adversary. In "Universalization and Union," for example, while Teilhard decries total war because of its unscrupulous choice of methods, he sees the total concentration of the life of a nation for defense or attack as pointing toward the growing unification of human life. Moreover, he affirms his hope and conviction that if men on opposing sides will only continue to probe for the truly universal in what they are fighting for, they will emerge from the conflict ultimately discovering that they are striving for the same goals, and hence strife against each other will cease. To bolster his argument here he refers to his own personal experience of finding himself in unexpected agreement with people he at first considered opponents.[24] Consequently, by putting all of his statements together and noting the qualifications he himself introduces (the use of "may," "perhaps," etc.), one can formulate a theory of *gradual* development toward fullness of love and freedom in society. This gradual progress would be, for an unknown period of time, mixed with mortal struggle and coercion.

At this point objection must be made to the firmness of Teilhard's assurance that peace ultimately will emerge, even though gradually, through the final sublimation of aggression in constructive love. The reason for objecting is that Teilhard's argument here is a formulation in a particular context of his fundamental thesis on ultimate human unification. The flaw in his logic, which vitiates his position on that point and which

24. *AE* (1942), pp. 79-95.

has been critically examined in chapter 3, likewise vitiates his conclusion here.

On the other hand, his moral exhortations as to what men should do if war is to be surmounted and sublimated, can be accepted as genuinely helpful, even if limited in scope. Were he to have gone more deeply into the causes and remedies for war as such, it would seem that he would have been required to marshal, in this particular context, all the other factors examined in chapter 4 regarding obstacles to love, and their respective counterparts. It goes without saying that Teilhard's attribution of the causes of human strife in the modern world to the split between the progressive and immobilist cast of mind is open to the charge of oversimplification.[25]

*Nonviolence and Pacifism.* If one grants that Teilhard's theory of the place of aggression in human growth is, at least, consistent with his own evolutionary theory, there is still, nevertheless, a vexing question he never probed. Is the sense of attack and victory—the experience of war—really *necessary*, as he avers, to build the sense of sustained resolve called for in persistent constructive effort?

In view of the growing body of thought about the arguments for nonviolence as a basic philosophy with practical techniques for constructive social change, his failure to give the matter serious consideration would seem to be a formidable gap in his thinking. It is true that the term *nonviolence* has different shades of meaning, ranging from simple nonresistance, which could be an attempt merely to persuade an adversary or call attention

25. That Teilhard was particularly sensitive to divisions among men proceeding from these contrasting attitudes shows up with considerable force in his "A Note on Progress" (1920), *FM*, pp. 11-24. As has been seen in the study of his moral theory, it is at the heart of his distinction between a morality of equilibrium and a morality of movement. For specific correlations with the war phenomenon, see "The Salvation of Mankind" (1936), *SC*, pp. 144-45, and "Faith in Peace" (1947), *FM*, p. 154.

to divergence of positions, to a type of nonviolent, direct action, which, while not invoking physical force, could really be a genuine attack in the form of psychological coercion.[26] Teilhard gives no evidence of being aware of the range of such approaches, nor of the implications they would have within the context of his personalism, which calls for the use of any force as a last resort, be it psychological or physical coercion. His 1953 comment on nonviolence as a doctrine lacking faith and dynamism, presenting simply the negative face of unanimity, shows a regrettable unfamiliarity with the history and ramifications of the concept.[27]

It is also surprising that he never met head-on the radical pacifist position that human life is of such value that one is never justified in taking another human life, even in self-defense.[28] It may well be that he was so thoroughly conditioned by his family and traditional French military background that he never became really aware of the existence of a serious theoretical problem in this sector. His World War I reference to his being a priest ordained for war would indicate he even viewed his Christian priesthood against this background. What is to his credit is that despite narrowness of vision here,

26. For an excellent comprehensive study of various approaches to nonviolence, ranging from nonresistance to dynamic nonviolent direct action, see William Robert Miller, *Nonviolence: A Christian Interpretation* (New York: Schocken Books, 1966). The section of Miller's book dealing with "The Dynamics of Nonviolence," pp. 131-214, contains ideas that, I believe, could well be used to fill in the Teilhardian gap on the potential of nonviolent resistance as a constructive, dynamic, evolutionary force, love-imbued, yet at the same time striving toward conquest of evil, dehumanizing powers. The position Miller outlines seems compatible with Teilhard's fundamental ethical stance as contained in his theory about a morality of movement, as well as his particularization of it regarding resistance to evil in *DM*.
27. See Teilhard's letter of January 21, 1953, quoted by Mathieu, *La pensée politique de Teilhard*, pp. 261-62.
28. For a good short sketch of the bases for certain radical pacifist positions, see René Coste, "Pacifism and Legitimate Defense," trans. Theodore L. Westow, in *Moral Problems and Christian Personalism, Concilium* (New York: Paulist Press, 1965), 5, 80-94. A more complete anthology type of presentation, including opinions by John C. Bennett, Gordon, Zahn, Daniel Berrigan, A. J. Muste, Paul Ramsey, *et al.*, may be found in James Finn, *Protest, Pacifism and Politics*, Vintage Books (New York: Random House, 1968).

he did work to a position, as indicated in his reflections on the atomic bomb, that in effect involved a renunciation of war.

What his final thinking was on the future role of actual warfare of some sort is not perfectly clear, regardless of the strong language in the essay just referred to. The question arises because of some ambiguous language in "The Singularities of the Human Species," written in 1954. He does not speak of war by name but he does refer to the probability of "inner conflicts more violent than any we are now familiar with" as humanity continues in its quest for unanimization. However, when he speaks of these, he does so in such a context that they can be interpreted as not necessarily referring to warfare. Here is the latter part of the text:

> since they [the inner conflicts of humanity] will develop in a human milieu much more strongly polarised towards the future than we can yet imagine, these phenomena of tension will very likely lose the sterile bitterness peculiar to our present struggles. Moreover, in the midst of such an atmosphere of "conspiration," certain operations of a universal character may be envisaged as realisable, which would be out of the question in the state of psychic disaggregation in which we still vegetate today.[29]

*War Experience—the Grand Monad and the Noosphere.* In addition to the positive by-product experience of attack and victory, with regard to which Teilhard reluctantly conceded some sort of need for war in mankind's past and present state, there was another positive result of his World War I life in the trenches, which in an important manner altered his world view, but which he does not relate to any pragmatic, psychological need for war. What is involved here is the intuition he received at the Front that moved him to write "La Grande Monade," expressing his consciousness of the large human reality

29. *AM*, p. 258.

knit together into one "being," which he later would call the "noosphere."[30] The originally suppressed final paragraph of "La nostalgie du Front" is a forerunner of this concept, the germination of which he assigns to his wartime experience in "Le coeur de la matière," written toward the end of his life.[31]

*Teilhard as War Sympathizer*. When all the texts are in and weighed, Charbonneau's indictment of Teilhard as being a war promoter and sympathizer can hardly be substantiated.[32] His moral stance on war was clearly that it was wrong, unless definite conditions were met. That he could be faulted for inaccurate judgment about the existence of these conditions in a given war situation is another question. But mistakes in moral judgment with the best of intentions are quite different from holding an indefensible moral attitude. If one were to raise the question about pushing moral analysis into the matter of whether, in the present situation, with the risk of nuclear holocaust along with the total war practice of obliteration bombing, excessive force looms as a factor ruling out the possibility of just warfare, Teilhard's own statements—definite enough, it would seem, about excessive force in atomic weaponry and the reprehensible brutality of total war—would provide suasive evidence in his defense. To claim that his appeal for sublimating aggression in the direction of research betrays an insensitivity to the need for developing human respect and love among human persons, fails to take into account that in the last analysis this sublimation is, in his theory, to be motivated by a strong sense of universal human love, rooted in an awareness of human solidarity and co-responsibility for the progress of mankind. His language in passages about war may be the language of sublimating aggression for research, but the spirit per-

30. *EG* (1918), pp. 237-48.
31. *EG* (1917), pp. 213-14; *I*, (1950): p. 14, n3.
32. See Bernard Charbonneau, *Teilhard de Chardin, prophète d'un âge totalitaire* (n.p.: Editions denöel, 1963), cited by Mathieu, *La pensée politique de Teilhard*, p. 255.

vading what he says is, for those who will read and ponder his ideas in their complete context, the spirit of deep and profound love.

The most serious lacuna in his moral thinking about aggression and strife among men seems to lie in his failure to perceive the dynamic, constructive potential in certain forms of nonviolent protest. Had he been aware of the possibility in this type of action of a peculiar mixture of attack against injustice, sustained by a conscious and highly disciplined love, he might well have revised his thinking about the psychological need for the physically coercive struggle of war, recognition of which by him, it must be emphasized, was in no way an indication of moral approval of cruelty or barbarity.

*Teilhard and Liberative War.* If the question is asked, "What follows from Teilhard's premises on aggression, with regard to 'wars of liberation?' " the answer could be debated somewhat. If one accepts his cast of mind as incorporating the fundamental tenets of just-war theory, then the answer would run in favor of such struggles, with the proviso that the necessary conditions be met, and, in the setting of his morality of movement, that strife of this type be genuinely directed toward the ultimate effective realization of more personalized love in the world, despite the suffering inevitable in the struggle. As d'Ouince has pointed out, however, Teilhard, in looking ahead, did not anticipate struggle precisely in the form of protest against dehumanization in a technological world as it broke out among French university students after his time. He was explicitly more concerned with the probability of another type of struggle against forces reactionary to progress.[33] What he did envision was men "striking" out of loss of zest for

---

33. See d'Ouince, *Teilhard: la pensée chrétienne*, pp. 84-85. At this point, d'Ouince is commenting on the significance of the youth protests in France in 1968. For an American analysis of countercultural motivation in the context of technological society, see Gibson Winter, *Being Free: The Possibilities of Freedom in an Overorganized World*, Macmillan Paperback (New York: The Macmillan Co., 1970), pp. 80-96.

growth, and, as has been noted on his comments to Léontine Zanta, he saw value in the use of force to elevate backward elements of humanity.

The resolution of the problem as proposed would seem to point, then, to the legitimacy, and at times the urgent necessity, however regrettable, of liberative war, with one final proviso.[34] And the proviso would be that one could assume that a more enlightened Teilhard would have been forced to insist, prior to the ultimate invocation of physical force, on the use of dynamic nonviolence to the full in resisting evil and seeking liberation.

## C. The Meaning and Place of Research

That research has an all-important part to play in mankind's efforts to overcome war and construct a peaceful world is clear enough from what has been seen above. But Teilhard did not speak of research only in this context. Of the moral imperatives that he did in fact speak about from a consciously moral stance, the duty of research was one of his main preoccupations. He spoke of it as a fundamental human obligation, quite apart from the context of sublimated aggression in which it has been viewed in the immediately preceding considera-

34. What inclines one to this proviso, in addition to his expressed views about the unthinkableness of war after the discovery of the atomic bomb, is the implication of his own lived position regarding what to many seemed unjust restrictions imposed by ecclesiastical authorities on his freedom to publish. His criticism of pacifism in the civil political sphere has been noted (see above, n28). However, analysis of what he actually did in the ecclesial sphere reveals at least an analogous pacifist, or nonviolent-resistance approach regarding these restrictions. His repeated presentation of manuscripts, or requests for permission to talk, or teach, and his subsequent acceptance of refusal, and even exile, by church authority—all this is clearly parallel to the nonviolent-resistance pattern in civil matters of insistent petition and peaceful acceptance of rejection, and worse. It is true that Teilhard gives no evidence of having seen the parallel, and viewed his own problems in the context of his understanding of religious obedience (see below, chap. 9 n80).

tions.[35] What should be borne in mind also is that, as will presently emerge, research for Teilhard extended to more than mere intellectual inquiry, and in the last analysis was closely allied to the orientational thrust of dynamic love.

## 1. TEILHARD'S APPROACH

In what follows, attention will be directed mainly toward clarifying the range of meaning Teilhard assigns to research, and why he considers what he does speak of as so imperative. Some thought, however, will be given to certain directions and emphases regarding the objects to which he thought research should be directed. Some of his ideas on the orientation of research are very explicit. But there are also important corollaries to be drawn that he did not draw himself.

A letter to an American friend in 1938 contains an important expression of his thought about the moral and ethical aspects of research. It will be a good starting point. Speaking of what his plans are for the future, he writes:

> In any case, a large part of my activities will surely be absorbed by "parascientific" efforts. Along this line, I believe to see more and more clearly the aim: to develop a *new psychology and ethics of research*, or, if you prefer, a new type

35. Although the term *research* does not get explicit emphasis in "Cosmic Life" (1916), the first of Teilhard's major papers, the concept and his attitude toward it shows clearly in *WW*, pp. 33-34. For indications of his explicit concern and the main lines of an approach that was with him through the years, see, of the other World War I writings, "Mastery of the World and the Kingdom of God" (1916), *WW*, pp. 80,83,88; "The Priest" (1918), *WW*, p. 220, 220, n25; "Forma Christi" (1918), *WW*, p. 260; "Note pour l'évangélisation des temps nouveaux" (1919), *EG*, pp. 272-73; and "The Promised Land" (1919), *WW*, p. 285. For his correspondence of the period see *MM* (1916), pp. 114, 116, 124, 126, and (1918), p. 213.

Commentators on Teilhard's ethical thought have noted the significance of research in his ethic. See, for example, Mermod, *La morale chez Teilhard*, pp. 84-89; de Solages, *Teilhard: étude*, pp. 217-19; Barthélemy-Madaule, *Bergson-Teilhard*, pp. 398-403.

of scientist, who would carry on his task with the consciousness of his function, which is to achieve the World as a
faithful servant of Evolution. I am more and more convinced that this new spirit is essential to the future of Man.
This future is obviously bound to be more and more under
the spiritual and material control of research. But so far research is still egoistic, meaningless. Scientists have a narrow
soul, a short sight, and generally an underdeveloped heart.
They are dry and inhuman, and so often ugly. All that because they are burrowing without looking at any sky. I
dream to open this sky, right in the line of their tunnels![36]

In various places he presents a clearer, more developed view of what he has in mind by the concept of
research. In "The Mysticism of Science," one finds his
most extensive contrast of modern research with that of
previous ages.[37] After an opening disclaimer as to his
credentials regarding the history of science, he describes
what he considers were three discernible stages through
which humanity passed before developing the "modern
mysticism for discovery."

*Esoterism*, according to Teilhard, is exemplified in the
ancient Egyptian approach to science, where, despite
evidence of positive insights, "a single vague notion of
something hidden seems to have covered and confused
nature and the gods." The Greek sense of observation
and experiment obviously opened the way to the modern world, yet the Greek notion of *kosmos* wherein everything could be discovered as fixed and harmoniously
regulated according to canons of a static eternity or of
the past, led to an *aestheticism*, by which inquiry termi-
nated in some understanding and contemplation of the
ordering of reality, but did not lead on, really, beyond
enjoyment to conquest. Under the subtle influence of a

36. *LF*, p. 125. Also, on the lack of adequate orientational vision behind
much scientific research, see "The Mysticism of Science" (1939), *HE*, pp.
171-76, and "Réflexions sur le bonheur" (1943), *DA*, p. 138. Likewise, *LF*, letter of August 2, 1939, p. 132.

37. *HE* (1939), pp. 163-81. The pages of most significance for understanding his analysis of research are pp. 165-73. What immediately follows is drawn
from these.

beyond-looking Christianity and the concrete impact of the development of optics, a sense of *curiosity* took hold powerfully at the time of the Renaissance. With infinite vistas of the micro and the macro opening up, the circumscribed yielded to the limitless. If science had once been "speculative," it now became "discovery."

However, another major step was necessary for mankind to reach the threshold of the modern research mentality: the discovery of time. By this Teilhard means the discovery of the indefinite reaches of the past, opening up the roots of evolutionary theory, which, in turn, led to serious thinking about the possibility and probability of a similarly endless future of growth and development. Now, at last, man could explain his need for knowledge.

> No longer only to know out of curiosity, to know for knowing's sake, but to know out of faith in a universal development which was becoming conscious of itself in the human spirit, to know in order to create, to know in order to be. Henceforth science recognized itself as a means of extending and completing in man a world still incompletely formed. It assumed the shape and grandeur of a sacred duty.[38]

In *Man's Place in Nature* he contrasts research as he views it today with two, more fundamental, senses: 1) "an effort to feel our way toward the continual discovery of better biological arrangements," in which case it is one of the fundamental properties of living matter, and 2) "*reflective* groping," according to which it would be coextensive with the origin of human thought. Today, after two centuries of escalating impact by science and technology together, along with intensified socialization, we find no longer individual invention, born of isolated, tentative search, but another, a third approach, collective invention, born of "totalised research," research carried

---

38. *HE*, p. 171. On the creativity of research, see also *PM* (1940), p. 249. Likewise immediately below.

on by an increasing number of human beings more and more organized into highly complicated teams. Hence research today emerges as the all-important, inner, radical hunger and thirst of human consciousness to expand by conquest of the mysteries of the material universe, and, no less, the mysteries of its own social unification in the still evolving, perhaps now yet-embryonic noospheric organism.[39]

## 2. FURTHER IMPLICATIONS ABOUT THE MEANING OF RESEARCH

### a. *Comprehensiveness of Teilhard's Approach*

The clarifications of the notion of research seen so far were made by Teilhard as conscious clarifications. There are, in addition, important inferences to be drawn from other expressions of his thought. Implicit in what has already been seen is a concept of research that is inclusive of both pure, or basic, and applied research. From his earliest reflections on the topic down to his last, this comprehensive approach can be found. Obviously, he knew the difference between the two styles, since his own paleontological work to which he devoted long years of effort was clearly not "inventive" in the sense in which he uses the term when he talks about it with a view to man's using scientific discoveries to build a better world. Even here though, there is a certain type of creation, in that something new has surfaced in human consciousness with each new insight.[40] But it is clear enough, from the context in which he speaks about man's continuing evolution through research, that he is talking about the mastery of matter and the improvement of mankind itself through a variety of technological tools and instruments. Architects and engineers designing a cyclotron, industrial workers, psychologists

39. *MPN* (1949), pp. 105-7.
40. *PM* (1940), p. 249. In this text he is speaking of mathematics as creative discovery. The principle declared would apply equally well to paleontology.

seeking to expand human perception, as well as organizers striving to bring individuals to a higher style of group life and action—all these would be responding to what he has in mind when he speaks of the sacred call or duty of research. Not the least also to be included would seem to be the moralists, dedicated to the discovery and implementation of an improved human love-energetic, developing along the lines of his morality of movement, ultimately "Christified" in the conscious growth of The Divine Milieu.[41]

*b. Research and Art*

In view of Teilhard's stress on the constructive aspects of research, on the responsibility of scientists, technicians, and moralists to seek and develop new ways of enlarging human consciousness and thus increase the vitality of human spiritualized energy, one is impelled, for the sake of thorough inquiry, to ask, in the context of research, about the character of Teilhard's thought on art.

41. This comprehensive notion of research occurs, in one form or other, throughout his writings when he works with the concept. In addition to the World War I texts cited above, n35, see: "My Universe" (1924), *SC*, p. 68; *LF*, letter of April 20, 1927, p. 70 (particularly significant for the observation of the trend he sees in theoretical research's being "transformed into a need to influence and manipulate which leads logically to social conflicts and struggles"); "Modern Unbelief" (1933), *SC*, p. 114; *LF*, letter of September 18, 1935, pp. 88-89 (why his research into the past has led him to concern about research occupied with the future and its development); "The Phenomenon of Spirituality" (1937), *HE*, p. 108 (integration of the research concept into his ethical theory of an ethic of movement, development, conquest); "Human Energy" (1937), *HE*, p. 126 (the thrust of research toward developmental organization of human energy); *PM* (1940), pp. 249, 278-83 (specifically on the organization of research); "The Formation of the Noosphere" (1947), *FM*, pp. 172-74; "The Human Rebound of Evolution" (1947), pp. 201-2 ("The Control and Preservation of Purposive Thinking"), pp. 202-4 ("The Moral Ordering of Invention"); "The Religious Value of Research" (1947), *SC*, p. 199; "From the Pre-Human to the Ultra-Human" (1951), *FM*, pp. 293, 296 (on responsible invention and the reflective power of invention); "On Looking at a Cyclotron" (1953), *AE*, pp. 349-57 (particularly significant as a powerful, poetic, reflective synthesis of his fundamental approach to constructive, developmental research; and "Research, Work, and Worship" (1955), *SC*, p. 218, esp. n2 (important, in addition to its fundamental material on religion and research, for correlation of his thinking on priest-workers and priest-scientists, and the connection he sees between the former's concern for *better life* with the neohumanistic hope for *fuller life*).

Earlier, in exploring Teilhard's methodology, what he had to say about art was noted in the immediate context of his own use of a poetic manner of thought and expression in pursuing the development of his vision.[42] One may recall that, quantitatively, Teilhard said very little about art. Available for analysis in the present study were only two brief texts. One was a footnote, from *Man's Place in Nature* (1949), in which he expressed his opinion that what he stressed about the need for scientific research would apply across the board with regard to the need for artistic research in the growth of the noosphere.[43] The other text, from ten years earlier, consisted of some brief remarks, analytic of the function of art as a form of human energy, addressed to a gathering of artists in Paris.[44] Important sections of this text are included in the discussion in chapter 2, but it will be helpful at this point to recall the gist of their import in the present context.

It can be recalled that Teilhard did not see artistic activity as a useless appendage to the mainstream of human effort. He judged art to have a triple function of vital importance for the growth of human spiritualized energy, in a manner distinct from that of science and philosophy. He saw art as giving a body to, in some manner materializing, human hopes, fears, and enthusiasms. At the same time, he pointed to the injection of an intellectual element, but one dominated by intuition rather than by reason, and, in its embodied form, generative of still further thought-energy. Thirdly, he contrasted the originality of individual personal insight in artistic activity with a more collective thought-growth in science and philosophy. It was in this context that he affirmed: "The more the world becomes rationalized and mechanized, the more it needs 'poets' as the saviors

42. Above, chap. 2C (3).
43. *MPN*, p. 107, n1.
44. "Comment comprendre et utiliser l'art dans la ligne de l'énergie humaine" (1939), *DA*, pp. 95-97.

and ferment of its personality."[45] In summarizing his position, he asserted that art represented the extreme advance zone in the field of expanding human energy.[46]

Clearly, then, from what little he did say, it can be seen that he assigned art an important place in the framework of research. On the other hand, the question immediately comes to mind as to why, if he judged it important, he did not stress it more. Again the problem arises of dealing with a writer who never synthesized his thought with a view to incorporating all the elements pertaining to fundamental ethical questions—of dealing with a writer who tucked away, moreover, certain pieces of important material in occasional observations. For sure, he had given the matter of the significance of art some thought, but in writing his most carefully elaborated statements of his theories on the human phenomenon, such as *The Phenomenon of Man* and *Man's Place in Nature*, he limited himself to what he judged pertinent to the scientific-minded audience he anticipated.

Where he can be faulted at this point is that he was unaware of the extent to which, in attempting to reach scientists, he was using what scientific critics would describe as a poetic approach. The underlying problem remains, as was seen in examining his methodology earlier, that Teilhard was not reflexively aware, with sufficient clarity, of precisely what manner of thought processes he was using. Consequently, he did not explain his theory of knowledge satisfactorily, and he left himself open to the charge of confusing methods of thought, rather than producing a clear-cut integration or synthesis of disciplines. With this charge, I concur.

There is yet a further problem with regard to Teilhard's fundamental approach to research. It shows up both in all that he said about constructive scientific research and in the little he said about artistic research.

45. *DA*, p. 97.
46. *Ibid*.

The problem is that of his pragmatic, or utilitarian orientation. What does he hold about the value of intellectual activity *not* subordinated to some constructive goal? Does he admit the value of scientific, philosophic, artistic—even religious—contemplation as an end in itself, or must it always be subordinated to the evolutionary process?

His language is unblushingly utilitarian and work oriented. The problem as posed here is related to the problem of leisure in Teilhard's thought, and is, in effect, a formulation of the same problem in a different context. Since it is taken up at some length in chapter 8, it will not be explored here.[47] In passing, though, it can be noted that if Teilhard were to be called a Puritan at heart because of his effort-orientation, what appears is a peculiar type of Puritan—one who wrote much on love, but nothing on justice, who looked very much to the responsibility of the individual beyond himself to the larger society, and who would undoubtedly have drawn anathemas from Calvin for neglecting to put enough stress on human sinfulness.

### 3. THE ORGANIZATION OF RESEARCH

For further clarification as to how his mind was operating with regard to the direction in which he thought research should press forward on the scientific, phenomenological level, two significant texts from the latter part of his life should be examined.

The first is his description of what he understood by "geobiology," and is contained in a piece he wrote for the publication issued by the Institute of Geobiology, which he himself founded in Peking in the early forties. He saw it as an independent discipline, not *juxtaposed* to paleontology, ecology (in the older, narrow sense), biogeography, or other similar disciplines, but *superim-*

47. See below, chap. 8B (2).

*posed* "as a totalizing principle of a different order, tying them together, directing, and concentrating them in a single bundle, without possible interference, on a double object specifically and incommunicably its own." This double object would involve, first, the study of the organic ties among living beings taken as comprising in their totality a single system closed in on itself, and secondly, the study of physico-chemical bonds tying the origin and growth of this living layer to planetary history.[48]

What is particularly noteworthy in this description is that if one interjects the impact of technological development on this planetary life system, what emerges is accurate description of the major thrust of research taken up by the ecological movement in its larger amplified sense, developed since Teilhard's time.

The second text comes from the early fifties and reflects Teilhard's later concentration of focus on global anthropology and all it implied. It consists of a memo to Julian Huxley in March 1951, reacting to two reports sketching plans for a specialized research group to study human ideology. In his memorandum Teilhard suggests setting up an "institute for Human Studies," which would focus on the study of human self-evolution, with both a theoretical and an applied branch. The theoretical branch would seek both to establish the existence of human progress toward a higher form of human life and to define the direction of this progress. Some specific matters to be researched would be: "Evidence for a planetary 'rise in psychic temperature'"; "Effects on human arrangement of planetary compression"; "Totalization and personalization"; along with "General conditions, either physical (the question of resources) or psychic (the problem of maintaining the appetite for

48. Quoted by Claude Cuénot, "L'apport scientifique de Pierre Teilhard de Chardin," *Cahiers, Pierre Teilhard de Chardin, 4, La parole attendue*, pp. 64-65, (hereafter referred to as *Cahiers 4*). The original location is "Geobiologie et Geobiologia," in *Géobiologie: Revue de l'Institute de Géobiologie*, (Pekin, 1943), p. 1-2. (My translation.)

evolution) necessary for self ultra-hominization." The applied branch would have three sections—one for energetics, one for eugenics, and another as a steering, presumably, coordinating section.[49]

If such an Institute for Human Studies were put together with his Institute of Geobiology, the end product could well be an Institute for the Total Human Environment, of the sort much needed to meet the ever-increasing environmental crisis on a global scale.

### 4. RESEARCH AND RELIGION

There remains another enormously significant style of research as he conceived of it, and that is the profound probing into the mysteries of religion and their correlation with the spirit of scientific, technological, organizational, and artistic effort considered up to this point. As he looks ahead, in *The Phenomenon of Man*, toward the main lines of human quest in the future, he sees three principal axes of development in human consciousness, ultimately synthesizing into one: a fundamental intensification of research, focusing more and more on mankind, which in turn would bring science and religion

49. Huxley refers to such an Institute, in passing, in his "Introduction" (1958), to *PM*, p. 21. He seems to have in mind the memorandum reproduced in Cuénot, *Teilhard-Biography*, p. 305, the outline of which is embodied in the text above. Likewise to be noted, in this context of interdisciplinary scientific research, was Teilhard's plan, after World War II, to establish in Paris a small community of Jesuit scientists that would be in open communication with other scientific workers of varied ideological and religious concerns. A roster of priests was drawn up, and a possible residence located, but the project fell through, apparently, for reasons mostly financial. On this see d'Ouince, *Teilhard dans l'Église*, p. 254. Other texts clarificatory and confirmatory of Teilhard's thought on the direction of research in the early fifties would be "A Major Problem for Anthropology" (1951), *AE*, pp. 313-18 (this could almost be considered a commentary on the plan for the Institute he sketched in his memo to Huxley), and his letter of December 4, 1951, *LT*, pp. 320-21, where he outlines his view of three levels of work while engaged by the Wenner Gren Foundation in New York. The letter is significant for indicating how he was attempting, as a research associate for a secular organization, to continue his work on human origins, to initiate a new type of research in the direction of his hypothesis on human convergence, and at the same time, privately to pursue his longstanding quest of a rethought Christology and Christianity in terms of human biological convergence.

into a convergent action of searching, creative adoration with adoring, creative searching. In this book, it is true, his overt concern is about the convergence of scientific faith with religious faith, and he comes at the question from the vantage point of a scientist, ultimately transcending, yet firmly rooted in empirical scientific thought. It would be important to keep in mind here the particular value he assigned to Christianity as he interpreted it, namely, as eminently suited to become the terminal and universal religion.[50]

In his interpretation of Christianity, in his rethinking of the major elements of Christian faith in the light of science and technology in an evolving world, one finds him putting into practice his own theory about the character of religious research. Here he can be observed seeking, as a firm believer, a more profound grasp of the meaning of his faith and how it can be presented to the modern world, how it can grow in an intellectual and affective climate vastly different from that of its origins and development down to the present.[51] To his efforts here could be added his pleas for more organized inquiry in the Church, about which more below in chapter 9.

If one were to ask what was the technique he used in his religious inquiry and in the application of his insights, the answer, in effect, lies in all that was examined above in chapter 2 pertinent to his ethical methodology. In other words, his adaptation of Ignatian active-contemplative spirituality, when viewed from one angle,

50. See *PM* (1940), pp. 291-99, "Epilogue: The Christian Phenomenon." The thesis is central in Teilhard's thinking and occurs over and over again. Other significant examples of its statement can be found in "How I Believe" (1934), *CE*, pp. 126-30; "The Universal Christ and the Convergence of Religions"; "Human Energy" (1937), *HE*, pp. 156-58; "The Phenomenon of Christianity"; and "The Singularities of the Human Species" (1954), *AM*, pp. 271-73; "Appendix: Complementary Remarks on the Nature of the Point Omega, or, The Unique Nature of the Christian Phenomenon."

51. See *MM, SC,* and *CE, passim.* Likewise, "Comment je vois" (1948), *DA*, pp. 179-223, and the unpublished papers, "Le coeur de la matière" (1950) and "Le Christique" (1955). The remaining unpublished essays, hopefully soon to be published in France, would also have pertinent material.

can be seen to provide his ethical methodology, and from another, presents a picture of what in the last analysis would be meant by religious research dedicated to continuing evolution, through a divinized morality of movement.[52]

## 5. RESEARCH AND HUMAN RESPONSIBILITY

The underlying phenomenological base for the urgency of research stands out quite clearly from what has already been said about the way in which he interprets the concept itself. In a world where mankind has the responsibility to strive toward ever-higher forms of consciousness and human unity, research becomes the overriding essential human activity, since it is precisely through love-motivated seeking and searching that men will acquire the vision of human unification and discover the vast range of implements that must be fashioned to effect it. The argument could be formulated somewhat differently by saying that, if the main evolutionary thrust is toward man-developed higher consciousness, then that type of human activity which is itself the fully aware quest of higher consciousness must of necessity be the most urgent task of mankind. Research, in the broad Teilhardian sense, is precisely such activity.[53]

It is not surprising then, that Teilhard should be concerned about what affects man's fundamental disposition toward research. In the last analysis, what he has to say about "the zest for living" relates closely to his thoughts on the meaning of love as the central evolutionary ener-

52. See above, chap. 2.
53. The line of argument is clear from all that has been seen about Teilhard's thinking on research. A capital text, summing it up in his own words, can be found in a letter of December 10, 1933, "You ask yourself: 'Is scientific research a derivation or a deviation?'—I think that it is one form (one of the most perfect, of the most direct) of what we call being, or life, or Evolution. I cannot define the World otherwise than by a gradual awakening of consciousness: research is precisely the frontier in the spreading of this universal consciousness." The letter is quoted in Cuénot, *Teilhard-Biography*, p. 217, n10.

gy.[54] As a matter of fact, at the very end of this essay he explicitly correlates the two when he speaks of love as a higher form of zest. What he says about zest for living, actually, is similar to what he has to say about cosmic love in all its implications, except that his slant and focus differ. Of special significance here is the explicit direction he emphasizes for research.

What bothers him greatly is that all over the earth engineers and economists concentrate on the problem of natural resources, but no one is sufficiently concerned to survey the zest for life, "to take its 'temperature', to feed it, to look after it, and (why not, indeed?) to increase it."[55] But, if this zest withers away, and if mankind does not maintain and increase its inward appetite for growth, there is serious danger that the human race will go on strike and cease to develop.

Consequently, Teilhard makes the following plea, with a summation of his argument.

> In the end the ultra-human cannot be built except with the human; and the human is, essentially, nothing but a will to subsist and grow greater, which can equally well be intensified or wither away.
>
> It is then, to the theoretical and practical study of this will (a will that radically conditions all our forms of power) that a new science—the most important, perhaps, of all sciences—must be devoted: and tomorrow it will inevitably be so devoted. Its problem will be, "How to maintain deep in the heart of man the source of his vital impulse, and open it up ever more widely."[56]

Particularly significant for the present study on his moral thought and the methodology behind it is how he goes on to urge exploration of the elements in the main religious currents of the earth as of paramount importance in the type of research he is advocating, and that, furthermore, speaking from his own personal conviction,

54. "The Zest for Living" (1950), *AE*, pp. 231-43.
55. *Ibid.*, pp. 236-37.
56. *Ibid.*, p. 237.

he views Catholicism as having a central-axis function in the entire process.[57]

Finally, contrapuntal to the urgency for research derived from phenomenological grounds, he sees an impelling need for the responsible Christian to immerse himself in it. The Christian has a call, from Christ, determinative of his very essence as a Christian, to build the Body of Christ and bring the Incarnation to fulfillment. But the Body of Christ can now be seen to be a cosmogenetic Body, which cannot be built without the marshaling of all the energies required for human continuation of cosmogenesis in the noosphere. Research energy motivated by love is indispensable for the process.

### 6. CONCLUDING OBSERVATIONS

With regard to the character and scope of his thought about research, Teilhard lacks adequate clarity in distinguishing between the areas of pure and applied research. Likewise, he would have done better to incorporate in his major writings, and apply to an analysis of his

---

57. *Ibid.*, pp. 238-43. The principal essays which Teilhard devoted explicitly to comparing religious currents of East and West are "La route de l'Ouest," 1932, *DA*, pp. 47-64, and "L'apport spirituel de l'Extrême-Orient: quelques réflexions personnelles" (1947), *DA*, pp. 149-60. For other expressions of his thought on the matter, see: "Christianity in the World" (1933), *SC*, pp. 105-6; "How I Believe" (1934), *CE*, pp. 121-23; "Comment je vois" (1948), *DA*, pp. 215-16; "A Clarification: Reflections on Two Converse Forms of Spirit" (1950), *AE*, pp. 217-27. In "L'apport spirituel de l'Extrême-Orient," Teilhard takes a less negative view regarding Eastern Mysticism than in most of his other writings. He would undoubtedly have welcomed, if it had been available to him, William Johnston's *The Still Point: Reflections on Zen and Christian Mysticism*, Perennial Library (New York: Harper & Row, Pub., 1971). While Johnston does devote considerable space to Teilhard as a Christian Mystic, unfortunately he has no comment on Teilhard's comparative reflections on Eastern and Western Mystical thought. Had he done so, he probably would have put Teilhard's thinking in the category of those who read the East, regrettably, but unavoidably, because of cultural conditioning, with too Western eyes. Teilhard would probably have agreed with Johnston's stress on working from phenomenological experience, rather than concepts, and would probably have been particularly interested in his conclusions about "Zen and Christianity," pp. 183-93, which point to a highly nuanced possible synthesis of certain aspects of Zen with Christian prayer.

own thought, the position about art that he did put forth in his 1939 observations about the meaning and function of art. In this particular address, Teilhard's clarifications about the differences between art and science and philosophy stand in need of much greater development and exposition. Moreover, it can again be emphasized that his failure to do this adequately anywhere is a key factor in explaining negative criticism of the Teilhardian approach to knowledge.

On the credit side there would be his stress on the social-responsibility aspect of research activity. To give him good marks here would, for the moment prescind from a final judgment on the "Puritanical" character of his fundamental stance, for reasons indicated above, to be elaborated more at length in chapter 8. Also to Teilhard's credit would be his argumentation and effort in favor of interdisciplinary research, both on the level of the various scientific disciplines as they looked to the development of human personalization, and on the level of pursuing the relationship between science and religion. Finally, regardless of what the judgment is about the results of his efforts to research and interpret the meaning of Christianity in an evolutionary age, there is good reason to endorse his insistence on the need to make the attempt.

6

# The Organization
# of Spiritualized Energy:
# (b) Global Harmony in the
# Geopolitics of Complementarity

## A. Teilhard's Approach to Politics

The reason for considering Teilhard's political thought in the context of "spiritualized energy" is that, ultimately, political processes can be shown to derive from the raw stuff of human interpersonal relations as they embrace a complicated pattern of intellectual, volitional, and affective energies interacting within the sphere of civic life.

It goes without saying that the concept of the political has, over the years, acquired considerable range of meaning. This present study in its entirety might, for example, be called a "political" work in the large, fundamental, Aristotelian sense of the term, since it is concerned with those factors, elements, and facets of human existence which contribute to the well-being of society as a whole. To say this does, in effect, equate political concern with social moral concern, and to so speak is not without precedent or value. At the other end of the spectrum one finds the day-to-day work of practical politics. Included in this would be the processes of executive, legislative, and judicial branches of governmental bodies, with all the fact-finding, framing, and revising of legislation, the many painstaking details of administration, not to mention the periodic sallies before the general public, getting the sense of the popular mind, the pulse of its heart, and attempting to diagnose whatever ills may assail it and to improve its general and particular civic health. At some point in between, closer to the larger concept than the narrower, there is the work of devising the more immediate theoretical background for the day-to-day practical chores. The ideas of Teilhard that will be examined here fall in this in-between sector.

He was, admittedly, no political activist in the commonly accepted use of the term. That he was not stems in part from his own conviction as to what his own particular role was in the overall process of helping to improve society. A clear expression of this attitude is found in a letter to his brother Joseph, written from Burma in February 1938. While it is true that this letter is a comment on his interpretation of his role at a particular time, still, it expresses a mind-set characteristic of his approach in general.[1]

After describing the setting in which he was working, he remarks:

> You see, then, how I am spending in the calm of ancient nature the hours that are so full of tension for China and Europe; and you may well imagine that I am not too

---

·1. The generic character of his approach to political matters is documented both by the texts shortly to be examined and by the absence in his life of personal involvement in concrete political questions. However, despite the lack of development or progress from theorizing to practical implementation, there was a definite development in his theoretical thought from a sort of inherited, so to speak, authoritarianism of the Right, to the democratic sympathies of his later years. On this point, see Mathieu, *La pensée politique de Teilhard*, pp. 99-106.

pleased at being a deserter. Still, I am biding my time—
should it ever come—and I am working patiently to clarify
my "message" (?) and strengthen my platform. It seems to
me more important to create a new concept of human activity than to plunge into the feverish intoxication of a political drive which already has its leaders and will never lack
followers. At the same time I am watching with great anxiety the strange transmutations we are undergoing but fail
to understand.[2]

This does not mean that he did not have his own observations about current political happenings, which surface from time to time in his correspondence.[3] But it
does mean that his main preoccupation was with the underlying currents upon which these happenings were
borne, and that he felt that his principal political effort
should be directed toward chaneling the current rather
than guiding one or another particular boat on its surface.

A serious gap in his political thinking, which some
might attribute to this distance from the raw experience
of practical politics, is the absence in his writings of any
specific observations on the psychological and ethical
dangers for personalization involved in the exercise of
political power. He did recognize the legitimacy of the
use of coercive force in certain circumstances. This point
has already been established from the preceding analysis
of his thought on war. As will be seen again shortly, he
was no advocate of total *laissez-faire* democracy, or of
limiting educational direction to suasive power alone.
But his treatment of power stops short with his indication of the types of power he judged feasible. It ignores
altogether the enormously important question of the
psychological and ethical obstacle to the growth of
societal love found in the pride, arrogance, and ten-

2. See *LT*, letter of February 13, 1938, p. 238.
3. See *MM*, pp. 253, 258; *LZ*, pp. 73, 75, 78-80, 116; *LF*, pp. 45, 199; *LT*,
pp. 200, 219, 267, 273, 328, 335, 336.

dency to dehumanizing domination so readily attendant upon the exercise of power in human relationships.

To attribute this gap in his ethical thought to his distance from the political arena does not seem an adequate explanation, however. What does help to explain both the distance and lack of concern for the evil potential latent in the use of political power is once again Teilhard's failure to be moved to the point of explicit concern by the corrosive impact of human sinfulness in a particular sector. Whether a keener awareness of sinfulness would have led him to more active involvement in politics is debatable, however much one can see the plausibility of increasing involvement stemming from just such an awareness. But it is difficult to see how, if he had been more profoundly aware of the strength of the divisive thrust of human pride in power, he could have avoided coming to grips with it in his reflective writing.

## B. The Fundamental Political Texts

Teilhard's thought about the fundamental currents of political life is found principally in a number of essays written between the mid-thirties and the late forties. To be singled out here especially are "The Salvation of Mankind (Some Thoughts on the Present Crisis)" (1936); "The Natural Units of Humanity: An Attempt to Outline a Racial Biology and Morality" (1939), "Reflections on the Rights of Man" (1947), and "The Essence of the Democratic Idea" (1949). These will be examined in sequence, except that "The Natural Units of Humanity" will be taken separately, after the others, both because it has a special focus on the racial question, and because, despite its early date, it shows a certain depth and comprehensiveness helpful for bringing his other ideas into better perspective.

## 1. "THE SALVATION OF MANKIND"

The most comprehensive of the more overtly political essays is the first, "The Salvation of Mankind" (1936), written in the period of turmoil leading up to World War II.[4] The post-World War II writings provide clarifications, mainly of the democratic concept, with implications for the others broached at the time.

As he viewed the world in those critical days of the middle thirties, he saw three principal influences (apart from Christianity) striving for mastery of the earth: democracy, communism, and fascism. He looked at all of these against a background of mankind striving toward convergence along three core axes: a fundamental faith in progress toward a more human *future*, a drive toward the *universal* (the total life of the planet), and a thrust ever more toward recognition of the importance of the human *person*. He finds evidence of these axes in each of the principal influences, yet also judges each of them to be seriously failing in its present form.

Democracy he faults on two main counts: personalism and universalism. As a consequence of excesses following the developments of 1789, the individual role was exaggerated. Each human cell came to be considered a center for itself alone. From this came excessive fragmentation and an egalitarianism that denied the organic and hierarchic character of true universalism. His charge is that democracy confused the individual and the person, the mob with the totality. As a reaction to this extreme fragmentation and leveling-down process, communism arose on the left and fascism on the right.

In communism he sees a vision of totalitarian civilization rooted in the cosmic powers of matter, with an atmosphere of newness and universality. The communist reaction, however, to anarchistic liberalism brought in its train two disastrous effects: 1) the destruction of the

4. *SC*, pp. 128-50.

person, with man reduced to a termite, and 2) the death of spirit, through an unbalanced enthusiasm for matter. The mechanical development of a soulless collectivity obscured the human spirit and a pseudo-determinism killed off human love.

Fascism, while in some forms holding to a static world view in reaction to revolution, still was, as he saw it, open to the future, to vast wholes emerging. Moreover, it preserved an element Teilhard consistently held critical: the importance of an elite, and with this, the personal and spirit. He even went so far as to say that within the fields it sought to cover, fascism did perhaps satisfy the basic conditions (the universal, personal, and concern for the future). But, because it ignored a genuine internationalism, he pronounced it ridiculously limited on the score of universalism. Even if one were to grant it a place as a small-scale model of the future, a necessary stage, training man to learn a larger role, still, its narrow, exclusive nationalism made it grossly inadequate.

In the interplay of these struggling forces, Teilhard saw the world on the defensive, striving for light. Because of the positive components each contained, he interpreted the contest as not radically divergent, but in a hidden way working toward convergence in a common future. For this convergence to mature, he maintained that a fourth spirit must emerge, described as the *human front*. This fourth spirit would combine the democratic zeal for the rights of man with the communist vision of the power of matter and the fascist ideal of organized elites. It would have a kind of catalytic impact, helping the "good" and the "bad" to sort each other out. In the long run, the type of struggle he saw emerging with more sharply drawn lines of battle was a contest between two root forces of mind, the progressive and the immobile.

Two important implications of the development of this human front would be, he thought, first, the appearance of "engineers" devoted to the conquest of the resources of the earth, and, second, other "technicians" who would concentrate exclusively on the definition and extension of knowledge about the ever-more-lofty concrete objectives that should absorb human energy. In this way he saw the construction of an "energetics of spirit." His conclusion here amounts to another formulation, this time in a broadly political context, of his central thesis about morality in the evolutionary process, with definite ties to what has been seen above about research.

## 2. "SOME REFLECTIONS ON THE RIGHTS OF MAN"

"Some Reflections on the Rights of Man" was written in 1947, apparently in the context of discussion by the United Nations of the new Declaration on the Rights of Man, and was, in fact published in *UNESCO* in 1949.[5] It amounts to an expansion and clarification of some of his observations on democracy, seen in "The Salvation of Mankind." In the earlier piece he pointed up the problem arising from the fragmentation of excessive individualism. Here he strives to show some fundamental concepts that should be operative in reconciling the contemporary sharpening tension between the individual and the demands of an increasingly collective society. The premise from which he works is a familiar one: men can fully develop as persons only in association with others; men do not become completely "reflective," which in effect means "human," unless they are reflected in each other. The collective and the individual are not, therefore, essentially antagonistic. A critical problem, though, is to bring about totalization not through external force, but rather by sympathy and internal harmonization. For this to be done, he advocates three fundamental principles that must underlie any new declaration of human rights:

5. *FM*, pp. 193-95.

The absolute duty of the individual to develop his own personality.

The relative right of the individual to be placed in circumstances as favourable as possible to his personal development.

The absolute right of the individual, within the social organism, not to be deformed by external coercion but inwardly super-organised by persuasion, that is to say, in conformity with his personal endowments and aspirations.[6]

### 3. "THE ESSENCE OF THE DEMOCRATIC IDEA"

In "The Essence of the Democratic Idea," drafted as a response to a UNESCO Questionnaire in 1949 but never published, there is a more detailed analysis of what these concepts mean in the context of what he perceives to be at the heart of democracy.[7] The central question to which he directs himself is not simply "What is Democracy?" but, as he rephrases it, "What exactly is hidden *behind* the idea of democracy?"

To get at this, he first presents a sketch of "The Present Evolutionary State of Mankind." The main ideas are again familiar. Mankind, with continual planetary compression and psychic interpenetration, is irresistibly unifying, organizing itself. But it is doing so with a vital condition operative: the exaltation, in the unification process, of the incommunicable uniqueness of each separate element. To show that this type of organizing can be done, he appeals to the experience of every successful team or association. Hence he reads the present turmoil of democratic aspirations as something coming out of compressive socialization in its steady movement toward personalizing totalization.

Next, he elaborates on a "Biological Definition and Interpretation of the Spirit of Democracy." At the outset

6. *Ibid.*, p. 195.
7. *Ibid.*, pp. 238-43.

he restates what he has just said in different language. From his biological vantage point he formulates the principle that the spirit of democracy is equivalent to the "evolutionary sense" or the "sense of the species," which for mankind means not merely the drive to propagate, but also the will to grow through the organized arrangement of the species upon itself.

After this he develops two main lines of thought. First he applies the principle just declared to the concepts of liberty, equality, and fraternity. Then he examines the conflict between the liberal and socialist democratic factions.

He explains the three "magical words" as follows:

> Liberty: that is to say, the chance offered to every man (by removing obstacles and placing the appropriate means at his disposal) of "trans-humanising" himself by developing his potentialities to the fullest extent.

> Equality: the right of every man to participate, according to his aptitudes and powers, in the common endeavour to promote, each by way of the other, the future of the individual and the species. Indeed, is it not this need and legitimate demand to *participate* in the Human Affair (the need felt by every man to live co-extensively with Mankind) which, deeper than any desire for material gain, is today agitating those classes and races that have hitherto been left "out of the game"?

> Fraternity: as between man and man, in the sense of an organic interrelation based not merely on our more or less accidental coexistence on the surface of the earth, or even on our common origin, but on the fact that we represent, all of us together, the *front line*, the crest of an evolutionary wave still in full flood.[8]

Interpreting these concepts in the light of his guiding principle enables him to bring them out of the realm of the "indeterminate, amorphous, and inert" and to pro-

8. *Ibid.*, p. 241.

vide guidance and dynamism, arising from the underlying, sustaining impulse.

The conflict between liberal and directed democracy he finds to be no clash between contradictory social ideals, but rather an interaction process between two natural components, personalization and totalization. A biologically true democracy must have a balanced combination of these two factors, complementary rather than antagonistic. An attempt to build a democratic society on either one of these in its pure state produces an inadequate type, individualist on the one hand, authoritarian on the other.

The harmonization of these two is what he discusses in his final section, "The Technique of Democracies." Disavowing competence to criticize existing forms and methods of democracy, he offers three remarks from his "biological" standpoint.

First, he insists on two general conditions: 1) allowing the individual the widest possible freedom of choice for the development of personal qualities (with the proviso that choice be directed toward heightened reflection and consciousness), and 2) promotion of "currents of convergence," by which he means collective organizations, the sole environment wherein individual action can reach fulfillment. It is at this point that he speaks of the need for "a judicious mixture of *laissez-faire* and firmness," worked out with moderation, tact, and art, by people with a sufficiently developed progressive instinct.

His second remark takes off from the last thought expressed in his first remark and highlights the necessity of innumerable *experiments and probings* if the democratic ideal is to find itself. Compression and unification to date have left a wide range of heterogeneity and unequal maturation, which cannot be democratized without imagination and adaptation, conforming to the diversified habits and customs of the human components.

Finally, he stresses the need for maintaining and fostering growth in men's minds of the "sense of the Species." Using the term *polarization* not in the sense of separating toward opposite poles, but of centering on one, he concludes:

> Only a powerful polarization of human wills, after each fragment of humanity has been led to the discovery of his own particular form of freedom, can ensure the convergence and unified working of this plurality in a single, co-ordinated planetary system. Above all, only this polarization, through the unity thus constituted, can create the atmosphere of non-coercion—unanimity—which is, when all is said, the rare essence of Democracy.[9]

## C. Implications and Further Developments

Such, then, are the thought-lines in what could be called his more or less specifically political essays. What they come down to is a transposition of his central ideas on morality, human responsibility, and societal love into the language of political theorizing. But there is more than mere transposition. There is also particularization, a practical application of his leading themes on human evolutionary process, which results in a distinctively Teilhardian critique of democracy, fascism, and communism, his sympathies ultimately lodging with his interpretation of democracy.

### 1. DEMOCRACY

It is clearly, however, not an across-the-board egalitarian democracy for which he opts. He affirms the need for leading evolutionary human shoots, for elite groups functioning within an organic democratic framework, wherein his basic concept of organic complementarity plays an important role. (Further specification of this

9. *Ibid.*, p. 243.

important idea will be seen in his essay "The Natural Units of Humanity.") When he talks of participating in the human affair, he does not clarify what his stand would be precisely on participation in the decision-making process. His insistence on the absolute right of the individual not to be coerced, but to be persuaded in conformity with his responsibility for self-development has important implications, which would seem to lead to maximization of decision-making participation. The problem lies with the criterion for the maximum and with structuring its implementation. That the criterion is to be drawn from fundamental ideas on organically complementary personal talents and their place in contributing toward increased Omegalization seems clear. But how determination of these talents and endowments would be structured within organized political society, he leaves for others to decide.

## 2. FASCISM

The fundamental critique of fascism seen in "The Salvation of Mankind" was not enlarged upon much in his other writings and correspondence. The Zanta letter of 1936 is admittedly embarrassing with regard to the positive aspects of his assessment of Mussolini's Ethiopian invasion. However, it is by no means a blanket approval of fascism and does not in the last analysis provide adequate evidence for leveling the charge of "Fascist!" against him.[10] True, in keeping with his other analyses

10. See *LZ*, pp. 115-17. In this letter Teilhard is condemnatory of what he speaks of as Mussolini's cowardly and gratuitous use of force, as well as of fascist narrow nationalism. The sense in which he aligns himself with Mussolini and "against the liberals of the left and the missiologists" has to do with his belief that the earth (mankind evolving) has the right "to organise itself by reducing, even by *force*, the refractory and backward elements." Although he does not use the term *fascist* in his 1939 essay "The Moment of Choice," (*AE*, pp. 13-20), he is clearly condemning, in strong language, the Axis powers when he talks of fighting to destroy the barbaric "divine right" of war (pp. 15-16). For further analysis of Teilhard's approach to Fascism, and confirmation of the position that he was strongly anti-fascist, see Mathieu, *La pensée politique de Teilhard*, chap. 3, "Teilhard et les Fascismes," pp. 99-117.

along this line, it does highlight his basic conviction of the need for elite groups of some sort to provide direction for evolution in the political process. It is also another piece of evidence documenting his lack of deep concern about the potential evil in the abuse of power by such an elite. His later stress on the maximization of persuasion and self-development, as seen above, definitely rules out, in theory, a strongly coercive elitism, although he never seems to have excluded, as a practically necessary measure, the use of force at certain times and in certain instances, at least during man's present evolutionary phase.[11]

### 3. MARXISM

With regard to Marxism, however, there are later significant amplifications and clarifications.[12] The principal criticisms seen above were that communism on the one hand destroyed the human person by reducing him to a termite, and on the other, through its over-emphasis on matter, veiled the reality of spirit and in effect killed love. (The second point can be read as a reformulation of the first, or clarification of it.) On the positive side, Teilhard recognized the value of Marxist enthusiasm for the earth and its future development.

When he develops his ideas on "The Planetisation of Mankind," almost ten years later, there is at the conclusion of the essay a reference to Marxism in his descrip-

11. In the last analysis, this is what his "judicious mixture of *laissez-faire* and firmness" (*FM*, p. 243, "The Essence of the Democratic Idea" [1949]) seems to come to. It goes without saying that what is mentioned here should be considered against the backdrop of Teilhard's thought on aggression, examined in the previous chapter.
12. For an excellent study of Teilhard's approach to Marxism, and the development of his thought about it, see Mathieu, *La pensée politique de Teilhard*, chap. 2, "Teilhard Juge de Marx," pp. 52-97. Mathieu's work is particularly valuable for its information concerning Teilhard's contacts with Marxist thought, through personal dialogue and, admittedly, limited reading. Likewise, his critical remarks about Teilhard's interpretation of Marxism contain significant observations regarding his greater familiarity with Marxist anthropology than with problems of surplus value, economic alienation, and class struggle (pp. 68-84).

tion of what he sees as the dichotomized elements in humanity today. The analysis by Marx about conflict between producers and exploiters Teilhard views as outdated, or "at the best a misplaced approximation." There is no longer to be a division of men into two camps on the basis of class. The question is one of attitude of mind. The bourgeois spirit he takes to be reflected in the attitude that simply seeks to make the world a comfortable home, whereas the true "toilers of the earth" are those who look on the world as a progressively developing organism. One of his favorite points, the opposition between immobilism and mobilism, is driven home again, but this time as a correction of Marxist analysis.[13]

With "Faith in Man" (1947), he broaches an aspect not introduced previously—the possible convergence, ultimately, of Marxism and Christianity.[14] One could argue that something of this was implied or could be derived from the concluding section of "The Salvation of Mankind," in which, discussing "The Place of Christianity," he makes the case for a properly interpreted Christianity providing the essential elements of Personalism, Futurism, and Universalism missing in the other contending forces of ideas. Be that as it may, he does bring Marxism and Christianity into direct juxtaposition in the present essay (as well as in "The Heart of the Problem," about which more shortly).

Ultimate convergence is predicated on the foundation of a common Faith in Man. To Teilhard, it is a matter beyond argument, a matter of ordinary experience, that to the extent Marxists and Christians hold this type of faith and are aware that both groups hold it, there exists a fundamental mutual sympathy, despite obvious differences. Moreover, he does not believe that the Marxist drive of faith, even though materialist, can lose every

13. *FM* (1945), p. 139.
14. *Ibid.*, pp. 185-92.

upward surge toward spirit. Here he summarizes with his well-known and much-quoted argument:

> Followed to their conclusion the two paths must certainly end by coming together: for in the nature of things everything that is faith must rise, and everything that rises must converge.[15]

Particularly significant in his approach at this time is the affirmation of the drive toward spirit that he perceives in Marxism, a drive that his severe negative criticism of ten years before did not see.

Two years later, in "The Heart of the Problem" (1949), he directs attention to the specific character of the contemporary opposition between Marxist and Christian views, and how the two can be brought into alignment.[16] Christianity as commonly interpreted concerns itself almost exclusively with the "above" and neglects the human. Marxism is devoted entirely to the "ahead" and admits no transcendent focus of aspiration. Both at present have complementary inadequacies. Moreover, Teilhard's personal conversations with Marxist intellectuals led him to hold them not wholly atheistic. They manifest a genuine, basic "faith," in that they are willing to sacrifice and abandon self for something greater, which ultimately implies "worship" and a sense of the "divine." The "God" to whom they object is an extrinsicalist God, a "deus ex machina," demeaning both the glory of the universe and the splendor of human effort. On the other hand, a genuinely incarnational Christianity must, of its own interior logic, make its own whatever is authentically human. Reconciliation of the two is symbolized by Teilhard's resultant vector, whereby mankind pushes above and ahead at the same time, believing "*at the same time wholly* in God *and* the World, the one through the other."[17]

15. *FM*, p. 192.
16. *Ibid.*, pp. 260-69.
17. *Ibid.*, pp. 268-69. It should be noted in this context that while Marxist

In the previous writings Teilhard has not given a description of how Marxism can get along, or tries to get along, without the personal Center he considers essential. Two essays from 1950 do this, each putting the matter in somewhat different language. In "The Probable Coming of an Ultra-Humanity," although he does not speak of Marxism by name, what he says about the collectivist stand clearly applies. He presents this type of answer to the question of mankind's terminal condition as follows:

> it will suffice to ensure the biological success of our evolution if Man organises himself gradually on a global scale in a sort of closed circuit, within which each thinking element, intellectually and affectively connected with every other, will attain to a maximum of individual mastery by participating in a certain ultimate clarity of vision and extreme warmth of sympathy proper to the system as a whole. A higher state of consciousness diffused through the ultra-technified, ultra-socialised, ultra-cerebralised layers of the human mass, but without the emergence (neither necessary nor conceivable) at any point in the system of a universal, defined and autonomous Centre of Reflection.[18]

In "Human Unanimisation," he comes to substantially the same point in treating of the positive attributes emerging in the developing human "Sense of Species."

> Those who think on Marxist lines believe that all that is necessary to inspire and polarise the human molecules is that they should look forward to an eventual state of *collective* reflection and sympathy, at the culmination of anthropogenesis, from which all will benefit through *participa-*

theoreticians such as Roger Garaudy admit the value of Teilhard's thought as a basis for Marxist-Christian dialogue, Garaudy at the present time finds the two approaches still very antithetic: "Teilhard's thought is fundamentally opposed to Marxism." See Roger Garaudy, "Le Père Teilhard, le concile et les marxistes," *Europe* 431-32 (mars–avril 1965):186-87. Cuénot is appreciative of Garaudy's attempts to open up Marxist thought to rapport with concepts such as those of Teilhard, while recognizing radical differences. See the perceptive critical essay by Claude Cuénot, "Teilhard et le marxisme," *Europe* 431-32 (mars–avril 1965):164-85.

18. *FM*, p. 278.

*tion*: as it were, a vault of inter-mingled thoughts, a closed circuit of attachments in which the individual will achieve intellectual and affective wholeness to the extent that he is one with the whole system.[19]

In both places he contrasts these views with the Christian super-centration on Christ Incarnate, psychologically necessary for true human unity. It is his fundamental criticism of the impersonal character of Marxism, set in a particularized context. Moreover, in the last essay he makes the claim that in both Camus and Wells he finds evidence of a view approaching the Christian one.

Was it not Camus who wrote in *Sysyphe*, "If Man found that the Universe could love he would be reconciled?" And did not Wells, through his exponent the humanitarian biologist Steel in *The Anatomy of Frustration*, express his need to find, above and beyond humanity, a "universal love"?[20]

Two principal lines of thought stand out in these later reflections on Marxism: a sharpening of his analysis on the nature of collective consciousness in the Marxist sense, and a penetration into possible spiritual resources of Marxist thought that would provide the base for an eventual convergence with Incarnational Christianity. They also serve to highlight the fundamentally personalist approach in Teilhard's political ethic.

For personalists, it is not hard to agree with Teilhard's personalist objections to Marxism. His optimism about the two rising faiths converging with "necessity" is another matter. The possibility and actuality of increasing collaboration between well-disposed Marxists and Christians on urgent problems of human need, and also the more widespread use by Christians of certain aspects of Marxist social analysis are acceptable enough to many. But Teilhard's glowing affirmation of convergence makes one pause. If all that he meant by the statement

19. *Ibid.*, p. 286.
20. *Ibid.*, p. 287.

was that persons who sincerely strove to do what was right and were loyal to the deepest demands of their consciences would find, somehow, the saving grace of Christ and ultimately find union in God, then a "necessity" of convergence would be agreeable. But such convergence is clearly conditioned, and unfortunately Teilhard's language in the passage in question, as in others similar, does not affirm this condition. In the last analysis, the problem turns out to be the same underlying problem, with a different nuance, as was analyzed above in chapter 3, when Teilhard's basis for predicting ultimate human unification was rejected.[21]

4. TEILHARD'S PERSONALISM AND TOTALITARIANISM

Teilhard's personalist approach to matters political needs considerable stress, particularly in view of the fact that severe criticism has been directed toward his political thought as tending toward a totalitarianism that would ruthlessly engulf the individual and his precious uniqueness through a cold subordination of individual human persons to the needs of an evolving collective humanity.

That Teilhard abhorred the prospect of an ant-hill depersonalized society is clear enough from his concern expressed on more than one occasion.[22] Yet the charges of totalitarianism have been leveled by critics who are presumably aware of these texts. How account for this phenomenon in Teilhardian criticism? It cannot be denied that if one leans heavily on certain texts preoccupied with the concept of the noosphere and the need for a global, total vision of human development, it is possible to derive the impression that the individual hu-

21. See above, chap. 3B.
22. See, for example, "Sketch of a Personalistic Universe" (1936), *HE*, p. 81; *PM* (1940), pp. 256-57; "The Grand Option" (1939), *FM*, p. 49; *MPN* (1949), pp. 100-101; "Does Mankind Move Biologically on Itself?" (1949), *FM*, p. 250.

man person gets lost in this sweeping vision of humanity as a whole.[23] On the other hand, it would seem that sufficient attention to the implications of Teilhard's fundamental thought that union in genuine love differentiates by fostering personal uniqueness should allay these fears. For the precise point of *differentiating* union, on the level of the sexual love of the couple, the broad human love of all men, or the love between man and God, is that such love union not only safeguards, but is directed toward developing individual personal uniqueness, no matter what the type of association with other human or divine persons. It is true that Teilhard does stress the responsibility of the individual person to dedicate himself to developing the whole, the totality of society. It is also true that he insists that this be done in conformity with his principle of differentiating union. Hence the dedication he has in mind involves a basic duty and right of self-development to be exercised by individuals, and *to be respected by all others in their dealings with each other*. It is precisely this respect of individual personal rights and duties that seems to have been ignored, or not sufficiently weighted, by those who accuse Teilhard of totalitarianism.

Moreover, Teilhard's understanding of the function of an elite in social development must likewise be ap-

---

23. Such would seem to be the explanation of the stand taken by Victor C. Ferkiss, *Technological Man: The Myth and the Reality*, pp. 86-89. The critique by Ferkiss would seem to be based on an incomplete marshaling of texts, failing to take into account the force of other texts clearly declaring Teilhard's anti-totalitarian personalism. A similar shortage of texts would seem to be at the root of the attack by Ernst Benz, which sees Teilhard tending to justify Marxism and advocating an idea of love incompatible with Christian respect for the "thou." See Ernst Benz, *Evolution and Christian Hope*, trans. Heinz G. Frank, Anchor Books (Garden City, N.Y.: Doubleday — Co., Inc., 1968), pp. 234, 240. For a French misreading of Teilhard and a good corrective analysis, see Mathieu's comments on Bernard Charbonneau, *Teilhard de Chardin, prophète d'un âge totalitaire*, in Mathieu, *La pensée politique de Teilhard*, pp. 90-95, where he is speaking of Teilhard and Marxism, and also p. 146, where he treats of Teilhard's concept of an elite and its implications. One could also note Claude Cuénot's comments in "Teilhard et le Marxisme," *Europe* 431-432 (mars–avril 1965):172. "Teilhard was horrified by totalitarianism; the defense of the rights of the human person preoccupied him to the point of being an obsession. . . ." (My translation.)

proached with the implications of this essential principle in view. For him, an elite, leading evolutionary group does not emerge as a *coercive* body, but as a preeminently *suasive* corps, seeking the development of its own members and all it attempts to influence in accord with the principle of creative, searching, striving, *differentiating* human love. In this context, what will be seen shortly about his thought on the complementarity of human groups in the evolutionary process is important. The ruthless fascist or Marxist type of elitism as it has appeared is then seen to be opposed to the Teilhardian concept of the function of an elite, which is best associated with the evangelical notion of a leaven in the mass, as formulated in modern times by men such as Cardijn in the theory and tactics of the Jocist movement. What should not be overlooked, above all, is Teilhard's wish, paradoxical as it might seem, for the growth of a kind of "universalized elite" as the democratic concept of human social development more and more takes hold in human consciousness.[24]

24. The text where he expresses this concept is an early one. It is found in a letter to his cousin Marguerite, September 9, 1918, *MM*, pp. 232-33: "The whole difficulty (and secret) of real democracy is to encourage the renewal and the recruitment of the elite, and to make inclusion in it as universal as possible." Such a thought seems to go far toward putting Teilhard on the side of the democratic angels; unfortunately his next thought is disconcerting: "But *in itself*, the mass of humanity is profoundly inferior and repulsive. Don't you find it so?" Teilhard's honest confrontation with the problem of loving everyone has already been noted, in considering his theory of "the human sense." In the light of what he clearly holds about the possibility of and responsibility for universal love, it seems best to take these disconcerting ideas from an early letter as a reflection of a problem that was ultimately to be more psychological than theoretical as to universal human dignity and lovableness. Notwithstanding the evidence that can be noted indicating a similarity between Teilhard's theory of the need for an elite and Marxist-Leninist theory, it seems more in keeping with Teilhard's bent to stress the ties of resemblance to evangelical and later Christian concepts. On this point, see Mathieu, *La pensée politique de Teilhard*, pp. 143-44. Mathieu's observations on this matter seem somewhat inconsistent with his insistence on Teilhard's antitotalitarian personalism. What similarity one can find between Teilhardian and Marxist theory on the elite question would have to be limited more to what the two approaches have in common regarding the function of an elite, but not with regard to its ultimate motivating spirit. This for Teilhard would have to be personalist, with prime emphasis on suasive love.

## 5. POLITICS AND RELIGION

Another important question is provoked by the stance taken in the pieces just examined above. It has to do with why Teilhard examines Marxism in direct juxtaposition to Christianity, rather than to democracy and fascism, as he did in "The Salvation of Mankind." To a certain extent and implicitly, as has been noted, Marxism is set alongside Christianity in the earlier work. The historical expansion and impact of Marxism after World War II (along with the apparent waning of fascism) undoubtedly provides part of the answer. Moreover, it would seem valid to infer that in his discussion of a socialist type of democracy, as in "The Essence of the Democratic Idea," he is bringing Marxist and democratic ideas together. But apparently he never saw fit to pursue the avenues of inquiry opened up here.

The underlying reason for this approach seems to be what was referred to at the beginning of the present chapter, namely, that Teilhard's concern about political matters found its outlet in inquiry directed to fundamental, orientational world outlooks, rather than to the more practical details of political organization. Another way in which this mind-set of Teilhard appears is the absence of any essay, or even side remarks, on the enormous problem of concrete Church-State relations. In the large and fundamental sense, he was obviously concerned about the implications of his Christian faith with regard to man's temporal life, and he was seriously concerned about how the Church should present itself to modern temporal and political man. But he did fail to extend his practical thoughts on the apostolate into this area. Perhaps this is understandable enough when one takes into account his long years removed from the European scene and his general style of life, as well as his strong negative feelings about the highly juridical approach to the Kingship of Christ as evidenced in Pius XI's Encyclical and much of the professional theologizing of the time.[25] But it is disappointing to find little that would approximate observations of the sort made by his confrere Alfred Delp, S.J., in his *Prison Meditations* about the role of the Church in social and political life.[26]

## D. Geopolitics and Human Complementarity

In the political writings considered up to this point, the question of the politics of race or of racial nationalism has not come up for explicit discussion. The matter was of concern to Teilhard as far back as the First World War and reflections on the problem show in his correspondence through the years.[27] His basic position was clarified for him in the thirties and shows no change down to the last years of his life. A grasp of how he works with the notion of complementarity is of the utmost importance for appreciating this position, which led him to part company with even so close and esteemed an associate as the Louvain missiologist Père Charles.[28]

### 1. "THE NATURAL UNITS OF HUMANITY"

The most detailed and developed formulation of his thought along these lines is found in "The Natural Units of Humanity" (1939), the essay mentioned earlier in the

25. For Teilhard's reaction to the encyclical on Christ the King, see d'Ouince, *Teilhard: la pensée chrétienne*, p. 155, n18. On rereading the encyclical during his retreat of 1939, he noted in his retreat journal, ". . . how static! juridical! inferior to the thesis of Colossians!" (My translation.)

26. As a sociologist, Delp was by professional bent more inclined to social analysis. His criticism of Church responsibility for emergence of the bureaucratic type of man would undoubtedly have won approval from Teilhard, with his sensitivity to juridicism. See Alfred Delp, S.J., *The Prison Meditations of Father Delp*, Intro. by Thomas Merton, Macmillan Paperback (New York: The Macmillan Co., 1963), p. 152. Delp's strong plea for a Church more involved with basic human concerns would have struck a responsive chord in Teilhard.

27. See *MM*, pp. 253, 258; *LZ*, pp. 78-80, 116-17; *LF*, pp. 67, 71, 196; *LT*, pp. 86-133, 216, 219.

28. See *LZ*, p. 116; *LT*, p. 220. Charles was one of the "Missiologues" to whom Teilhard refers.

present chapter.[29] A close look at it is important (even with the risk of going over ideas now perhaps over-familiar), in view of the fact that, as he saw the evidence, there was no complete equality of racial or national groups, but rather complementarity. How can he escape the charge, therefore, of being a racist in the final analysis? Ultimately, in the same way that his explanation of the role of an elite in democratic society could be said to enable him to avoid being categorized as a fascist.

The bulk of the essay is devoted to laying out the groundwork for the concluding section on "The Foundations of a Racial Morality." In the earlier pages he summarizes the biological reasoning for anticipating that the ramification process occurring throughout the ascending stages of living beings should be expected to operate also on the human level. Human ramification he finds characterized by two main properties, the preeminence of the psychic over the somatic, and unlimited mutual fertility among the various branches. Furthermore, the intermingling of these two properties in human development provides a human ramification process of extraordinary complexity, whereby the cross-breeding carried on involves mixing the somatic in varying degrees with correspondingly varying styles of the psychic. The upshot of this is that the natural unit of humanity is neither the anthropological race nor the sociological nation or culture, but an amalgam that he describes as a *branch of humanity*. It is an ethnico-politico-moral combination that must be taken *as a whole and in movement* to be understood. Moreover, the number of combinations in which the psychic and somatic mingle in varying proportions leads to extreme diversity, with different elements predominating in different ways, depending on the particular thrust in a particular environment of genetic factors, soil and climate, political

29. *VP*, pp. 192-215. For a later summary of his thought on racial complementarity, see his letter to Torrês-Bodet of *UNESCO*, July 27, 1950, quoted by Cuénot, *Teilhard-Biography*, pp. 300-301.

structure, and language and culture, with all their multiple interactions. At this point he asks the directional question: where does science see all this leading—toward purposeless diversification or convergent harmonization? He begins interpreting the phenomena by a statement of his basic evolutionary law, the law of progressive growth toward higher states of complexity and consciousness. Here he draws two related corollaries: 1) evolution is coming to a head, with the emergence of reflection in man, and 2) further progress in life is going to be in the spiritual realm. He accepts as a factual starting point the growth of humanity, insofar as it can be measured by power and consciousness, in fixed and limited regions. In this progress, certain ethnic groups have made up the advance wing. This reality, however, is not to be explained solely on the grounds of "blood and mind," nor on grounds of economic resources and climate. What is especially significant is that the most vigorous human branches are not those in which the purest genes have spawned in isolation, but those in which much interfecundation has taken place.

*The most humanized human collectivities always appear in the last resort, to be the product not of segregation but of synthesis.* [30]

The geographical loci of outstanding human development have been places on earth where different human strains have run together and easily intermingled. Then Teilhard generalizes on this observation by affirming that divergent influences surfacing in human evolution not only do not ultimately prevent the branches from falling apart, but use diversity to effect by combination superior forms of human awareness. The distinctive traits of the branches are not destroyed, but, with man, since convergence is on the ascendance, multiplication develops and completes itself by synthesis. Coalescence is achieved, not confusion, and once again the organic

30. *VP*, p. 207. (Emphasis Teilhard's.)

principle, "union differentiates," comes into play on a new and higher level. For many today, repulsion, isolation, and fragmentation seem to be the real life cycle for the human shoot. Once high hopes of growing human unity have been dashed by the tension and strife in the world brought on by clashing human groups. Teilhard, however, does not read the evidence in that way. He sees the struggle going on as one not to fight and devour, but to rejoin and to fertilize. In the recent past, men have been prematurely hopeful of what could be brought about by attempts such as The League of Nations to unify different peoples. For a genuinely united earth, one must first have nations fully conscious of their own unique identity. The extreme divergence of the present time is the necessary prelude to a convergence never before witnessed on earth. If one only gets high enough for a broad perspective on the evidence, one can, he claims, see this is happening. Arms developments, industrial inventions, psychological and social readjustments, worked out in one country, spread far and wide. All mankind profits from the contagion of whatever is valid and progressive in discoveries and awakenings of consciousness.

At this point he focuses on the fundamental ethical question. With all the preceding as his working foundation, indicating where humanity is tending, he makes his claim that what human action stands most in need of at the present time is an international ethic.

Here he is admittedly on difficult ground and one can sense his awareness of the texture of the soil as he leads into his consideration of "The Foundations of a Racial Morality," the final section of the essay.[31]

He accepts racial differences as existing, but urges that these differences are no reason for antagonism. The cause of true human dignity does not seem to him to be at stake by acknowledging what evidence points to as

31. *VP*, pp. 211-15.

manifest ethnic variations. Children of one family are not all equally strong or intelligent. Correspondingly, people can be biologically equal as "thought phyla," who in the long run will gradually be integrated into a unified whole, but who are not yet altogether equal in physical gifts and mental acumen. He pleads that the original errors of feminism and democracy be not repeated. Man's need for woman is rooted precisely in the fact that woman is not man. A national organism can function only because a mechanic is not an athlete, a painter, or a financier. The fact that the Chinese, French, Kaffir, and Japanese are not the same accounts for the richness in the future of man not otherwise possible. When inequalities of various sorts are seen in their *essential complementarity*, their positive value is manifest. It is only when they are viewed statistically and in isolation that they seem to be damaging.

His two main ethical imperatives are then derived from this acceptance of functional diversity in the total human organism. The first is that each human branch should strive to complete itself *in the future*, according to its own qualities and genius, rather than strain to preserve or recover some original purity. The second is that the drive toward collective personalization should find the neighboring branches mutually seeking aid from each other in the common quest. Here he rejects, as has been seen earlier in the analysis of aggression, all that implies the validity of the law of the jungle and internecine strife among human beings. Human teamwork, whereby each develops in sympathy with all others, and spiritual energies are gradually organized to a higher pitch of perfection. This is the style of cooperation in convergence as opposed to a mechanical balance of material forces, that appears as mandatory.

When he says this he does not intend to gloss over the complicated technical problems of implementation, which he lists: definition of zones of occupation and zones of influence to the best advantage of the totality and the component elements; establishment of a certain distinction and rank or hierarchy, without which there would be unavoidable disorder or fragmentation between unevenly individualized or vigorous branches; a certain amount of living space and a sorting-out process of outside contributions, so that the progress and peculiar genius of each natural group would be assured (something needed for the self-maintenance of any organism); the right of each nation to live and yet not infringe on the rights of other nations; a sufficiently pliable arrangement to allow for adjustment to new situations, the extent to which, throughout the necessary adjustments, one can expect balance to develop on its own by the natural play of forces, or be pushed by rational planning in a calculated direction. He asks, finally, whether there should be totalitarianism or liberalism, the preeminence of one group or democracy.

One fundamental manner of resolving all these problems is ultimately advocated, namely, the method life has used from the very beginning in its steady ascent to higher consciousness. Here he describes it as the method of slow and patient exploration, operative in the context of one necessary condition: an atmosphere of unity. In this atmosphere, he claims, one political solution seems about as good as another, at least as a start, whereas apart from it catastrophe will be inevitable.[32]

## 2. CRITIQUE AND ANALYSIS

Despite the terminology, what comes to the fore here is not a variation from Teilhard's habitual thinking, but a formulation in different language of his constant plea for courageous, love-motivated research, this time particularized in the political realm. His final argument is

32. *Ibid.*, p. 214. This statement is a puzzling overemphasis, so it would seem, of the impact of "atmosphere," and, it is hoped, would have been revised later by Teilhard along the lines of his thought-development about the urgency of a type of democracy.

likewise in line with his approach as seen previously. In it he points to the need of a unifying center of attraction for this love energy, which needs organization in all the complicated situations he has enumerated: a unifying Center that must be personal—Someone, not just Something.

What should be noted at the outset in analyzing the meaning of his thought in this essay is that his working concept of "race" as a "human branch" already embraces a complex process of synthesis, involving a host of factors beyond genetic transmission of anthropological (in the narrow sense), racial characteristics. This immediately sets his position apart from that of a Nazi type of racial purists and also from a Marxist style of environmental determinism.

Prior to a more detailed examination of certain aspects of his position as outlined here, it should be borne in mind that in it he is concerned with a more immediate future and avoids the eschatological question about what would be the ultimate result of the processes he describes. Logically, one would expect some ultimate synthesis, which somehow would still enable, out of respect for the differentiation of function of component groups and individual persons, his ideas on complementarity to be operative, both on the individual personal and on the group level. How he approached the eschatological question will be considered more closely in chapter 9, but even then, it will be seen that his vision of the ultimate future is not a detailed one, and, in fact, leaves the problem as just posed answered in only a very general way.

Critique of his position on complementarity here must consider two basic issues: 1) does the actual history of the development of human branches, in his sense, reveal the existence *in fact* of the complementary differentiation he describes? and 2) *if* this complementarity is accepted as established, does it lead to any conflict with what he holds about the radical dignity of the human person? Another way of phrasing the second question would be to ask whether complementarity as he explains it can at the same time mean a gradation, and hence relative inferiority or superiority of roles, without negating a more fundamental equality of personal dignity. It seems, on the strength of what he says about the equality of "thought phyla," that he himself would answer in the affirmative the second question as phrased, and that, ultimately, through this distinction, he would attempt to free himself from holding racial distinctions in a pejorative sense. The ultimate judgment on the first issue will have to be left to the hands of cultural anthropologists, social psychologists, and historians.

With regard to the second issue, careful reading of what Teilhard has to say about it reveals a position that can be summarized as follows: inequalities, in the sense of different levels of cultural development, have existed and continue to exist among the various branches of humanity; but all branches of humanity are equal in their fundamental dignity and responsibility for collaboration to build a better world, with full recognition that different groups have different complementary functions in this task. Understood in this way, his position can no more be judged a denial of equality of human dignity than can the teaching of St. Paul about diversity of members in the Body of Christ.

There is, however, a more serious difficulty with the manner in which Teilhard builds his argument toward his international ethical norms, and it has to do with another aspect of his analysis of the process of human progress. The difficulty is closely tied to the problem analyzed in chapter 3 about the connection between predictive accuracy and ethical validity. In the present context it has a different initial form, in that it arises not from his predictive accuracy, but from the accuracy of his assessment about past and present convergence by humanity in differentiating social union, and the relationship of this accuracy to the ethical norms he states (the development of national identity simultaneously with efforts toward cross-fertilizing collaboration in a common global task).

As Teilhard leads into his statement of ethical imperatives, he does so on the assumption that they are to be formulated toward the continuation of an *established and existing* process. In other words, the directions for future choice are made dependent upon discernible directions of past choice. In all candor, one must admit that the difficulty lies at the very roots of his fundamental premises for his morality of movement, based on the acceptance of the reality of constructive evolution. The way in which he presents his argument in the essay at hand simply brings it more sharply into focus.

For Teilhard himself, there seems to be little question but that he accepted his analysis of the past as valid grounds for his projections of future imperatives, whether they be general or more particular moral directives. However, his sweeping statements that all past developments have taken place along the lines he described, and that the human race is of evolutionary necessity unifying now along the same lines, must be questioned both on grounds of universality and necessity. There are those (the present writer among them) who would argue, on the records of history, that there is no certainty humanity has in fact been unifying down through the centuries in the manner he alleges. There are also those who would seriously question, on the grounds of the contingency of human freedom, against the inevitability he professes to see. This second point has been raised earlier, and the conclusions drawn then would hold in the present context as well.[33]

In the earlier analysis the conclusion was reached that the flawed logic in his predictions did not ultimately undermine his ethic, because the ethical directives did not have of necessity to be based on absolute predictive ac-

33. See above, chap. 3B.

curacy, but could be seen to make good sense against a highly contingent future as well. Similarly, in the present context, one could argue that the ethical imperatives he advocates make good sense, even though the record of past history does not substantiate his generalization. There seems to be enough evidence that where and when people have acted as he described, human unification has proceeded satisfactorily, and that where and when these conditions have not been realized, the opposite has taken place. Consequently, one could argue from *partial* and *conditioned* past success to the same imperatives Teilhard would like to base on *universal* and *inevitable* progress.

When his directives, formulated more than thirty years ago, are viewed against the background of developments in recent years, they take on added significance. This is especially so in the light of the importance attributed to them by Léopold Senghor of Senegal, who has found Teilhard's thought appropriate for inclusion in his writing about "negritude" in African consciousness, and who has judged Teilhard's fundamental political concepts better suited to African needs than those of Karl Marx.[34] Latin American interest in Teilhardian thought, as attested to by Ivan Illich, Dom Helder Camara, and Francisco Bravo, is also not without relevance.[35]

## E.  Teilhard and World Government

On the question of the ultimate development of some type of international political structure, or world government, Teilhard's thought was consistent with his dis-

34. See Léopold Sédar Senghor, "Pierre Teilhard de Chardin et la politique africaine," *Cahiers* 3, pp. 13-65.
35. See Francisco Bravo, *Christ in the Thought of Teilhard de Chardin*, trans. Cathryn B. Larme (Notre Dame, Ind.: University of Notre Dame Press, 1967). The Preface is by Ivan Illich, who quotes with approval Dom Helder Camara's laudatory comments on Teilhard as an example of the impact of Teilhardian thought on Latin America (p. vi).

position, if not as fully elaborated as one might wish by way of the implications of the Law of Complexity-Consciousness applied to noospheric political anatomy. As is clear from texts already seen, his concern is almost exclusively with political ethos, with root orientational principles, rather than the morphology of political structure. It is not that he did not recognize the need for organizational form and procedure. He knew and lived within the organizational patterns of a definite area of big science, as well as the societal structures of his Order and his Church. But his anti-juridicism is well known. It may well have been this psychological antipathy to juridical form that inhibited his pursuing his observations on the consequences of the Law of Complexity-Consciousness into the area of local, national, or international government, with little more than recognition of their existence as a sector of life, outside his particular competence as analyst or creative designer.[36]

What he has to say is limited and ambivalent. He speaks of geopolitics in the same breath as geoeconomics, which he definitely admitted needed international organization.[37] He also, in one of his 1946 essays, quotes with approval an excerpt from *The New Yorker*, August, 1945:

36. Such a disposition would be consistent with, and might be said to flow from his attitude toward organizational matters in general. To quote Cuénot, "It is safe to say that Teilhard was by no means a first-class organizer. His intelligence kept him out of trouble, but he had endless difficulty in organizing an expedition, getting lost in practical details. He was only really at ease when he had to draw up plans for research. Then he did a wonderful job, taking views that were both grandiose and correct, and choosing the right way to set about things." See Claude Cuénot, "Pierre Teilhard de Chardin: Sketch for a Portrait," trans. W. E. O'Hea, *The Teilhard Review* 6, no. 1 (Summer 1971):5-7.

37. See *PM* (1940), p. 283. The same thoughts on this subject occur, word for word, in "Pré-humain, humain, ultra-humain," in *Idées et Forces* 2, no. 5 (Oct.-Déc. 1949): 68. It may well be that, since it was about this time that Teilhard, with the help of Henri de Lubac and Bruno de Solages, undertook a careful revision of *The Phenomenon of Man*, the text in its substance should be assigned to the later date. On the other hand, the content of the passage is not such as would seem to warrant revision for the eyes of censors. The appearance, then, of the same text in a later piece could be taken to point to continuity in his thought on the subject.

Political plans for the new world, as shaped by statesmen, are not fantastic enough. The only conceivable way to catch up with atomic energy is with political energy directed to a universal structure.[38]

Moreover, in an essay of the following year, he further observes:

Although the form is not yet discernible, mankind tomorrow will awaken to a "pan-organised" world.

But, and we must make no mistake about this, there will be an essential difference, a difference of order, between the unitary state towards which we are moving and everything we have hitherto known.[39]

However, Pierre Louis Mathieu reads Teilhard as ultimately not putting much weight on the importance of world governmental structure, but rather inclining to the value of international economic, scientific, and cultural collaboration apart from such a framework.[40] As confirmatory of his judgment, Mathieu refers to a personal journal entry of February 12, 1946, which would call for, in the interests of planetary unity, not so much a government in the juridical and constitutional sense, as a polarity—a directional thrust that would serve as a higher control and criterion of action.[41]

Such an observation cannot be ignored, but it seems that Mathieu's analysis does not pay enough attention to the texts referred to immediately above, nor distinguish between Teilhard's bent to distrust the efficacy of the

38. See "Some Reflections on the Spiritual Repercussions of the Atom Bomb" (September 1946), *FM*, p. 141.
39. See "The Formation of the Noosphere" (1947), *FM*, p. 176.
40. Mathieu, *La pensée politique de Teilhard*, p. 263.
41. *Ibid.*, p. 265. Mathieu discusses the matter in approximately two pages of text, bottom of p. 262 to the top of p. 265, under the heading, "Perspectives d'un mondialisme politique." The personal note, it should be marked for what it is worth, is dated February 1946, and the essay on "The Spiritual Repercussions of the Atom Bomb" more than six months later. Unfortunately, Mathieu's discussion makes no reference to this later text with definite implications about world political structure. Because of what is known about Teilhard's consistent fundamental attitudes, the dating of these two texts seems less significant than the failure to consider the content of the text from the essay on the atom bomb.

juridical and his recognition, as the texts seem clearly to indicate, that some form of it, on a planetary scale, would sooner or later come into existence. If this distinction is kept in mind, the journal entry to which Mathieu alludes would retain its force as expressing Teilhard's skepticism with regard to the relative subordinate importance of world governmental structures, but would not have to be read as contradictory to his other expressed thoughts that they would ultimately come to be—out of evolutionary necessity. With this interpretation, the evolution of planetary complex political structures could be seen as, not a utopian terminal condition of world society, necessarily, but the normal societal implementation of the Law of Complexity-Consciousness, whereby a unified global noospheric political spirit would have its corresponding political anatomical structure and nervous system. Teilhard's stress on the primacy of a controlling, directive, critical spirit would then lose none of its force. The apparent differences in his thoughts as just examined would then be "both-and" rather than an "either-or."

In conclusion, Teilhard's political concerns as reviewed in the present chapter corroborate Madeleine Barthélemy-Madaule's observation that his thought moved in the realm of *le politique* (political theory) rather than *la politique* (practical politics).[42] A further precision, however, seems in order, namely, that in the area of political theory, his overriding emphasis was on fundamental outlook or basic philosophy, in the broad sense of the term, and that he showed indifference to the questions of theory pertaining to governmental form and structure. That his personalist convictions did not lead him to the same level of practical involvement as an Emmanuel Mounier may well be regretted, but this fact should not impinge on the ultimate evaluation of his thought on the particular level he judged himself com-

---

42. See Barthélemy-Madaule, *La personne chez Teilhard*, p. 196.

petent and inclined to develop it.[43] Admitting his
shortcomings and lacunae, one can still make a strong
case that contemporary political life would improve by
taking his thought seriously, criticizing it more in depth,
and applying it, especially along the lines he advocated
for the development of democratic process and for the
growth of an international community sincerely groping
toward harmony while recognizing and positively fostering personalizing complementary diversity.

43. *Ibid.*, pp. 302-21, "Epilogue: L'univers personnel d'Emmanuel Mounier
et de Pierre Teilhard de Chardin." Also, André Ligneul, *Teilhard and Personalism*, trans. Paul Joseph Oligny, O.F.M. and Michael D. Meilhach, O.F.M.,
Deus Books (New York: Paulist Press, 1968), pp. 47-63, "The Involvement of
the Person."

# 7

# Education as the Transmission and Development of Spiritualized Energy

## A. Education and Spiritualized Energy

When Teilhard speaks of spiritualized energy, he does not once bring up the question of the importance of education as such. Nevertheless, his concern about the organization of human energy can be seen to have an educational orientation in its most fundamental sense. When Teilhard talks about organizing human energy on all levels, and preeminently on the level of spiritualized energy, he is concerned about how human beings can help each other to develop their potential. It seems clear enough, then, that what he does have to say about education, limited as it is, should come up for analysis in the present context.

## B. The Basic Sources

Of Teilhard's writings available for analysis here, there

251

is only one that devotes itself explicitly to the matter of education. It is entitled "Social Heredity and Progress," with the subtitle "Notes on the Humanist-Christian Value of Education."[1] Although written in 1938 and published in *Études* in 1945, the late date should not be taken as indication that he had no earlier interest in the subject. His World War I letters to his cousin Marguerite contain significant observations on educational questions, and it seems that during that time he wrote a short essay on "L'education de l'amour," only an incomplete copy of which has survived.[2] He speaks of education in a number of places, mostly in passing, but the most important sources for his explicit thought about it are the published essay and his early letters.

His fundamental theme about education is that its primary function is to operate as a special form of biological development through addition to serve as an essential organic process of transmission of vital developments in the evolution of human collective consciousness. He speaks of it as heredity become socialized in a special way in the consciousness of mankind, as distinguished from mere chromosomal heredity. The present consideration will draw mainly on his elaboration of this concept as found in "Social Heredity and Progress," with supplementary material from other sources.[3]

The essay is divided into three parts: 1) "Education and Life," 2) "Education and Mankind," and 3) "Educa-

1. *FM*, pp. 25-36.

2. See Cuénot, *Teilhard-Biography*, p. 476, Bibliography, item #503. The text is not dated, but there seems to be evidence for locating it among the early writings. On this point see Claude Soucy, *Pensée logique et pensée politique chez Teilhard de Chardin* (Paris: Presses Universitaires de France, 1967), p. 20, n1. Unfortunately, a copy of the text was unavailable for the present study.

3. The principal texts in addition to "Social Heredity and Progress" where Teilhard works with either the notions of transmission, heredity, or additivity in an educational context are the following: "The Promised Land" (1919), *WW*, p. 285; "Hominization" (1925), *VP*, p. 58; *PM* (1940), pp. 224-25; "The Formation of the Noosphere" (1947), *FM*, pp. 161-63; "Reflections on Original Sin" (1947), *CE*, p. 197; "Comment je vois" (1948), *DA*, p. 195; *MPN* (1949), p. 87; "The Energy of Evolution" (1953), *AE*, p. 364; and "The Singularities of the Human Species" (1954), *AM*, p. 242. Most of them have little or no development.

tion and Christianity." As can be seen, the third part goes beyong the phenomenological plane. It will be considered in the present context, however, because, as was seen earlier in the discussion of the conscience-decision process, important inferences can be drawn for secular-humanist, and other religious minds from Teilhard's thinking about Christianity.

In the first part, "Education and Life," he spends some time on the question of whether, or to what extent, there is evidence of acquired characteristics being transmitted germinally to descendants. He leaves the question unresolved, despite his inclination toward germinal transmission, and urges attention to a phenomenon open for contemporary observation: education. This he describes as: "The transmission by example of an improvement, an action, and its reproduction by imitation."[4] (The definition gives rise to some significant practical applications, not all of which he highlighted.) What perturbs him is that education, operative in this way, seems to be dismissed as an unimportant "epiphenomenon," so far as the larger biological picture is viewed. He insists that observation of the animal kingdom provides evidence of its universality, so that, ". . . at least for practical purposes, education is a universal biological function, co-existent with the totality of the living world. . . ." And he is strong in his affirmation that educational activity is organically integrated into the entire generative process. "At what point," he asks, "does the mother cease to engender her child? Is it when she first feeds it, after giving it birth? Or is it when, having weaned it, she teaches it to know and hunt its prey?" (p. 28).

At all events, he concludes that education is not artificial, accidental, or accessory, but an essential, natural form of biological additivity. In it he also sees a possible indication of germinal heredity taking shape, with or-

4. *FM*, p. 27.

ganic mutation appearing at this stage in the form of psychic invention, arising in the parents and handed on by them. He likewise views heredity as passing, through education, beyond the individual and into the collective, social phase.

What this implies with regard to the education of human persons is taken up in the next part. Central to his argument at this level is what he presents as the following fact:

> Mankind, as we find it in its present state and present functioning, is organically inseparable from that which has been slowly added to it, and which is propagated through education. This "additive zone," gradually created and transmitted through collective experience, is for each of us a sort of matrix, as real in its own way as our mother's womb. It is a true racial memory, upon which our individual memories draw and through which they complete themselves. (pp. 30-31)

This is no mere "snowball" additivity, however, but organic evolutionary growth, proceeding in an observable direction toward maturation. Gradually through time there has evolved a state of collective human consciousness handed down from generation to generation, but with continual increment. Although sustained by the individual, this consciousness reaches out into the group and with formative impact works toward the shaping of a kind of generalized human personality.

> It seems that where Man is concerned the specific function of education is to ensure the continued development of this personality by transmitting it to the endlessly changing mass: in other words, to extend and ensure in collective mankind a consciousness which may already have reached its limit in the individual. (p. 32)

All this is quite general, it is true, and heavy with biological analogy. But it does amount to the lengthiest explanation available from him about the biologically additive aspect of education, which in other writings he refers to with only brief formulas. What he presents here is hardly much more than that, but it does contain some Teilhardian additivity.

When, in the third part, he explores the implications of the preceding ideas for Christian education, he goes beyond mere general application. In this section he strikes certain notes which, despite their religious context, have practical consequences for secular humanist education, and which bring his additive, transmissive ideas of education in line with what he has also said about the importance of creative, inventive research and love in human progress.

For Teilhard, Christianity is in essence the religion of the Incarnation: "God uniting Himself with the world which He created, to unify it and in some sort incorporate it in Himself." Consequently, for the worshipper of Christ, this act expresses the history of the universe. What is more, this incorporation takes place by both quantitative and qualitative steps. There is numerical growth of the body of Christians, and also growth of a collective Christological consciousness. It is in his reflections on the latter that one finds implications for research. He puts the point most directly when he makes the simple statement: "We cannot continue to love Christ without discovering Him more and more" (p. 33).

The discovery element in this statement is significant, since his use of the transmission notion with such frequency could convey the impression that Teilhard viewed education as something of a mechanical pipe-line process of transfer. To read him in this way would be to miss all that is involved in his analogical use of ideas, and above all, what is contained in *human* transmission of previous psychic human growth. Clearly, for Teilhard, among the foremost developments of contemporary man to be increased by those now alive and handed on is a profoundly grasped *zest for discovery*.

What has just been said is defensible enough in the light of Teilhard's ideas in the essay under examination, and the same essay contains other corroborative material. One could also infer it from other texts previously seen on the importance of research in the evolutionary process. If this spirit of inquiry is one of the outstanding human evolutionary developments, obviously strenuous effort to foster and communicate it in the educational process would be one of mankind's most precious legacies for the future. Oddly enough, though, Teilhard did not draw out the inference. A plausible explanation seems to be that to him it was so obvious as to be taken for granted, and that his own distance from the scene of actual controversies about the relative roles of teaching and research in schooling did not provoke in his thinking the need to make clarifications pertinent to what remains a thorny problem in the educational world.

His own purpose in introducing the ideas of numerical growth and increased awareness of Christ active in the world was to enable him to integrate what he observed in Christianity with what he had previously observed as proper to the entire process of life—to show that in Christianity as with all living organisms, the mysterious law of additivity and social heredity was operative.

At this point there appears the critical question, one of his central preoccupations, as to whether human effort, tending toward a "natural" collective personality, is really divorced from the Christic endeavor, seeking a mystical oneness in Christ, or whether the two are "simply related phases, on different levels, of the same event." To take up the second option and accept their correlation is for him to affirm the correct notion of Christian humanism, which he sums up in language reminiscent of Augustine: "Life for Man. Man for Christ. Christ for God." Here he states emphatically:

> to ensure the psychic continuity, at every phase of this vast development embracing myriads of elements strewn throughout the immensity of time, there is a single mechanism–education. (p. 34; emphasis Teilhard's)

Several points come to light in his concluding summation that indicate what were to him the gravity and unity, as well as the complexity of the work of the Christian teacher. They contain more food for thought on the role of zest for research and also some provocative suggestions on the place of love.

The first point he makes is something of an explication of the basic premise that through education biological heredity is furthered in a reflective form and in its social dimensions. But note the practical slant.

> The educator, as an instrument of Creation, should derive respect, and ardour for his efforts from a profound communicative sense of the developments already achieved or awaited by Nature. Every lesson he gives should express love for, and cause to be loved, all that is more irresistible and definitive in the conquests of Life. (p. 35)

From what is known about what he judged the most important developments achieved or awaited by nature, as the most irresistible and definitive conquests of Life, one could paraphrase his words here to read that the educator should above all strive to communicate an awareness of the meaning of love in human evolution, as well as a spirit of research and discovery.

His second point, however, bears more directly on the concept of love and its importance, although he comes at it with different words. As he sees the work of education, the necessary if gradual convergence of minds and hearts is being realized through educational effort to spread common viewpoints and attitudes.

> Directly charged with the task of achieving this unanimity of mankind, the educator, whether his subject be literature, history, science, or philosophy, must constantly live with it and consciously strive for its realisation. A passionate faith in the purpose and splendour of human aspirations must be the flame that illumines his teaching. (p. 35)

Granted, the word "love" does not appear in the above, but it hardly seems straining the text to read it as referring to the need for developing precisely that form of human energy which Teilhard considered indispensable for bringing about human unity in unanimity. For him so to speak definitely puts him in the camp of those who link character formation and development of morals and values to the core of the educational process. His earlier correspondence with his cousin, moreover, bears this out.[5]

More on the role of love in education appears in his final point, where he expands on the direct and indirect incorporation of the world in the Word Incarnate, to be brought about through the medium of education. Indirect incorporation would derive from the dispositive activity of increased humanization itself, which, in the light of what has already been seen concerning Teilhard's understanding of the human, would involve inculcating a sense of moral responsibility for continuing evolution, with all that implies regarding the development and organization of human energy on all levels. A point not yet explored, but one that was enormously important for Teilhard and is relevant here, would be technological education in an atmosphere of authentic evolutionary humanism.[6]

The direct incorporative role for the Christian educator would be that of an instrument or channel of a living-faith tradition. What Teilhard emphasizes as of capital importance for the mentality of one so employed is that the connection between humanization and religious faith be grasped as an inseparable structural relation. He then adds a sentence that could at first blush be disconcerting:

5. See, for example, *MM*, pp. 86, 108, 204, 257.
6. When Teilhard touches on the issue—in fact, he merely skirts it—he is mainly concerned about education for the leisure he envisions from technological advances. See "The Phyletic Structure of the Human Group" (1951), *AM*, pp. 161-62. Here, as elsewhere, he shows no concern with technological or vocational training as such, other than that he assumes it is taking place.

To have experienced and understood, in order to teach others to experience and understand, that all human enrichment is but dross except inasmuch as it becomes the most precious and incorruptible of all things by adding itself to an immortal centre of love: such is the supreme knowledge and the ultimate lesson to be imparted by the Christian educator.[7]

What disconcerts is that he seems to express here an almost a Kempis contempt of the world right after having stressed its value. Obviously Teilhard was no late-medieval anti-intellectual. But he did have a definite hierarchy of values. What comes through his strong language is his conviction that mere research and technological growth will never bring human life to maturation. The world, whatever its technical sophistication, without a vital core and center of love energy, without Christ-Omega, would simply not be an evolving world, for it would have nothing to draw it effectively onward and upward.

More important than the paradox of his language, however, is the stress again on love in the context of education. Education, if it be Christian, must strive mightily to engender a deep personal love of Christ. By analogy, stretching his Omega theory to the fullest and applying the implications to educators who are not Christian, one could say that the educator, no matter what his religion, would be expected to strive heart and soul to foster a love of whatever would personally unify those with whom he was dealing, however he might describe the ultimate Loving Center of human aspiration.

From what has just been seen, one can affirm that Teilhard's concern in his writing is on the level of educational philosophy rather than the techniques of administration, curriculum development, or pedagogical method. As it was with matters political, here, too, his

7. *FM*, p. 36.

concern is more with the main current and its direction than with what rides on its surface. One could say also that he is writing a basic ethic of education, in that, without putting it in so many words, he lays strong ethical imperatives on the educator's conscience, whoever he or she may be. In a real sense, educators would be among the foremost of those engineers and technicians of the future upon whose shoulders so much depends.

## C. Analysis and Comment

What is surprising, in view of the crucial role of education in the evolutionary enterprise, is that Teilhard wrote so little about it. He did have other significant thoughts pertinent to it, but they have to be gathered from various places and pieced together in much the same manner as must be done with the rest of what belongs to his moral theorizing.

While it is true that "Social Heredity and Progress" was written with school people in mind, it would be inaccurate to hold that he viewed the school as the sole educational channel. This is not only implied in his stress on the transmission of a collective consciousness, which of its very nature depends on a large environmental context for impact, but also can be derived from how he carried on his own educational vocation. He himself spent relatively little time in the formal classroom as a teacher. But he devoted an enormous amount of time and energy to writing, lecturing, and conversing—all of which would correctly fall under the classification of educational activity as he described it. The thrust of his apostolate, as he conceived and practiced it, by wilderness camp fire or at diplomatic receptions, in his voluminous personal correspondence or in the midst of scholarly congresses, was in itself an excellent object lesson exemplifying the theory examined above.

As for the perennially thorny educational problem of

freedom versus authority or student spontaneity and initiative versus administrative discipline and control, Teilhard declares a basic principle in "Human Energy," but stops short, as usual, of the practicalities entailed in implementation. Writing specifically about the problem of the relation of individual noospheric elements to the totality, he notes that because of the spiritual nature of the noosphere, these elements are not the direct counterparts of the faceless and interchangeable components of a gaseous mass, but rather are like cells of a highly specialized organism.

This means that the perfection and utility of each nucleus of human energy in relation to the whole, definitely depend on what is unique and incommunicable in the achievement of each. The final preoccupation of any specialist in spirit, therefore, when dealing with human units who are undergoing any kind of transformation under his direction, is to leave them the possibility of self-discovery and the freedom of self-differentiation, both to an ever-increasing extent.[8]

Taken by itself, and also in the context of certain other statements already seen about the condition of no coercion for the development of love, the sense of this passage points to minimizing external discipline and control. Moreover, it is clear from his correspondence with his cousin that he was sympathetic with her efforts to work toward more freedom of choice and spontaneity for the students with whom she dealt.[9]

But there are complications that arise from what he also wrote to Marguerite about the need for constraint (even the *Index*) in education and a certain amount of force, in view of the fact that it did not seem to him that all men were really ripe for rational autonomy, particularly younger members of the species.[10] One should also keep in mind in this context what has been seen previ-

8. *HE* (1937), p. 131.
9. *MM*, pp. 128, 142.
10. *Ibid.*, p. 108.

ously about his letter to Léontine Zanta, in which he commented on the need for the use of force in the context of the Italian Ethiopian campaign of the thirties, as well as his remark in "The Essence of the Democratic Idea," where he speaks of balancing "*laissez-faire* with firmness." Despite the fact that education in the strict academic sense of schooling is not the focus of attention in these texts, their implications for education in both the larger and narrower sense are obvious enough. Willy nilly, the question of coercive force must be faced again, this time in the context not of warfare, but education.

When the various expressions of Teilhard's thought are weighed in their different contexts and considered against the background of his own manner of dealing with people who came to him for advice and also against his other comments to Marguerite about doing one's best to develop an educational environment without coercion (granted the difficulty of "motivating from within"), one comes to the conclusion that at times, reluctantly and as a last resort, coercive force is required in educating young human beings (as well as peoples), but that every effort should be made to avoid it.[11]

Criticism has been directed against Teilhard for his lack of compassion for those suffering from hunger, for a supposed lack of social conscience.[12] Right off one could counter by arguing that the main thrust of his educational principles is directed toward developing a highly sensitive social conscience if it is directed at anything, although he does not put his ideas in so many words. Moreover, there is in one of his letters to Marguerite an illuminating passage that could be said to reflect this attitude quite well. It is contained in a letter dated January 8, 1916.

> You are absolutely right in working to make love of the poor supreme in the Institute: it's the most Christian attitude, the most social, the most educative, that you could

11. For Teilhard's comments to Marguerite, see *ibid.*, p. 142.
12. See Ferkiss, *Technological Man*, p. 89.

make your pupils adopt. To make them turn with real sympathy to the destitute is in some way to give them, in one single habit of mind, the quintessence of all humane and Catholic training. You can never go too far along those lines.[13]

Although it seems that he never elaborated specifically on this point, there is no evidence that Teilhard ever reflected any change in attitude. In fact, the cumulative impression, stemming again from his personal dealings with individuals, as well as his theoretical writings seen in their total context, was that he was deeply sensitive to human suffering in all its forms and strove as best he could to get at the roots of it to extirpate it.[14]

A problem in the educational world has always been that of how faculty and students relate on a personal level. What Teilhard's attitude could be expected to reveal regarding professorial responsibilities both to teaching and research could easily enough be predicted on the basis of his ultimately quite practical socially responsible approach to research and his fundamental personalism. What he said about scientists without a heart can well be recalled at this point.[15] But there is a clear statement of his concept of teacher-student relations, again from a wartime letter to his cousin, from the Front:

> Yes, go out, with all your heart, to the students whom providence seems to send your way. . . . Having known their difficulties and shared their way of living you can, more closely than anyone else, teach them to find all around them the God whom you yourself can now see more clearly in everything.[16]

13. *MM*, p. 87.
14. Ferkiss, *Technological Man*, p. 89, seems to have been unaware of the implications of Teilhard's thought in *DM* on resistance to evil, to say nothing of the compassion evidenced in his writing about the passivities of diminishment. See *DM* (1927), pp. 80-94. One could also note, regarding Teilhard's sensitivity to the sufferings of others, the opening pages of his essay "Reflections on the Compression of Mankind" (1953), *AE*, pp. 341-42. For excerpts from this text, see above, chap. 1C, near end.
15. See above, chap. 5C (1) for the quotation from *LF*, p. 125.
16. *MM*, p. 190.

Important in this text is not only Teilhard's sense of compassion and sympathy for students as human beings, but also his awareness of the educational impact of teachers in sharing life experience with their students, and not living in remote professorial isolation from them.

## D. Educational Content

The only place in which Teilhard goes specifically into the matter of educational content is in an overtly religious paper, his last, in fact, before he died. It is called "Research, Work, and Worship," and was written in New York, March 1955.[17] His main purpose was not to outline any educational curriculum, but rather to point up what to him was an inescapable psychological fact as well as an essential aspect of working for the greater glory of God: that a scientific research worker must think through the implications of his research for his faith and his faith for his research. The same would hold, correspondingly, for industrial workers. The thought is hardly a new one for him, and is in itself another formulation of his basic concepts about research.

His ideas about education are found in the third section of the paper: "A practical step to be considered: specialised religious training for scientific and industrial workers" (pp. 218-20). Here he has two recommendations that clearly fit into the educational picture, plus a third with educational implications. The first would be for specialized schools in which young research students or workers would be given an intellectual theological training "more concerned than it is now to make plain the genetic links between the Kingdom of God and human effort" (p. 219). Second, and to him equally important, would be spiritual education in which the Spiritual

17. *SC*, pp. 214-20.

Exercises of Ignatius of Loyola would be clearly and sharply adapted to take into account the shift from a static to a dynamic world view, in which the researcher and the worker meet and complete the Total Christ through divinized human effort. Finally, he advocates "a new and higher form of worship to be gradually disclosed by Christian thought and prayer, adapted to the needs of all tomorrow's believers without exception" (p. 220).

His first recommendation is not really a new thought, but a statement in this particular context of his basic approach to Christian humanism. The second can rank as one of his most important recommendations, and, as has been seen above with regard to the adaptations he made in his own religious prayer life, was a recommendation that flowed from his own experience of many years. The reason for assigning it top priority is that reflective, prayerful meditation on the meaningful orientation of human life would seem to be a key and decisive activity in personal development, an essential condition for the indispensable assimilation of life experience into a transformed consciousness, and thus a *sine qua non* if basic educational goals are to be achieved. What this recommendation amounts to is to incorporate into the educational process practical training in the type of ethical methodology that enabled Teilhard to construct his own synthesis of his scientific humanist and religious faith, and to derive and sustain the radical zest and love energy necessary for implementing this synthesis in the daily task of striving to push human evolution forward and upward. Moreover, it provides further evidence of the claim made previously about his lining up on the side of formational, rather than merely informational educators. And, for once at least, Teilhard is revealed as getting into the process of practical implementation itself, even though he stops at naming the process and does not expand on how it should work.

His third recommendation is not clear and one can only speculate as to its correct interpretation. Judging from the centrality of the Eucharist in his own life, and the manner in which he interpreted it in "The Priest," "The Mass on the World," and *The Divine Milieu*, one seems justified in assuming that he had in mind a revamping of liturgical language to bring it in line with his own interpretive adaptations in the writings just mentioned.[18] Taken in this sense, his recommendation about worship becomes an essential continuation of his second recommendation about the adaptation of the Exercises, and would play an important part in the educational function of developing a Christified sense of evolutionary community. It would thus relate closely to his basic educational thesis about the need for improving and hightening collective consciousness, and would likewise reveal its compatibility with an important thesis about the educative function of liturgy and sacrament.

What the educational implications of these recommendations would be for those who did not share his religious convictions would have to be drawn out by analogy, as was attempted in the previous chapter on his ethical methodology when treating of the conscience-decision process. In so doing, some form of reflective meditation on the ultimate meaning of life and its relation to the evolutionary process would be involved. Likewise, the incorporation of these meditative insights into a "liturgy," a public ceremonial, symbolic of human unification—perhaps not ultimately dissimilar from the Marxist adaptations of Christian Confirmation rituals, which in East Germany resulted in the mass coming-of-age ceremonials.

Drawing out these analogical implications cannot be done without the risk of putting ideas into Teilhard's mind that he might well never have had. Moreover, there is a further problem arising from the implications as drawn. It is the risk of encouraging the development

18. For "The Priest" (1918), see *WW*, pp. 205-24; "The Mass on the World" (1923), *HU*, pp. 19-37. In *DM* (1927), note especially "The Nature of the Divine Milieu: the Universal Christ and the Great Communion," pp. 121-28, and "The Growth of the Divine Milieu," pp. 128-49.

of a kind of civic religion, with all the attendant problems arising from the inevitability of such a religion closing off the human mind from the transcendent, rather than being disposed toward it. To bring up such a barrier would clearly go against Teilhard's concerns, even on the phenomenological plane, about the need for human life to focus on a transcendent as well as immanent Omega. It would also go counter to his deepest convictions about the need for human activity to lead to Christ, rather than cut one off from him.

## E. Concluding Observations

First, by way of overview, Teilhard was relatively unconcerned about stressing what the logic of his evolutionary theory would seem to have put in a position of prime importance. He devoted very little space to education, despite the significance he gave it when he did write about it.

Second, the main emphasis in his explanation, formally, was on the *transmissive* aspect rather than on the *stimulative*, unless one give overriding weight to the one essay in which he did treat of the formative impact of Christian education. He seems not to have seen the implications of how his thinking on research bore on education, unless, again, one focus sharply on what is contained in his recommendations found in "Research, Work, and Worship." But here again he is not himself focusing on what would be the specific problem of teaching related to research, but on the basic human need to think through a particular life situation in the context of faith.

Finally, in only one place—in a letter to his cousin about helping her students to develop a love of the poor—does he even touch on the enormous educational problem of how to educate human persons, young and old, to face realistically the problem of evil in human existence, to understand and to cope with the manifold dimensions of human sinfulness.

To mention these strictures by way of concluding is not to deny significance to his writings on matters educational. Teilhard's attempt to view education as part of the large evolutionary process does have value, as does his thrust toward educating for human solidarity and the love of Christ, with all that entails. Not least, perhaps, would be his plea for the educator to really try to identify with and understand his students, to share their lives and aspirations, and to try genuinely to lead them toward higher divine-human development, rather than coerce them into a predetermined pattern of life and thought. Once again, regret can only be expressed that about these matters he said so little.

8

# Extensions and Foundations of Spiritualized Energy. Technology as Controlled Energy and Its Socioeconomic Aspects: The Incorporated Energy of Individual and Social Eugenics

### A. Spiritualized Human Energy and Controlled Energy

Up to this point, focus has been on the main facets of what Teilhard called spiritualized human energy, on how in various ways thought, choice, and feeling would be organized in line with his morality of movement, of conquest, and development. He also spelled out two other levels, neither of which was unrelated nor capable of being totally separated from the spiritualized level. These were his levels of controlled and incorporated energy.

When he spoke of controlled energy, what he had in mind, in the simplest sense of the expression, was the material energies of the universe that had been subjected to human control in the form of instruments, made to extend or support the energies contained spatially within the human body-person. Because he accepted a Bergsonian theory of the instrument, he assimilated these energies to the body-person itself, and hence considered them as genuine forms of human energy by way of supportive or extensive instrumentality, with regard to spiritualized energy, and not as sharply distinct artifacts. Hence he judged the wing of an airplane as "natural" to man as the wing of a bird was to a bird.

It goes without saying that this classification can be challenged, on the grounds that there are obvious differences between the living organism of a human being and the nonliving instruments he designs. At the very least, one would have to admit that the term *natural* is used analogically when applied to tools. Be that as it may, it was decided to accept Teilhard's classification as a working concept, despite its need for qualification.

As will shortly be seen, there are also problems in dealing with the concept that arise from how Teilhard himself worked with it. They have to do with the way he brought technology into his discussion of controlled energy, and the fact that at times he used the term in a sense closely aligned with the controlled-energy concept, and at times in a sense more closely tied in with what has been seen on the level of spiritualized energy when the questions of political and educational life were under scrutiny.

What he has to say about incorporated energy, the energy of the human-body "natural machine," will be examined in the latter part of this chapter. But one should bear in mind, in the context of the first part, what the fundamental line of interconnection is among the different levels of energy. Within the body-person unit, incorporated energy is in itself supportive and extensive of spiritualized energy. It is, then, intermediate, between the controlled and spiritualized levels. As one looks in the direction of controlled energy, it is the form

of human energy within the body-person that most immediately experiences the supportive influences and
outreaching potential of controlled energy.

## B. Technology as Controlled Energy and Its Socioeconomic Aspects

### 1. THE MEANING AND FUNCTION OF TECHNOLOGY

*Technology* in much contemporary thought has two
fundamental senses. At times it refers to the increasingly
sophisticated tools and instruments more or less
explicitly understood as extensions of the human hand,
arm, foot, eye, ear, or brain. At other times it looks to
those aspects of human society organized in a special
manner as a consequence of the discovery and development of machinery.

With Teilhard, both senses are found, with their own
Teilhardian nuances. He is explicit with regard to holding that tools of any sort, from the wheel to the wing of
an airplane, should be considered not as "artificial"
realities, but as natural organic inventions similar to the
foot itself or the wing of a bird. It is in this manner that
he speaks of technology in the first sense—as extending
the range, the outreach of human activity, and also,
through automatic machinery, as increasing the human
element's freedom and responsibility for a broader use
of his powers.

When he speaks of *general technology*, however, he has
more in mind than the sum total of a growingly indefinite number and styles of instruments—mechanical, electronic, chemical, or what have you. In the context of his
Law of Complexity-Consciousness, he observes:

> The whole of mankind may equally well be compared to an
> ellipse in which a focus of technical organization is allied to
> a focus of psychic knowledge. And from the fact that man-

kind is accepted as a reality with its two foci, this conclusion follows automatically—general technology is not merely a sum of commercial enterprises, a mechanical dead-weight on our shoulders, but rather the sum of processes combined reflectively in such a way as to preserve in men the state of consciousness which corresponds to our state of aggregation and conjunction.[1]

What should be noted here are his expressions "technical organization" and "sum of processes." Also the finality he includes, of the technical organizational processes being ordered to preserving a state of consciousness corresponding to a given state of human associational solidarity.

Linking technology in this sense to a condition of societal consciousness provides a clue to the relationship between technology as controlled energy and socioeconomic questions, the answers to which are, in great part, worked out on the level of orientation, function, and structure in economic life, expressing certain types of socioeconomic theory. It also points to the connection between the Teilhardian levels of controlled and spiritualized energy, in that, when he speaks of technology in the first sense, what he says pertains to the controlled level, whereas when he speaks of general technology he is moving on into the area of human affective, intellective, and volitional activities as they manifest themselves in social relationships. Hence general technology is in the sphere of spiritualized energy in much the same way as his thought about political and educational matters.

Finally, by way of clarification, there is another sense in which technology is used in contemporary writing, as when one speaks of trusting to technology to work out solutions to problems of population control by contraceptive methods, or of food and energy supplies, and the entire cluster of problems associated with planetary

1. "The Place of Technology in a General Biology of Mankind" (1947), *AE*, p. 159.

pollution and ecology. Although technological work of
this sort is clearly related to the other meanings, the ac-
cent in this context is heavily on what Teilhard commonly is thinking about when he talks about the role of
research—creative research directed responsibly toward
building the earth and enriching human life. Here again
one would be primarily in the sphere of spiritualized
energy. Certain elements of Teilhard's thought about
individual and social eugenics would also fit in here, to
the extent that in writing about these matters he would
be concerned about questions of medical research
technology.

His basic concepts along the line of controlled energy,
although he does not use the expression until a decade
and a half later, can be found in his "Hominization" essay of 1923, where he comments on the tool-making
phase of life, and the impact of extending and liberating
instruments on the organic unity of humanity as a
whole. To speak of artifice as *"nature humanized"* can be
seen as another form of describing human energy controlling the world around man. Looking beyond the individual to mankind taken as a whole (it was in this essay
he introduced the term "noosphere"), he sees the
transportation-communication system produced by industrial research and development as the creation of a
new nervous system for humanity. Much of what he says
in later writing about this matter is an elaboration of the
basic ideas found in this piece.[2]

Specific formulation, in terms of controlled energy,
occurs in "Human Energy" (1937):

> In the fields of controlled energy, by definition the efforts
> of the new techniques must on the one hand tend increas-
> ingly to strengthen, by appropriate measures (aeroplanes,
> radios, "movies") the ray of penetration action and there-
> fore connexion belonging to each individual element; and
> on the other hand to make available, by a judicious use of

2. See *VP*, pp. 56-64.

automatic machinery, an ever increasing portion of the activities contained in that element.[3]

Here one can readily see the two aspects of range-extension and power-liberation fundamental to Teilhard's approach to the problem of the machine.[4] The same thought underlies his reflections ten years later, in "The Place of Technology in a General Biology of Mankind" (1947), the only essay in which he takes up the question of technology itself, and the piece, it may be recalled, in which he formulates his description of general technology.[5] Particularly significant applications of his root themes to discoveries and inventions that were taking hold at the time can be found in his "Reflections on the Spiritual Repercussions of the Atomic Bomb" (1946), in his comments on television and the computer, in *Études* (1950), and in what amounts to a kind of prose lyric his "On Looking at a Cyclotron," embodying his reactions to a tour of the Berkeley Cyclotron in 1953.[6]

What should be noted at this point is Teilhard's fundamentally positive, optimistic, and even enthusiastic attitude regarding technological developments of the sort described on this level of controlled energy. That problems arise from their impact on the socioeconomic order, he was well aware. They present a respectable spectrum of questions about *how*, precisely, man in society will approach the matter of *control*, with due responsiveness to his psychic, spiritual energy needs and powers.

3. *HE*, p. 128.
4. For Teilhard's approach to these aspects in the context of human responsibility, see above, chapter 3 (the examination of his essay "The Evolution of Responsibility in the World" [1950]). Also see *AE* (the same essay), esp. pp. 210-13.
5. See *AE*, pp. 159-61.
6. For the reflections on the Atom Bomb, see *FM*, pp. 140-48; the comments on television and the computer, *Études* (1950): 264 (mars): 403-4, and 265 (mai): 251-52; for the comments on the cyclotron; *AE*, pp. 347-57. The observations in *Études* are unsigned, but see Cuénot, *Teilhard-Biography*, p. 453, nos. 383 and 384 of the Teilhard Bibliography.

## 2. SOCIOECONOMIC ASPECTS OF TECHNOLOGY

Of the significant problem areas in human society, the economic sector was one to which Teilhard devoted the least of his explicit reflective activity, except, perhaps, for the problems of war and aggression as such. However, as with war and aggression, he did have serious thoughts along this direction, scattered throughout his reading notes, journal entries, correspondence, and various essays. Often, in his essays, they surface in the context of technological development, which is the principal reason for taking them up in the present chapter.

### a. The Orientation of Economic Organization

Two expressions are central for understanding Teilhard's thought on the underlying guiding motivation he judged requisite in approaching economic matters. They are "more-being" as distinguished from "well-being."[7] The acceptance of one over the other implied for him enormous consequences for human society. The materialist, however sophisticated, he saw as fundamentally absorbed in well-being (although he did modify his position somewhat with regard to certain types of Marxists).[8] But others, of course, not formally materialist,

7. The expressions seem to contain, with a differently nuanced emphasis, the same basic concepts involved in Teilhard's thinking on fixists and mobilists, on those tied in with a morality of equilibrium and a morality of movement. What follows in the text is based on the texts directly to be cited, interpreted in the light of the concepts mentioned in the last sentence. The expressions appear first in his correspondence, reading notes, and personal notes of the mid-forties, and then are found in variant forms in several essays of the years following. See the letter of December 27, 1944, cited by Mathieu, *La pensée politique de Teilhard,* p. 228; reading notes of 1945, Mathieu, pp. 230, 232, n104; and personal notes of August 3, 1946 and February 10, 1946, Mathieu, p. 189. For Teilhard's essays, see *MPN* (1949), p. 107; "Pré-humain, humain, ultra-humain" (1949); *Idées et Forces* 2, no. 5 (oct.-déc.): 69; "The End of the Species" (1952), *FM*, p. 203; and "Research, Work, and Worship" (1955), *SC*, p. 218, n2.

8. See, for example, the reference to Paul Vaillant-Couturier in the note cited in the last text mentioned immediately above. Teilhard would have been gratified, had the article appeared in his lifetime, to have observed the position taken on freedom and creativity in Marxist thought, by Roger Garaudy,

could be trapped in the same type of basic disorienta-
tion. Their concern, whatever its underpinnings, was for
making the world a better place to live, in the sense of a
more comfortable planet, with no sense of evolutionary
drive. Such people tended to be static and "fixist" in
their views of the world, and would look to economic life
to provide them with a more or less stable, balanced order of development, production, and consumption.
Whatever dynamism their stance contained found its
term in a smooth-running organizational process with an
astmosphere either explicitly or implicitly hedonistic,
and, at times, individualistic.

On the other hand, the drive toward more-being in
economic life implied a drastically different cast of mind,
a psychic orientation, in effect imbued with the prime
directional thrust of his morality of movement, whereby
the controlling spiritual drive in economic life would
come from applying his basic moral premise in this
sector—to strive constantly for evolutionary progress toward higher consciousness, personalized, in expanded
knowledge and more intense love. It is true that in the
settings where the expression is used, the stress is more
on the mind and research activity, but correlating his
thoughts in these contexts with the main line of his
thought about love seems warranted, along with a certain amount of regret that he did not see fit to do so
himself. The regret is sharpened by the fact that unless
one reads into his language in these particular settings
the full range of his thought on the meaning of research, its relation to love, and its extension into art and
religious contemplation, one can come away with an im-

"Freedom and Creativity: Marxist and Christian," *The Teilhard Review* 3, no. 2
(Winter 1968-69): 42-49, especially with Garaudy's prediction about what man
would do with the leisure derived from new productive techniques, p. 49.
"Leisure will no longer be merely relaxation and amusement. It will be work
in its highest form, which is creative activity—limitless creativeness in the
realms of scientific research, of literature, of all the arts and of the unlimited
knowledge of mankind which is love."

pression that his approach was too highly intellectualized and hence unrealistically narrow.[9]

Against the background of this thought about fundamental orientation, it is not difficult to infer what Teilhard's judgment would be about the quasi-apotheosis of profit, money for itself, and possessions for mere status or pleasure, rather widespread in the economic attitudes of people in the more technologically developed nations. At this juncture it is not out of place to recall his basic approach to "money morality," laid down in explaining his morality of movement. What was once governed by the notion of exchange or fairness, must from now on be regulated by the idea of energy in movement. ". . . Riches only become good to the extent that they *work* for the benefit of the spirit."[10] That this implies a disciplined austerity of mind and heart, with little sympathy for either selfish hoarding, hedonistic consumerism, or production and marketing strategy catering to the latter, is quite evident.

On the other hand, Teilhard did admit a positive value of sorts for the profit motive in human life at its present state of evolution.[11] His position here, in terms of sublimation, would be similar to his position with regard to the relationship between physical sex and a higher love. As he expressed his hopes that physical sex would be sublimated in the direction of a higher love, so he would incline to hope that profit motivation would be sublimated into a drive for more-being through research.[12]

9. In this context, it is worth noting that Paul Chauchard has suggested, in view of the fact that the noosphere is a personalist society where social relations are based on love, that it is in reality an *agaposphere*. See Paul Chauchard, *Teilhard de Chardin on Love and Suffering*, trans. Marie Chêne, Deus Books (New York: Paulist Press, 1966), p. 31. Likewise, in *MPN* when Teilhard speaks of "to be more," his own footnote speaks of the importance of artistic research along with scientific research. See *MPN* (1949), p. 107, n1.

10. "The Phenomenon of Spirit" (1937), *HE*, p. 107.

11. For a more detailed analysis on the point see Mathieu, *La pensée politique de Teilhard*, "Critique du capitalisme," pp. 189-95.

12. Although Teilhard's vocabulary differs from that used by Ivan Illich

*b. Some Particular Aspects of Human Economic Activity—Unemployment, the Meaning of Work and Leisure*
    The problem of unemployment came to the surface, understandably enough, during the years of the great economic depression, in 1933. That this problem should arise as the consequence of machines more and more taking over the work of human hands does not surprise him. In fact, he considers such a development almost inevitable, and, in the long run, as pointing toward more liberation of spirit. Writing in "Christianity in the World" (1933), however, he does not speak about how to adjust work-force allocation to take account of the opportunities for using human energy freed by mechanization, but rather he tends to read the crisis of the time in terms of a fundamental spiritual emptiness, which, because of the absence of clear and compelling religious motivation, resulted in men's lacking the thrust to organize their manipulation of matter adequately so as not to leave great quantities of human energy idle or squandered in pointless activities.[13]
    Writing in "Human Energy" four years later in 1937, Teilhard approaches the problem on a different level. Speaking of unemployment from the evolutionary point of view as "the sudden appearance of a mass of human energy violently released by an internal adjustment of the noosphere," he puts this sudden energy surge down as the root cause, rather than the machine itself, or bad

when he speaks of "Tools for Conviviality," the spirit underlying Teilhard's approach to controlled energy and technology is quite similar, particularly if one keeps in mind that his thought about technology has to be viewed in the context of the thrust of his personalist, consciousness-enlarging, love-developing morality of movement. Illich's plea for responsible limitation of tools, subordinating modern technologies to politically interrelated individuals, rather than power-heavy managers, or mechanized, impersonal systems, seems definitely to rest on a type of personalist world view quite compatible with Teilhard's phenomenological and Christological personalism. The two thinkers can be said to complement each other rather well in this sector. Illich, unfortunately, does not spell out his philosophical base, while Teilhard does not get into a type of institutional analysis like Illich's. See Ivan Illich, *Tools for Conviviality*, World Perspectives (New York: Harper & Row, Pub., 1973), pp. xxiv-xxv, 10-45, on the meaning of "convivial."
    13. *SC*, pp. 100-102.

economic organization, or the lack of radically sound, ultimate life-motivation (as just seen above). He does not defend faulty economic organization, nor want to discount it, but rather points up what he judges should simply be faced as one of the central and inescapable challenges of man's conquest of matter through technology—overcoming dislocations and imbalances as they develop, rather than being unduly disconcerted or depressed by them.[14]

While Teilhard can be criticized for not manifesting sufficient explicit concern regarding the suffering of the unemployed and their families, it can be said in his defense that, by focusing this attention on the need for chaneling human energy rendered idle by the increase of mechanization into higher types of activity, he was indeed implicitly working toward more than alleviation of suffering—toward a far more enjoyable life for all. However, true as this defense might be, it ignores another aspect of the workers' life, still prevalent in highly industrialized society despite the advances of automation. This is the dehumanizing characteristic of routine assembly line and much clerical office work. When Teilhard speaks of the machine as freeing the hand for thought, he seems to be taking a great leap from the craft style of work with tools to automatic machinery. Moreover, when he speaks glowingly about workers and engineers (along with researchers) as the key creative agents of the future, he overlooks the consciousness-curtailing, subhuman, materializing aspects of the process of much industrial and commercial work in favor of the products in transportation, communica-

---

14. *HE*, pp. 123-24. Teilhard's lack of economic expertise in his analysis of the unemployment situation drew the following observations from a professional economist associate of the present writer: "Depression results from a crisis of nerves on the part of investors—influenced by some maldistribution, badly organized financial market, monetary policy, and poor fiscal policies. Technological unemployment (or "displaced employment") is real and a problem, but scarcity tends to eliminate it—i.e., the need for other things creates other jobs." (Private communication, July 1972, from Dr. Peter L. Danner, Chairman, Dept. of Economics, Marquette University, Milwaukee, Wis.)

tion, and other areas, with their obvious liberative effects for those who can afford them.

This failure to address himself to the dulling, thought-inhibiting characteristics of a great part of existing general technology can be taken as one of the most serious gaps in his socioeconomic thinking. It can be attributed in part to the fact that while he knew the world of scientific research intimately and was well acquainted with university and intellectual workers, he had relatively little knowledge from experience of the conditions of life and work endured by those in factory or office.[15] His fundamental theoretical approach to the meaning of work assumes the possibility of creativity and discovery—elements sadly lacking in the "work" of millions in the work force today. Consequently, much of what he has to say specifically about work that could be gathered together into a Teilhardian philosophy (and theology) of work, can be said to apply only to those not touched by the crippling routine of mechanized toil. If he had synthesized his thinking about detachment and communion with God (or Omega) in action with the ultimate positive elements of the passivities of diminishment as found in much existing routinized work activity, there would be a possibility of a quite realistic Teilhardian theory of work applicable to a large part of contemporary work life.[16] Unfortunately, he did not do this,

15. See d'Ouince, *Teilhard dans l'Église*, p. 162, n44. "Teilhard knew well the world of the university. . . . He was likewise concerned with certain large global problems (especially those of eugenics and culture) and he often discussed them with Julian Huxley, then Director of *UNESCO*. On the other hand, problems of the world of work (what we call the social question) and those of partisan politics remained relatively distant from him." (My translation.) This relative distance, however, should not be taken as cold lack of concern. Commenting on Teilhard's activities in Paris when he was well on in years, Claude Cuénot writes, ". . . he succeeded admirably in speaking to workers, manual or otherwise, and was later to be a warm partisan of the worker-priest movement. His spirituality, in fact had a spontaneous turn towards work and a natural attraction towards Christ the Worker." See Cuénot, *Teilhard-Biography*, p. 222.

16. See *DM* (1927), "Our Struggle with God against evil," pp. 83-84, and "True Resignation," pp. 90-93—all taken under the general heading of "The Divinisation of Our Passivities." What also would have made Teilhard's approach more realistic would have been analysis of the details of mechanization

and his writings as they stand, with regard to both the
painful aspects of unemployment and the dulling aspects
of factory work, leave him open to the charge of letting
his overoptimism show once again.

Further understanding of his approach to unemployment and work can be derived from his attitude toward
a problem area correlative to both of these, an element
of human life that is drawing increasing concern, particularly in the more technologically developed
societies—the question of leisure.

The fundamental question is whether Teilhard's ethical theory with its stress on work allows room for leisure
at all. Here, of course, much depends on the understanding of leisure. Teilhard in his writings did not leave
any formal discussion of the term. So, again one must
attempt to interpret what little he did say and to pro-
duce an acceptable construct of his thought by using the
evidence available—a certain number of not much more
than textual side remarks, along with the manner in
which he lived his own life, as an indication of what he
meant by the fragments he put in writing. Ultimately
one would have to evaluate this construct for consistency
with his stand on the importance and place of effort in
human life.

Teilhard's position on the matter is not easy to determine. One critic considers him to be ". . . as hostile to
pleasure and play as any Puritan deacon."[17] And, it is
true, if one were to rely solely on his strong phrases a-
bout "the true toilers of the earth" and the spirit that
should imbue them, as this particular critic seems to

and undiscerning technological development, such as Illich attempts when he
outlines the six ways in which abuse of technology threatens free, creative,
human existence. See *Tools for Conviviality*, chap. 3, "The Multiple Balance,"
pp. 45-83. Illich supplies specification of what Teilhard, in one of his earliest
writings, had described as the "re-forming of matter above us," in writing about his concern regarding the growth of collectivities. See "Cosmic Life"
(1916), *WW*, pp. 39-40. Later, Teilhard's approach was often expressed in
concern about "ant-hill" existence. See, for example, *PM* (1940), pp. 256-57.

17. Ferkiss, *Technological Man*, p. 87. The footnote that presumably would
directly document this refers to Harvey Cox, not Teilhard.

have done, such an impression would not be hard to derive.[18] But there are good reasons for seriously questioning the validity of seeing him with the stern hard face of a Puritan, apart from ample photographic and personal testimony to a ready twinkle in his eye, and his own description of how he danced arm in arm down the streets of Strasbourg with his confreres at the time of the victory celebrations in 1919.[19]

In addition to what he says about leisure in his essays, which is not very much, a great deal can be sought in the evidence contained in his World War I correspondence, which reflects a life-style that seems to have been with him all his days. When his other ideas are viewed in this context, their interpretation, however one may formulate it, hardly emerges to validate as grim a judgment as the one just alluded to.

First, what is the life-style reflected in these letters and incorporated in his living? What shows up consistently is a deep and abiding joy in the beauty of nature, long walks along the sea shore or through the forests, times and places for quiet, prayerful thought and writing, as well as reading. While he was thinking much of the time and thinking serious thoughts, the fact is that he enjoyed what he was doing and gives no evidence of being a harried, compulsive toiler striving to budget every moment under the watchful eye of a Calvinistic God. Not only did he enjoy long stretches of peace and calm in which his mind could freely follow its bent, but he also obvi-

18. See "The Planetisation of Mankind" (1945), *FM*, pp. 137-39. The criticism by Ferkiss seems to be developed mainly out of reading texts from *The Phenomenon of Man* and *The Future of Man*.

19. See Claude Cuénot, "Pierre Teilhard de Chardin: Sketch for a Portrait," *The Teilhard Review* 6, no. 1 (Summer 1971): 4, quoting a letter by one of Teilhard's friends, "Pere Teilhard was often genial, in a really playful and artless manner. It was one of his most attractive traits when we used to meet in 1939. After his infraction [(*sic*) read "infarction"] his physical fatigue and the increasing moral strain put upon him (by the prohibition, laid upon him in August 1947, from writing on any subject but science) made his bursts of gaiety rarer. . . ." For Teilhard's own account of the Strasbourg incident, see *MM*, p. 266.

ously relished conversation and letters with friends and family. Nor was he a dour ascetic who never enjoyed a poem, painting, sculpture, or novel.[20] In later years when he was traveling much in the course of his work, he looked forward to meetings with friends and the long talks they brought in an easy, relaxed atmosphere, such as that of Léontine Zanta's apartment.[21] His long sea voyages gave him great blocks of time for peaceful, quiet reflection and writing serious essays. He also enjoyed protracted periods of simple meditation and prayer.

One can counter, obviously, by saying that all this indicates that he could never really stop working. What it proves, however, is simply that he was active; it does not prove at all that his type of activity as described was a burden, a chore, or "work" in the pejorative sense. What this leads to is the admittedly difficult question of what one is going to say about the meaning of work, play, free time, recreation, and leisure.

The passages in Teilhard's correspondence where he uses the word *loisir* are not frequent. When he does use the word, it is in the context of being free to relax from ordinary duties and to have time to walk in the open air, to think, pray, read, and write.[22] That he should have time for these activities and for conversation, was important to him, as shows up in other passages where he does not use the term itself but speaks of what he would like to do or how he is enjoying what he is or has been doing.[23] To this extent one could say that he appreciated

20. For passages from his World War I correspondence, see *MM*, pp. 103-115, 141, 152, 159, 175, 198, 223, 302. On Teilhard's interest in the arts, see Cuénot, *Teilhard-Biography*, pp. 222-23, and, by the same author, "Sketch for a Portrait," *The Teilhard Review* 6, no. 1 (Summer 1971): 6. Teilhard's humble remark, "I am an idiot in musical matters," quoted in this article, did not mean he had no interest in them. His own expressed desire, written in a 1927 letter, to have been a shadow of Wagner rather than Darwin, is not without point in the present context. See *LF*, p. 59. (This text is quoted above, in chap. 2C (6).

21. See *LZ*, pp. 51, 59, 73, 85, 95-96.

22. See French text, *Genèse d'une pensée*, pp. 204, 205.

23. See texts cited from *MM*, above, n20.

both the freedom from necessity and the joys of contemplation, elements entering into the consideration of
leisure from Aristotle down to the present time.[24]

There is another aspect, too, that would enable one to
classify his life as leisurely, in accord with serious
thought about its meaning. It is the fertility of thought
that came out of his time off from either his medical
military work at the Front in the first World War or his
scientific research during the rest of his life. The point is
reinforced in that he was obviously not writing his
thoughtful essays for profit, did seem to write a great
deal to clarify his own thought, and seemed controllably
detached from the prospect of not having a large reading or listening public.

However, his theory of human effort, at least when
seen only partially, could make him look like a stern
ascetic, taking time off occasionally to breathe better and
thus drive on forward more vigorously.

What complicates matters more is not only the manner
in which he approaches the question of unemployment
and curtailed work time when he speaks of the impact of
mechanization, but the fact that the word *chomage* is ambiguous in the French and admits translation as "unemployment" (its usual meaning) in one context, but
"leisure" in another.[25] Further complication arises from
his stress on research as compatible with Aristotelian and
Platonic enthusiasm for contemplation, yet harboring an
essentially incompatible element in that his inclusion of
the idea of development in research seems to drag one
from lofty contemplation of truth and beauty down to
the mundanely practical task of improving human life
through continuing evolution.

24. For a good sketch of the development of thinking on leisure in the
West, see Sebastian de Grazia, *Of Time, Work, and Leisure*, Anchor Books (Garden City, N.Y.: Doubleday & Co., Inc., 1964), chap. I, "The Background of
Leisure," pp. 9-30.
25. See French text for *MPN*, *La Place de l'Homme dans la Nature*, p. 151.
The word *chomage* there is translated into English in *MPN*, p. 104, as "leisure."

At this point it is important to go back to his thinking on unemployment if one would understand his thinking in this area, since in the few places (mainly eight papers between 1933 and 1951) where the question of leisure comes to the fore at all, it is in this context.[26] The unemployment question, as was seen, surfaced in the midst of the economic crisis of the thirties. At that time he was concerned not to view it with excessive alarm, but to put it in its total spiritual perspective beyond mere economics.[27] In later years, notably after the initial developments of atomic energy, the question of how to handle the significance of this energy surge that research and technology had wrought forced him to face the problem of increased manual idleness again.[28] He admits that he is faced with the problem of leisure (*loisir*) and does not know precisely what to say about educating masses of humanity for the changes taking place in work life.[29] In general he is optimistic, as was noted above, about hands being freed so that brains could think, but he is nowhere specific as to how this should be done in revamping the organization of socioeconomic life. (His general thought on this matter will be seen shortly.)

26. See "Christianity in the World" (1933), *SC*, pp. 100-101; "Human Energy" (1937), *HE*, pp. 123-24; *PM* (1940), p. 279; "The Spiritual Repercussions of the Atom Bomb" (1946), *FM*, p. 146; "The Formation of the Noosphere" (1947), *FM*, pp. 172-73; *MPN* (1949), pp. 104-7; "Pré-humain, humain, ultra-humain" (1949), *Idées et Forces* 2, no. 5 (oct.-déc. 1949): 68; and "The Phyletic Structure of the Human Group" (1951), *AM*, p. 161.
27. "Christianity in the World" (1933), *SC*, pp. 100-101.
28. "The Spiritual Repercussions of the Atom Bomb" (1946), *FM*, p. 146; "The Formation of the Noosphere" (1947), *FM*, pp. 172-73. In the latter essay, the English rendering of the French passage where Teilhard is expressing his thought on the manner in which some would deal with unemployment derived from increased use of machinery, is awkward, to the point of being unintelligible. The original text reads: "De ce chef, essayer de refouler le chômage dans la Machine ne serait qu'un effort contre nature, une absurdité biologique." See *L'avenir de l'homme*. The meaning would seem to be, "So that to attempt to suppress unemployment *by suppressing the machine* would be against the purpose of Nature and a biological absurdity." To read, "So that to attempt to suppress unemployment by *incorporating the unemployed in the machine* . . ." hardly makes sense (and could give rise to distracting images of Donderbeck and his sausages). (Emphasis added.)
29. "The Phyletic Structure of the Human Group" (1951), *AM*, pp. 161-62. (French text, *L'apparition de l'homme*, pp. 222-23.)

That the organization of society should take place in the direction of increasing the number of research workers, he sees as desirable and inevitable, even to the extent that in his reflections on the Berkeley Cyclotron he went so far as to find the laboratory and the factory already coalesced.[30]

The evidence, consequently, points toward an absence of concern about what man should do in his time away from serious work, still less toward a preoccupation with how this time should be described. The main thrust of his thought was toward freeing mankind from less spiritual and intellectual work activity so that people would be free for more intellectual and creative work, with the admittedly serious goal of improving the totality of human life. Because of this controlling concern, despite his reference to the question of leisure, it does not seem that the problem of leisure as formulated by certain contemporary theorists surfaced in his mind.[31]

One could argue, moreover, that for an almost habitual contemplative in action—inclined that way, it could be said, by temperament and trained in it through Ignatian spirituality—the problem of leisure in such terms would have seemed to him, in effect, a false problem. If the inner peace and tranquility for complete human fulfillment and happiness demand no isolation from purposeful activity, if the joy of loving union with God is not only possible but actual in work as well as in activity apart from work, then an Aristotelian type of leisure not only becomes unnecessary, but ultimately is judged to be based on an erroneous philosophy of human life and happiness. Play, recreation, and relaxation, yes, and admittedly for practical purposes—to better assist human creative thought. But leisure as a quasi-absolute end in itself, no, particularly since the only ab-

30. *AE* (1953), p. 354.
31. See, for example, de Grazia, *Of Time, Work, and Leisure*, pp. 393-416, where a good summary of the problematic can be found in his discussion of "Leisure's Future."

solute he acknowledged for his own interior life was the absolute of the Omegalizing, Christogenetic process, unifying mankind, in hopeful, joyful evolutionary effort, while collaborating with the ultimate Personal Center, Christ-Omega.[32]
In the end, it would be Teilhard's theoretical and practical preoccupation with zest for life, with creative thought and love, that would take the cold glint of the Puritan deacon out of his eye and reveal something much more like the kind and gentle warmth of a Francis of Assisi. Despite obvious differences, there is, as a matter of fact, an almost Franciscan lyricism in his approach to nature, to God in nature, and to enjoyment of the world. Nor should one overlook here the *joie de vivre* observed in him by the French Marxist Garaudy.[33]
What judgment, finally, does the evidence point to with regard to the place of leisure in his morality of constructive effort? As has been seen above, most of what he said about leisure in a serious context had to do with the orientation of effort from less spiritualized to more spiritualized constructive activity. The term *leisure* would then not be used in the sense of play, but of freedom to be active in some better and more satisfying way than previously. Consequently, on the basis of written words alone, one would have to say that he did not develop a theoretical place for leisure, in the sense of play or in the sense of contemplation divorced from some life-goal.
One would also have to say that his constructive, action-oriented understanding of research and contem-

32. If it is true that one man's meat can be another's poison, it can also turn out that one man's work can be another man's play. Herman Kahn, of the Hudson Institute, has been known to smile benignly when someone referred to the Institute as "Kahn's playpen on the Hudson." Moreover, despite the fact that Teilhard never developed the comparison, one could, borrowing from the C. S. Lewis concept of heaven as "The Great Dance," trace out the implications of participating in the Risen Life through realized eschatology, and reach an understanding of the activity of Christogenesis in terms of "Christogenetic play."
33. See Claude Cuénot, *Science and Faith in Teilhard de Chardin*, with a comment by Roger Garaudy, p. 82. Garaudy speaks of Teilhard's profound vision making him "a master both of *joie de vivre* and of human unity."

plation would be incompatible with a theory of leisure that would demand that contemplation has no end beyond the experience of its own action. Leisure of that type would be inconsistent with his morality of development.

However, if one were to accept the pragmatic concept of leisure as play in the sense Aquinas used it when he affirmed the moral duty of play and relaxation to enable one to work well, then one could argue, not from what Teilhard theorized, but from his life-style, that in practice he exemplified such a theory of leisure.[34] One could further argue that such an understanding of leisure would not be incompatible with his morality of effort.

*c. The Organization of Economic Life*

Despite the absence of specific ideas on socioeconomic structures, Teilhard's thought does contain important observations on the role of planning, research, and management—determinative elements in all of these structures. Moreover, flowing from these concepts and others seen above, it is possible to derive criteria, not for a technical economic evaluation, but for a fundamental ethical critique of certain types of capitalist and socialist approaches.

A personal note of 1947 sums up his orientational stance and sets the stage for the next step in the present inquiry.

> The aim of political economy is no longer the chicken in the pot, but the liberation (through organization and mechanization) of the immense store of human energy up to now absorbed in the work of material production.[35]

How the development of mechanization would be achieved and how the results derived would be incorporated into the life of human society depend in great part

34. See Thomas Aquinas, *Summa Theologica* 2-2ae, q. 168, art. 4.
35. Personal note, August 22, 1947, cited by Mathieu, *La pensée politique de Teilhard*, p. 193.

on how one situates the role of research and planning in the socioeconomic process.

Teilhard's thought on the essential character of research in human progress has already been considered. What should be noted in the present context is the liaison he saw developing, toward the end of his life, between the laboratory and the factory, and the ascendance of the laboratory that he judged to be emerging. Likewise especially significant is the awareness he manifested of and the importance he assigned to the critical questions of planetary energy reserves and sufficiency of food supply. He was familiar with the writings of Fairfield Osborn, Josue de Castro, and Charles Galton-Darwin, and was deeply concerned about the problems to which they directed their efforts.[36] Commenting on Osborn's *Our Plundered Planet* in *Études* (1949), he wrote, ". . . Osborn's pages do not make pleasant reading, but every man ought to read them . . . so as to become accustomed to discern beyond the individual details of daily life, the vast currents drawing us onward and the inexorable ties binding us together on a planetary scale."[37] Problems of the economic order were clearly, for Teilhard, among the prime objects toward which research must be directed if mankind's responsibilities for survival and development were to be met.

The questions of planning and management present special problems, the solutions to which in the socioeconomic order are closely tied to the main lines of his political thinking seen above, and could be said to be economic corollaries of it. The basic need for foresight and planning can be found in his fundamental thesis about the character of human responsibility for continuing evolution. Since man's responsibility for economic progress is an important element in the larger picture of responsibility for total human progress, and since re-

36. For more extended treatment of the subsistence problem as seen by Teilhard, see Mathieu, *La pensée politique de Teilhard*, pp. 212-16.
37. *Études* 262 (déc. 1949): 402-3. (My translation.)

sponsible progress calls for seeking out and weighing all possible alternatives, it follows that applying the fruits of economic research to plans for the human economic future is one of mankind's most important responsibilities, heightened immeasurably in modern times by growing understanding of the limitations of energy and food supply, as well as the consequences of industrial pollution.[38]

The problem, though, is not that man should plan, but how this planning should be directed and

38. To get at the function of economic planning in Teilhard's thought one must work mostly by inference from certain passages and the drift of certain essays, as well as from fragments of personal notes, and some comment in his correspondence. The fundamental thrust of his essay "Human Energy" (which has provided the framework for synthesizing his ethical thought in this study), with its concern for the *organization* of human energy, is clearly in this direction. Moreover, with regard to economic matters he has these significant specific comments in the elaboration of his thought on "controlled energy": "Seemingly, no less urgent than the question of sources of energy is the world wide installation of a general economy of production and labour, reinforced by the establishment of a rational gold policy. Financial and social crises are at pains to remind us how confused our theories are in these matters and how barbarous our conduct. But when will men decide to recognize that no serious progress can be made in these directions except under two conditions: first that the proposed organization must be international and in the end totalitarian; and secondly, that it must be conceived on a very large scale. What is ruining our present day economics and politics is not only their persistent segmentation of the world into tight compartments. More lethal still is their stubborn conservation of a static form and ideal: reciprocal areas of exchange whose perfection it seems would consist in a private short circuit." *HE* (1937), pp. 133-34. (With regard to the term *totalitarian*, the French editor of the text saw fit to remark: "Obviously this adjective is intended to convey a general notion of totality, not a so-called 'totalitarian' regime." Teilhard's choice of words here is unhappy, and the correction seems necessary, and coherent with the rest of his thinking.) The point of this text in the present setting is that if Teilhard was not thinking about international economic organization and the planning integral to it here, it is hard to say what else he was writing about. Moreover, his later observations on the implications of the discovery of techniques for mastering atomic energy, in his essay on the spiritual implications of the Atomic Bomb (1946) along with his detailed analysis of the meaning of the Berkeley Cyclotron (1953) clearly point in the same direction. Likewise significant would be the plan he suggested to Julian Huxley, in March 1951, for an "Institute for human studies" (see above, chap. 5), with its Applied Branch looking to energetics, eugenics, and steering. The personal notes that can be found, of January 7, 1946 (Mathieu, *La pensée politique de Teilhard*, p. 221), and March 23, 1946 (*ibid.*, p. 225), are relatively insignificant confirmatory observations of ideas seen elsewhere. More significant are his sympathetic comments in his correspondence on Roosevelt's attempts with the New Deal (*LT*, Sept. 1933, p. 200.), and his discontent with the developments at the time of Eisenhower. (*LT*, Nov. 22, 1952, pp. 334-35; also letters of Oct. 5, Oct. 22, Nov. 9, and Nov. 21, 1952, Mathieu, p. 188.)

organized—which projects one straightway into the realm of political economy. Teilhard's thinking in this realm is an extension of his views on the essentials of the Democratic idea. His global consciousness points in the direction of some type of worldwide structure for economic planning that presumably would ultimately be incorporated in a type of world government. His sympathy for the goals of the earlier League of Nations, for which he judged the earth not yet sufficiently matured, and the United Nations are clear enough, as they are in particular for UNESCO, with which he had particular personal ties, but with which he experienced some regrettable disillusionment. He does not say much specifically about the world-government concept as such, but the trend of his thought is toward it, as was seen in chapter 6.[39] More particularly, he did not think that the operation of economic energies and forces could be left to the play of chance or uncontrolled individual enterprise. On the other hand, he was steadfastly against, as always, anything that would establish the ant-hill or beehive style of mechanized bureaucracy and inhibit the full development of the uniqueness of the individual person, or, as has been seen, the particular national or human branch, in its peculiar complexity.[40]

It is here, again, that the problem of the elite—and a particular type of elite, the managerial elite—comes to the fore.[41] Teilhard's personal humanism, faithful to the

39. See above, chap. 6C.
40. See Mathieu, *La pensée politique de Teilhard*, p. 225, and the citation of Teilhard's personal notes, March 23, 1946.
41. Teilhard read James Burnham's *The Managerial Revolution* in its original English version, while in Peking during December 1944, and was quite taken by it, while at the same time disagreeing radically with Burnham's concept of the function of an ideology. See his personal notes, December 16, 1944, Mathieu, *La pensée politique de Teilhard*, p. 229, and his letter of December 27, 1944, *ibid.*, p. 228. The following year, his notes show comments on Saint-Simon and Prosper Enfantin. See *ibid.*, pp. 229-32, for analysis and comment pertinent to Teilhard's agreement and disagreement with these seminal "technocratic" writers. On fundamental world-view matters that would involve Teilhard's basic concepts on Omegalization, there was, of course, radical disagreement, regardless of his sympathy for their scientific, human-development concerns.

principle of differentiating unity as expressed in the organizational structures and functions imbued with his
sense of species, human sense, or societal love, would
put him beyond the pale of an arrogant technocratic
oligarchy precisely because of the weight he assigns to
individual personal development and responsibility, in
keeping with his governing principle of complementarity
with differentiating union. In this context, however, he
still held that there are some who know better than
others what is best for all, and that they should have authority and power, after all means of rational persuasion
and consultation have been exhausted, to effectively control social developments when and where necessary.[42]

This position distinguishes him from both the old and
neo-liberal individualistic capitalists and the doctrinaire
materialistic socialists. His emphasis on social solidarity
and authoritative managerial planning cuts him off from
the former, and his stress on the need for the fullness of
unique personal and human development separates him
from the latter.[43] But he would seem to be in line with a

42. The basis for this statement is Teilhard's sympathy for such attempts as
the Roosevelt Brain Trust, as well as his declaration, when writing about the
essence of the democratic idea, that there is needed a mixture of firmness and
*laissez-faire* in society governed by democratic principles, and his contention
that refractory segments of humanity could legitimately be subjected to enlightened higher control, when necessary. To save Teilhard from inconsistency here, his remarks about the Brain Trust—which come to approval of a
special kind of elitism—have to be tempered with the considerations seen
above, chap. 6C (4), regarding elite groups in a political context. If his coun-
terweighting thought there is taken into account, Teilhard's notion of an
evolutionary elite resembles, closely enough, Illich's concept of the type of
special groups needed for political transformation to a convivial society. See
*Tools for Conviviality*, pp. 105-6. Further correlative comparison of the two
thinkers would be valuable by way of filling in what Teilhard has to say about
planning (above, B (2) ) with Illich's views on the use of the legal system for
bringing about a convivial society. See *Ibid.*, pp. 92-99, 108-10. Illich does
have some harsh words about "planning" in the centralized, Big-Brother
sense, but he is clearly talking about the reality of a planning process when he
describes what is needed by way of framing legislation to free persons for
convivial living. In the same context, see Pearce Young, "Law in the Age of
Planetization," *Teilhard Symposium*, pp. 210-25.
43. The following quotation, which he copied out in his personal notes,
Jan. 9, 1946, from a *Life* article, J. M. Keynes's preface to his *Essays in Persuasion*, is important for confirming the tendencies of his thought: "The
economic struggle between classes and nations is . . . a transitory and *unneces-*

strain of social thought close to home—and likewise close
to his heart, had he lived to see its formulation—the social thought in the sociopoliticoeconomic realm as found
in the writings of Pope John XXIII, the Second Vatican
Council, and Pope Paul VI, particularly as expressed in
*Mater et Magistra*, *Pacem et Terris*, *The Pastoral Constitution
on the Church in the Modern World*, *The Development of
Peoples*, and *A Call to Action*, Pope Paul's letter issued on
the eightieth anniversary of *Rerum Novarum*. Although
his thought was by no means so specific in details as
these writings, general as some find them, it is quite compatible with their orientation and expressed concerns.

## C. The Incorporated Energy of Individual and Social Eugenics

Teilhard's concern about the development of the human body and "that great body made of all our bodies"
is rooted in his perception of the connection between
thought and the living organism in which it occurs. "So
long as its phase of immersion in the 'tangential' lasts,
thought can only be built up on this material basis."[44] In
his earlier writings, he was not preoccupied with the
precise demands of this relationship between incorporated energy and spiritualized energy, but in the late

*sary* muddle. For the Western World already has the resources and the
technique if we could create the *organization* to use them, capable of reducing
the Economic problem, which now absorbs our moral and material energies,
to a position of secondary importance. Thus the author of this *Essays* still
hopes and believes that the day is not far off when . . . the arena of the heart
and the head will be occupied or re-occupied by our real problems—the problem of life and human relations, of creation and behavior and religion." See
Mathieu, *La pensée politique de Teilhard*, pp. 183-84, for further comments on
the text, and its inclusion in Teilhard's notes. In general, Teilhard works
within the framework of problems arising within an economy of abundance,
and does not address himself directly to problems of underdeveloped, or developing nations, although his thought has definite implications for them,
especially when his notions of global responsibility and complementarity are
pursued to their conclusions.

44. *PM* (1940), p. 282; "Pré-humain, humain, ultra-humain" (1949), *Idées et
Forces* 2, no. 5 (oct.-déc. 1949): 67.

thirties the question arises and it was to continue to show itself from time to time thereafter.[45] From the beginning he reveals an awareness of the complexities and risks involved in exploring the implications of such a concern, but unfortunately he does not probe as deeply into them as might be desired, and in the course of what are really not much more than passing remarks, makes certain provocative observations which at first reading are disturbing. If taken out of the context of the other elements in his thought, they could be considered indefensible as they stand. Even when taken in a larger context, they still give rise to what, for a good number, would be agonizing perplexities about both the extent of human dominion over the human body and the relative priority of individual personal dignity and rights viewed against the background of a general social biological good, however much the biological has an impact on and extends into the personal.

Some of his observations in a eugenic context are more directly pertinent to the socioeconomic area, such as those about land and resource distribution, but they are understandable enough in the light of what gives rise to them—his concern about the matter of hunger and the possibility of famine.[46] With regard to another question, also, when he talks about psychoanalytic concern for disease, he is broaching the area of interaction between incorporated and spiritualized energy. His recommendations here to go beyond healing to the psychoenergetics of developing man's transindividual as-

45. The main texts available are the following: "Human Energy" (1937), HE, pp. 126-27, 131-32; PM (1940), p. 282; "The Spiritual Repercussions of the Atom Bomb" (1946), FM, p. 144; "Comment je vois" (1948), DA, pp. 196-97; Letter of Sept. 18, 1948, LF, pp. 186-87 (reflects Teilhard's thought on the risks, yet inevitability of genetic planning "because planning is of the essence of Life"; "The Directions and Conditions of the Future" (1948), FM, p. 233; "The Psychological Conditions of Human Unification" (1949), AE, p. 176-77; MPN (1949), pp. 110-11; "Pré-humain, humain, ultra-humain" (1949), Idées et Forces 2, no. 5 (oct.-déc. 1949): 67-68; and "The Convergence of the Universe" (1951), AE, pp. 295-96.
46. PM (1940), pp. 282-83; also the companion text from "Pré-humain, humain, ultra-humain." See above, n43.

pirations are a good example of how he saw the bearing and importance of incorporated energy for the development of love, even though he does not use the vocabulary of love in his remarks at this point.[47] These particular socioeconomic and psychological concerns, tied in as they are with incorporated energy, are, nevertheless more on the periphery than at the heart of the present concern.

What he has to say about the protection, development, and improvement of the human body itself, and of ethnic types of human bodies, is the center of present focus, and his thought here presents special problems. That there should be serious attention directed to fighting disease on all fronts and improving conditions of individual and general hygiene, he seems to take for granted as not needing special advocacy. There is an atmosphere of more intense urgency, however, coupled with a sense of crisis, when he brings up the improvement of the human body by means of working on the nervous system, through mechanical, chemical, or biological stimulation, or pushes into the area of genetic control, the selection and balance of sexes, hormonal manipulation, and population control.[48] Without being specific, he seems to assume that there are inferior ethnic types, and that these should not supplant superior types, but should be subjected to qualitative population control. To the extent necessary, moreover, literal suffocation on the planet would be under quantitative population control.[49] And there is the question, raised only once, to be sure, but nevertheless definitely put, about the relative rights of the physically diseased and weak in comparison to the rights of the strong in the onward evolutionary struggle—the rights of the

47. "The Psychological Conditions for Human Unification" (1949), *AE*, pp. 176-77.

48. See "Human Energy" (1937), *HE*, p. 127; "The Directions and Conditions of the Future" (1948), *FM*, p. 234.

49. "Human Energy" (1937), *HE*, p. 132; "Comment je vois" (1948), *DA*, p. 197; "The Directions and Conditions of the Future" (1948), *FM*, p. 234.

wounded in juxtaposition to the rights of the fighters at the front.[50]

From the character of observations such as these, the existence of the two central problems alluded to earlier can be seen to emerge. How should man approach the question of the extent of human dominion over the human body? How does one deal, in matters of social eugenics, with the rights of the individual person or of particular groups of persons? This is not the first time that the second problem has been noted in Teilhard's thought, but it presses home with sharp immediacy in the present context.

## 1. HUMAN DOMINION OVER THE HUMAN BODY

The first problem is not treated at length. Teilhard's earliest approach is an *a fortiori* argument, resting on an undeveloped assumption. When speaking of incorporated energy itself, in "Human Energy" (1937), he adverts to the reaction some express with regard to direct work on improvement of the human body.

> Such an ambition has long appeared, and still appears to man, fantastic or even blasphemous. Some refuse to imagine any profound change in what seems "to have always been"; others have a false religious fear of violating the Creator's irrevocable rights over His work both of flesh and thought. For a complex of obscure reasons, our generation still regards with distrust all efforts proposed by science for controlling the machinery of heredity, of sex-determination, and development of the nervous system. It is as if man had the right and power to interfere with all the channels in the world except those which make him himself. And yet it is eminently on this ground that we must try *everything*, to its conclusion.[51]

The kernel of his argument is in the last two sentences: man has the right and power to experiment on and de-

50. "Human Energy" (1937), *HE*, p. 132.
51. "Human Energy" (1937), *HE*, p. 127.

velop all subhuman energies; *a fortiori*, he must have the right and power to experiment on and develop those energies which properly make him man. The undeveloped assumption would be that the right to control the physical and biological energies around man must include the right to control the physical and biological energies in man. At this point many nonbelievers as well as believers would feel impelled to insist that he moderate the sweeping character of his statements, on grounds that they would draw from his own insistence that life had passed a critical threshold in reaching the human level, and that the human person simply cannot be treated across the board as a plant or animal.

Without meeting this specific objection, it must be admitted that he does immediately add some restraining qualifications:

A delicate undertaking, if ever there was one; but precisely because of their delicacy, these undertakings require, if they are to be soundly, reverently and religiously pursued, the precautions and surveyance of methodically conducted research. No longer only man experimenting on his fellows; but humanity feeling out in order to give its members a higher quality of life.[52]

He is, furthermore, aware of the satirical pictures drawn by H. G. Wells and Aldous Huxley of attempts by man to improve man biologically, but is not deterred by them, and urges holding to what he sees as a fundamentally sound idea, in the hope that ". . . its realization, like all life's actions will defy caricature."[53]

These qualifications give rise to two critical questions: 1) what enters into the precautions and "surveyance" of methodically conducted research to ensure sound, reverent, and religious pursuit of human biological research, and 2) how does humanity feeling out in order to give

52. "Human Energy" (1937), *HE*, p. 127.
53. *Ibid.*, pp. 127-28.

its members a higher quality of life, differ from man experimenting on his fellows?[54]

In the particular essay under discussion he does not expand on these two points, but from the extent to which later in the same essay he explores the meaning of love as the highest form of human energy, one could infer that his theory of human love and personalism would have important implications regarding problems he raised earlier.[55]

## 2. PERSONAL RIGHTS AND SOCIAL NEEDS

What this theory does lead to and also how the implications involved tie this problem in with the second major problem under scrutiny, can be derived from a passage in *The Phenomenon of Man* (1940). Writing on the care and improvement of the human body, he notes the difference between mankind, "so full of misshapen subjects," and animal societies with flawless members. Granted that human evolution is bent toward suppleness and freedom rather than geometrical perfection, he observes: "All the same, suitably subordinated to other values, it may well appear as an indication and a lesson."

54. These questions would seem to be, obviously enough, two of the basic questions of medical ethics pertaining to eugenic research. The literature is growing on how to answer them in concrete lines of research, involving such matters as artificial insemination, ovarian transplants, use of sperm bank, cloning, in vitro fertilization, etc. Since Teilhard approached these concrete questions only from the distance of general principles, comparison or contrast of his thought with the issues currently under debate would not be to the point of the present study. For a recent study of important problems in this area, see Charles E. Curran, *Contemporary Problems in Moral Theology* (Notre Dame, Ind.: Fides Publishers, 1970), "Moral Theology and Genetics: A Dialogue," pp. 189-224. For a somewhat repetitious but nevertheless insightful article on a specific question, one could consult Paul Ramsey, "Shall we 'Reproduce?'" Part I: "The Medical Ethics of In Vitro Fertilization," *The Journal of the American Medical Association* 220, no. 10 (June 5, 1972): 1346-50, and Part II: "Rejoinders and Future Forecast" 220, no. 11 (June 12, 1972): 1480-85. Ramsey's main point is one compatible with Teilhard's personalism, namely, that unjustifiable risk is taken because it is impossible to obtain the needed consent of the person most directly involved, the child to be born. Also, note *Theological Studies* 33, no. 3 (Sept. 1973). The issue focuses on genetics.

55. The entire last, and rather lengthy, section of the essay is a development of this topic: "Love, a Higher Form of Human Energy." See *HE*, pp. 145-60.

Up to the present, the human race has been allowed to develop at random, and little thought has been given to the medical and moral factors needed to replace crude forces of natural selection if they are to be suppressed. He concludes that what is indispensable for the future is "a nobly human form of eugenics, on a standard worthy of our personalities." Passing on from individual to social eugenics, he counters the opinion that urges noninterference with the forces of the world.

> Once more we are up against the mirage of instinct, the so-called infallibility of nature. But is it not precisely the world itself which, culminating in thought, expects us to think out again the instinctive impulses of nature so as to perfect them? Reflective substance requires reflective treatment. If there is a future for mankind, it can only be imagined in terms of a harmonious conciliation of what is free with what is planned and totalised.[56]

Some particular points involved in this planning would be those already mentioned at the beginning of the present discussion—distribution of global resources, population migration, the physiology of nations and races, and other matters, sociopoliticoeconomic as well as eugenic in the strict sense.

The question of limitations on research is not treated directly in this passage either, but there are key expressions, with relevant implications. He speaks of the suitable subordination of values; then, shortly after, of a nobly human form of eugenics on a standard worthy of personality; and, later, of the harmonious conciliation of what is free with what is planned. The crux of the matter would quite clearly seem to be meaning of "a standard worthy of personality." He does not elaborate on this point but it should be noted that he does raise the important question of the implications of the dignity of the human person for the entire eugenic process, individual as well as social.

56. See *PM* (1940), pp. 282-83. "Pré-humain, humain, ultra-humain" (1949), contains a counterpart passage. See above, n43.

A second approach to the question of the extent of human dominion over human life is likewise tucked away in this passage from *The Phenomenon of Man*. It differs from the first in that it does contain the nub of an argument that could be used to sustain the flat assumption upon which the first formulation rests. It also prescinds from the element of religious value. The argument, phrased as a rhetorical question, occurs in the last quotation cited, where Teilhard objects to the principle of noninterference with the forces of the world. His answer rests on the inference to be drawn from the fact that in man the evolution of the world culminates in thought capable of critical, reflective, and perfective action on the instinctive impulses of nature. The inference would be that since thought has replaced instinct, and since, with thought, responsible control of evolution is in man's hand, man should exercise reflective management of himself as reflective substance, keeping in mind all the implications of reflective substance regarding personal autonomy and dignity.

Put in this fashion and developed somewhat beyond Teilhard's own language, the argument rests squarely on the meaning and range of human responsibility, now that factors of chance and instinct can be rationally supplemented. However, even if his basic position can be accepted, his thinking in this problem area is inadequate on the phenomenological level alone for want of clarification about how to apply personalistic norms to delicate concrete cases, as well as to institutionalized health care. On religious grounds it can be seriously faulted for not indicating even recognition of the debate, discussions, and pronouncements by his theological confreres and the Vatican on such matters as contraception or organic transplantation, to mention only two. These problems of human dominion over the human body were being discussed in his lifetime by experts within the Church to which, by his own admission, he looked for guidance. It is surprising, therefore, that he says nothing of the discussions going on in this area.

To return to the question of personalistic and religious norms governing individual and social eugenic research and development. What is disturbing about Teilhard's manner of speaking in the context of eugenics is that he seems to be leaning very heavily on the biological aspects of man, in the narrow sense of biological, which would focus more on his continuity with lower animals than on his discontinuity as person. As has been noted above, this is characteristic of enough of his writing about social man to be disturbing there as well. If one is to save his thought from an over-crude biologism, one is forced to make correlations with his eugenic thinking by drawing on other sources, where his personalism, phenomenological or religious, contributes a different perspective—with the by-now-customary lament that Teilhard never got around to doing this himself.

A particular case in point is his easily shocking questions that appear in the text of "Human Energy" (1937), when he is considering incorporated energy in its social dimension. He is speaking of questions related to eugenics, urgent but scarcely yet raised, and he asks:

> What fundamental attitude, for example, should the advancing wing of humanity take to fixed or definitely unprogressive ethnical groups? The earth is a closed and limited surface. To what extent should it tolerate, racially or nationally, areas of lesser activity? More generally still, how should we judge the efforts we lavish in all kinds of hospitals on saving what is so often no more than one of life's rejects? Something profoundly true and beautiful (I mean faith in the irreplaceable value and unpredictable resources contained in each personal unity) is evidently concealed in persistent sacrifice to save a human existence. But should not this solicitude of man for his individual neighbour be balanced by a higher passion, born of the faith in that other higher personality that is to be expected, as we shall see,

from the world-wide achievements of our evolution? To what extent should not the development of the strong (to the extent that we can define this quality) take precedence over the preservation of the weak? How can we reconcile, in a state of maximum efficiency, the care lavished on the wounded with the more urgent necessities of battle? In what does true charity consist?[57]

It is true that he immediately continues by asserting that such a serious complex of problems can only be handled by preliminary establishment of a scale and plan of distribution of human values on a very broad base—which presumably would include the main tenets of his personalism, alluded to in passing fashion in the questions. It is also true that the editor of the French text saw fit at this point to append a footnote attesting to Teilhard's constant efforts to encourage the weak and inspire the strong as evidence of his own expertise in making the necessary reconciliation about which he spoke.[58]

But the fact remains that the passage as it stands does convey an impression of intolerance both for weak peoples and sick and weak individuals. His thinking on racial, or human-branch, complementarity, as seen above in chapter 6, mitigates the brusqueness of the questions just quoted, as does his emphasis on love and universal sympathy, as well as his insistence on personal autonomy as a fundamental human right, and on persuasion over coercion in his understanding of democracy, educational theory, and religious conversion. However, the occurrence of passages such as the above indicates that despite the inner satisfaction he seems to have experienced from the resolution, for himself, of his basic synthetic problem, his general theoretical statements at times convey an incompletely resolved tension between a kind of scientist biologism on the one hand and phenomenological and religious personalism on the other.

On the strength of what is known to have been the

57. *HE*, pp. 132-33.
58. *HE*, p. 133, n1.

controlling force of Teilhard's own religious commitment, it seems reasonable that wherever the tension appears to be irreconcilable, the interpretive balance should be tipped in the direction called for by his religious personalism. This would hold particularly in the case of his questions about the evolutionary significance of the sick, weak, and suffering. What can also be mustered to his defense is his lifelong insistence on the spiritually energizing power of suffering associated with the suffering of Christ on the Cross, and clarified in application to the meaning of human illness at least twice in his mature years in the early thirties and early fifties.[59] He did not take up the subject often, or bring it in where doing so seems to have been required to anticipate serious objections. But, as will be seen in the next chapter, his preoccupation with the constructive, evolutionary power of suffering runs consistently from his earliest writings down to his last.

As a consequence, those who would seem to be weak and useless, from the point of view of animal biology, are, when evaluated in accord with Teilhard's clear position on the spiritual power of suffering, not necessarily weak at all, but capable of strong, vital, constructive effort. On this particular point, however, his phenomenology does not supply the solidly hopeful element, but rather his religious interpretation of the meaning of the Cross. His complete phenomenology does have a strong personalistic tone which, when taken into account, militates against a ruthless sacrifice of the individual to the good of the whole. But it does not provide the base for such a distinctively positive esteem of the struggling poor and weak as is present in the Christian faith-judgments flowing from his appreciation of Christ's suffering.

59. "The Significance and Positive Value of Suffering" (1933), *HE*, pp. 48-52; "The Spiritual Energy of Suffering" (1950), *AE*, pp. 245-49.

9

# Teilhard's Christological Ethic: The Fulfillment of a Morality of Movement in Divinized Human Love

## A. Orientation of Chapter

The present study was designed to follow a manner of progression in Teilhard's thought that he frequently adopted, a progression from his type of phenomenological considerations into a consideration of the meaning of Christ for an evolutionary world. Because Teilhard often brought the two into close juxtaposition, some of his Christological thinking inevitably appears in the process of an attempt to sift out, clarify, and develop the main lines of what could be called his phenomenological ethic. The preceding chapters have borne out in a number of instances the intermingling of these two strains of his thought. His Christological thought could also have been used as a working base toward development of a synthesis incorporating his phenomenological humanism. But since little of his writing in which he developed his thinking on moral matters went this way, I decided not to follow such an approach.

In much of his earliest writing, however, where he tried to clarify the principal elements of his synthetic position, he used another approach, whereby, so to speak, he held the love of the world in one hand, his love of God in the other, and sought to determine, by examining each in close proximity, how they could be brought into a genuine union of synthesis.[1]

Examination of his thought in the present chapter has some resemblance to this early Teilhardian approach, in that consideration of his ethical thought in his Christological setting will entail constant attention to the connection between his phenomenological humanism and his Christian convictions with their base in revelation, and to the character of the ethical synthesis that emerges in this running comparison seeking integration.

Teilhard's method of integrating revelation and his scientific humanist experience was seen in chapter 2. The present chapter is concerned with the results of that method toward what can be called the synthetic character of his Christological ethic. The controlling question can be phrased, therefore, as follows: "What is the relation between his interpretation of Christianity and his ethical thought?" One could also put it more specifically: "Does his Christianity merely animate and provide motivation for moral content derived from his phenomenological humanism, or does it also provide distinctively Christian lines of conduct, or, the counterpart of this last, is it his "Christian" ethic that is modified by his phenomenology?"

## B. Summary of Teilhard's Christological Thought

As background for answering this basic question and the other questions that flow from it, it will be useful,

1. Most of the World War I essays reveal this approach. In several instances, even their titles give indication of it: "Mastery of the World and the Kingdom of God," "Le Christ dans la matière," "Operative Faith," "Note pour servir à l'évangélisation des temps nouveaux," "La puissance spirituelle de la matière."

despite the risk of oversimplification, to recall certain key elements of Teilhard's Christological thought, some of which will need elaboration shortly in their ethical context.[2]

The foundation of Teilhard's Christology was the historical Jesus given meaning by the grace of faith. For Teilhard, Jesus of Nazareth, born of the Virgin Mary, was true God and true man, who lived, suffered, died, and rose from the dead for the salvation of mankind. The Omega Point and Personal Center of his phenomenological extrapolation was given the certainty and warmth of both heart and face in this historical Jesus, the immanent and transcendant God who entered human history at a particular point of fullness in time to draw evolution onward and upward through the attractive power of his love toward completion in Creative Union. It was this Jesus who established his Church. For Teilhard this was the Roman Catholic Church, which in biological terms he described as a Phylum of Love, the lead shoot in continuing evolution, or the head of the axis-arrow moving toward fulfillment in the Parousia. The union between Christ and the members of his Mystical Body is not the mere juridical bond of a voluntary sacral monarchy, but an organic, "physical" ontological, real union, howevermuch it defies adequate description or explanation. Infallibility of the Church and of the Pope in the Church is taken as one of the characteristics compatible with and called for by its leading role in phyletic evolution. Christ's Second Coming, the Parousia, is depicted as conceivably occurring at the critical maturation point of the total evolutive socialization process. Yet, it should be noted, for Teilhard this does not take

2. The corpus of primary sources that could be considered the base for the following sketch of Teilhard's Christological thought would be, *WW, EG, HU, SC,* and *CE* of the published works, plus *"Comment je vois" (1948),* from *DA,* and the unpublished papers "Le coeur de la matière" (1950), and "Le Christique" (1955). Critiques and commentaries particularly helpful have been those by Mooney, de Solages, de Lubac, d'Ouince, Faricy, Rideau, Smulders, Bravo, and Wildiers.

place within history but at its term, and the desired maturation is, in his explicit words, a condition necessary but insufficient, which is in need of God's transforming action for complete fulfillment.[3]

Through the Incarnation extended in the Church and in a special way in the Eucharist, the entire process of cosmogenesis or Omegalization is divinized and becomes Christogenesis.

Human effort and suffering are affected remarkably. Autoevolution now becomes a joint divine-human task in which love of Christ-Omega draws men to share as co-workers in the labor of Christogenesis, fulfilling the universe, building the Mystical Body to maturation in its totality—the Pleroma of Christ. The expiatory and satisfactory functions of suffering are accepted as part of the mystery of redemption, but the constructive value of the Cross, and suffering associated with it, is stressed. This emphasis on constructive suffering is closely tied with a reinterpretation of the meaning of Original Sin in the light of evolutionary theory about human origins. The reality of Original Sin is affirmed, but its meaning is taken to be the inevitable primeval condition of widespread failings attendant upon mankind's struggle to ascend the evolutionary slope, the impact of which has been transmitted to the psychic atmosphere of our own time.

The task of Christogenesis cannot be achieved by raw human effort alone. Christ's divinizing grace transforms men's minds and hearts, making them capable of seeing and accepting, through faith, hope, and charity, the realities and challenges of this task. Grace vitalizes the essential zest for life and fuller being, giving it new dimensions of divine-human consciousness. But grace, and the attractiveness of God perceived through it, do not take away human freedom. Men do sin, and, ultimately, if enough do, evolution will fail. Sin is the contra-unitive,

3. See below, F.

fragmenting limitation or negation of the evolutionary force or energy that in the concrete, on the human level, is love energy. By implication, sin thus becomes a refusal to love, although Teilhard did not describe it in these very words. The mystery of Hell is an awe-inspiring, sobering reality, a necessary "structural element" in God's total universe. Christ's victory in his resurrection is interpreted by Teilhard to corroborate his phenomenologically based optimism about the ultimate success of evolution, despite the moral failures of many along the way.

From what appears in this summary view of Teilhard's Christology and from the earlier examination of his method, a general answer to the tripartite form of the present controlling question can be formulated, before going into details. The answer would be that, in all areas of decision, Teilhard's Christianity would provide the ultimate vitalizing motivation, but that in some it would be energizing types of conduct derived from phenomenological thought, in some it would activate revelation based lines of internal and external behavior, and in others its influence would work on patterns of action of mixed origin, either phenomenological lines affected by revelation, or faith-derived lines interpreted from a phenomenological stance.

## C. Revelation and Teilhard's Morality of Movement

First of all, how does his theory on a morality of movement fit in with his religious beliefs? In the 1937 essay where he explains what he means by such a morality, he is writing in a phenomenological vein, and does not refer to religion, much less revelation, as a source for his fundamental concepts. When he does speak of religion and God, it is not of God disclosing a moral code, but of God toward whom, in love, one directs constructive moral life. God is presented as the motive for moral action, but not as a lawgiver of moral content.[4] Moreover, almost two decades before this, in a piece written specifically about the presentation of Christianity to the modern world, Teilhard has some definite notions about the limitations of scriptural writing concerning the development of humanity, with emphasis on the goal provided through revelation.[5]

But his position does not involve a simple dichotomy between a goal from revelation and paths to the goal from reason alone. Fundamentally, the thrust of human morality toward constructive effort has roots in both revelation and reason. His underlying premise for this is that the God of the Bible is no different from the God of nature. Appealing to St. John and St. Paul, he affirms that the fulfillment of every creature, in development, determination, and personality cannot be found except in Christ Jesus. Everything in the cosmos for the spirit, and everything spiritual for Christ, are his order of progression. For Teilhard, a thoroughly Christian orientation for a morality of effort and development can be derived from the revealed imperative to build the Body of Christ, to achieve the Pleroma.[6]

What emerges, then, is that Teilhard derives his developmental *orientation* of moral choice from both reason and revelation. The ultimate, completely fulfilling *term* of this orientation, however, is to be found in the Christ of revelation alone. The particular *lines of action*, concretizing this orientation, or the specific *content* of judgments about moral conduct are another matter. Evolutionary phenomenology can lay bare the organic ties of responsibility, and hence the moral imperatives in specific areas of personal and societal development. One

4. See "The Phenomenon of Spirituality" (1937), *HE*, pp. 108-12. Also, above, chap. 3C and C (1).
5. "Note pour l'évangélisation des temps nouveaux" (1919), *EG*, p. 376.
6. *Ibid.*, p. 376. Also, *DM* (1927), pp. 56-64, "Le coeur de la matière" (1950), *I*, pp. 10-20, and "Le Christique" (1955), *I*, pp. 6-10.

can, therefore, by adhering to this style of thought, develop an independent Teilhardian phenomenological ethic in terms of cosmogenetic Omegalization.

Can one, correspondingly, proceed from his Christogenetic orientation toward the Pleroma, and derive a revelation-based Christogenetic body of ethical content? For Teilhard, even for something so peculiarly rooted in revelation as his acceptance of evangelical poverty, chastity, and obedience in the religious life, the answer would be mixed. Certain Christian virtues, such as charity and chastity, are for him to be given a *new* interpretation that will maintain continuity with the essence of what the Scriptures contain, but at the same time will be altered in the light of new insights about person and society derived from evolutionary phenomenology. A noteworthy instance of this is his gradual clarification of the *dynamic* meaning he assigned to Christian charity, wherein the specific type of dynamism was clearly influenced by his understanding of human interrelationships in an evolutionary context.[7] Moreover, there are important areas of moral decision regarding man's collective social and political life about which revelation says nothing.[8] In these areas, the Christian may have his distinc-

7. On the development in Teilhard's thought about love, see above, chap. 4B. For early texts on charity, see above, chap. 4, nn7 and 10. Representative and significant later texts would be: *DM* (1927), pp. 142-46; "Le sens humain" (1929), *DA*, pp. 39, 42-44; "Christology and Evolution" (1933), *CE*, p. 92; "Human Energy" (1937), *HE*, pp. 192-93; *PM* (1940), pp. 295-96; "The Atomism of Spirit" (1941), *AE*, pp. 52-53; "Super-Humanity, Super-Christ, Super-Charity" (1943), *SC*, pp. 168-72; "Christianity and Evolution" (1945), *CE*, pp. 184-85; "Comment je vois" (1948), *DA*, pp. 217-20; "Le coeur de la matière" (1950), *I*, pp. 21-32; "Le Christique" (1955), I, pp. 5, 7, 9, 12. For Faricy's treatment of charity, see *Teilhard: Theology*, pp. 192-96.

8. The clearest formulation on this point is found in an early essay, "The Mastery of the World and the Kingdom of God" (1918), *WW*, pp. 82-83. Speaking of the function of revelation, he says, "It's commandments and counsels solve problems of a general order. It provides a basis and a goal for speculation, and breathes a Spirit into Action; but it has nothing to say about the nature of cosmic energies and the promises they hold, about details of politics and the social state, or about the definitive forms of thought and human organization." All of which leads Teilhard to appeal for the effort of research to supply what is wanting. His attitude remained consistent on this point throughout his life. For a late expression of the basic idea, in more condensed form, see his insistence on the function of revelation not to duplicate, but to animate research, in "The Death-Barrier and Co-Reflection" (1955), *AE*, p. 405, n6.

tive motivation, but in regard to content he has to develop avenues of conduct with the same rational tools as the nonbeliever.

## 1. ETHICAL SIGNIFICANCE OF THE DIVINE MILIEU

Teilhard's most complete development of the basic lines of what could be called the Christogenetic form of his morality of movement is found in *The Divine Milieu*, written in the late twenties in China. It elaborates at some length on fundamental themes of activity and passivity, the sanctification of the human and the humanization of the Christian, attachment and detachment, effort, suffering, and resignation, the meaning of faith, purity, and charity—all with the conscious intent of presenting a coherent synthesis of what Teilhard judged to be the highest contemporary human aspiration with an authentic, if different, interpretation of Christian life. The differences in his interpretation derived, quite as one would expect, from his manner of reading and understanding the character of the human in the light of his evolutionary thinking, which at that time had not reached the clarity of detail regarding the vision of the social human universe he was later to develop, particularly in his writings of the late thirties and forties. The principal emphases can be found running through his writings down through the years. Not long before he died, he reaffirmed his consistent adherence to what he had expressed long before, while commenting on its fundamentally general character, due in part to the fact that at the time of writing he had not experienced the insights into noospheric function and structure that would have provided the background for more particularized treatment.[9]

If one were to attempt a collection and synthesis of his ethic from a Christological base, rather than, as has been done in the present study, from the phenomenological

9. See "Le coeur de la matière" (1950), *I*, p. 26.

base of his thought on energy organization, a pattern for arranging materials could be taken from *The Divine Milieu*, using its treatment of themes and virtues as the framework, which could then be particularized from his phenomenological thinking.

What is especially important with regard to *The Divine Milieu* as a Christogenetic statement of Teilhard's morality of movement in its main outlines, is that despite its generic character, it goes into far more detail about fundamental attitudes and directions than do his phenomenological writings. Particularly significant as specifications of how the underlying thrust of an ethic of constructive effort would manifest itself in a Christian context are his thoughts on communion through action and detachment though action, when he is writing about the divinization of activities, and, in his reflections on the divinization of passivities, what he has to say about the passivities of diminishment, which covers such important concepts as struggling with God against evil, the transfiguration of apparent failure, and the meaning of true resignation.[10]

His thoughts on communion with God through action are the Christological version of what has been marked earlier as the totalization of one's actions through the synthetic power of love. More will be said about this similarity shortly in the section on love in *Christogenesis*. There is nothing particularly original in the content of his fundamental thoughts about communion through action.[11] What gives them a different cast is their setting in a context that throws emphasis on action as being constructive action, developmental of the universe.

Nor, in the last analysis, is Teilhard's thought on detachment through action a radically new insight. What

10. *DM* (1927), "The Divinisation of Our Activities," pp. 49-73, "The Divinisation of our Passivities," pp. 74-94.

11. Ultimately, they can be said to be rooted in his understanding of St. Paul's expression that Christ would be "All in all." Proximately they would seem to be an adaptation for use in his own thought framework of the traditional Ignatian concepts about contemplation in action, which were the core of his ascetical and spiritual training in the Jesuit Order.

he says about overcoming inertia at the beginning of action and the readiness to abandon what one has achieved in pursuit of further achievement can be put down as a logical corollary drawn from the Ignatian concept of active indifference as noted in the First Principle and Foundation of *The Spiritual Exercises*, where it is taken as given that the concerned Christian should be ready to move toward whatever use or nonuse of creatures will lead to the greater glory of God.[12] It is the context in which he situates his formulation of a time-honored concept that gives it a fresh note. There is, however, another aspect to mark at this point. He is, in effect, by speaking of *detachment* through action, meeting the objection of a type of Christian mentality that would read his insistence on concern for absorption in developmental action as self-glorifying egoism, leading to neglect or abandonment of the traditional Christian concern for self-denial in the pursuit of holiness.

When Teilhard develops his thought on the passivities of growth and the passivities of diminishment, he brings in important concepts for understanding the context of his insistence on effort to commune with God in action and to be detached in action—and to counterbalance what some would see as a kind of Christian Prometheanism. When he talks about the passivities of growth, he is affirming his sense of weakness, fragility, and dependence on God. His thought here has strong Pauline and Augustinian resonances about man's total need for divine help even to want to do good. Moreover, his discussion of the passivities of diminishment, of struggling with God against evil, of the transfiguration of apparent failure, communion through diminishment, and the meaning of true resignation, shows him coming to grips, although with his own peculiar vocabulary, with key elements of evil and human sinfulness so important for a realistic appraisal of the human condition.

12. See *The Spiritual Exercises of St. Ignatius*, trans. Louis J. Puhl, S.J. (Westminster, Md.: The Newman Press, 1957), "First Principle and Foundation," p. 12.

In these pages on the passivities of diminishment he faces the brute facts of what happens to the meaning of human existence when effort fails, catastrophe strikes, moral failures enervate, and death itself is imminent. Here are perhaps his strongest expressions about what it means to have faith in the providence of a loving God and in the redemptive meaning of Christ's suffering. While it is risky, and perhaps impossible, to select a single passage to epitomize his thought, the following is presented as capturing, if any segment of his thought could do so, the main thrust of his message here. It occurs at the end of the section on "Communion through diminishment," which is cast in the form of a single long prayer:

> The more deeply and incurably the evil is encrusted in my flesh, the more it will be you that I am harbouring—you as a loving, active principle of purification and detachment. The more the future opens before me like some dizzy abyss or dark tunnel, the more confident I may be—if I venture forward on the strength of your word—of losing myself and surrendering myself in you, of being assimilated by your body, Jesus.
>
> You are the irresistible and vivifying force, O Lord, and because yours is the energy, because, of the two of us, you are infinitely the stronger, it is on you that falls the part of consuming me in the union that should weld us together. Vouchsafe, therefore, something more precious still than the grace for which all the faithful pray. It is not enough that I should die while communicating. Teach me *to treat my death as an act of communion.*[13]

Although the word *detachment* does not appear, one can see that he is, both here and in what he says about the meaning of resignation, expressing ideas more traditionally associated with the concept of detachment before the elements of evil in human life. So far, therefore, as the reality of subject matter goes, it would be in-

13. *DM* (1927), pp. 89-90.

accurate to assert that he treats of detachment only in the context of active striving, and has nothing to say about how to be detached in suffering. What is regrettable, since the objection will inevitably arise, is that Teilhard did not stress this approach to evil more. However, as was noted above, *The Divine Milieu* was the development and distillation of ten years of prayerful reflection, and almost three decades later, shortly before he died, he still looked on it as an authentic expression of his fundamental Christian outlook toward activity and suffering, as well as the other matters contained in it. Moreover, the outlines of his basic concepts in it can easily be found in his World War I essays and later writings.[14]

## 2. ORIGINAL SIN AND ITS IMPORT

In the earlier treatment of freedom in his ethical thought, what was said about the question of sin and human sinfulness had to do mainly with establishing their possibility and fact as background for responsible choice. What Teilhard had to say about the revealed doctrine of Original Sin and its consequences would have been out of place in the phenomenological setting of chapter 3. It is, however, of considerable import in the present context, and must be taken up now.

While his speculative probes into how he could reconcile his scientific studies on human origins with the essential core of Roman Catholic thought on Original Sin were never advanced by Teilhard as a definitive answer to one of the most vexing theological mysteries, they struck an extraordinarily sensitive nerve in official circles. It was, in fact, a short explanatory note of the early twenties, which somehow found its way to the Vatican,

14. See, for example, "The Mystical Milieu" (1917), *WW*, pp. 128-32 (passivity), 132-36 (action); "My Universe" (1924), *SC*, pp. 69-70 (death through action), 70-73 (death through passivity); "Le coeur de la matière" (1950), *I*, pp. 27-29 ("Le Milieu Divin").

led to his forced withdrawal from teaching in Paris, and ironically enough, situated him for many years in China, where he did some of his most important scientific work on human origins.[15]

His closest and sympathetic associates, as de Solages has pointed out, parted company with him on this matter, not simply because of the problem of interpreting the Genesis account of Adam against scientific evidence pointing to polygenetic or polyphyletic evolution.[16] On this point, Teilhard allowed that scientific evidence could never prove or disprove conclusively at this great distance in time precisely how, or in what numbers, the distinctively human first appeared on earth. While he admitted the possibility of some primordial moral catastrophe to account for the extent of evil in the human world today, he definitely inclined to an interpretation of the origin of sin that put its root in the very character of the evolutionary process itself, and hence Original Sin as he would describe it would 'become the *consequence* of the internal statistical necessity of evolutionary process, rather than as a primordial moral fault, the cause, in some way, of subsequent moral corruption.[17] Moreover, he inclined toward an explanation of the transmission of Original Sin that would make use of the negative educational impact of a human environment whereby older human beings by example would establish a corrosive moral atmosphere for the young.[18]

15. Although Teilhard's "Fall, Redemption, and Geocentrism" (1920), *CE*, pp. 36-44, contains some ideas on "The First Adam," pp. 39-41, that would have been upsetting in Rome, it seems that the essay that found its way there and brought on his exile was "Note on Some Possible Historical Representations of Original Sin" (1922), *CE*, pp. 45-55. It was over twenty years before he devoted his efforts to another essay specifically on the subject. See "Reflections on Original Sin" (1947), *CE*, pp. 187-98. For a good inventory of other pertinent texts, consult Faricy, *Teilhard: Theology*, p. 157, n44.

16. See de Solages, *Teilhard: étude*, pp. 323-28.

17. For a late statement of his views on primordial fault, see *PM*, "Appendix" (1948), p. 313.

18. See "Reflections on Original Sin" (1947), *CE*, p. 197. Teilhard's concepts on original sin, in this essay and in his other writings, have not been without constructive impact in the theological world. See, for example, Piet Schoonenberg, S.J., *Man and Sin*, trans. Joseph Donceel, S.J., Logos Books

At this juncture, implications of Teilhard's preferred position, which he failed to see, must be noted. It has been objected that his turn-about explanation of Original Sin, which inserts evil by statistical necessity in the likewise statistically determined upward movement of evolution toward progress, does, in a sense, provide a base for not being too concerned about it since, from such a distant statistical vantage point, it cannot in the last analysis really vitiate the onward movement of humanity. With this objection I would concur, to the extent that it is in effect corollary to my objection to Teilhard's illogical extrapolation predictive of ultimate human unity.

What complicates matters from the standpoint of Teilhard's ethics is the apparent inconsistency of holding, on the one hand, a position that says sin cannot really destroy evolution, and, on the other hand, exhorting people to fight against evil, to recognize their responsibility to take control of evolution or it will be destroyed. What saved him, in his own mind, from looking on this as inconsistent, was what he judged was the significance

(Chicago: Henry Regnery Co., 1968), "Epilogue: Sin and Redemption in our Present View of the World," p. 192: "Roughly speaking, the difference between our present view of the world and of man and that which prevailed until quite recently is the difference between an evolutionary or historical picture and a static picture. Thus we speak in the spirit of Pierre Teilhard de Chardin. Even if this book has occasionally criticized some of his views, it has been deeply affected by his inspiration. The following pages are not a copy of his ideas, but rather the attempt of a confrontation with the view of the world which he has put before us. Only his conception of human nature has been completed by more emphasis upon man's typical historicity and freedom." There is something of an ironical paradox in the situation arising out of Teilhard's treatment of the problem of evil, in that on the one hand he is accused of paying insufficient attention to it, through his stress on optimism about the evolutionary process, and on the other hand his theory about the origins of evil puts the reality of sinfulness in evolution by necessity—statistical necessity, if you will, but nonetheless definite. In the last analysis, he does not deny the existence, or the importance of evil in his evolutionary theory, but affirms its inevitability. His optimism derives more from the long-range view of the process, than from ignorance of present evil. The problem is that this long-range view leads him at times to neglect the urgency of present evil. For example, he did not neglect the urgency of fear and anxiety about futility in human life, but he did neglect, among other things, to show concern about the immediate stress of unemployment, and the frustration of the assembly line.

of his use of the term *statistical* necessity. As he read the concept, this enabled him to maintain the *metaphysical* integrity of human freedom and responsibility, and at the same time work with extrapolative probability in examining large numbers on the phenomenological, non-metaphysical plane.

The distinction seems as valid as the traditional Roman Catholic theological insistence that it is morally impossible for man to avoid mortal sin without grace, and yet maintain his ontological freedom and responsibility, by which he would be "physically" free not to sin. But Teilhard's position is open to misunderstanding and in need of more clarification than he gave it, particularly in the area of the manner in which love operates through attractiveness and has a bearing on this particular problem. The root of the deterministic problem with Teilhard lies here, rather than in his statistical determinism, the reason being that the foundation for his predictions that men would overcome evil can be found in his opinion that attraction toward good will be more influential than the propensity toward the bad. In this area both clarification and modification are needed to bring his theory of love and his theory of responsibility into harmony.

There are then, admittedly, problems with regard to the relationship between Teilhard's thought on Original Sin and his ethical theory.

Against his understanding of the meaning of the Fall, there is clearly a different consciousness of the meaning of Redemption, both the prototype redemptive act of Christ and its continuation in the life of Christian believers today. The conscious motivation is not that of trying to restore, in union with Christ, some sort of satisfactory penalty balance before a monarchical type of God. It was noted earlier that Teilhard did not intend to replace or rule out the notions of satisfaction and expiation in his concept of Redemption, but rather to give more stress to what he considered to be the constructive value of suffering.[19] It was also noted that he nowhere explains how expiation and satisfaction would have specific meaning content against the background of his theory of Original Sin. It is possible, if one makes explicit what he does not express, to translate his language about sin as disruptive of unity into language expressing rejection of love and then go on further to formulate restoration of unity in terms of repentance on the part of the sinner and forgiveness on the part of God. In so doing one would have a workable equivalent of satisfaction and expiation not inconsistent with his premises. But this is yet another formulation that he did not undertake.

One reason for his not doing so was probably, as has been indicated, his strong reaction against what he judged to be an excessively juridical approach to the redemptive process. Another reason was very likely his bent to bring together, with what de Solages describes as his tendency for ultra-synthesis, his understanding of Creation, Incarnation, and Redemption in one unified vision.[20] In view of the dominant positive tones of the first two concepts, it is understandable that an attempt at synthesis of the three would play down the negative aspects of Redemption.

Teilhard's theory on the origin of evil in human life cannot be said to have direct impact on the content of his Christological ethic, because to assert that human moral failure must occur by statistical necessity in the evolutionary process has nothing to say directly about what specific moral failures would be involved, nor about what one should do to work against them. If, however, one accepts as a consequence of such an explanation the tendency to be less concerned about the dangers from sinfulness in human existence—since evolution will inevitably overcome these, in some way—then the orien-

19. See "Cosmic Life" (1916), WW, pp. 70-71; "Christology and Evolution" (1933), CE, p. 85; "Some Reflections on the Conversion of the World" (1936), SC, p. 123; "What the World is Looking for from the Church" (1952), CE, pp. 218-19.
20. See de Solages, Teilhard: étude, pp. 328-32.

tation toward moral content would be more positive and optimistic in tone. But note that the base for the optimism is not the statistical necessity at the root of evil but the statistical necessity calling for ultimate triumph over it. The optimism would be colored by the fact that the evils to be overcome had to be there and had to be fought, but would not derive fundamentally from a particular explanation of the origin of such evils.

However, one cannot say that in Teilhard's thought there is an unqualified optimism regarding the negative impact of human sinfulness. Regardless of satisfaction or dissatisfaction with the extent of his emphasis, the fact is that he does urge constant effort to overcome the fragmentation of the individual person and society through neglect of love. He recognized that men could sin by excessive individualistic self-centeredness as well as by failure to try, and he knew that men could lose heart before failure, suffering, and death.[21] What he says about evolution's succeeding if men keep on trying must be taken against the background of what was seen above about how he saw real success for evolution in a Christian sense when a person would find communion with Christ through resignation and communion in diminishment, even the diminishment of death. In other words, the Christian dimension of his struggle against evil points to success not only when evil is overcome, but when, in union with Christ's suffering, inevitable evil is accepted without being overcome. His explanation by way of his thought on the passivities of diminishment does take into account the mystery of Christ's victory in the Crucifixion. To the extent that he did say this, one cannot say that he ignored the problem of what to do with human failure. Where he is open to criticism is that he did not correlate sufficiently the thoughts he expressed

21. On the need for struggle toward personalizing unity, see "The Struggle against the Multitude" (1917), *WW*, pp. 98-105; *DM* (1927), "Detachment through Action," pp. 70-73; "Our Struggle with God against Evil," pp. 83-84; "Sketch of a Personalistic Universe" (1936), *HE*, "The Pains of Personalization," pp. 84-89.

in *The Divine Milieu*, and elsewhere, with other statements about the ultimate success of the evolutionary process. However, his omission of these concepts in certain texts must be evaluated on the basis of the anticipated reader in a particular context. When Teilhard's apologetic purpose is to gain acceptance for the reasonableness of a transcendent Omega by an entrenched scientific empiricist, it is unrealistic to blame him for not speaking about the Mystery of the Cross.[22]

## D. Love in Christogenesis

As was noted above, the dynamic aspect of charity as Teilhard developed it seems to have been derived from the input of his evolutionary theory, leading him to look to a broadened concept of concern for one's neighbor.[23] But it should also be recalled that this dynamic aspect amounts to a transfer to the area of love of the underlying concept of movement and development incorporated in his general moral theory, and that this, as has been seen, can find roots in his faith-understanding of what is needed to build the Mystical Body of Christ to maturity. What has happened here seems to be somewhat the reverse of what he describes in his account of his reaching a phenomenological insight into the existence of Omega.[24] He admitted that he had the model of Omega in his mind from revelation, although he developed a phenomenological path to recognition of its existence. Regarding the dynamism of charity, he seems to have come to a deeper understanding of charity by using insights drawn from evolutionary phenomenology, although he could well have done so by working from revealed materials alone.

22. Regarding Teilhard's adaptation of his writing to his audience, note his important explanation on this point in "The Outline of a Dialectic of Spirit" (1946), *AE*, p. 150, where he asserts that, in his writing for nonbelievers, he limited himself to the phenomenon of man and Omega.
23. See above, C.
24. *PM* (1940), p. 294.

As one reflects on what he has to say about the general aspects of love (attraction, affinity, sympathy, power of synthesis), the bulk of input appears to have come from his phenomenology, until, as was pointed out, one reaches what he has to say about the totalizing or synthesizing power of love, where his thoughts, put in phenomenological language, look very much like a transposition of Christian—and, more immediately, Ignatian—spirituality describing the character of contemplation in action, or, simply, finding God in all things.[25] Since his thought about totalization is corollary to his thought about Omega, Teilhard would have insisted, had he ever been moved to a methodological justification for it, on the soundness of a purely phenomenological base. By virtue of the same parallel, although there is no evidence that he mentioned the fact, he would have been forced to admit the similarity between totalization and contemplation in action.

## 1. TEILHARD AND AGAPEIC LOVE

From what has been seen thus far about the content of Teilhard's theory of love, one may say that regarding two points just considered—the dynamism of charity and the meaning of the synthetic power of love—different styles of possible methodological cross-fertilization have appeared. However, from the extent to which much of his writing about the basic character of love has a strong phenomenological flavor in his stress on communion through attraction, affinity, and sympathy, there arises a serious question about the possibility that in regard to one important aspect of Christian love, the influence of his phenomenology has been so strong as to delete, or at least obscure a type of loving that seems to derive uniquely, both as to knowledge and activation, from divine

25. See above, chap. 4C.

revelation and the power of grace. The problem is that of agapeic love in Teilhard's thought.

Although discussion about eros and agape and its impact on understanding the meaning of Christian love arose in Teilhard's lifetime, he does not allude to it.[26] In recent years, however, analysis of his thought has put his ideas in the eros-agape setting, with the clear implication, in at least one instance, that Teilhardian love is all eros and no agape. In response to this position, it has been noted that desire is not so simple a notion as one might think. There can be an egoistic desire of greed and pleasure and a nonegoistic desire of aspiration and union, in which self-giving is incorporated. The observation has also been made, and with it I at least partially concur, that quantitatively Teilhard treats more often of "Eros by which man rises to God" than of agape in the sense of divine charity, but that agape does enter into Teilhard's spiritual and mystical writings.[27] It is not difficult to substantiate the claim that Teilhard's basic

26. Part I of Nygren's seminal *Agape and Eros* was first published in 1930. By 1953, such extensive literature had appeared on what earlier was judged a neglected topic, that Nygren, in his "Author's Preface" to the revised English version of his work, admitted that he could not, within the compass of such a preface, even list the books and articles that would be pertinent to the problem.

27. See Christian d'Armagnac, "Teilhard est-il gidien?" *Les Études Philosophiques* 21 (Paris, 1966): 536, which is a response to an earlier article in the same journal by Jean Brun, which leveled the charge. D'Armagnac's distinction between egoistic desire and nonegoistic desire is derived from Jean Mouroux, in his critique of Nygren, "Eros et Agape," *La vie intellectuelle* (avril 1946), pp. 28-38. Mouroux, in *The Meaning of Man*, trans. A. H. C. Downes, Image Books (Garden City, N.Y.: Doubleday and Co., Inc., 1961), without speaking in eros-agape terminology, has a rather lengthy treatment of these pertinent concepts, on love as desire and gift, in his chapters on "Love," pp. 182-209, and on "Charity," pp. 210-41. According to Smulders, Teilhard probably knew Mouroux's thought, and in the formulation of his concept of person, may have been influenced by him. See Smulders, *Design of Teilhard*, pp. 69, 273, n33. What influence he may have had on Teilhard's thinking on love is not clear. Mouroux pursues his analysis to much greater depth than Teilhard, with more explicit treatment of the effect of human sinfulness on human love and liberty. It is worth noting that according to Smulders, in the same study, p. 279, n78, a certain amount of misunderstanding about Teilhard's thought on love is attributable to the fact that *The Phenomenon of Man* does not develop his thought on the subject fully, and that as a consequence evaluation based in good part on this source alone would and could not be accurate.

thought on love contains the note of self-giving, of leaving one's narrow egoism behind, both in collaborative evolutionary effort with other human persons and in genuine, "sur-centric," loving adoration of God.[28] Nor is it difficult to document his clear awareness of the need and the reality of divine initiative for bringing human love to fulfillment.[29]

But the critical point with regard to agapeic love is not the aspect of self-donation or of God's initiative. It is above all the motivation for this donation and initiative, and the peculiarly creative character of divine and hence divinized human love. Teilhard's stress on the need of the lover to respond to a preexisting attractiveness in the beloved, thus leading to communion, seems to run counter to an essential element in the love of God for man, namely, that at its root God's love in creating man responds to no attractiveness in man, since whatever good ultimately might emerge in man is there precisely because God's free action has put it there, and, moreover, God's redeeming love of sinful man is actually directed toward one who, precisely as sinner, is not attractive at all, but repulsive, as one rejecting divine love.

Here certain aspects of Teilhard's theory about crea-

28. For this particular vocabulary of Teilhard, see "Réflexions sur le Bonheur" (1943), *DA*, pp. 130-32. For the outgoing character of love, see the analysis above in chap. 4C (2) for certain qualifications.

29. For an emphatic statement from what Teilhard considered his most important spiritual effort, see *DM* (1927), p. 44: "Not only as a theoretically admitted entity, but rather as a living reality, the notion of grace impregnates the whole atmosphere of my book.

"And in fact *the divine milieu would lose all its grandeur and all its savour* for the 'mystic' if he did not feel—with his whole 'participated' being, with his whole soul made receptive of the divine favour freely poured out upon it, with his whole will strengthened and encouraged—if he did not feel *so completely swept away* in the divine ocean that *no initial point of support* would be left him in the end, of his own, within himself, from which he could act." Also note "The Humanity of Christ and the Faithful" (1920), *CE*, p. 17; "Pantheism and Christianity" (1923), *CE*, p. 68; "My Universe" (1924), *SC*, pp. 57-58; "Super-Humanity, Super-Christ, Super-Charity" (1943), *SC*, p. 166; and "Introduction to the Christian Life" (1944), *CE*, pp. 152-53, 161-62. For a somewhat extensive study of the problem of divine initiative in Teilhard's thought, see Henri de Lubac, "'Ascent' and 'Descent' in the Work of Teilhard de Chardin," *CB*, pp. 143-68. (The essay is incorporated in the correspondence volume, for which de Lubac wrote notes and commentary.)

tion and redemption can, with its implications regarding the nature of love, give rise to the serious question as to whether, despite his insistence on God's transcendence and man's weakness and dependence on God's action, his theory of love really admits the existence of authentic, agapeic, divine love.

If, as Teilhard has said, love arises from an ontological need for union, and does not preexist to create this need, and if, God, in exercising his creative love, was responding to an inner need to unite himself with creatures—man, preeminently—then it is difficult to see how God emerges as radically and sovereignly free.[30] Moreover, Teilhard's synthesis of Redemption with creation, with its attendant stress on the constructive meaning of redemption and, in effect, total bypass of explanation about the process of metanoia, of conversion from sinful rejection of love to healed acceptance and then offering of love—this particular redemption theory, to the extent he developed it, completely ignores the traditional Judeo-Christian central theme of God's selfless love for the recalcitrant sinner.

What can be said in Teilhard's defense with regard to the need of God to love man and to even receive his love is that what is at issue underlying his writing in this area is the God-to-man relationship looked at in the context of building the Pleroma.[31] Hence he would be talking about God's love not at the origin of the entire creative process, but at a point subsequent to the initial act of creation, or, better, as he sees it in the process of

30. See "The Soul of the World" (1918), *WW*, p. 189, n3. This particular bald formulation occurs only once, to the knowledge of the present writer, and then in a marginal note to a text where it is quite clear that Teilhard has no intention of denying God's gratuity in action. But the phraseology is unfortunate. Regarding the problem of divine gratuity in creation, see above, chap. 2, n34. As was noted there, sympathetic critics freely admit the awkwardness of Teilhard's expression in this problem area, while maintaining, nevertheless, his firm intent to uphold divine transcendence.

31. See "Pantheism and Christianity" (1923), *CE*, pp. 67-70; *DM* (1927), pp. 57, 62, 122, 125, 143, 151; "Suggestions for a New Theology" (1945), *CE*, pp. 177-78, 183; "The Contingence of the Universe" (1953), *CE*, pp. 226-27. On the Pleroma's "completing" God, see Mooney, *Mystery of Christ*, pp. 185-88.

God's *continuing creation*, after he has initiated the entire process. What this would have to convey, then, would be that despite his statements about getting away from the notion of "creatio ex nihilo," he really did not ultimately deny it, but sought to avoid a misplaced stress on it in understanding God's creative action in the world here and now, where there is, as St. Paul attests, a mysterious but real need in the God-man, Christ, for human love, divinized to be sure, if the Body of Christ is to grow to maturation.

If Teilhard's thought is given this interpretation, then it is possible to free him from the charge that his affirmation of God's independence, sovereign freedom, and transcendence is inconsistent to the point of contradicting his theory of creative union. The fact that in writing about creative union he wants to approach the problem of creation at the level of observable phenomena lends weight to his defense with regard to the problem of ultimate inconsistency.[32] But it is seriously to be regretted that he himself did not seem to be enough aware of the type of problem his position was generating to provide the necessary clarifications in his own writing.

The problem arising from the nature of God's free, agapeic, redemptive love of the sinner, who, turned away from God by refusal to love, is turned around to accept and give love as a consequence of God's free extension of love, is a problem of a different order. What gives pause is not that Teilhard's solution is inconsistent with other expressions of his thought, or contradictory to traditional Christianity, but that he does not really address himself to the problem at all.[33]

32. On the advisability of situating Teilhard's thought on Creative Union in a theological rather than a philosophical context, see Mooney, *Mystery of Christ*, pp. 180-85.

33. To my mind, the most likely explanation as to why he did not develop a body of theory in this area is not that he held any serious convictions about its unimportance, but that he did not judge the problem as such to be of immediate psychological importance for the particular audience he envisioned. He may have misjudged his readers, or his potential readers, but the error would be then in the realm of psychological fact rather than speculative truth.

Once more, then, the critic is forced to ask, "Does Teilhard's theory of Christian love, despite its incompleteness in this area, contain the elements from which a satisfactory rationale of redemptive agapeic love could be constructed?" Such a work of construction is made particularly difficult because of the failure on Teilhard's part to pursue to any depth an analysis of the meaning of hatred and enmity that would be the counterpart of his analysis of personal love.[34] The absence of such analysis was what necessitated, in chapter 4, looking into the evidence of his thought from his own personal life in order to put down some indication as to what his thinking was about forgiveness in human relations as a means to overcoming obstacles to love.[35]

To construct such a rationale, one would have to start with his definite position on the need for God's grace if man is to respond with genuine Christogenetic love to divine initiatives. The next step would be to recall his affirmation of man's sinfulness. His urging to resist evil, which implies resistance of moral evil within oneself, would be the introduction of the repentance element on the human side, although, as was noted, he says next to nothing specifically about repentance.[36] The need for God's grace for divinized human love would obviously extend also to divinized, repentant human love.

As one follows this line of reasoning down to the end, it can be seen that the same problem emerges ultimately as emerged in consideration of God's creative love—the problem of Teilhard's consistency in firmly avowing God's supreme transcendence. The rationale, then, for a divine, agapeic, redemptive love capable of being pieced together from various sources in Teilhard's thought

Note, for example, his comment in the preface to *DM* (1927), p. 44: "The reader need not, therefore, be surprised at the apparently small space allotted to moral evil and sin: the soul with which we are dealing is assumed to have already turned away from the path of error."
34. See above, chap. 4, n69.
35. See above, chap. 4, n68.
36. *Ibid.*

would then rest on the same problematic grounds as the rationale for God's creative agapeic love.[37] In my opinion, it is possible to accept this rationale by giving overriding weight to Teilhard's definite and strong language about God's transcendent sovereignty and the fact of human dependence on God. If one is ultimately pushed to the wall on grounds of consistency, it would seem reasonable to hope that Teilhard would have modified his thinking where necessary to assure a clear statement of what was certainly his firm conviction about God's being all in all and man's being nothing by himself.

Furthermore, it goes without saying that he would have had to make explicit modifications in his practical recommendations for human conduct, to the extent that to avoid being misunderstood as too Promethean, his thought on the meaning of passivities, of both growth and diminishment, would have drawn more stress.[38]

37. In speaking of both God's creative and redemptive love as agapeic, rather than limiting the term to God's redemptive love alone, there is recognition of a sufficiently prevalent extension of the term, which can embrace both aspects, without confusing creation and redemption. What is stressed in this usage is the common fundamental reality of God's transcendently free, autonomous self-giving, whether it be initially to bring creatures into existence, or to attempt to win back the love of rebellious, sinful creatures who have rejected his love. For an understanding of agape in line with such a reading, see Karl Rahner and Herbert Vorgrimler, *Theological Dictionary*, trans. Richard Strachan (New York: Herder and Herder, 1965), pp. 72-73. The distinctive mode of New Testament charity, agapeic love, stressed by Rahner and Vorgrimler, is that it is realized by the Spirit of God—that it is ultimately of divine rather than human origin. As a matter of fact, Nygren himself, in listing differences between eros and agape, presents a picture of agape with much the same emphasis, although more amplification. Nygren's statements of particular significance in the present context would be the following: "Agape is primarily God's love; 'God is Agape.' Even when it is attributed to man, Agape is patterned on Divine love. Agape is sovereign in relation to its object, and is directed to both 'the evil and the good'; it is spontaneous, 'overflowing,' 'unmotivated.' Agape loves—and *creates value* in its object." See Anders Nygren, *Agape and Eros*, rev. trans. by Philip S. Watson (London: S.P.C.K. and Philadelphia: Westminster, 1953), p. 210, cited by Bernhard Erling, "Agape and Eros in the Thought of Nygren, D'Arcy and De Rougement" (paper presented at the Convention of the College Theology Society, St. Paul, Minn., April, 1971), pp. 4-5.

38. In this context one should not overlook the image that recurs in his writings about Jacob's struggling with the angel, and adoring the God whose emissary vanquished him. See "Cosmic Life" (1916), *WW*, pp. 14, 62, 65; "The Mysticism of Science" (1939), *HE*, p. 181; and "The Spiritual Repercussions of the Atom Bomb" (1946), *FM*, p. 148.

## 2. REVELATION AND SEXUAL LOVE

Teilhard's approach to human sexual love contains a peculiar paradox, the details of which have been noted in chapter 4.[39] What can be recalled here is the way his use of a humanistic psychology of intersexual spiritual energization runs counter to one style of Christian approach to chastity, which lays heavy stress on the need for separation of the sexes in many instances for the maintenance of purity, whereas Teilhard would stress communication (sans physical sex for the celibate) with sublimation through an intense shared love of Christ-Omega. What can be noted as the special impact of his Christian-faith values on his ethic of sexual love is his emphasis on the development of a celibate relationship, even within marriage. The origin of this emphasis seems to be his own personal experience of sublimating heterosexual attraction in the relationships he had with women—all of which derived both theoretical content and psychological motivation from his understanding of the meaning of Christ's celibacy and his celibate followers'. Teilhard's approach, then, to celibate love seems to be an approach that would be a prime example of an element of his love ethic, which derives both content and motivation from a revealed source whiie at the same time incorporating certain aspects of humanistic psychology.[40]

## 3. SOCIETAL LOVE AND AGAPE

Teilhard's theory of societal love, the human sense, sense of the species, or universal human love, brings one

---

39. See above, chap. 4D (1).
40. A contemporary case for celibate marriage can be found argued by Mary and Robert Joyce, *New Dynamics in Sexual Love: A Revolutionary Approach to Marriage and Celibacy*. (Collegeville, Minn.: The Liturgical Press, 1970). The Joyces pursue their point in a theological context, but the question of the positive value of celibacy has been raised in a nontheological setting by Jessie Bernard, "Women, Marriage, and the Future," *The Futurist* (April 1970), pp. 41-43.

up squarely again before the agape question—this time
in the manner in which Christian charity as divinized
human love would involve participation through grace in
a special type of universal human love, a humanized
form of the love with which God loves man both as creature and as sinner, as well as collaborator in bringing
Christ's Pleroma to completion. On the phenomenological level, Teilhard's thinking about universal human love
carries a strong emphasis on a sense of oneness with all
other human beings as co-workers in the common task
of continuing evolution. The risk entailed in this emphasis is that it tends to obscure respect for the individual person in his uniqueness and weakness. But this
risk can be countered on the theoretical plane within the
framework of Teilhard's basic principles by giving due
weight to his insistence on the meaning of sympathy,
differentiating union, and sharing in the common love
of an all-loving Omega.

What should be noted here is that the preceding
paragraph hides two distinct questions. One has to do
with the implications of a theory of love based on attraction, and how such a theory can provide love for those
who are attractive—the poor, the outcast, the sinners,
and, at times, at least, children. It is here that the most
critical aspect of altruistic agape enters in, where one
must seek how to establish a relationship with those toward whom one feels no affection, nor senses any mutuality. The second question is more theoretical, and asks
what happens to prevent the individual from becoming a
meaningless cipher in a theoretical view of society that
places strong emphasis on the goal of society as a whole.
This second question has been alluded to immediately
above at the end of the paragraph, and the general lines
of a Teilhardian phenomenological solution were indicated there.

While the two questions can be phrased as distinct,
they are not unrelated. To provide a rationale for loving
the unattractive means that one cannot ultimately allow

any individual to lose meaning and be considered unimportant in a vast human social whole. On the other hand, if there is a satisfactory place for the individual in a social theory emphasizing the development of society as a whole, one ultimately faces the question of where the unattractive, at least apparent social misfit, enters into this picture.

The second question is really the fundamental totalitarian political question, examined above in chapter 6.[41] Christian revelation itself does not deal with this question directly. However, Christian agapeic personalism has clear-enough implications about the distinctively unique value of even the most unattractive individual sinner when seen with eyes enlightened by the grace of Christ. And while it is true that Teilhard does have certain phenomenological principles that can protect the individual before the whole of society, and can even be drawn out to extend to the weak and seemingly unattractive, still it is likewise true that if one relies mainly on these phenomenological texts, it is difficult to emerge on the practical level with a comprehensive, warm, compassionate human love extending to all, particularly the physically, psychologically, or morally weak. Teilhard's phenomenology is incomplete—he admitted this clearly enough—and needs completion through revelation.[42]

What is of special significance here is his thought on the scope and motivation he saw in Christian charity.[43]

41. See above, chap. 6C (4).
42. See, for example, "Le coeur de la matière," *I*, (1950): 21.
43. In Teilhard's writings available for this study, the inventory of passages concerned with charity runs to well over ninety. In the present context, it is hoped that a sampling of his more vigorous language will satisfy. See, for example, "The Priest" (1918), *WW*, p. 212:

> By you, [Jesus] and you alone, who are the entire and proper object of our love and the creative energy that fathoms the secrets of our hearts and the mystery of our growth, our souls are awakened, sensitized, enlarged, to the utmost limit of their latent potentialities.
>
> And under your influence, and yours alone, the integument of organic isolation and wilful egoism which separates the monads from one another is torn asunder and dissolves, and the multitude of souls rushes on towards that union which is essential to the maturity of the world.
>
> Thus a third plenitude is added to the other two. In a very real

In it one finds depth in intensity of concrete, personal-motivation focus and also breadth in range, which enables one to fill in gaps left open by his phenomenology, and to see how he approached the problem of loving the unlovable, and hence indirectly, if no less definitely, the problem of finding a place for the individual—every individual—in a vast human social whole, which, in the light of his faith becomes personalized as the Whole Christ.

However, Teilhard's thought on fraternal charity stands in need of further elaboration than he gave it,

sense, Lord Jesus, you are the *plenitudo entium*, the full assemblage of all beings who shelter, and meet, are for ever united, within the mystical bonds of your body. In your breast, my God, better than in any embrace, I possess all those whom I love and who are illumined by your beauty and in turn illumine you with the rays of light (so powerful in their effect upon our hearts) which they receive from you and send back to you. That multitude of beings, so daunting in its magnitude, that I long to help, to enlighten, to lead to you: it is already there, Lord, gathered together within you. Through you I can reach into the inmost depths of every being and endow them with whatever I will—provided that I know how to ask you and that you permit it.

Perhaps the most powerful expression of his thought on charity directly is contained in prayer form in *DM* (1927), pp. 145-46. It is a lengthy prayer, and is concerned, quite realistically in the first part, with the all-too-human experience of repugnance toward others. Consequently, Teilhard asks of God:

Grant that I may see you, even and above all, in the souls of my brothers, at their most personal, and most true, and most distant. . . .

You do not ask for the psychologically impossible—since what I am asked to cherish in the vast and unknown crowd is never anything save one and the same personal being which is yours.

Nor do you call for any hypocritical protestations of love for my neighbour, because—since my heart cannot reach your person except at the depths of all that is most individually and concretely personal in every "other"—it is to the "other" himself, and not to some vague entity around him, that my charity is addressed.

No, you do not ask anything false or unattainable of me. You merely, through your revelation and your grace, force what is most human in me to become conscious of itself at last. Humanity was sleeping—it is still sleeping—imprisoned in the narrow joys of its little closed love. A tremendous spiritual power is slumbering in the depths of our multitude, which will manifest itself only when we have learnt *to break down the barriers* of our egoisms and, by a fundamental recasting of our outlook, raise ourselves up to the habitual and practical vision of universal realities.

Jesus, Saviour of human activity to which you have given meaning, Saviour of human suffering to which you have given living value, be also the Saviour of human unity; compel us to discard our pettinesses, and to venture forth, resting upon you, into the uncharted ocean of charity.

particularly in the area of human agapeic love directed toward sinners, above all the slothful, and, to a certain extent with regard to the role of those suffering from psychological and physical weakness.

"To a certain extent," applies particularly to this last group, a view of the fact that he does have clear statements about the spiritual energy capable of being released as Christic redemptive and constructive energy by those who unite their suffering and weakness with Christ in his passion, and that as a consequence of this aspect of the possible and in many instances actual divinization of their passivities, people in this group are deserving of all the compassionate love, esteem, and assistance one can extend to them as co-workers with an extraordinarily difficult share of the enterprise. The strongest criticism that could be made of Teilhard's thought in this particular area is that he did not elaborate enough on what he actually expressed in certain isolated contexts, principally those which arose out of his association with his invalid sister and her work with similar invalids through her activity in the Catholic Union of the Sick.[44]

But the presupposition that underlies his writing about the weak and suffering of this sort is that they were really trying, making an effort to find meaning for their condition. How to extend creative, agapeic love to the slothful sinner, strong or weak, and what its special evolutionary function would be constitute another problem. It is really the same problem seen earlier about God's agapeic love for the sinner and its character, except that in the present instance the question has to do with man's divinized capacity for and practice of this same type of love directed toward fellow human beings. The solution to the problem would consequently be of the same type. To the extent that one can legitimately infer genuine creative freedom in the action of God's love toward the sinner, and not mere response to a di-

44. See above, chap. 7, n58.

vine need to give toward an existing attractiveness of some sort, to the same extent one can read the same type of creative freedom in Christian fraternal charity, which would be extended toward all sinners, including the slothful. Even if one grants that this could be done—and it seems it is possible—the serious objection remains that it has to be elaborated, almost *ab ovo*, as can be seen from the considerations just advanced, which flow from Teilhard's failure to supply more than the bare groundwork, and that none too firmly.

### 4. THE COSMIC CHRIST AND COSMIC LOVE

If one manages to surmount the difficulties in Teilhard's approach to the agapeic nature of Christian charity, which arise ultimately from certain implications of his admittedly unsatisfactory attempts to wrestle with metaphysics of creation and from his neglect in probing the mystery of human malice and its conversion into love, one can find enormous positive, Christic, motivational material in his thought about the Cosmic Christ and the manner in which he developed his thought and feeling about Christ seen in this way, especially in pieces such as "The Priest" from his earliest writings, "The Mass on the World" a few years later, and above all in *The Divine Milieu*. It is in writings of this sort that one finds the all-important central position of the Eucharist as the focal ritual and experience of contact whereby human love becomes divinized and divine love humanized to provide the authentic fullness of evolutionary energy, reaching out into all lines of human endeavor.

It is in these writings also that one finds the completion of meaning for his understanding of Cosmic Love. In these, the extrapolated, probable, lovable, but silent Omega appears not only with the heart and face necessary for truly personal love, but with a living voice, sharing, as the revealing Word, his inmost thoughts, feelings, and even human fears with those he loves. Some, it is true, have been troubled by Teilhard's extension of the Eucharistic consecration beyond the limits of the sacramental species themselves. However, it seems clear enough that when he was speaking of Eucharistic radiance as extending outward from host and chalice, he was definitely thinking of a *different kind* of Eucharistic presence throughout the cosmos, although it would be in some mysterious fashion ontologically tied in with Christ's presence in the bread and wine. One way of clarifying the character of this radiant influence would be to juxtapose Teilhard's thoughts from his "Mass on the World" with the main line of thought from his syllogism in *The Divine Milieu*, and his subsequent development of the meaning of that syllogism.[45] In this manner it can be seen how the material universe, existing for the human person and the human person existing for Christ, can through Eucharistic communion bring the universe to Christ, through human beings. It can likewise bring Christ, in a special way, out into the universe, over and above the manner of his divine immanence apart from the Eucharist, precisely through the extension of his creative effort by divinized human love, energized in a special way by Eucharistic grace-energy.

## 5. CHRISTIC HUMANISM

Finally, there is a paradox that shows up in the type of writing Teilhard uses in much of his important material on Christian charity. One of his main preoccupations throughout his life was to strive to build up the human foundations and components of religious faith through reflecting on the import of scientific thought. Yet this type of human effort on his part resulted in writing ab-

45. For "The Mass on the World" (1923), see *HU*, pp. 19-37. Exposition of the syllogism in *DM* is found in pp. 56-62.

out love that lacks a warm human flavor because of his frequent use of geometric imagery.[46] On the other hand, his overtly religious writing such as is found in his prayers, especially in "The Mass on the World" and *The Divine Milieu*, wherein he was *expressing* his own personal love and not consciously writing *about* it, manifests a deeply human quality.[47] His conscious effort to elaborate on the human comes off as less than human, whereas his conscious effort to express his love of Christ, who is human and beyond human, draws out aspects of human goodness surpassing those stimulated by the human sphere alone. The situation presents intriguing corroborative evidence, by application, of the contention of his confrere Emile Mersch about the Incarnation's not altering the humanity of Christ, but stretching it to its fullest potential.[48] In this instance, of course, it is Teilhard's, not Christ's humanity that is in question. But it is precisely the response to the Incarnate Christ—and hence one could say it is an extension of that Incarnation—that enriches Teilhard's humanity through his own love-imbued, prayerful, response to that love.

## E. The Relation of Faith to Love and Hope

Divinized human love in Teilhard's thought is obviously rooted in his faith in Christ, in his Christology. A closer look at what he means by faith and how it is related to hope and love will be helpful for a better grasp of the substructure upon which he built his theory of love.

46. The most conspicuous instance of this would be "Centrology" (1944), *AE*, pp. 99-127.
47. The principal prayer texts in *DM* (1927), are the following: pp. 55-56, 78-79, 80, 89-90, 106-7, 110-111, 126-28; p. 132; pp. 135-37, 145-46, 147,49.
48. See Emile Mersch, *The Theology of the Mystical Body*, trans. Cyril Vollert, S.J. (St. Louis, Mo.: B. Herder Book Co., 1951), pp. 216-26. Also see Christopher F. Mooney, S.J., "Christianity and the Change in Human Consciousness," *Teilhard: Symposium*, pp. 143-61. This is an excellent short study of Teilhard's thought about Christ's role in human fulfilment.

The summary of his Christology can be said to contain the principal elements of *content* in his religious faith. But what did he have in mind by the *process* of believing?

In his earliest writing devoted explicitly to faith itself, he speaks of "operative faith," of faith from the aspect of its energy-activating impact on human life. In this sense he is writing about a loving, trusting, and hence hope-imbued adherence to God, who is revealing himself and calling for a response in human effort under the influence of grace.[49] Almost two decades later, in answer to a request for a declaration of his personal apologetic approach, he speaks of faith in a more general psychological sense as effecting an intellectual synthesis, the roots of which are ultimately buried beneath the level of man's conscious apprehension.[50] Faith of this sort can be found in a humanistic faith experience, such as he describes when delineating the meaning of "faith in the world," and it can also apply to an integrated vision of the world and its meaning, synthesized under the influence of the revealing action of God.

Teilhard's most specific description of faith as man's response to God's revealing action appears in his important "The Outline of a Dialectic of Spirit" a dozen years later. In the early stages of this essay he traces man's ascent to fuller being through successive intuitions of a scientific-hypothesis framework. In explanation of what happens when God in his transcendence becomes immanent in a special way through revelation, he remarks:

As soon, however, as we admit the reality of a *reply* coming

49. See "Operative Faith" (1918), *WW*, pp. 226-48. In this essay Teilhard's main emphasis is on a dynamic interpretation of Christian faith, although he has a section in which he explains his understanding of natural faith, pp. 231-37.

50. See "How I Believe" (1934), *CE*, pp. 96-132. What he describes here, in speaking of "Faith in the World," pp. 99-102, has a resemblance to his earlier writing on "natural faith," but in this piece he is approaching the entire faith question more from the angle of intellectual synthetic vision than from that of energizing dynamics. With Teilhard, obviously, the two views are not incompatible, in that his theory of human energetics demands an activating, meaningful, total vision.

from on high, we in some way enter the order of certainty. This, however, comes about only through a mechanism not of mere subject-to-object confrontation but of contact between two centres of consciousness: it is no longer an act of *cognition* but of *recognition*: 'the whole complex inter-action of two beings who freely open themselves to one another and give themselves—the emergence, under the influence of grace of theological faith.[51]

Despite the fact that this is the only text of this sort to be found analytic of theological faith, it is significant on two counts. First, it provides an excellent description of how his own religious faith found expression both in his lived commitment and in prayers of the type mentioned above. Second, it is a *personalist* explanation of the understanding of theological faith, with a clear statement of such important elements as freedom, openness, and commitment. Furthermore, it gets to the heart of the theological faith-act itself and provides the foundation for understanding both the consequences of such an act in "operative faith," and also the consequences of faith taken in the sense of the synthetic psychological process under the influence of revelation.

When theological faith is taken in the manner just explained, it can be seen how it includes, as an integral element, hope in the form of trust extended to God, who is revealing himself as one whose assistance can be relied on consistently throughout the struggle to collaborate in Christogenesis, and whose promise of ultimate victory through sharing in Christ's Resurrection at the Second Coming provides firm motivational assurance as one looks to the future beyond death. Faith in this sense also includes personal love, since it contains an openness implying sympathy and free self-giving leading to communion.

That faith of this sort embodied obscurity along with certainty, Teilhard did not deny, as can be seen from

---

51. "Outline of a Dialectic of Spirit" (1946), *AE*, p. 148.

the concluding portion of "How I Believe," as well as notations in his personal retreat notes.[52] In these latter, especially, there is a genuine poignancy in his prayerful pleading for light, a pleading stemming from the paradoxical certainty that he was calling out to the One who could, and who he trusted ultimately would, answer his prayer.

## F. Hope and Christogenetic Eschatology

The phenomenological grounds for his assurance that human evolution would succeed have been questioned earlier, with the judgment being that, because of the logical weakness of Teilhard's argument, a firm phenomenological base for hope in some eventual success of mankind, was wanting.[53] In the last analysis, the foundation for solid hope in the victory of mankind over a host of evils, physical as well as moral, rests on the revelation of Christ's Resurrection and his ultimate victory at the Second Coming. Since Teilhard accepts the reality of Hell as a structural element in the universe, where "waste" of this sort must be considered possible and to an unknown extent actual, how large the number of human beings ultimately to succeed would be is a question for which neither his phenomenology nor Christian faith could provide an answer.[54] Nor can he, drawing from either source, determine when in time the final

52. See "How I Believe," "Epilogue: The Shadows of Faith" (1934), *CE*, pp. 131-32, and the editorial note, p. 132, which refers to later writings that indicate greater clarity of vision as Teilhard's life drew to a close. There is some question, however, as to the extent to which the vision was clarified or Teilhard's serenity became firmer in the midst of a kind of accepted ambiguity. In his unpublished retreat notes for 1944 and 1945, he shows definite concern about faith, especially in the entries for the First Day of each retreat: on June 30, 1952, he registers concern over the compatibility of his "Christique" with Christianity, and in the last retreat of his life, August 19-26, 1954, he writes, at the very beginning, of his objective to recover and accentuate his balance and *élan*.

53. See above, chap. 3B.

54. Teilhard does not say much about Hell, but what he has written is definite enough. See "Cosmic Life" (1916), *WW*, pp. 68-69; *DM* (1927), pp. 147-49; "Introduction to the Christian Life" (1944), *CE*, pp. 164-65.

developments would take place. What he does construct, however, drawing on the certainty of the Second Coming from revelation and on the probable course of human development through the compressive socialization stage to the extent that he can extrapolate on phenomenological grounds, is a hypothetical picture of what the final condition of the human race would be like, whenever that would be reached. His conjectural presentation of the coincidence of the Parousia with the coming to term of the entire human evolutionary process, is, then, a synthesis of revealed certainty with extrapolated probability.

As was noted above, in the summary of Teilhard's Christological thought, his understanding of the coincidence of the Parousia with the terminal maturation of the evolutionary process did not mean that the Parousia was achieved within history by human effort alone.[55] He conceived this type of maturation as analogous to the fullness of time" mentioned with regard to Christ's first coming, and looked on it as a necessary condition for the Second Coming, but he explicitly referred to its insufficiency in itself. There was therefore, in Teilhard's thought, denial that the final perfection of humanity was possible *within* history. In other words, he did affirm *discontinuity* between evolutionary process and the final coming of Christ—just as all along he affirmed the need for divine grace to Christify human action. It would be God's sovereign action alone that would energize the ultimate transformation and lead a sufficiently matured humanity through and across the time barrier of human history into the ultimate Promised Land and a new, transfigured mode of human existence, now divinized to its fullest capacity in the Risen Life.

Since Teilhard's position on this point is open to misunderstanding, it is important to look closely at what he says. If it is not possible to defend him against the

55. Above, B.

charge that he holds a Pelagian type of eschatology, then the possibility of a genuine, supernatural, Christological ethic is vitiated at its roots, for the ultimate moving force would be reduced, in such a setting, to humanity's lifting itself to completion by its own bootstraps.[56]

An important early text that sets forth the underlying orientation to be found in other, later, texts is found in Teilhard's essay "The Priest," written at the Front in 1918. Although it does not deal specifically with the Parousia, it does treat of the discontinuity between the world left to itself and God.

> The whole world is concentrated, is exalted, in expectation of union with God . . . and yet it is pulled up short by an impassible barrier. Nothing can attain Christ except he take it up and enfold it.

> Thus the universe groans, caught between its passionate desire, and its impotence.[57]

Six years after, in his second essay entitled "My Universe," there occurs a lengthy passage, too long to quote

56. The most extensive treatment of the Parousia, which looks into the specific problem of discontinuity, can be found in Mooney, *The Mystery of Christ*, pp. 192-99. Especially significant would be p. 194, n85, which appears on pp. 278-79. It reads in part: "One thing which de Lubac does not point out must be insisted upon here: it is not possible for Teilhard to conceive of a 'super-humanity' within history. The reason is that planetary maturation is to be brought about by contact with Omega, as is clear from *PH*, 302, 341 [Eng. trans., pp. 272, 307]; and Omega for Teilhard is always the Person of Christ, whose Parousia will bring an end to human history and whose Pleroma is clearly a transhistoric reality." De Lubac's treatment of the Parousia, to which Mooney refers, occurs in *Religion of Teilhard*, pp. 153-65. While de Lubac does not broach the question in the precise language about which Mooney speaks, he does present evidence that can lead to the same conclusion. Faricy's clarification pertinent to the question is worth noting: "Teilhard has no intention whatever of denying the gratuity of God's intervention in the world at the end of time, or denying the gratuity of the Parousia. Christ's second coming could never be brought about merely by the powers of natural evolution and human effort. The Parousia is a supernatural event. What Teilhard does deny is that the Parousia will be an *arbitrary* event, unconnected with human evolutionary progress . . . just as the Incarnation took place in 'the fullness of time,' so will the Parousia take place only in a greater and ultimate fullness of time." See Faricy, *Teilhard: Theology*, pp. 211-12. Also important to note on the question would be de Solages, *Teilhard: étude*, pp. 303-4. His position is in line with that of Mooney, de Lubac, and Faricy, but worded more tersely.

57. *WW*, p. 206. The editorial note on this page is significant also.

in its entirety, on the Parousia. It is representative of his basic thought on the question. Particularly significant regarding the issue of discontinuity is the following paragraph:

> When the end of time is at hand, a terrifying spiritual pressure will be exerted on the confines of the real, built up by the desperate efforts of souls tense with longing to escape from the earth. This pressure will be unanimous. Scripture, however, tells us that at the same time the world will be infected by a profound schism—some trying to emerge from themselves in order to dominate the world even more completely—others, relying on the words of Christ, waiting passionately for the world to die, so that they may be absorbed with it in God.[58]

True, Teilhard's position as outlined describing "The Ultimate," in *The Phenomenon of Man* (1940), could be read in a naturalistically human way.[59] However, when this and other texts are taken in the context of his understanding of the transcendence of Christ-Omega, the evidence points to his awareness of discontinuity in the fulfillment process at the end of time, since union with Christ-Omega calls for a break with time and history.[60]

Moreover, in two essays almost a decade later, "Trois choses que je vois" (February 1948) and the important synthesis of his thought, "Comment je vois," written in August of the same year, one finds definite formulation of his thinking on human maturation at the end of time as being a necessary, but not sufficient condition for Christ's action in the Parousia.[61]

Hence, evidence is lacking to condemn Teilhard on the grounds that he holds that humanity can reach its fulfillment through its own efforts and without passing

58. *SC* (1924), p. 84. Note likewise, from shortly after this time, *DM* (1927), pp. 150-55.
59. *PM*, pp. 285-89.
60. Mooney, The *Mystery of Christ*, pp. 278-79, argues strongly along this line. He cites an abundance of back-up texts.
61. "Trois choses que je vois," *DA*, p. 169; "Comment je vois," *DA*, p. 206, n1.

beyond history into a new and distinctively different mode of existence in the Risen Life at the Second Coming. To say this, however, does not remove objections to the faulty logic used by Teilhard to extrapolate a probable picture of what ultimate human maturation would be. It merely points to the judgment that Teilhard can be relieved of the charge that he does not allow the intervention of Christ's supernatural action at the end of time—and this on the basis of his consistent expressions affirming the need for God's supernaturally transforming action.

As can be seen from the considerable input of revealed material into the motivational picture along the central lines of love, faith, and hope, it is Teilhard's synthetic, Christogenetic ethic that alone supplies sufficient definite, concrete, activation power to achieve the type of noospheric development he held so important. What happens to the other major areas of human energy organization when they are viewed in the context of his Christological thought?

## G. Revelation and Sublimated Aggression

Aggression, as was noted in chapter 5, can be looked at from three principal variations of movement against an obstruction.[62] One can struggle against the impersonal forces of nature in an attempt to master and control; or one can resist an unjust personal adversary with or without personal enmity directed toward him; or there can be attack motivated by personal pride, arrogance, and hatred, to subjugate other persons to one's control and hence eliminate them as obstacles to one's own personal will.

What revelation has to say about the first (struggle against natural obstacles, for mastery of matter in order

62. See above, chap. 5A.

to further Omegalization) has, in effect, been considered above in the present chapter in the context of revealed input into Teilhard's concepts on a morality of movement, or a religion of conquest and development.[63] Where his Christology has significant impact with regard to the other two types of aggression is principally in the manner by which anger against an unjust aggressor is controlled in accord with the dictates of Christian charity, and also, obviously enough, by the manner in which Christian charity and humility rule out the third type of aggressivity altogether. In both areas what would be provided to supplement a phenomenological ethic containing content recommendations or imperatives, for the sublimation of aggression, would be the distinctive motivational element of Christian love. Moreover, with regard to these two particular areas, Christian revelation has definite content prescriptions. One is urged to love enemies, even though they be unjust; unjust aggression is clearly condemned.

Because aggression is in especial need of control by Christian kindness and gentleness, it is particularly to be regretted that the concern Teilhard shows about this matter was limited in its expression, apart from his life, to his correspondence and personal notes. That he was aware of the need to be gentle, and of its significance for him as a Christian, is clear enough from these sources, but unfortunately he saw no urgency to develop his theorizing on love in this direction.[64]

63. See above, C and C (1).
64. Writing to his cousin Marguerite, May 28, 1915, he comments: "If there is one thing of which I have become convinced just recently, it is that in relations with others you can never be too kind and gentle in your manner; gentleness is our first source of strength, the first also, perhaps of the visible virtues. I have always repented when I have allowed harshness or contempt to show—and yet it is so agreeable a temptation" (MM, p. 55). Likewise, on October 15, 1915: "May our Lord unite us so thoroughly with himself that he may be seen in all that we do, above all through his kindness and great love . . ." (MM, p. 75); and, June 25, 1916: "My need is great to steep my soul in him [Christ] again, so that I may have more faith, more devotion, more kindness" (MM, p. 105). The concern continues through the years. See LT, p. 206 (no exact date is assigned, but the excerpt would seem to be from late in 1934): "May the Lord only preserve in me a passionate taste for the world,

## H. Revelation and Research

The manner in which the duty of research can be tied in with a revealed source of knowledge, particularly along the lines of channeling energy into research as a consequence of sublimating aggression, presents a complex problem.

The obligation for research, in the broad, multidimensional sense in which Teilhard considers research, can be derived as a fundamental corollary to the obligation for constructive evolutionary effort toward expansion of consciousness. Intellectual inquiry, along scientific, philosophical, and artistic lines, falls neatly into place as a prime form of human expenditure of energy called for to meet the demands of continuing evolution. As has been seen with regard to the fundamental thrust of a morality of movement, general content imperatives for working to improve human existence can be derived from the revealed need to build the Body of Christ. The Scriptures themselves say nothing directly about concrete imperatives regarding research as Teilhard takes the term. Christian tradition, however, from the earliest efforts toward speculative theology in the primitive Christian community, has taken a direction along lines corroborative of what Teilhard was urging, at least to the extent that it urged believers to seek understanding of the faith through available instruments of human experience.[65]

Relating all this to the sublimation of aggression is another matter. This particular aspect of the imperative toward research seems to be derived, with regard to its contents, from Teilhard's phenomenological analysis of

and a great gentleness. . . ." In his retreat of 1943, asking himself how he will be recognized as a witness to God, he wrote: "1. Gentleness, peace, before everything. 2. To love better, to fear less. 3. Disinterestedness." (Cited by de Lubac, Teilhard: *Man and Meaning*, p. 81, n7.) For de Lubac's comments on this matter, see *ibid.*, pp. 80-81. Also see above, chap. 4, esp. n68.

65. In this context it would be useful to recall Teilhard's dictum, from "Social Heredity and Progress" (1938) (45), *FM*, p. 33: "We cannot continue to love Christ without discovering Him more and more."

human experience, probable motivation for which could be drawn from his phenomenology, but for which the most compelling motivation would again be sought in the love of Christ.

His insistent plea that the Church itself should be more active in the promotion of research, even to the extent of instituting under its auspices an "organ of research," seems to come from a synthetic process, with input from reason and revelation.[66] The Church, needless to say, has an obligation to do all possible to increase its vitality and further its growth as an extension of Christ as his Body. Human experience today points to the urgency of research in all forms for this constructive process. Consequently, the Church should devote special energy toward the promotion of research. So would run the argument in logical form, with the first premise derived from revelation and the minor appearing out of human experience, which for Teilhard was his specific experience of contemporary scientific humanism.

## 1. RESEARCH AND ADORATION

His correlation of research with adoration would be another instance of his synthesis of the revealed and human sources of knowledge.[67] The religious mystic's

66. The expression "organ of research" appears in a letter quoted by Teilhard to Victor Fontoynant, July 26, 1917. The text is quoted at some length by de Lubac, *Religion of Teilhard*, appendix 1, pp. 288-89. The suggestion Teilhard made for a special group of scholars for interdisciplinary work under Church auspices was in line with his attempt in Paris thirty years later to assemble such a group. See above, chap. 5, n49. The duty of the Christian as Christian, and hence priest as priest, or Church, as Church, to be concerned about furthering research was a lifelong preoccupation with him, see his earliest writings: "Mastery of the World and the Kingdom of God" (1916), *WW*, p. 88; "The Priest" (1918), *WW*, p. 220; "Forma Christi" (1918), *WW*, p. 260. Much of his own writing, as assembled in the collections *SC* and *CE* is evidence of how he attempted to perform in response to his own understanding of research into the contemporary meaning of Christianity, as well as the meaning of scientific research for Christianity. Of particular importance regarding the expression of his own thought on the process of research in a religious context are the papers "The Religious Value of Research" (1947), *SC*, pp. 199-205, and "Research, Work, and Worship" (1955), *SC*, pp. 214-23.

67. See *PM* (1940), pp. 283-85. This seems to be the clearest statement of a kind of equivalence that Teilhard would abhor seeing associated with "concordism." The juxtaposition would seem to be in the last analysis another

search to expand his consciousness by seeking ever new avenues to experience the goodness and beauty of God and to express this experience in worship does not seem to be what Teilhard had in mind primarily when he formulated his equation of research and adoration, although this particular type of seeking experience seems to provide the prime analogue for what he did have in mind. What he was thinking of first and foremost seems to have been the, to many, startling equivalence of scientific research itself with adoration of the divine.

In what way can the process of empirical scientific questioning, hypothesis formulation, and test, be said to be the same as standing in reverent awe before the power, knowledge, and love of Omega? How can one equate the drive to empirical scientific knowledge, and the process of satisfying that drive, with "Alleluja"? Is Teilhard speaking of an ontological identity, or is he speaking figuratively? If figuratively, by what type of figure?

By the canons of strict empirical inquiry—which in themselves limit inquiry to the *how* of observable phenomena and do not push into the metaphysical *why*, or the transcendent—empirical scientific research can not be ontologically paired with standing in awe before the transcendent for the obvious reason that it is simply not looking for or at the transcendent. However, generalized scientific research, the scientific phenomenology of Teilhard's devising, in that it looks into the total human phenomenon with a spirit of reverence for the possibility of an Omega-Center and would rejoice in discovering Omega's presence as, to say the least, highly probable—*this* type of scientific research can be said to have, dominating its vital *élan*, a spirit that has much in common with the adoration of the religious mystic. Hence, on the phenomenological plane alone, one could say that for Teilhard, generalized scientific re-

"groping" by Teilhard toward resolution of his basic faith problem. One may note, also, the trend of thought in the following passages: "Science and Christ" (1921), *SC*, pp. 31-36; "Modern Unbelief" (1933), *SC*, pp. 114-15; "The Religious Value of Research" (1947), *SC*, pp. 199-205.

search, *analogous* to strict empirical research, would incorporate a spirit of awe before the Omega-factor *analogous* to the adoration of the religious mystic.

For the religious researcher in the scientific world, the type of person Teilhard had in mind in his "Research, Work, and Worship," still another interpretation of the formula is possible.[68] Here again, one is in the province of a particularized area of contemplation in action. The situation, in fact, is Teilhard's own life-situation, that of a scientific researcher schooled in Ignatian mysticism to find God in all things. It is the situation of a seer who, striving for a more complete vision of *The Divine Milieu*, is, for much of his conscious working life, seeking empirical truths *in which* he can find reflected some facet of the Cosmic Christ, whom he can adore as a humble believer. Empirical scientific research, along with generalized scientific thinking, would for such a person both be motivated by loving adoration of Christ, and hence *caused by* adoration, and be a source of insight into the splendor of God's work, on the empirical level, and of Omega—Christ working, on the generalized scientific level—and hence, ultimately contributory to adoration.[69]

## I. The Mystical Christ and the Political Order, Education, Technological Economics, and Eugenics

The principal reason for considering under one heading aspects of Teilhard's Christogenetic ethic as it pertains to the organization of human energy, spiritualized, controlled, and incorporated in these particular areas, is that they all, with certain exceptions to be noted shortly,

68. *SC* (1955), pp. 214-20.
69. When it is borne in mind that Teilhardian "research" is comprehensive to the extent of including the notion of technological development and much that comes under the heading of "engineering," what would emerge here would be a special variety of contemplation in action—contemplation in cosmogenetic action, or, if one should so wish to speak, in creative autoevolution of noospheric anatomy and physiology.

feed ethical content from a phenomenological base into his integrated synthetic ethic where the prime motivation comes from Christic love. What the phenomenological content is, for the most part has already been seen in the preceding chapters. What remains for examination is how Teilhard's divinized human love would penetrate into these sectors, what modifications it might introduce, and to what extent the end product, so to speak, in each of these areas would have been subjected, with varying degrees of intensity, to cross-fertilization of the phenomenological by the Christological and vice versa.

The general mode of penetration into these areas by divinized human love has already been seen in this chapter, where reference has been made to the type of thinking manifested in such writings as "The Mass on the World" and *The Divine Milieu*. One would, then, use the main directives on the divinization of activities and passivities, on the incorporation of all human effort in Eucharistic offering, as major premises, so to speak, in a wide variety of prudential syllogisms, the minor premises of which would come from his phenomenological thinking, and in which the practical conclusions would ultimately embody a phenomenologically based directive to action, or acceptance motivated by Christic, or divinized human love. With St. Paul, Teilhard would say that, globally, everything should be done *in Christ Jesus*. In these areas, particularly, most of what should be done in the concrete would have to be discovered through the efforts of his scientific phenomenological humanism. The action finally placed would be, then, a phenomenologically derived yet Christogenetically motivated action.

## 1. TEILHARD AND THE "SECULAR INSTITUTE" CONCEPT

A particularization of how this would take place institutionally in society can be found in an illuminating passage from *The Divine Milieu*:

Within the Church we observe all sorts of groups whose members are vowed to the perfect practice of this or that particular virtue: mercy, detachment, the splendour of the liturgy, the missions, contemplation. Why should there not be men vowed to the task of exemplifying, by their lives, the general sanctification of human endeavor?—men whose common religious ideal would be to give a full and conscious explanation of the divine possibilities or demands which any wordly occupation implies—men, in a word, who would devote themselves, in the fields of thought, art, industry, commerce and politics, etc. to carrying out in the sublime spirit these demands—the basic tasks which form the very bonework of human society?[70]

His continuing thoughts are particularly important for throwing light on the divinizing character of Christian work in these areas:

Around us the "natural" progress which nourishes the sanctity of each new age is all too often left to the children of the world, that is to say to agnostics or the irreligious. Unconsciously or involuntarily such men collaborate in the kingdom of God and in the fulfillment of the elect: their efforts, going beyond or correcting their incomplete or bad intentions, are gathered in by him "whose energy subjects all things to itself." But that is no more than second best, a temporary phase in the organization of human activity. Right from the hands that knead the dough, to those that consecrate it, the great and universal Host should be prepared and handled in a spirit of *adoration*.[71]

When one says that in the preceding passages there is contained an approach to getting the motivation of divinized human love into the very fabric of human society, into "all trades, their gear, and tackle and trim," he is pointing to the fact that these texts and those associated with them are conveying an approach to effort in the material world akin to considerable thought expressed in recent decades about a theology of work, a theology of politics, and, fundamentally, a theology of the laity as

70. *DM* (1927), pp. 66-67.
71. *Ibid.*, p. 67.

well.[72] True, what Teilhard was writing about in *The Divine Milieu* is more immediately applicable to the Secular Institute concept in Roman Catholicism as it has been developing in the last quarter century or more. Also, his immediate concern, as evidenced in his own writings, was in the direction of priest-worker, priest-researcher concepts.[73] But it is not difficult to move from here into the Secular Institute area, and then into the divinizing mission of all sharing in the priestly, prophetic, and kingly roles of Christ through baptism.[74]

Moreover, even though in all these areas there is a Christogenetic informing influence extending into tasks, the basic human content of which would be derived from his phenomenology, it should be noted that what is involved here is not simply addition of a Christian motive to a purely secular task. The tasks themselves, taken in the light of his thinking on the nature of the Cosmic Christ, the Divine Milieu, and the extensions, in some way, of the Eucharist into all the elements and processes of cosmogenesis—these tasks are no longer purely secular or worldly tasks. Hence, in their materials and content they assume an added dimension. They are performed out of love *for* the living God and the completion of his Mystical Body, but also in the awareness that this same God, both above and ahead, is also *within* the materials used and is co-activating the processes of hu-

72. The literature in these areas continues to grow. One could call attention above all to the efforts of Chenu, Congar, Kaiser, Cardijn, Metz, Novak, Cox, and Stringfellow—to say nothing of Reinhold Niebuhr, and, much earlier, Rauschenbusch.

73. "Research, Work, and Worship" (1955), *SC*, pp. 214-20, was drafted with the problems of priest-researchers and priest-workers specifically in mind. His "Le néo-humanisme moderne et ses réactions sur le Christianisme" (1948), *I*, was a conference given before chaplains of "L'Action Catholique Ouvrière," at Versailles, Sept. 1948.

74. Although the texts cited in the section immediately above, were from the late twenties, Teilhard's journal entries from the World War I years and shortly after contain similar thoughts. See de Solages, *Teilhard: étude*, p. 215, n19, entry of November 17, 1916, and p. 218, n34, entry of October 24, 1919. With regard to the operations of *Opus Dei* in the practical order, Teilhard seems to have had definite reservations, however much the concept was compatible with his thought. See, Mathieu, *La pensée politique de Teilhard*, p. 106, letter of October 12, 1952.

man effort. In other words, while a secular humanist
and a believing Christian of Teilhard's bent might agree
on common rational grounds *that* something should be
done in scientific eugenic research, or economic or political life, the Teilhardian view would see what should be
done itself as suffused with a Christic radiance, as well as
something which should be done in response to the love
of Christ as the center of cosmogenesis.

In the last analysis what this means is that one can still
hold a common-content core for a secular humanist and
Christian ethic, but Christian motivation lies not only in
the *ultimate* motive of the act, but in its *proximate value* as
well. Not only is the act directed *toward* the divine, but
the *act itself becomes divine-human*.

## 2. UNIVERSALISM. FUTURISM. PERSONALISM.

With regard to Teilhard's political thought, in particular, an argument could be proposed that his main
emphases on universalism, futurism, and personalism
may represent an unconscious phenomenologizing of
aspects of human societal life, derived at their roots
from his religious experience of the meaning of the
Mystical Body. Of the three, the first two could have
stemmed from a common scientific humanist approach.
But it would seem that his strong personalist emphasis,
both in human societal relationships as well as in ultimate human meaning found in a supreme, personal
Center-Omega, could very well have come through a
subtle permeation of basic concepts on Christian charity.
Just as Julian Huxley parted company with him on
Omega, so Teilhard parted company with Marxists on
personalism in society—a differentiation that, in the latter instance as well, is associated with the Omega concept. Since his humanist colleagues, who could agree
with him on much of his societal theory, could not agree
here, and since his faith-vision in the background could

be assigned as a probable differentiating variable on the formation of his own consciousness, the evidence points to the judgment that in this particular area there is another example of subtle influence on his phenomenology by his Christology.

What especially needs expansion and stress, far beyond what Teilhard himself gave, is the importance of concern for the poor, the suffering, the unwanted. Teilhard's failure to pursue his personal concern about gentleness by way of clear elaboration in his reflective essays has been noted above.[75] One could say that this concern is implied to a point in what he did say about charity, likewise noted above, but the fact is that he did not clarify his thought by way of much concrete detail.[76] The absence of such follow-through can, of course, be read as another indication of the risk involved in working with a large, overall picture, stressing global human growth and solidarity. The needs of little people too easily get left out of the picture, and one can get the impression that they do not really matter too much. Teilhard would undoubtedly have voiced his regrets that his thought would be interpreted in this way, but he did not seem to be aware of the steps he could have taken to prevent such a reading of his ideas.

### 3. THE PROBLEM OF ELITES

There is likewise a problem regarding Teilhard's position on the importance of elites for social development. Here the background is more complex. His own somewhat aristocratic French origins, coupled with his evolutionary conclusions on leading shoots, could well have blended with his Christian understanding of the leaven in the mass in such a way as to make it impossible to unravel the epistemological genesis of his final think-

75. See above, H.
76. See above, D (3), esp. n43.

ing on the matter. His move toward a particular type of democratic political philosophy, recognizing the importance of rights of the individual person, while at the same time holding for the legitimate value of elite groups, would seem, again, to have been conditioned by his understanding of the value of the individual person and the complementary functioning of persons and groups as can be found in analysis of the implications of the Mystical Body doctrine. On the other hand, one could also argue that his particular approach to understanding the Mystical Body in an organic, nonjuridical fashion alone, may well have been influenced by his phenomenological thinking.

Again there is need for a corrective coming from his fundamental thinking on gentleness, kindness, and charity, to meet the problem arising, inevitably it would seem, from the tension between personalism and elitism. The records of church history are filled with accounts of factional strife among elite Christian groups and the tragic wounds inflicted by the intolerance of the dedicated. Here, too, is evidence of Teilhard's lack of a sense of human sinfulness operative in the historical process, and of the serious need to balance stress on effort, courage, and leadership with humility and consideration for others and their human wants and failings.

## 4. EDUCATION

His educational thought, so far as its short formulations in terms of biological additivity are concerned, is clearly phenomenological. However, the one lengthy essay he devoted to education was an essay precisely on the meaning of Christian education, and, in it, as has been seen, his understanding of the apostolic, missionary orientation of education came in for heavy emphasis.[77]

77. "Social Heredity and Progress" (1938) (45), *FM*, pp. 25-36. See above, chap. 7B. For a study of the implications of Teilhard's thought in general for religious education, see Robert Faricy, "Religious Education," *The Teilhard Re-*

In the largest and most complete sense, his educational ethic emerges as a mixture of phenomenology and Christology, providing the same methodological obscurities as the immediately preceding questions, and for the same reasons.

## 5. EUGENICS

Finally, the compatibility, incompatibility, or mutual cross-fecundation of his thought on eugenics with his Christology calls for investigation. Here, it seems, is an area where concrete imperatives come from phenomenology alone, through careful searching for means to improve the biological quality of human existence on individual and social levels. The reason for saying this is, basically, that this is one area that revelation has not opened up at all. The Holy Spirit, it seems clear enough, has not moved the traditional inspired writers to talk of genes, chromosomes, or hormones.

But, once again, in confronting scientific experimentation involving human persons, whether individually, or in groups, the personalist factor becomes a demurring factor. Teilhard never went into this problem area at great length, and his purely phenomenological observations, as has been noted, have a chilling atmosphere about them. With regard to the rights of the weak as balanced off against the needs of the strong, there is need of correction or at least qualification drawn from his Christologically inspired ideas on charity and the value of suffering for Christogenesis. As a consequence, one is inclined to hold that, of all the areas regarding the organization of human energy, Teilhard's thought on the divinization of the organization of incorporated energy is an area which could be ranked first among under- or un-developed areas.

*view* 5, no. 2 (Winter 1970-1971): 85-93. The article contains a wealth of textual citation from Teilhard, brought to bear on contemporary catechetical foci, but, surprisingly, does not even mention Teilhard's piece written for religious educators.

## J. Ethical Imperatives in Christogenesis for the Christian as Christian

There are certain things to be done that can be said to be the responsibility of a Christian as a Christian—ethical imperatives that derive from God's revealing and revealed Word alone—precisely because they deal with that sphere of human action which pertains to how a person responds to Christ revealing himself.

### 1. THE CHRISTIAN DUTY TO BELIEVE, HOPE, AND LOVE

At the top of the list would be the initial and most fundamental obligation to believe, to accept God and his message.[78] To say this is not to claim that the moment when this obligation exists can be given a precise point in time easily discernible by the one obliged, for the simple reason that the empowering grace of faith operates in a subtle and often obscure fashion, as can be discovered from the records of countless conversions, as well as the records of progressive growth in faith, once the initial step of acceptance has been taken. What can be said about the moment when this duty exists must then be put out conditionally. Once a person grasps the fact that God is and is speaking to him, then the obligatory moment has arrived.

In view of what Teilhard held about the need of faith in Christ for full human maturation, it would seem that he would have recognized and agreed to this fundamental duty as just indicated. But the fact is that, while he never denied it, he did not approach the emergence of faith from this angle. He recognized, for himself and

78. Teilhard does not express his thought in just this language, but it would seem to flow from what he does say in "La morale peut-elle se passer de soubassements métaphysiques avoués ou inavoués?" (1945), *DA*, pp. 144-45, where he speaks of the obligation of loving obedience to the will of God, which stems from a philosophy in which a personal and transcendent Being stands at the head of the universe.

others, the radical need to search for meaning, for a synthetic vision of human existence. The duty to believe in Christ, to perform an act accepting him, would be implicitly contained in the duty to accept what one discovered as the fruit of earnest seeking. Teilhard's advice to others, and his own path, seem to have run along this line of encouragement to search, with the underlying assumption that he was dealing with a person of good will who would accept the results of serious inquiry the moment those results became clear.[79]

The same can be said with regard to the existence of ethical imperatives to hope and to love. Their existence can be established as compatible with man's Christogenetic needs, once the foundation has been set up through the initial act of faith-acceptance. But again, Teilhard's approach was not that of calling attention to a duty, but rather of pointing to an answer to a deep human hunger and thirst for an issue, a meaningful end for the universe, and a real, living Person to love at its heart and core, as well as at the end of time.

## 2. RELIGIOUS RESEARCH AND THE APOSTOLATE

Where he was aware of a note of duty as such and expressed this awareness was with regard to the duty of the Christian and hence the Church toward research into both the meaning of traditional Christianity for modern times and the manner and style of communicating that meaning. This type of religious research was for Teilhard a Christian duty of prime urgency. From his earliest years, his writings directed toward his fellow believers explicitly attest to his concern about this particu-

79. Note, for example, his advice to a correspondent, June 11, 1926, *LF*, p. 31: "In any case, for you, as everyone, there is only one road that can lead to God, and this is the fidelity to remain constantly true to yourself, to what you feel is highest in you. Do not worry about the rest. The road will open before you as you go." Also see *LZ*, pp. 50, 56.

lar Christian duty—all within the context of his understanding of fidelity in religious obedience.[80]

### 3. EUCHARISTIC PRAYER

Another specifically Christian duty (which finds its fullest expression in *The Divine Milieu*, although the concept
is a constant throughout his life), is that which can be
described as the duty to *pray eucharistically*. This work,
and other expressions of Teilhard's thought in the same
vein, have more to say about such things as effort, attachment, detachment, struggling with God against evil,
and true resignation, than about prayer as such, about
quiet, reflective, meditative thought in God's presence,
pondering the meaning of life before Him. But despite
the few explicit words about this, the book is written and
reads as the communication of a meditative, prayerful
experience, complete with personal, explicit prayer passages at critical stages in its development.[81] Apart from
what he says about the need for set times of prayer, his
strongest affirmation of the Christian responsibility to
pray *effectively* in union with the Eucharistic Cosmic
Christ would be derived by inference from the cogency
of its entire message.[82] The process of inference may be

80. With regard to Teilhard's thought about the role of teaching authority
in the Church, see above, chap. 2, n7. Also, Emily Binns, "The Very Quick
of the Life of the Church Today," *The Teilhard Review* 6, no. 2 (Winter 1971-72):
88-91. More specifically, with regard to his understanding of the meaning of
fidelity in religious obedience, and all it implied, see d'Ouince, *Teilhard dans
l'Église*, esp. pp. 120-37, "L'épreuve de l'obeissance," but the whole book is
significant in this context. Also, Barjon, *Le combat de Teilhard*, pp. 274-83,
"L'épreuve de la fidélité," with significant quotes from Teilhard's correspondence with Auguste Valensin, and pp. 283-88, " 'Bien Finir,' " for pertinent
citations from retreat notes about Teilhard's concern with regard to his fidelity. An excellent expression of his own thought about how he interpreted his
obediential relationship to superiors is found in his letter to Fr. Janssens, the
Jesuit General, October 12, 1951. See Pierre Leroy, S.J., "Teilhard de Chardin: The Man," printed at the beginning of *DM*, pp. 37-40. The letter is a
frank manifestation of his conscience to the General, with a summary of his
main convictions, along with a firm profession of his obedience.
81. For the principal prayer texts, see above, n47. The prime example, to
be sure, of how Teilhard did this in writing is his "The Mass on the World"
(1923), *HU*, pp. 19-37, the forerunner of which is his "The Priest" (1918),
*WW*, pp. 205-24.
82. On specific attention to prayer, see *DM* (1927), pp. 64-65, 131-32.

formulated as follows. From understanding Teilhard's communication of his own experience, a person would see how his own life could find meaning only through consistent incorporation of a comparable prayerful vision into the details of his own life. Hence he would see the need to strive to see Christian life for himself as Teilhard described it. This would mean that he would be aware of a duty to learn to pray in a manner exemplified by the total vision of *The Divine Milieu*.

There would be, then, the following main, peculiarly Christian, ethical imperatives for the Christian, either explicit or implicit. The Christian as a Christian has a duty to grow in faith, hope, and love; to strive to understand, within the framework of Church guidance, the traditional core of his beliefs in the light of the human cultural experience of his own time; and to communicate this understanding to others. Finally, the Christian has, as a correlative duty, the duty of Eucharistic prayer, of the large, all-embracing scope such as Teilhard described.

10

# Conclusion. Compressive Socialization and Teilhard's Synthesized Ethic

When, by way of summation and critical evaluation, one looks back over the Teilhardian ethical materials examined in the preceding chapters and asks, "What kind of Christological ethical solution does he present for the problem of compressive socialization?"—the answer is complex, with several positive and several negative components.

## A. Reservations

The fundamental problem underlying all others pertinent to answering this question is the problem of determining with some precision what his answer was. It should be recalled that he never put the question in so many words, and consequently never elaborated a fully developed synthesized ethic, pulling together his phenomenological ethical ideas with what elements he left of an ethic looking to revelation for its base. Nor have previous studies of his thought attempted such an elaboration in any detail.

Previously published approaches to the study of Teilhard's ethical ideas have either been short segments of larger works, such as can be found in the writings of de Solages, Barthélemy-Madaule, and Faricy, or they have explored only the phenomenological line, as did Mermod, or his spirituality alone, as, for example, de Lubac.[1] While most of the other approaches have located his ethics in close proximity to his thinking on socialization, none has synthesized the widely scattered elements into a comprehensive whole, utilizing the framework presented in "Human Energy" as a base, nor have they correlated these elements with his Christological thought, nor attempted an analysis of his methodology in an ethical setting.

Since the present study was followed out within the limits of a critical analytic synthesis of materials Teilhard actually did provide, and did not proceed, beyond the point of synthesis, to develop what he left undeveloped, its results offer more the elements from which one could construct a complete answer to the question put above, rather than the answer itself. The first negative component, then, to the question as put, would be that Teilhard left an incomplete Christological ethical solution to the problem of compressive socialization. To say this is not to condemn him formally as a superficial ethicist, but rather to describe an aspect of his thought that a formal ethicist finds regrettable, if challenging.

When one looks closely at the elements that Teilhard did leave, however, there are reservations that must be made about the quality of his ethical thinking.

The root flaw, in my view, is found in his phenomenological methodology, and it has to do with his han-

---

1. Mathieu's work, *La pensée politique de Teilhard*, was not designed to be a formally ethical study. However, much in it pertains to ethics. His section on "Un néo-Christianisme de l'action," pp. 162-82, could, as a matter of fact, be categorized as dealing with Christian social ethics, although Mathieu does not so label it.

dling of analogy. To say this is to affirm again the absence in Teilhard of self-analysis directed toward his theory of knowledge, and to locate a critical area of deficiency within his intellectual process. The problem is not that Teilhard ignored the function of analogous thought, but in how he handled it. His fundamental error in working with the dynamic analogy he advocated was to project the deterministic *continuity* of evolutionary process in subhuman biological evolution into the indeterminate areas of human freedom and responsibility— areas that he himself insisted were areas of evolutionary development *discontinuous* with what preceded.

If one accepts this as an explanation of what was happening in his reasoning process, then one can without difficulty account for two major consequences, unfortunately also negative, in his ethical thought. These consequences have unfortunate consequences of their own.

The first is his emphasis on the element of attractiveness toward communion in his theory of love. It is the foundation for his extrapolations about ultimate human convergence in love, and the base of his phenomenological hope. As a consequence, it was logical—along this line of logic—for him to be relatively unconcerned about the element of moral evil seriously obstructing evolutionary progress, when he was thinking on the phenomenological plane. What is more, his assumption of this kind of understanding as background for his interpretation of revelation can be seen to lead easily into his relative neglect of the theological factors of both Original Sin and personal sin in his explanation of Christ's redemptive activity and of the Christian's share in it. His melioristic approach to both phenomenological and Christological ethics is likewise explained on these grounds. If one can depend on the power of love-attraction to be as strong as he described, it would be reasonable to lay stress on doing the better thing, ethically, and to be less concerned about what would be necessary for ethical survival alone, or about the peculiar danger of malice and sinfulness as corrosive of evolutionary process.

The second major consequence, which likewise has unfortunate results to follow, is the distance from the individual person's needs and wants that flows from viewing humanity with strong emphasis on its global, planetary character, as seen in terms of large numbers of people and great stretches of time. In its extreme form this shows up in the tendency to subordinate the individual person to society.

Of these two deficiencies (the overstress on attractive force in love, and the tendency to view humanity as an individual-obscuring, massive organism), the first is the more serious, because it is a defect of which Teilhard does not seem to have been aware. He gives no evidence of seeing that there was a serious problem of basic logic in the way he argued analogically.[2]

The second problem he did recognize. His abiding concern about avoiding an ant-hill existence for human being attests to this, as well as his insistence that the union of human persons through love, on all levels of love, was a *differentiating* union, which would carefully safeguard, and in fact develop, the unique prerogatives of the human person. He was aware, then, of the tension between person and society, and, ironically enough, his fundamental concept of differentiating union seems to rest, when it is applied to human society, on an assumption of individual personal uniqueness that could only be derived from the free, discontinuous element in humanity that his theory of love tended to neglect. With regard to the person-society dilemma, the problem with Teilhard's thought was not so much that he did not have a workable theory for resolving it, but that he did not pursue it fully enough in certain contexts to prevent certain critics from condemning him as totalitarian.[3]

2. See above, chap. 3B.
3. See above, chaps. 1E; 3C (1); 4D (1) (2); 6B (2) (3), C (1) (2) (4), D (2); 7C; 8B (2), C (2); 9D (3).

On the Christological side, a consequence, again unfortunate, of the global approach is the neglect of expressed concern for the individual weak, sinful, suffering human person. It is known that Teilhard personally was concerned for the moral and physical suffering of those he knew, but his theoretical writings do not bring out this particular facet of essential Christian charity, howevermuch he may have practiced it.

## B.  Positive Elements

If the preceding criticisms have pointed to aspects of Teilhard's ethical thought that would stand against him and would call for modifications in his approach, what can be said for him? It goes without saying that in pointing to those aspects of his thought which have positive value, the impression could be left that one is glossing over defects, or discounting negative criticisms. Such is not the intent in what follows, but, in view of the at times strong adverse criticism argued in the preceding study, some highlighting of discernible good ideas is in order—both in the interests of critical objectivity, to the extent that such is possible, and also to give a better overall perspective to the complexities of Teilhard's approach.

As a beginning, it can be claimed that Teilhard does ask, and does attack with vigor, certain fundamentally correct, important questions regarding both secular humanist and Christian theological ethics. His fundamental orientational question, which is of obvious ethical import, is twofold: 1) how can the believing Christian integrate his Christian faith in a theoretical and practical way with scientific, technological, evolutionary humanism? and 2) how can a scientific, technological, evolutionary humanist integrate his deepest convictions in a theoretical and practical manner with an orthodox interpretation of Christianity? Also to be noted, by way of preliminary observation, is the question he asks about the importance of morality in the evolutionary process. Further, one could point to the inquiry he makes about the organic tie between morality and "metaphysic," in the sense of a basic *weltanschauung*, or understanding of the world.

His generic answer to the orientational question is that Christ can be properly viewed as the energizing Personal Center, radiating outward into the sphere of cosmogenetic process, and that the sphere of cosmogenetic process, in order to be activated, requires an immanent, yet transcendent Personal Center, Omega. The answer is obviously one to provide more satisfaction for the searching Christian than for a convinced secular humanist, but it is not difficult to see how a secular humanist, open to the possibility, at least, of valid religious phenomena, could find the position worth pondering.

From the point of view of those who are convinced that morality and ethics are important, Teilhard's stress on the paramount importance of morality for evolutionary progress is congenial. Moreover, his argumentation to support this contention, for those who accept the reality of responsible freedom and its impact on social progress, seems valid. Also, his linking morality organically with a fundamental world view could, if sufficient attention were paid to its implications, do much to help clarify considerable debate about ethical questions, which at times is carried on without clearly attending to the philosophical bases expressed or implied upon which opposing, or variant, ethical positions rest. What is involved here holds not only for Christian-secular dialogue, but for all ethical discussions, which frequently enough get bogged down because of undetected or unexpressed underlying premises.

When one focuses on certain specifics of the ethical implications in Teilhard's Christological position, the following positive elements can be noted.

The central Christological dogma is that of the Mystical Body. Consequently, his Christological ethic is basically an ethic directed by concern for promoting growth of the Mystical Christ. As this is spelled out, one finds strong emphases on hope in the assistance of Christ Risen, yet involved in the cosmogenetic process, particularly through human persons in their response to his love, in a dynamic Eucharist-centered quest for bringing human beings and the totality of the universe to fulfillment beyond time and in union with him.

The dimensions of the human to which Teilhard gives special attention in his exploration of the meaning of Christ's full humanity are precisely those which were brought strongly to his mind by the significance of his life experience in war, close friendships with keen minds of both sexes and varying philosophical convictions, and the evolutionary import of social process derived from his professional work in a particular branch of the scientific community.

His interpretation of the growth of the Mystical Body, therefore, is one that is presented against the backdrop of his grasp of the meaning of global socialization, the sublimation of sexuality and aggression, the urgent need for research applied to human betterment, and a profound respect for the dangers and humanizing potential of science.[4]

Especially to be singled out here as key elements in his Christogenetic ethic are the concept of charity as dynamic and constructive, not merely palliative, and the importance of his radical personalism as affecting his recurrent stress on an authentic love union that exercises differentiating effect on the people involved, whether they be a couple, citizens of a nation, or different nations of the world. Likewise, calling for special attention are his unfortunately often-neglected ideas on the pas-

---

4. A recent work that points up the impact of Teilhard's thought on Christian social theorizing is Gustova Gutiérrez, *A Theology of Liberation*, trans. and ed. Sister Caridad Inda and John Eagleson (Maryknoll, N.Y.: Orbis Books, 1973), pp. 32, 76 n35, 173, 175, 261.

sivities of growth and diminishment, with their special implications regarding recognition of the need for divine grace for full humanization, as well as the significance of suffering, failure, and death in leading to union with Christ. Nor should what he had to say about the significance of the ecclesial community for theoretical and practical guidance be overlooked.

Although Teilhard never did develop his thought on the details of ethical methodology, his method of prayerful, contemplative seeking for meaningful action should also be mentioned. To the extent that he did have something to say about this, his ideas can be looked on as pointing toward valuable adaptations of one traditionally acceptable and fruitful tradition—the Ignatian—in the light of social and intellectual developments in the modern world.

Finally, it is important to note the method by which he strove to communicate his ideas and the ethical implications contained in it. It has been described above as a method of personalistic sharing, by which he strove not to force his concepts on anyone, but to present his vision as a communication of himself and his understanding of the world in the light of Christ. What is of significant ethical import here is the respect for the intellectual and moral integrity of conscience he conveyed through this approach.

## C. Concluding Remarks

There is good reason to believe that it will be a long time, if ever, before the last synthesizing and critical efforts are in with respect to Teilhard's ethical thought. The fragmentary and scattered character of his ethical concepts makes the task of putting together *the* authentic Teilhardian ethic a synthesizing task colored by the peculiar concerns of the synthesizer, and precludes universal agreement as to organizational plan and selection.

Moreover, the criticisms advanced, both pro and con, must likewise be affected by the particular world view of the critic making the analysis.

In addition, there is the admittedly tentative and exploratory quality of Teilhard's thought itself, even in such a work as *The Phenomenon of Man*, over which he labored hard and long, with careful revision.

Within and without his own Church he has met with a broad spectrum of reaction, ranging from strong, if at times undiscerning opposition, to enthusiastic approval, equally lacking in critical discernment. Because of the reservations summarized at the beginning of this chapter, and others expanded on in preceding chapters, my own position is not one of unqualified approval. On the other hand, the positive elements are, in my judgment, of such significance as to be well deserving of acceptance where they can be satisfactorily validated, and of continued exploratory probing where there are ambiguities and gaps.

Perhaps it would not be out of place to leave the last word as to how to approach evaluation of Teilhard's work to the man himself. In one of his earliest essays, he wrote:

> It is infinitely preferable to offer, provisionally, a mixture of truth and error than to mutilate reality by trying prematurely to separate the wheat from the tares.[5]

Throughout his life he was willing to take the risks implied in such a stance, and it is well known at what cost. Many years later, toward the close of *The Phenomenon of Man*, he left what may be read as a well-modulated challenge to those who would find more tares than wheat in his offerings:

> In this arrangement of values I may have gone astray at

5. "Creative Union" (1917), *WW*, p. 153.

many points. It is up to others to try to do better. My one hope is that I have made the reader feel both the reality, difficulty, and urgency of the problem and, at the same time, the scale and the form which the solution cannot escape.[6]

6. *PM* (1940), p. 290.

# Bibliography

BIBLIOGRAPHICAL NOTE. The following bibliography contains a complete inventory of the Teilhard primary sources available for the present study. Apart from actual writings of Teilhard, the listing is selective and limited to works cited or consulted as pertinent to a critical inquiry into his ethical thought.

The most complete and detailed bibliography of Teilhard's published and unpublished writings is that by Claude Cuénot, and can be found in his *Teilhard-Biography*, pp. 407-85. An excellent comprehensive general bibliography of Teilhard materials is Joan E. Jarque's *Bibliographie générale de oeuvres et articles sur Pierre Teilhard de Chardin* (Fribourg, Suisse: Éditions Universitaires, 1970). It contains well over two thousand entries and runs to the end of December 1969. For materials after that date, one could consult *Archivum Historicum Societatis Jesu* 39 (1970), and subsequent issues.

## Works by Pierre Teilhard de Chardin

### BOOKS BY TEILHARD AND COLLECTIONS OF HIS WRITINGS

Oeuvres de Pierre Teilhard de Chardin
1. *Le phénomène humain*. Paris: Éditions du Seuil, 1955. American edition, *The Phenomenon of Man*. Revised translation by Bernard Wall, with Introduction by Julian Huxley. Harper Torchbooks. New York: Harper & Row,

Pub., 1965. English edition, London: Collins.
2. *L'apparition de l'homme*. Paris: Éditions du Seuil, 1956. English edition, *The Appearance of Man*. Translated by J. M. Cohen. London: Collins, 1965. American edition, New York: Harper & Row, Pub.
3. *La vision du passé*. Paris: Éditions du Seuil, 1957. English edition, *The Vision of the Past*. Translated by J. M. Cohen. London: Collins, 1966. American edition, New York: Harper & Row, Pub.
4. *Le milieu divin*. Paris: Éditions du Seuil, 1957. American edition, *The Divine Milieu*. Translated by Bernard Wall, Alick Dru, Noel Lindsay, *et al*. Harper Torchbooks. New York: Harper & Row, Pub., 1965. English edition, London: Collins.
5. *L'avenir de l'homme*. Paris: Éditions du Seuil, 1959. American edition, *The Future of Man*. Translated by Norman Denny. New York: Harper & Row, Pub., 1964. English edition, London: Collins.
6. *L'énergie humaine*. Paris: Éditions du Seuil, 1962. English edition, *Human Energy*. Translated by J. M. Cohen. London: Collins, 1969. American edition, New York: Harcourt, Brace, Jovanovich.
7. *L'activation de l'énergie*. Paris: Éditions du Seuil, 1963. English edition, *The Activation of Energy*. Translated by René Hague. London: Collins, 1970. American edition, New York: Harcourt, Brace, Jovanovich.
8. *La place de l'homme dans la nature* (Le groupe zoologique humain). Paris: Éditions du Seuil, 1956. English edition, *Man's Place in Nature*. Translated by René Hague. London: Collins, 1966. American edition, New York: Harper & Row, Pub.
9. *Science et Christ*. Paris: Éditions du Seuil, 1965. American edition, *Science and Christ*. Translated by René Hague. New York: Harper & Row, Pub., 1965. English edition, London: Collins.
10. *Comment je crois*. Paris: Éditions du Seuil, 1969. American edition, *Christianity and Evolution*. Translated by René Hague. New York: Harcourt Brace Jovanovich, Inc., 1971. English edition, London: Collins.
11. *Les directions de l'avenir*. Paris: Éditions du Seuil, 1973.

OTHER COLLECTIONS

*Écrits du temps de la guerre* (1916-1919). Paris: Bernard Grasset, Éditeur, 1965. American edition, *Writings in Time of War*. Translated by René Hague. New York: Harper & Row, Pub., 1968. (The American and English editions do not contain all the essays found in the French.) English edition, London: Collins.

*Hymne de l'univers*. Paris: Éditions du Seuil, 1961. American edition, *Hymn of the Universe*. Translated by Simon Bartholomew. New York: Harper & Row, Pub., 1965. English edition, London: Collins.

*Sur le bonheur*. Paris: Éditions du Seuil, 1966.

*Je m'explique*. Textes choisis et ordonnés par J.-P. Demoulin. Paris: Éditions du Seuil, 1966. English edition, *Let Me Explain*. Texts selected and arranged by Jean-Pierre Domoulin. Translated by René Hague, *et al*. London: Collins, 1970. American edition, New York: Harper & Row, Pub.


ESSAYS AND NOTES PUBLISHED IN VARIOUS PLACES

"Géobiologie et Geobiologia," 1943. Cité par Claude Cuénot, "L'apport scientifique de Pierre Teilhard de Chardin," *Cahiers Pierre Teilhard de Chardin 4, La Parole Attendue*. Paris: Éditions du Seuil, 1963, 64-65. Originally printed in *Geobiologia, Revue de l'Institut de Géobiologie* (Pékin) 1 (1943): 1-2.

"La pensée de Père Teilhard de Chardin," 1948. *Les études philosophiques* 10, no. 4 (oct.-déc. 1955): 580-81.

"Pré-humain, humain, ultra-humain," 1949 *Idées et Forces* 2, no. 5 (oct.-déc. 1949): 59-69.

Compte rendu: "La planète au pillage." *Études* 263 (déc. 1949): 402-3. (Review of Fairfield Osborn's *Our Plundered Planet*. Boston: Little, Brown, 1948.)

"Machines à combiner et super-cerveaux." *Études* 264 (mars 1950): 403-4. (The text is not signed, but see Cuénot, *Teilhard-Biography*, p. 453, bibliographic entry #383.)

"L'invasion de la télévision." *Études* 265 (mai 1950): 251-52. (The text is not signed, but see Cuénot, *Teilhard-*

*Biography*, p. 453, bibliographic entry #384.)
"The Antiquity and World Expansion of Human Culture,"
1954. *Man's Role in Changing the Face of the Earth*.
Edited by William L. Thomas, Jr. Chicago: The University of Chicago Press, 1956.

### PUBLISHED LETTERS

*Genèse d'une pensée* (lettres, 1914-1919). Paris: Bernard Grasset,
Éditeur, 1961. American edition, *The Making of a
Mind*. Translated by René Hague. New York: Harper
& Row, Pub., 1965. English edition, London: Collins.
*Blondel et Teilhard de Chardin*. Commentaire par Henri de
Lubac, S.J. Paris: Beauchesne, 1965. American edition,
*Pierre Teilhard de Chardin, Maurice Blondel: Correspondence*. Notes and Commentary by Henri de Lubac, S.J.
Translated by William Whitman. New York: Herder
and Herder, 1967.
*Lettres à Léontine Zanta*. Introduction par Robert Garric et
Henri de Lubac. N.p.: Desclée de Brouwer, 1965.
American edition, *Letters to Leontine Zanta*. Introduction by Robert Garric and Henri de Lubac. Translated
by Bernard Wall. New York: Harper & Row, Pub.,
1969. English edition, London: Collins.
*Lettres de voyage* (1923-1955). Recueillies et présentées par
Claude Aragonnès. Paris: Bernard Grasset, 1956.
American edition, *Letters from a Traveller*. Introductory
materials by Julian Huxley, Pierre Leroy, S.J., and
Claude Aragonnès. Translated by René Hague, *et al*.
New York: Harper & Brothers, Pub., 1962. English
edition, London: Collins.
*Accomplir l'homme: Lettres inédites (1926-1952)*. Préface du Père
d'Ouince. Paris: Éditions Bernard Grasset, 1968.
American edition, *Letters to Two Friends: 1926-1952*.
Prologue by René d'Ouince, S.J. Supplementary essay:
"Pierre Teilhard de Chardin as a Scientist," by
Theodosius Dobzhansky. Translated by Helen Weaver.
New York: The New American Library, 1968.
"Two Unpublished Letters of Teilhard," Article, with text and
commentary, by T. V. Fleming, S.J. *The Heythrop Journal* 6 (1965): 36-45.

### UNPUBLISHED MATERIALS

"Essai d' intégration de l'homme dans l'univers," 1930. (Incomplete copy.)

Notes de retraite: 21-29 oct., 1944 (Pékin); 20-28 oct., 1945 (Pékin); 23-30 juin, 1952 (Purchase); 24 juin, 1953 (Purchase); sept. 1953 (sur le bateau, au retour du Transvaal); 19-26 août, 1954 (Purchase).

"Le néo-humanisme moderne et ses réactions sur le Christianisme," 1948. (Notes prises à la conference faite aux Aumôniers de l'Action Catholique Ouvrière, Versailles, 21 sept.)

"Le coeur de la matière," 1950.

"On the Biological Meaning of Human Socialization," 1952.

"Le Christique," 1955.

## Works on the Thought of Teilhard

### BOOKS

Allegra, Gabriel M. O.F.M. *My Conversations with Teilhard de Chardin on the Primacy of Christ: Peking, 1942-1945.* Translated by Bernardino M. Bonansea, O.F.M. Chicago: Franciscan Herald Press, 1971.

Barbour, George B. *In the Field with Teilhard de Chardin.* New York: Herder and Herder, 1965.

Barjon, Louis. *Le Combat de Pierre Teilhard de Chardin.* Québec: Les Presses de l'université Laval, 1971.

Barthélemy-Madaule, Madeleine. *Bergson et Teilhard de Chardin.* Paris: Éditions du Seuil, 1963.

————. *La Personne et le drame humain chez Teilhard de Chardin.* Paris: Éditions du Seuil, 1966.

Benz, Ernst. *Evolution and Christian Hope.* Translated by Heinz G. Frank. Anchor Books. Garden City, N.Y.: Doubleday & Co., Inc., 1968.

Blanchard, Abbé J.-P. *Méthode et principes du Père Teilhard de Chardin.* Paris: La Colombe, 1961.

Bravo, Francisco. *Christ in the Thought of Teilhard de Chardin.* Translated by Cathryn B. Larme. Notre Dame, Ind.: University of Notre Dame Press, 1967.

Browning, Geraldine O., Alioto, Joseph L., and Farber, Seymour M., M.D., eds. and comps. *Teilhard de Chardin: In Quest of the Perfection of Man.* An International Symposium. Rutherford, N.J.: Fairleigh Dickinson University Press, 1973.

Chauchard, Paul, *Man and Cosmos.* Translated by George Courtright. New York: Herder and Herder, 1965.

————. *Teilhard de Chardin on Love and Suffering.* Translated by Marie Chêne. Deus Books. New York: Paulist Press, 1966.

Crespy, George. *From Science to Theology: The Evolutionary Design of Teilhard de Chardin.* Translated by George H. Shriver. Nashville, Tenn.: Abingdon Press, 1968.

Cuénot, Claude. *Nouveau Lexique: Teilhard de Chardin.* Paris: Éditions du Seuil, 1968.

————. *Science and Faith in Teilhard de Chardin*, with a comment by Roger Garaudy. Translated by Noel Lindsay. London: Garnstone Press, 1967.

————. *Teilhard de Chardin: A Biographical Study.* Translated by Vincent Colimore and edited by René Hague. Baltimore, Md.: Helicon, 1965.

Devaux, André A. *Teilhard and Womanhood.* Translated by Paul Joseph Oligny, O.F.M. and Michael D. Meilach, O.F.M. Deus Books. New York: Paulist Press, 1968.

Dobzhansky, Theodosius. *The Biology of Ultimate Concern.* Meridian Books. New York: The New American Library, 1967.

Faricy, Robert L., S.J. *Teilhard de Chardin's Theology of the Christian in the World.* New York: Sheed and Ward, 1967.

Ferkiss, Victor C. *Technological Man.* Mentor Books. New York: The New American Library, 1969.

Gray, Donald P. *The One and the Many: Teilhard de Chardin's Vision of Unity.* New York: Herder and Herder, 1969.

Grenet, Paul-Bernard. *Pierre Teilhard de Chardin ou le philosophe malgré lui.* Paris: Beauchesne, 1961.

Gutiérrez, Gustavo. *A Theology of Liberation.* Translated and edited by Sister Caridad Inda and John Eagleson. Maryknoll, N.Y.: Orbis Books, 1973.

Johnston, William. *The Still Point: Reflections on Zen and Christian Mysticism.* Perennial Library. New York: Harper & Row, Publishers, 1971.

Ligneul, André. *Teilhard and Personalism.* Translated by Paul

Joseph Oligny, O.F.M. and Michael D. Meilach, O.F.M. Deus Books. New York: Paulist Press, 1968.

de Lubac, Henri, S.J. *The Eternal Feminine: A Study on the Poem by Teilhard de Chardin*. Translated by René Hague. New York: Harper & Row, Publishers, 1970.

———. *The Religion of Teilhard de Chardin*. Translated by René Hague. Image Books. Garden City, N.Y.: Doubleday & Co., Inc., 1968.

———. *Teilhard Explained*. Translated by Anthony Buono. Deus Books. New York: Paulist Press, 1968.

———. *Teilhard de Chardin: The Man and His Meaning*. Translated by René Hague. Mentor-Omega Books. New York: The New American Library, Inc., 1967.

Maloney, George A., S.J. *The Cosmic Christ: from Paul to Teilhard*. New York: Sheed and Ward, 1968.

Mathieu, Pierre-Louis. *La pensée politique et économique de Teilhard de Chardin*. Paris: Éditions du Seuil, 1969.

Mermod, Denis. *La morale chez Teilhard*. Paris: Éditions Universitaires, 1967.

Mooney, Christopher F., S.J. *Teilhard de Chardin and the Mystery of Christ*. Image Books. Garden City, N.Y.: Doubleday and Co., Inc., 1968.

North, Robert, S.J. *Teilhard and the Creation of the Soul*. Milwaukee, Wis.: Bruce, 1967.

d'Ouince, René. *un prophète en procès: Teilhard de Chardin*. Vol. 1: *dans l'Église de son temps*. Vol. 2: *et l'avenir de la pensée chrétienne*. Paris: Aubier-Montaigne, 1970.

Rabut, Olivier, O.P. *Teilhard de Chardin: A Critical Study*. New York: Sheed and Ward, 1961.

Raven, Charles E. *Teilhard de Chardin: Scientist and Seer*. New York: Harper & Row, Pub., 1962.

Rideau, Emile. *Teilhard de Chardin: A Guide to His Thought*. Translated by René Hague. London: Collins, 1967.

Smulders, Piet, S.J. *The Design of Teilhard de Chardin*. Translated by Arthur Gibson. Westminster, Md.: The Newman Press, 1967.

Speaight, Robert. *The Life of Teilhard de Chardin*. New York: Harper & Row, Pub., 1967.

de Solages, Mgr. Bruno. *Teilhard de Chardin: témoignage et étude sur le dévelopement de sa pensée*. N.p.: Édouard Privat, Éditeur, 1967.

Soucy, Claude. *Pensée logique et pensée politique chez Teilhard de*

*Chardin*. Paris: Presses Universitaires de France, 1967.

Tresmontant, Claude. *Introduction à la pensée de Pierre Teilhard de Chardin*. Paris: Éditions du Seuil, 1956. English translation, *Pierre Teilhard de Chardin, His Thought*. Baltimore, Md.: Helicon Press, 1959.

Wildiers, N. M. *An Introduction to Teilhard de Chardin*. Translated by Hubert Hoskins. Fontana Books. London: Collins, 1968.

ARTICLES

d'Armagnac, Christian, S.J. "De Blondel à Teilhard nature et intériorité." *Archives de philosophie* 21 (avril-juin 1958): 298-312.

————. "Teilhard Est-il Gidien?" *Les études philosophiques* 21 (1966): 533-37.

Barthélemy-Madaule, Madeleine. "Réflexions sur la méthode et la perspective teilhardienne." *Les études philosophiques* 21 (1966): 510-32.

Bastide, Georges. "Naturalisme et spiritualité: Le statut de la réflexion dans la pensée de Teilhard de Chardin." *Les études philosophiques* 20 (1965): 409-47.

Binns, Emily. "The Very Quick of the Life of the Church Today." *The Teilhard Review* 6, no. 2 (Winter 1971-72): 84-93.

Brun, Jean. "Un Gnostique Gidien: Teilhard de Chardin." *Les études philosophiques* 20 (1965): 465-82.

Cuénot, Claude. "L'apport scientifique de Pierre Teilhard de Chardin." In *Cahiers Pierre Teilhard de Chardin* 4, *La parole attendue*. Paris: Éditions du Seuil, 1963.

————. "Teilhard et le marxisme." *Europe* 431-32 (mars-avril, 1965): 164-85.

————. "Teilhard de Chardin: Sketch for a Portrait." Translated by W. E. O'Hea. *The Teilhard Review* 6, no. 1 (Summer 1971): 1-10.

Danielou, Jean, S.J. "Signification de Teilhard de Chardin." *Études* 312 (fév. 1962): 146-61.

Faricy, Robert. "Religious Education." *The Teilhard Review* 5, no. 2 (Winter 1970-71): 85-93.

Freible, C. W., S.J. "Teilhard, Sexual Love and Celibacy." *Review for Religious* 26 (1967): 282-94.

Garaudy, Roger. "Le Père Teilhard, le concile, et les marxistes."

*Europe* 431-32 (mars-avril 1965): 185-208.

Gray, Donald P. "Teilhard's Vision of Love." In *Dimensions of the Future*. Edited by Marvin Kessler, S.J. and Bernard Brown, S.J. Washington: Corpus Books, 1968.

Journet, Charles. "Pierre Teilhard de Chardin, penseur religieux: de quelques jugements récents." *Nova et Vetera* 37 (oct.-déc. 1962): 284-313.

des Lauriers, Guérard, "La démarche de Teilhard de Chardin." *Divinitas* 3 (1959): 221-68.

Medawar, Sir Peter. "Teilhard de Chardin in 'The Phenomenon of Man.' " *Mind* 277 (1961): 99-106.

*Monitum*, restricting the use of Teilhard's writings. Issued by the Sacred Congregation of the Holy Office, June 30, 1962. *AAS* 54 (1962): 526.

O'Day, Michael. "Lacuna or Breakthrough: Review Article." *The Teilhard Review* 4, no. 2 (Winter 1969-70): 93-97.

Perlinski, Jerome. "Teilhard's Vision of Peace and War." *The Teilhard Review* 3, no. 2 (Winter 1968-69): 52-59.

Rideau, Emile, S.J. "La sexualité selon le Père Teilhard de Chardin." *Nouvelle revue théologique* 90 (1968): 173-90.

Russo, François, S.J. "La Socialisation selon Teilhard de Chardin." In *Teilhard de Chardin et la pensée catholique: Colloque de Venisse*. Texte Établi par Claude Cuénot. Paris: Éditions du Seuil, 1965.

Senghor, Léopold Sédar. "Pierre Teilhard de Chardin et la politique africaine." In *Cahiers Pierre Teilhard de Chardin 3, Pierre Teilhard de Chardin et la politique africaine*. Paris: Éditions du Seuil, 1962, pp. 13-65.

Sullivan, Dan. "Psychosexuality: The Teilhard Lacunae [*sic*]." *Continuum* 2 (1967): 254-78.

Swan, Lucile. "Memories and Letters." In *Teilhard de Chardin: Pilgrim of the Future*. Edited by Neville Braybrooke. Libra Books. London: Darton, Longman & Todd Ltd., 1965.

## Other Pertinent Materials

### BOOKS

Bainton, Roland H. *Christian Attitudes Towards War and Peace*. New York: Abingdon Press, 1960.

Bouillard, Henri. *Blondel et le Christianisme*. Paris: Éditions du Seuil, 1961.

Bourke, Vernon J. *History of Ethics*. 2 vols. Image Books. Garden City, N.Y.: Doubleday and Co., Inc., 1970.

Clarkson, John F., S.J.; Edwards, John H., S.J.; Kelly, William J., S.J.; and Welch, John J., S.J.; trans. and eds. *The Church Teaches: Documents of the Church in English Translation*. St. Louis: B. Herder Book Co., 1955.

Coste, René. "Pacifism and Legitimate Defense." Translated by Theodore L. Westow. *Moral Problems and Christian Personalism*. Vol. 5 of *Concilium*. Editorial Director, Franz Böckle. New York: The Paulist Press, 1965.

Curran, Charles E. *Catholic Moral Theology in Dialogue*. Notre Dame, Ind.: Fides Publishers, 1972.

————. *Contemporary Problems in Moral Theology*. Notre Dame, Ind.: Fides Publishers, 1970.

Davitt, Thomas E. *Ethics in the Situation*. New York: Appleton-Century-Crofts, 1970.

Delp, Alfred, S.J. *The Prison Meditations of Father Delp*. Macmillan Paperback. New York: The Macmillan Co., 1963.

Dostoyevsky, Fyodor. *The Brothers Karamazov*. Translated by Constance Garnett. Signet Books. New York: The New American Library, 1957.

Finn, James, ed. *Protest: Pacifism and Politics*. Vintage Books. New York: Random House, 1968.

de Grazia, Sebastian. *Of Time, Work, and Leisure*. Anchor Books. Garden City, N.Y.: Doubleday & Co., Inc., 1964.

Illich, Ivan. *Tools for Conviviality*. World Perspectives. New York: Harper & Row, Pub., 1973.

The Jesuit Provincials, American Assistancy. *Consensus Positions and Recommendations of the Santa Clara Conference*. Santa Clara, Calif., August, 1967.

Johann, Robert O. *Building the Human*. New York: Herder and Herder, 1968.

Joyce, Mary and Robert. *New Dynamics in Sexual Love: A Revolutionary Approach to Marriage and Celibacy*. Collegeville, Minn.: The Liturgical Press, 1970.

Lepp. Ignace. *Atheism in Our Time*. Translated by Bernard Murchland, C.S.C. Macmillan Paperback. New York: The Macmillan Co., 1964.

Long, Edward LeRoy, Jr. *A Survey of Christian Ethics*. New York: Oxford University Press, 1967.

Mersch, Emile, S.J. *The Theology of the Mystical Body*. Translated by Cyril Vollert, S.J. St. Louis, Mo.: B. Herder Book Co., 1951.

Miller, William Robert. *Nonviolence: a Christian Interpretation*. New York: Schocken Books, 1966.

Mouroux, Jean. *The Meaning of Man*. Translated by A. H. C. Downes. Image Books. Garden City, N.Y.: Doubleday & Co., Inc., 1961.

Niebuhr, H. Richard. *The Responsible Self*. New York: Harper & Row, Pub., 1963.

Rahner, Karl, S.J. *The Dynamic Element in the Church*. Translated by W. J. O'Hara. New York: Herder and Herder, 1964.

Rahner, Karl and Vorgrimler, Herbert. *Theological Dictionary*. Translated by Richard Strachan. New York: Herder and Herder, 1965.

Richardson, Alan. *History: Sacred and Profane*. Philadelphia: The Westminster Press, 1964.

Ryan, Mary Perkins and John Julian. *Love and Sexuality: A Christian Approach*. Image Books. Garden City, N.Y.: Doubleday and Co., Inc., 1969.

Schoonenberg, Piet, S.J. *Man and Sin*. Translated by Joseph Donceel, S.J. Logos Books. Chicago: Henry Regnery and Co., 1968.

*The Spiritual Exercises of St. Ignatius*. Translated by Louis J. Puhl, S.J. Westminster, Md.: The Newman Press, 1957.

Winter, Gibson. *Being Free: Reflections on America's Cultural Revolution*. New York: The Macmillan Co., 1970.

### ARTICLES

Bernard, Jessie. "Women, Marriage, and the Future." *The Futurist* (April 1970), pp. 41-43.

Danner, Peter L. Chairman, Dept. of Economics, Marquette University, Milwaukee, Wisconsin. Private communication to the writer of the present study, July, 1972.

Erling, Bernhard. "Agape and Eros in the Thought of Nygren, D'Arcy and De Rougement." Paper presented at the Convention of the College Theology Society, St. Paul, Minn., April, 1971.

Fletcher, Joseph. "Situation Ethics Under Fire." In *Storm Over Ethics*. Philadelphia: United Church Press, 1967.

Garaudy, Roger. "Freedom and Creativity: Marxist and Christian." Translated by W. E. O'Hea *The Teilhard Review* 3, no. 2 (Winter 1968-69): 42-49.

Gustafson, James M. "Context Versus Principles: A Misplaced Debate in Christian Ethics." In *New Theology: No. 3*. Edited by Martin E. Marty and Dean G. Peerman. New York: The Macmillan Co., 1965.

————. "Love Monism: How Does Love Reign?" *Storm Over Ethics*. Philadelphia: United Church Press, 1967.

Johann, Robert, S.J. "Love and Justice." *Ethics and Society*. Edited by Richard T. De George. Anchor Books. Garden City, N.Y.: Doubleday & Co., Inc., 1966.

Ramsey, Paul. "Shall We 'Reproduce?' " Part I: "The Medical Ethics of In Vitro Fertilization." *The Journal of the American Medical Association* 220, no. 10 (June 5, 1972): 1346-50. Part II: "Rejoinders and Future Forecast." *JAMA* 220, no. 11 (June 12, 1972): 1480-85.

Saslaw, William C. "Entropy and the Universe." *The Teilhard Review* 3, no. 2 (Winter 1968-69): 76-79.

*Theological Studies* 33, no. 3 (Sept. 1972). Special issue devoted to genetics and ethics.

# Index